# THE
# TECHNOLOGICAL
# SYSTEM

*By the Author*

The Technological Society
Propaganda
The Political Illusion
A Critique of the New Commonplaces
The Presence of the Kingdom
The Theological Foundation of Law
Violence
To Will and to Do
The Meaning of the City
Prayer and Modern Man
The Judgment of Jonah
The Politics of God and the Politics of Man
False Presence of the Kingdom
The New Demons
Apocalypse
Hope in Time of Abandonment

*Jacques Ellul*

# THE TECHNOLOGICAL SYSTEM

Translated from the French by
Joachim Neugroschel

With a new foreword by Daniel Cerezuelle
(translated by Lisa Richmond)

WIPF & STOCK · Eugene, Oregon

Wipf and Stock Publishers
199 W 8th Ave, Suite 3
Eugene, OR 97401

The Technological System
By Ellul, Jacques
Copyright©1980 Le Cherche Midi Editeur
ISBN 13: 978-1-5326-1525-2

Publication date 5/30/2018
Previously published by Continuum, 1980

# CONTENTS

| | | |
|---|---|---|
| | Foreword by Daniel Cérézuelle | vii |
| | Translation Addendum | xv |
| | Introduction | 1 |

*Part One:* WHAT IS TECHNOLOGY 21

1. Technology As a Concept — 23
2. Technology As an Environment — 34
3. Technology As a Determining Factor — 51
4. Technology As a System — 76
   General Idea — 76
   Defining the System — 82
   Features of the System — 108
   The Absence of Feedback — 117

*Part Two:* THE CHARACTERISTICS OF THE TECHNOLOGICAL PHENOMENON 123

5. Autonomy — 125
6. Unity — 156
7. Universality — 169
8. Totalization — 199

*Part Three:* THE CHARACTERISTICS OF
TECHNOLOGICAL PROGRESS                              205

    9  Self-Augmentation                          209
  10  Automatism                                 232
  11  Causal Progression and
      Absence of Finality                         256
  12  The Problem
      of Acceleration                             283

*Conclusion:* Man in the
  Technological System                              310
Postscript                                           326
Notes                                                327
Bibliography                                         361

# FOREWORD TO THE 2018 EDITION

## *The Technological System*

JACQUES ELLUL (1912–1994) HAD a lifelong concern with what he called "Technique." Over the course of four decades, he published three major books on the role of technology in the contemporary world: *The Technological Society* (French, 1954; English, 1964), *The Technological System* (French, 1977; English, 1980), and *The Technological Bluff* (French, 1988; English, 1990). These books are not disconnected but represent a constant deepening, by a mature thinker, of earlier intuitions.

In 1935, Jacques Ellul and Bernard Charbonneau, then just twenty-three and twenty-five years old respectively, composed a document that they called "Instructions for a Personalist Manifesto."[1] In this text of about fifteen typewritten pages, they protested the depersonalizing nature of modern daily life. The increasing power and concentration of vast structures, both physical (the factory, the city) and organizational (the State, corporations, finance), constrain us to live in a world that is no longer fit for mankind. Unable to control these structures, we are deprived of freedom and responsibility by their anonymous functioning; and thus we have all become proletarians. "Man, who has everywhere only a small and specific job to perform, and in which fate, rather than man, has become the manager, is made into a proletarian." "In a society of this kind, the type of man who acts consciously becomes extinct."

1. Bernard Charbonneau and Jacques Ellul, "Directives pour un manifeste personnaliste" (Bordeaux, 1935). Reproduced in Bernard Charbonneau and Jacques Ellul, *Nous sommes des révolutionnaires malgré nous: Textes pionniers de l'écologie politique*. Introduction by Quentin Hardy, texts transcribed by Sébastien Morillon, corrected and annotated by Christian Roy (Paris: Éditions du Seuil, 2014). Quotations from sections 17, 21, 25, and 26.

Charbonneau and Ellul were not content only to denounce this sorry condition of modern man. To improve it, they also pointed to its underlying cause, which they believed it was necessary to act upon. This cause is the uncontrolled development of Technique, and during the past two centuries it has become a determining social force. "Technique dominates man and all of man's reactions; against it, politics is powerless . . ." Technique's increasing power also abets totalitarianism and the wanton destruction of nature. It is urgent therefore to put Technique in its proper place, so that it might be managed by a commanding power.

This "necessary revolution" is assuredly not simple, for what Ellul and Charbonneau called Technique is not only machines but also the pursuit of efficiency in every field: "Technique is the means of producing concentration; it is not an industrial process but a way of acting in general." It is thus not only our tools and methods of production that must be changed but also our institutions and our style of life. Against the technicist and productivist ideology of their day, it was in the name of an objective of personal freedom and autonomy that our two young thinkers advocated for a limitation to our technological and economic power: "an ascetic city, so that man might live."

Charbonneau and Ellul did not invent the concept of Technique to describe the unified process of social transformation whose overall effect eludes our choices. From the close of the First World War, various thinkers had been sensing that something new was transforming the human world: Spengler, Berdayev, Junger, Huxley, Valéry, Bergson, and others. Yet our two "Gascon personalists" were probably among the first, long before Heidegger, to give Technique a central role in the transformations of the modern world and to perform a radical critique upon it in the name of a demand for freedom. The technicization of the world, just like the unfolding of capitalist logic, takes place beyond our control and sometimes even beyond our awareness. It proceeds according to its own logic, which confers on it a broad autonomy. This idea of an autonomy of Technique, just like an autonomy of the State, was common to Charbonneau and to Ellul. They both engaged in a critique of the State and of Technique, and often in the same terms. In a lecture given in 1936, Charbonneau explained that "our civilization is not identified by an 'ism.' It cannot be categorized; it is born of an age of technological changes."² In another talk given in 1945, a few months after Hiroshima, he invited his listeners to notice "the autonomy of technique" as the first step toward achieving a "control over techniques."³

Ellul later recounted that immediately following the Second World War, in a social context of euphoric fascination with State-directed economics and technological progress, the two friends decided to undertake an in-depth critique of the State and of Technique. As a legal scholar of the history of institutions, Ellul would have preferred to study the State, but Charbonneau had already begun to prepare a work on this subject and asked Ellul to start instead upon the part of their common program that had to do with Technique. This is how Ellul developed in *The Technological Society* a systematic analysis of Technique's decisive role in contemporary society.⁴

Ellul's analysis owed much to the influence of Marx, which Ellul always acknowledged. But whereas in the nineteenth century Marx had insisted on the role of capital, and on the autonomous logic of its development, to explain the social disorganization (general proletarization) and political disorganization (revolutions) of his day, Ellul believed that for the twentieth century it was Technique that had become the primary factor determining social life. Technique develops according to its own logic, which confers on it an autonomy analogous to that of capital in the previous century: "Technique conditions and calls forth the social, political, and economic changes. It is the driver of everything else, despite appearances and despite man's pride, which claims that his philosophical theories still have determining power and that his political regimes are decisive for progress. Technique is no longer determined by external necessities but by internal ones. It has become a reality in itself, sufficient unto itself, with its particular laws and its own decisions."⁵

This affirmation of Technique's developmental autonomy in modern society (and in this society alone) led to misunderstanding and numerous misinterpretations. In reading Ellul we must bear in mind that for him

---

2. Bernard Charbonneau, "Le progrès contre l'homme." In Charbonneau and Ellul, *Nous sommes des révolutionnaires malgré nous*, p. 96.

3. Charbonneau, "An deux mille." In Charbonneau and Ellul, *Nous sommes des révolutionnaires malgré nous*, pp. 202, 208.

4. Ellul, *La technique ou l'enjeu du siècle* (Paris: Librairie Armand Colin, 1954). Translated into English as *The Technological Society* (New York: Knopf, 1964).

5. Ellul, *La technique*, p. 121.

autonomy does not mean independence, and he never forgets that Technique develops in a society in which other non-technological forces are also at work. Ellul made use of the metaphor of cancer: this proliferation of harmful cells occurs according to a specific logic of self-generating growth. Biologists study its mechanism, and its results can be fatal to the organism in which the cancer develops. But the life of this organism, without which the cancer would not exist, follows another very different logic, and this logic can obstruct the cancerous cells' proliferation in such a way that many early cancers do not develop further.

For Ellul, Technique cannot develop except within certain social and cultural conditions. For Marx, economic laws are historically determined. Over the course of history, various societies have been acquainted with currency, banking, and private property, and yet they were not subject to the logic of what Marx calls "Capital" that characterizes industrial society. In the same way, for Ellul, Technique is not individual techniques. He distinguishes carefully between the technological *operation*, which is inseparable from man's mode of being in the world and is a sort of anthropological constant (which is why it is absurd to accuse Ellul of technophobia), and the technological *phenomenon*, which is specifically modern and might just as easily have not come to pass. Technique's autonomy is not a permanent and necessary attribute of all Technique; it is a social fact that is historically determined, particularly by the attitudes and values of men. "The technological phenomenon is the preoccupation of the great majority of the men of our day to seek out in all things the absolutely most efficient method."[6] Ellul's formulation is striking: he does not say that the technological phenomenon "requires" the preoccupation of men, but that it *is* this preoccupation. This preoccupation is inseparable from a conviction, namely, that all increase in the power to effect (efficiency) is good for man. But this is true only for our day; it was not always thus and may change again.

We find the same idea in *The Technological System*: "Self-generating growth rests upon Technique's *a priori* justification *in the consciousness*."[7] But it is clear that if for Ellul this is the conviction of our day, it may disappear, and the technological phenomenon may disappear with it. Autonomy is not an intrinsic and permanent characteristic of human Technique. It is

---

6. Ellul, *La technique*, 19.

7. Ellul, *Le système technicien* (Paris: Calmann-Lévy, 1977), 241. Translated into English as *The Technological System* (New York: Continuum, 1980). Italics mine.

relative to a particular state of the society and to the mindset that prevails in the civilization at the present time. This is why this alleged partisan of technological determinism writes, "There is no Technique in itself, but in its implacable advance it requires man's participation, for without him it is nothing."[8] Man's consent is what drives Technique's domination. So although relative, this idea of autonomy enables us to explain some of the difficulties that we all encounter in our individual and collective life. Technique is not a tool that we can use as we wish and that remains subject to our intentions. Rather, it has its own force of expansion and its own effects, whether social, cultural, political, or ecological. In particular, "it bends in its particular direction the wills that use it and the goals that are proposed for it,"[9] and our passion for technological power involuntarily brings into being particular situations that are especially hard to remedy. Without an understanding of this domination's overall logic, our specific actions will not succeed in freeing us from it.

Twenty years after the publication of *The Technological Society*, Ellul felt it necessary to complete and update his analysis, for the situation had gotten worse. Not only do we have techniques at our disposal that are more and more numerous and powerful, but the development of the electronic techniques of information and communication confer on the autonomy of Technique dimensions that are qualitatively new. Of course, such novelty is not absolute. When he first published *The Technological Society*, Ellul emphasized the tendency of modern Technique to eliminate human interventions, and he stressed the importance of the computer's appearance, which he called the "mathematical machine." The computer was enabling the development of servo-mechanisms capable of performing more and more subtle tasks, previously performed by men, by inserting into the machine the ability to recognize feedback action. Ellul warns the reader, "This is a beginning; all cybernetics is oriented in this direction,"[10] and it makes possible the rise of mass unemployment, which is a factor of war; but he does not extend his analysis of the role of informatics further.

In addition, Ellul clearly identified how technological systems tend to become constituted. Four years before the publication of Gilbert Simondon's

---

8. Ellul, *La technique*, 203.
9. Ellul, *La technique*, 128.
10. Ellul, *La technique*, 124.

book *Du mode d'existence des objets techniques*,[11] Ellul pointed out that one of the factors of Technique's autonomization is the tendency of technological elements to become constituted into groups and systems: "Technique obeys its specific laws, with each machine in functional obedience to the others. Thus each element of the technological whole follows laws that are determined in relation to the other elements of this whole, laws that are thus internal to the system and cannot in any way be influenced by external factors."[12] In the context of the 1950s, Ellul did not feel the need to take these prescient remarks further. In hindsight, with the rise of the computer, they took on a new meaning and needed to be deepened. *The Technological System* updated and renewed Ellul's reflection on the autonomy of Technique by drawing on the ideas of technological environment, information, and system, which thinkers such as Simondon and Leroi-Gourhan had been developing in the intervening years.[13]

Ellul shows first that the objective of mastering Technique is all the more difficult to attain because Technique has become man's environment. In the technological society, technical mediation becomes all-encompassing; it determines the relationship not only to nature but also to other men; it disqualifies the symbolic mediations that man had patiently built up. "Technique therefore forms a continuous interface on the one hand, and, on the other, a generalized mode of intervention."[14] With regard to this technological environment that orients his perception of reality and his desires, modern man has great difficulty maintaining a critical distance. This enfolding is all the more troubling given that Technique tends to transform itself into an overall technological system, whose different parts are in increasing functional interrelation and interdependence due to techniques that permit the constant treatment and exchange of information. On the one hand, this technological system is in permanent expansion and cannot be stabilized, and on the other, the informational integration of the technological holism produces a tendency to self-regulation and a level of complexity and inertia that makes correction more difficult.

11. Gilbert Simondon, *Du mode d'existence des objets techniques* (Paris: Aubier, 1958). It is unlikely that Ellul was aware of Simondon's work before 1954.

12. Ellul, *La technique*, 125.

13. André Leroy-Gourhan, *Milieu et techniques* (Paris: Albin Michel, 1945) and *Le geste et la parole* (Paris: Albin Michel, 1964–1965).

14. Ellul, *La technique*, 44.

FOREWORD TO THE 2018 REPRINT EDITION        xiii

To reorient this technological system by criteria that are no longer technological but ethical or spiritual seems more difficult than ever. Yet to interpret Ellul's analyses as a justification for fatalism would be to misunderstand him. On the contrary, "My attitude is no more pessimistic than that of a doctor who examines a patient and diagnoses a cancer. I have always tried to warn, to issue the alert. I am still persuaded that man remains free to initiate something other than what appears inevitable."[15]

To conclude, one could apply to this Ellulian analysis of Technique what Jacques Ellul said of Charbonneau's analysis of the State[16]

> Bernard Charbonneau seems to describe an abstract me.chanism, the State, that functions on its own, has its own consistency, its motive for development, its coherence. As if there were a cancer developing in society, in itself, on its own, beyond man's control. And this is the first impression that may arise when we read this subtitle: "By Force of Circumstance." I therefore am not involved. The avalanche is accumulating on the heights, but I am in the valley. There is nothing I can do about it. Yet it is precisely this illusion and this justification above all that Bernard Charbonneau is denouncing throughout this book. The State has developed on its own exactly to the extent that man has given in—and more: that man has wanted it this way. "Force of circumstance" functions blindly, to the precise degree to which man gives up. Power grows implacable because no man is capable of the smallest act of freedom. In other words, as the reader reads of this growth of the coldest of all cold monsters,[17] he stands before the mirror of his own complicity, his own irresponsibility. And this is why we have a book that takes up a position verging on the unbearable.[18]

**Daniel Cérézuelle**
Bordeaux, France
March 2018
*Translated by Lisa Richmond*

15. Jacques Ellul and Patrick Chastenet, À contre-courant (Paris: La Table Ronde, 1994), 75. Translated into English as *Jacques Ellul on Politics, Technology, and Christianity* (Eugene, OR: Wipf & Stock, 2005).

16. Charbonneau, Bernard, *L'État* (Paris: Economica, 1987). When this book was first circulated in 1951 as a mimeographed document, its full title was *L'État: Par la force des choses* (*The State: By Force of Circumstance*).

17. Friedrich Nietzsche's definition of the State in *Thus Spoke Zarathustra*.

18. Ellul, "Une introduction à la pensée de Bernard Charbonneau." *Cahiers du Sud-Ouest* #7 (January–March 1985).

# A NOTE ON TRANSLATING *TECHNIQUE AND TECHNICIEN*

JACQUES ELLUL EXPLORES MANY of the nuances of the English and French technology vocabulary on pages 24–27 and 32–33 of *The Technological System*. Nevertheless, you will still be reading this discussion in an English translation so a brief note on the translation issues may be helpful. Throughout this book, translator Joachim Neugroschel uses the English word "technology" for the French *la Technique* and the adjective "technological" for the French noun and adjective *technicien*. Neugroschel notes on page 33 that Ellul himself gave him his approval for this approach. But readers, especially newcomers to Jacques Ellul, need to be cautioned that "technology" and "technological" cannot quite capture the sense of Ellul's French original.

In general usage (English and French), a *technique* is a *means* or *method* of doing something. A technique may include the development and use of tools and machines, but could also just refer to the *process* by which one, for example, argues or debates, dances a fox trot, or wins at chess. In its historical etymology, *technology* (like other "ologies" such as biology, theology, psychology) refers to *the study of technique* (even more literally, "discourse about technique"). But over time this linguistic definition, its *denotation*, has been supplanted by a cultural *connotation:* "technology" is no longer the *study* of something; it is the *thing itself*. In popular usage today, *technology* refers even more narrowly to machines and computers—not including techniques, means, methods, processes, or simple tools.

*Technical* would not be much better than *technological* as a translation of *technicien* (as in *le Système technicien*). In common English usage, "technical" suggests "complex" or "detailed" (as in "a technical argument"). But *le Système technicien,* the term is characterized and ruled by the quest for the most efficient means—not necessarily by complexity. Note also that Ellul did not call his book *le Système technique* but *le Système technicien*. *Technicien* is also a noun referring to a technician, a "techie," not just to the abstraction suggested by technique and technology. The system is more than a system of technicians, but it also includes them. It is from one perspective a "technicist system" and another a "technician system."

But now to the main point. Ellul is always concerned with something much more fundamental than machines and computers, and more than engineers and technicians. For Ellul, *la Technique* is about means, methods, and process, indeed, about the "ensemble of means." It is "the totality of methods, rationally arrived at, and having absolute efficiency (for a given stage of development) in every field of human activity" (*The Technological Society*, p. xxv). To emphasize that this is not about particular individual methods or tools but about the whole "ensemble" and the logic common to them all, Ellul often uses a capital "T" in Technique, which, unfortunately, is not replicated in this English translation.

Human beings have always developed and used various techniques, Ellul says. What is distinctive about the 20th century is the triumph and proliferation of *one* way of thinking about techniques (means, methods, processes, tools, etc.). Technique subjects all of them to scientific, rational analysis in search of the one best, most measurably efficient way. Magic, tradition, mystery, faith . . . no means or methods on such foundations can endure. For all fields of human activity, all aspects of life, all corners of the globe, this phenomenon, collectively described as *La Technique*, is the dominating (though not the only) force. That was the argument of Ellul's *The Technological Society* (1954 French original, *La Technique, ou l'enjeu du siècle*).

In the book you are now holding, Ellul takes his theory to a new level. In *The Technological System* (1977 French original, *Le Système technicien*) he argues that *la Technique*, being more than just the most powerful *force* in our world, has evolved into (or generated) a networked *system* within which all of life takes place. Just remember that it is not only our computers and networks that comprise this system. It is our habits of thought, values, institutions, worldview, and culture. This System now raises the stakes still higher and makes our civilizational challenges greater than ever.

**David W. Gill**
March 2018

*Introduction*

# TECHNOLOGY AND SOCIETY

TECHNOLOGY is not content with *being*, or in our world, with being the *principal or determining factor.* Technology has become a system. This is what I will try to show in this analysis. But we have to be clear about the object of my research. Twenty-five years ago, I arrived at the notion of the "technological society"; but now, that stage is passed. Nevertheless, we are faced with the major problem of what makes up the specific nature of our society, its chief characteristic. Indeed, we have to track down the key to interpreting the modern age. But if we go through the field of definitions that are generally accepted today, we will see that every so-called specific trait is actually secondary and points ultimately to technology. Let us investigate.[1]

The best-known definition today is by Raymond Aron: the "industrial society." This term is very widespread, but I find it inadequate. Let us ignore the knotty question whether Raymond Aron is designating a model or the reality of our society. For a model, an ideal type, his description is rigorously exact, useful, and interesting. But it obviously does not correspond to present-day reality. In the nineteenth century, Western society was certainly an industrial one, and Aron is right in showing that once the industrial factor began to develop, it affected all societal relations. He is right in showing that the industrial factor led to a social model that was similar everywhere, no matter what the national traits, the political system, or the original differences. Now the industrial factor is characterized by the multiplication of machines and a certain organization of production. Both factors are technological. Today, however, the industrial factor may still be huge, but it does not have much in common with what it was in the nineteenth century.

Above all, it is drowned in a mass of other phenomena that are equally important. Although these phenomena are partially determined by the industrial factor, they have broken away from it, taking on a tremendous volume and a force of transformation which goes beyond industry in the strict sense of the word. Present-day society is still industrial; but that is not its essence.[2]

We need not dwell too long on this contrast between the industrial system and the technological system. Let us focus on two examples of analysis: Seurat's and Richta's.

The influence of technological systematics contrasting the industrial world with the new conception was very well analyzed by Georges Seurat, *Réalités du transfert technologigue* (1976). And his example is highly significant: What is the difference between the old factory and the new? In the former, the goal is to add value to raw material in a series of operations performed by a family of machines, each machine having its own function. If a problem crops up in one "family," it has no repercussions on any other. The machines are installed in partitioned workshops; the families of machines are kept independent of one another by stocks and interconnections. Human error has little weight. Seurat compares the structure of that factory to a beehive or anthill: an individual's mistake is unimportant.

The past fifty years have completed a metamorphosis in four ways: *The power of unitary machines has been growing incessantly.* A new machine costs less to buy, produce, and run than two old machines, but its output is twice that of *one* old machine. "Along the path of giantism, one can reasonably go to the limits of the possible, concentrating businesses in order to put them on the scale of the biggest machines imaginable." This assertion by a distinguished expert on technology rightly sweeps away the ideological conjectures about smaller sizes of companies, the dispersal of small factories in nature, etc. Such consoling ideologies came from Maoist ideas or from the unwarranted assumption that everything would shrink because certain devices are now so tiny. In the industrial reality, all we can expect is a theoretically indefinite growth of subsystems.

The second line of development emphasized by Seurat is *complexification:* "The problems raised by giantism require solutions that are often at the frontier of the universe explored by technology." However, this complexification includes an apparent simplification. The giant and complex machines can no longer be trivialized within a family of machines. The hookups are too burdensome or too fragile. An ideal structure is imposed: *One single* machine performs each stage of the process, and there has to be a continuous flow of raw material along the production line of the machines. Hence: no more separate workshops, no more stocks, no more interconnections. As a result, the earlier analogy to the anthill is passé, "the ants have disappeared." (Which shows how *simply* backward China actually is.) A factory now creates a vertical integration of successive machines, *each* having a different function. There is a "body"—enormous and complex, but it is *one* body. This in turn necessitates a greater circulation of information.

And that is the fourth characteristic: Information has to be automated and decentralized. Otherwise, nothing can function. Hence, the inevitable presence of the computer. Information circuits innervate the entire process at each stage, and all of them frequently wind up in a single control room. In biological terms, this structure could be likened to a cerebralization. We must bear in mind, however, that this is nothing but a simile and that this gigantic structure is not alive in any way. The whole thing cannot function without a human being who is properly trained, aware of his responsibility, capable of attention and solidarity, and proof against sabotage or striking. The damage done to all would be too immense.

Still, the most rigorous demonstration of the passage from industrial to technological society, of the radical difference between the two, is furnished by Radovan Richta's fundamental opus *Civilisation at the Crossroads* (1969). Richta even sees that difference as the key to interpreting the failure of socialism in the USSR. He maintains that the Soviets are clinging to the industrial model, unwilling to take the step that would bring them into the technological system. A system totally different from the earlier one.

At one time, technology and machine industry were connected; but for more than half a century now, a gap has widened between them. Industrialism developed a centralized, hierarchical system, with a linear growth, a division of labor, and a separation between the means and the ends. Mechanization created additional jobs and made human work more draining. It operated by means of steady reproduction, developing masses of men and integrating them in the industrialization.

Modern technology, however, contradicts each of those different points. If allowed to act, it leads to decentralization and flexibility; it does away with the hierarchy and the division of labor; it particularly has to bridge the gap between implementation and management; it presupposes a polyvalent and nonlinear growth; it reintegrates the ends into the means; it cuts down on labor and thus on the costs of labor. The value factor is no longer human work but scientific invention and technological innovation. Consequently, we can no longer apply Marx's analysis, which states that the economic totality is based on the surplus value produced by the salaried labor of the worker.

The industrial system is a closed, repetitive world, with a linear evolution. The technological system is inevitably open, nonrepetitive, with a polyvalent evolution. It can proceed only by the universal development of mankind, and that development is absolutely necessary for the development of the technological system. We are thus confronted with an ensemble that is totally different from any that has ever existed before. Technology may not yet be playing that role, but Richta has an explanation with which I agree by and large. He points out that neither capitalist nor socialist countries are managing to leave the industrial model of society. They jealously preserve industrialism and industrial production as dominant features, both economically and sociologically. Moreover, they force technology to serve this development, which goes against the very grain of modern technology. Hence, technology is all the more alienating, but only because of that fact. For technology, conceived in terms of its automation, its chemical transformation of the world, its economy of energy, its cybernation, its data processing, its biological intervention, and its indefinite output of nuclear energy, has little to do with the old industrial mechanization.

We are dealing here with a tremendous idea, with a decisive importance. However, rather than coming back to Richta later on, I would like to offer some criticism of his work—and his team—right away. First of all, I think, they completely failed to see that they were dealing with a system, and they failed to envisage the consequences of that. They were dominated by a humanism that is very appealing and very refreshing, but perhaps a bit sentimental and not too rigorous. They overemphasized the automative aspect of technology, as if that were a key to everything else. Finally, they displayed a vast idealism in regarding technology as something positive, so long as it is viewed on its own terms (not deformed) and is left alone. Hence, they believe, it is valid to apply pedagogical techniques toward an utterly new didactics for shaping a certain type of man. "The aim of education is not to form a certain type of man, but a man capable of forming himself according to such and such a type and to change that type. . . . Teaching should be oriented towards the structure of the object and be based . . . on generalizing the creative faculties."

We fully agree about the desirable goals. But according to these lines—and I could quote a hundred examples—Richta assumes that what is desirable from a humanist viewpoint has been virtually *realized* by technology. Such is his idealism, preventing him from bringing up the issue of power. He never once stops to think that technology is power, made up of instruments of power, hence producing phenomena and structures of power, i.e., of domination. For Richta, technology spells an enrichment of the human person and the mutual development of man by man. Yet we do not see how humanity is to pass from the control of man by others (and not by himself) to the situation that Richta visualizes—a situation of giving and loving. Technology does not make that possible. On the contrary!

Those are my chief criticisms. However, they do not detract from the depth of the analysis or the validity of the total orientation. What is needed is not so much a more precise knowledge of the system, but rather a way of relating it to mankind and the overall society and of examining the fundamental choices that must now be made.

Certain sociologists fully realize that we are no longer in an industrial society, for instance, Daniel Bell, and then also Alain Touraine. But they employ strange words: postindustrial, or advanced industrial society. I find it quite remarkable that in a time when the use of mathematics is being developed in the human sciences, people can employ such imprecise and meaningless words.

Bell pinpoints the five dimensions of postindustrial society as follows: (1) The creation of an economy of services. (2) The predominance of the class of specialists and technicians. (3) The importance of the theoretical service as a source of innovation and political elaboration in the society. (4) The possibility of autonomous technological growth. (5) The creation of a new intellectual technology. But how can one fail to see that these five traits are directly linked to the growth and predominance of technology and technicians? The very terms used by Bell imply as much. Furthermore, there is no reason why they would describe a "post" society.

Postindustrial? This simply means that we have passed the industrial stage. And now?

In what way does this indicate the slightest feature, render the slightest idea of what our society is like? If someone knew nothing about these things, one could precisely define the machine, industry, hence industrial society. But how can we communicate anything about a "post"?[3]

Would Bell ever dream of defining the political society of the seventeenth century as postfeudal, or that of the nineteenth century as postmonarchic? Likewise, the term "advanced or developed industrial society" makes no sense. "Developed"? This can only mean that industry has developed further. So we must still be living in a society that is industrial, only more so. Historical experience shows that the essential trend of industry is to develop. Hence, we can restrict ourselves to saying "a truly industrial industrial society." "Advanced"? But toward what? What has advanced? Where have we gotten to in this progression? What new trait has emerged? We are told nothing about all that. Consequently, those adjectives are perfectly useless, describe nothing in our society, and should therefore be resolutely discarded.

It must be emphasized that Touraine,[4] in contrast to Bell, hesitates about a qualifying term. Thus, he speaks of a "programmed society." In this case, I am far more in agreement. For he thereby joins the overall outlook of those people for whom the new thing about our society is the organization. He sharply distinguishes between the primary (capitalist) era of industrialization and our era. He qualifies this new society in terms of three features: (1) The emergence of new social "classes" (technicians, bureaucrats, efficiency experts). (2) The new trend of business, which is now based on organization and no longer on the relationship between economic power and productive labor. (3) Spare-time activities. All three characteristics boil down to a reduction and to the necessities of the technological system, which, as Touraine realizes, transforms the social struggles themselves. They are becoming more technological and are no longer subject to a takeover by the proletariat. Touraine adds one more essential feature of postindustrial society: the importance of the student movement with its deep contestation, its challenge, and its political weakness. But, as I have tried to show in my studies on revolution, I regard this feature as episodic and contingent. I feel that Touraine was influenced by the current events while writing his book.

There is another theme that is often developed under the label "bureaucratic society." Obviously, this is a major trait, shedding light on the form of power. It points out a development and it affects the entire social body. Let us leave aside the facile critique of bureaucracy. The things to be stressed are: the principles of order, method, neutrality, organization, and efficiency.

Administration becomes bureaucracy in the positive sense of the term when: the best possible people are hired; the social integration is complete; and the operation is active and efficient. Bureaucracy employs more and more complex machines and must itself function like a machine. The ideal administration is one that runs and works like an engine, with each office as a component and each individual as a part. The functioning has to be regular and continuous, beyond any opinions or influences.

Some observers therefore apply the phrase "organization society" to the society marked by such an administration. Undoubtedly, the term shows that the essence of bureaucracy is organization, and that this bureaucracy not only is governmental but also occurs in all forms of societal activity. Actually, though, the two terms overlap somewhat. However, one is narrower and pejorative. The other is broader and positive. In reality, though, all the marks and qualities of bureaucratic society come from the technologies of organization. The thing that has transformed administration into bureaucracy is the technology of efficiency. Bureaucracy depends on those technologies.

Furthermore, it is obvious that this definition does not take into account all the aspects, all the reality of our society. Organization and bureaucracy are indeed essential. But so are what they organize and administer! We cannot cut our society down to that single characteristic, distinguishing it from all other societies and covering all its activities.

There is a term that stems immediately from the above, with the term adopted by a certain number of economists (after C. Clark and J. Fourastié): a "society of services" or a "tertiary society." I will make the same comments here as before. If we have passed into a society of services, then the reasons are as follows. The productive technologies allowing the growth of industrial society were followed by technologies of organization, administration, leisure, etc., allowing the growth of services. Indeed, if one wishes to describe these three "orders," one refers to a certain number of technologies used in each of them. On the other hand, the notion of service, which validly designates the third aspect of economic activity, does not envelop all forms of this society. It does not take into account the complexity of life today, and it does not include what may be the most important aspect.

Plainly, we now have to deal with the shibboleth that was all the rage in 1968: the "consumer society." This slogan is useful for agitation and propaganda. To its credit, it accentuated an overly neglected aspect, and it focused the definition on the individual's life. But quite obviously, our society is characterized at least as much by work and production as by consumption! This is not the key word that covers everything, explains everything! If this term is aimed at the ideology inhabiting all of us, it is valid. If it is aimed at the economic or social reality, it is highly inadequate. However, there is one thing that strikes me as important: in consumption, we again find the technological element as the decisive one. What triggers consumption? Advertising, that is to say, the technologies of advertising. What is it that demands greater consumption? Mass production, which is possible only because of technology. What are we given to consume? Technological objects, because they are the things that are produced most. Hence, the consumer society, in all its aspects, is primarily characterized by various technologies.[5]

Close to the "consumer society," we find the famous "affluent society." Just how did we get to it, supposedly? By the development of certain technological factors, particularly automation. We must not forget, however, that this affluence is an affluence of technological products. And it is counterbalanced by the creation of new "shortages": of space, air, time, and the like. These shortages are all due to the application of technologies that are crucial to the existence of the affluent society. We will come back to this. Now affluence is certainly one of the important signs of the new society. But, in turn, it is dependent on and qualified by a certain number of technologies.

Next comes an attempt at synthesizing the above factors when H. Lefebvre offers his definition: a "bureaucratic society of "planned consumption." Actually, this denotes three of the characteristics following the industrial stage and perfectly consistent with certain functions and structures in our society. But this formula also reveals the same flaws as the earlier ones. It covers only certain aspects of our society: organization, consumption, psychological action. And it sacrifices others that are equally important: for instance, massification, production. Lefebvre's formula remains on a shallow level. He omits the factor common to all the included elements and constituting both their reason and their mode. Hence, his definition is no more scientific than the others, contrary to what he may claim. All he really offers is an addition of three characteristics rather than the results of a fundamental analysis.

Nevertheless, Lefebvre's formula directs us to a whole series of definitions that focus on a different category of phenomena: information. We can look at two of those definitions here.

One is by Marshal MacLuhan. For MacLuhan, the decisive fact is the appearance of new mass media, which transform not only the social fabric but, even more so, the way each individual thinks and lives. This is caused not so much by the sheer multiplication of information, but rather by the way this information is conveyed. Instead of delving into the countless aspects discussed by MacLuhan, we shall dwell on two elements. First of all, we have to point out the same thing as before. The new media are essentially and primarily technological media. They are produced by technological progress, they accompany it, they are closely tied to it, and they derive from *each* technological modification. It is not the media that bring forth technology, but rather the reverse. Furthermore, seductive as MacLuhan's theses may be, he obviously exaggerates the influence of the media by making them the sole explanation for everything happening in our society. His intellectual acrobatics are ingenious and admirable, but they fail to convince because they do not refer to any verifiable reality. The multiplying of media and information is certainly decisive today, but that single element cannot serve to describe everything. And even if we accept the modern analyses of language, we are left with the fact that technology is still the infrastructure, and permitting that multiplication in the first place.

Along the same lines, the situationists speak of a "society of spectacle." Because of bourgeois ideology, the watering-down of all serious things, the break in praxis, the multiplication of communications, the psychological action, everything in our society has become a spectacle. This term must not be taken in a simple and trivial sense; it has to be given its necessary breadth. Spectacle is a complete way of life. Consumption is a spectacle; so are political activity and leisure and work and family life and revolution. Modern man watches everything as a spectator. Everything is supplied to him as a spectacle, including the things he believes he is most deeply contributing to or participating in.

This analysis is assuredly the most profound. It is not fragmentary, and it may be praised for its coherent picture of observations concerning the individual and the social body. The individual is looked at as being *within* the social body. But how can this analysis fail to see that if there is a society of spectacle, then it exists because of, thanks to, and with a view to the technological transformation of our society! Technological methods are what make spectacle all-inclusive. Technological activity is "by nature" spectacular (excluding all internal reality): Technological activity is what waters down all serious things, since no action can be performed any longer unless by way of technologies. And the society of spectacle seems to be the ideal framework, the most favorable environment for developing technology because it is the milieu that is least disturbed by any untimely interference from autonomous man. Hence, technology is still the key to this present-day reality.

Z. Brzezinski (*Between Two Ages: America's Role in the Technetronic Era,* 1970) also figured he could add something absolutely new by coining the term "technetronic." He lists a number of differences between industrial and technetronic society.

In industrial society, the machine plays the essential role. The dominant social problems are unemployment and employment. Teaching is done through human relations. The ruling class is plutocratic. The university is an ivory tower isolated from reality. Reading favors a conceptual thinking proper to ideologies. Political conflicts are intrinsic; the masses are organized into trade unions; economic power is personalized; wealth is the object of activity.

The technetronic society may be contrasted to the above, point by point. There is a growth of "services," Automation replaces industrial employment. The central issue is that of qualifications. People give in to job security. Teaching is universal because of the communications technologies. Knowledge replaces wealth as a means of action. The university becomes the "reservoir of thinking," plunged into concrete life. The problem of participation in decision-making is generalized; it goes beyond political matters. Ideologies vanish, economic power is depersonalized, and wealth is no longer useful.

I certainly won't deny that Brzezinski has very accurately brought out new features of society in its present or imminent phase, but I don't see the need for coining a new term. "Technetronic" is a portmanteau word combining "technical" and "electronic." Come now! Isn't electronics technological? Does the word add anything to the early definitions of technology? Once again, technology equals the machine plus industry. Fine, then there is something new—according to the famous definition: In a machine, there are *material* parts that *move*. Electronics operates with no moving material parts. Granted. But if the computer is not a machine in the normal sense, then in what way is it not the product of a certain number of technologies? In what way is it not integrated in a technological system? There is no reason to distinguish between technology and electronics. The latter is merely part of the former. The traits that Brzezinski discerns in his technetronic society are actually the traits of a technological society. And much as I like his honest book, I am forced to admit that he simply went along with the fad of making up a—seemingly—esoteric vocabulary in order to give the impression of coming up with something new. What he says (in the first two sections of his book) is quite standard in regard to technological society. And all that is new here is the word "technetronic," which is unjustified. "Technology" amply suffices for everything he discusses.

* * *

In thus reviewing the most important current definitions of our society, we have been led to conclude in each case that the decisive fact, explaining the feature brought out, is the phenomenon of technology, and that this factor is common to all the definitions proposed.[6] Now each of these definitions is accurate. We cannot say that any of the authors is wrong, for each has detected an essential aspect of our time. We canot say that any of the definitions is flatly better than another. But each is limited. Generalizing is made possible by considering the common factor. This factor pays heed to all the aspects, and, since each one is accurate, the common factor must be accurate too. However, it exists at a deeper, more decisive level of analysis. Still, we need not wander off into philosophical abstraction since the relationship between that factor and the various traits is an actual and immediately verifiable relationship. Moreover, starting with the common factor, we could unearth other, equally important traits of our society.[7] This will become evident as we go along. However, by focusing on those that are commonly agreed on, we come to an unexpected result. We will be examining the "technological system," but we can say right now that these characteristics are intrinsic to the technological system itself. In other words, each author has tried, albeit unwittingly, to define our society through the technological system. Each time, light was shed on some element of the technological system. The latter *functions* in a nonstop circulation of "production and consumption." Nonetheless, these terms must be taken on all levels, for there is production not only of industrial goods, but also of symbols, individuals (by education), spare-time activities, ideologies, service signs, information. What is known as circulation (including that of human beings or information) always originates in production and winds up in consumption. However, this complex system is made possible only by improving an organization that leads to a more and more complete overlapping of production and consumption. Advancing constantly and necessarily, technology makes the technological system the agent of an inevitable affluent society. But, conversely, with everything thus being produced and consumed, the system presupposes a more and more thorough integration of each element, including man, as an object. Man can no longer be a subject. For, the system implies that, at least in regard to itself, man must always be treated as an object. Today, this phenomenon is far more important than the renowned Marxist interpretation of "commodity." The latter was defined by the capitalist system. But now, the capitalist system has been swallowed up by the technological system. And the category of commodity—still partly accurate and to be used with caution—does not explain very much. The category of the technicized object is far more crucial and—now—more rigorous. The technological system performs unintentionally. Hence, wherever it is applied, it produces a new kind of objectification which has nothing to do with Hegel's: it is no longer an objectification of the subject, and does not enter a subject-object dialectics. Now, anything that is incorporated, or seized, is treated as an object by the active system, which cannot develop or perform without acting upon a set of elements that have previously been rendered neutral and passive. Nothing can have an intrinsic sense; it is given meaning only by technological application. Nothing can lay claim to action; it is acted upon by technological process. Nothing can regard itself as autonomous; it is the technological system that is autonomous—as we shall demonstrate. Thus we can see that the famous theme of man's "reification" (now tending to replace "alienation") has its place and its explanation in an analysis of the technological system. We will come back to this. The preeminence and all-inclusiveness of the system allow us to describe modern society as the "technological society." This term, *société technicienne*, was first used in France by Georges Friedmann in 1938.[8] I would, however, like to add the word *technicized* (*technicisé*). The first adjective, technological (*technicien*), refers to the active character of the technological agent (*agent technicien*) and the second adjective to the resulting effect on society.

Nevertheless, this definition has been criticized by scholars like H. Lefebvre.[9] We can focus on three of his objections.

The first: Technology does not exist. It is important and effective only because of the urban milieu; outside that milieu, technology produces only isolated objects.

This criticism neglects the *correlation* between the "isolated objects," the creation of a complete technological system. The city is obviously the best *framework* for technology to develop in. But, as we have said, this framework is itself produced by technology, which also extends outside the city: the world of farming is becoming more and more technicized.

The second: Technology is becoming an autonomous and determining social object. This can take place only through a social stratum, which tends to become a caste or class: the technocrats, who act by way of organization. Hence, one must speak of a technocratic and bureaucratic society. And off we march to wage war against the technocracy.

I would say that this passage is a bit superficial! Technology operates only through a class? This remark overlooks the fact that each individual participates in the technological system on all levels. To neglect such a fact, one has to insist on the categories of Marxist interpretation of class and of the force acting through a class. One has to start by ignoring the dissolution of classes, as caused by the growth of the technological system. But even more than that, the claim of a transition from "technician to technocrat" is perfectly unacceptable. I do not see a real technocrat anywhere, as I have often written. And for me, the society of technicians is ultimately quite antitechnocratic. For no technician claims to be ruling society. There is no need to regard technicians as technocrats or to believe that a class *of that type* actually exists. Those two criticisms are based on a very shallow and hasty view of the technological reality.

The best response to Lefebvre's mythic view of the technocracy was offered by F. Hetman (*L'Europe de l'abondance*, 1967). In his book, there is an intelligent analysis of the effects of technology (as bringing affluence) on the social structures. Hetman very lucidly shows three effects, which dovetail with the sociological makeup of a technological society. Colin Clark's classification is replaced by a different one: at the bottom, the "unqualified afunctionals"; then the "functional operators"; and at the top, the "rulers-researchers-conceivers"; with perhaps a fourth sector for the activities of operational research. In other words, the social distribution is (already) less and less in terms of activities applied to the economy, and more and more in keeping with the technological capacity. As a result, we are entering—so we are told—the "era of clerks," and these clerks are the decision-makers in all domains because they have the knowledge and use of the technologies. Like it or not (and Hetman shows this so well), the experts, the specialists of diverse technologies are to be found everywhere, from business to administration, from government to agriculture. They form the true grid of society, the network holding the various pieces together. It is the technological coherence that now makes up the social coherence. But this is not a technocracy in the true sense of the word.

Finally, Lefebvre's last criticism: The theory of the technological society is really an illusion, a myth justifying the situation.[10] Its aim is to justify the privileged positions, divert the revolutionary forces, and disguise the unbearable aspects of the society. In other words, that theory plays the role of "ideology" in Marxist doctrine. I admit that I do not quite understand how a concrete analysis leading to a certain interpretation can be described in those terms. (Unless one starts out from another ideology, Marxism. This ideology turns the categories of class, exploitation, proletariat, commodity, etc., into definitive and scientific categories. Hence, it cannot understand anything outside its system, and it then attacks whatever it cannot fit into its explanatory schema!) Suppose a biologist detects the proliferation of cancer cells and examines their growth and spread, the mechanism of their production, the factors promoting the disease. If he tries to interpret what he observes, is he "justifying" it? The attempt to explain may be, but is not necessarily, a myth. Why is discerning something new an ideological illusion? As though discovering the technological system qua system could justify its reality. Actually, I have observed that all the people who have become aware of that reality have a negative attitude toward it; they are fearful, anxiety-ridden, and sometimes even panicky. The ascertained reality is the exact opposite of what Lefebvre maintains. Far from justifying the situation, the discovery of the technological system normally seems like an attack against technology, a criticism of technicity per se. Any shedding of light on the technological structure is always received by technologists and intellectuals as an indictment of that structure, even if absolutely no value judgement has been expressed. Hence, Lefebvre's vaguely Marxist denunciation is off-target. The various critiques of the notion of a technological society mainly expose the ideological character of their authors.

\* \* \*

But we have to transcend the idea of the technological society. For technology has reached a new scope and organization. This book will investigate its specific structuring. I realize technology exists as a system, that is to say, an organized whole. Further on, I will discuss that in detail. But for the moment, I would like to state that I also intend to elaborate on a model as well as describe a reality. The main difficulty will stem from the ambiguity between those two entities. When I investigate the specific features of technologies as an ensemble and the theoretical functioning of that ensemble, then I will obviously be dealing with a model. But this model is based only on real givens, and it takes an entire aspect of our world into account. The impression of a model will be heightened by my ignoring dysfunctions. The dysfunctions of the system and its feedback, its correction due to errors, will be the subject of another book. However, the concept of a technological system requires us to define our society more precisely. It is not enough to call it a "technological and technicized society." Yet, conversely, can we identify the society with the technological system? Is the latter everything? Or has the society itself become that very system? Has the society been so thoroughly transformed as to become—so some people think—a megamachine? A mechanism expressing the technology in everything, translating it into all aspects and forms?

All the things making up the societal life—work, leisure, religion, culture, institutions—all the things forming a loose, complex whole, enclosing real life and giving man both a reason to live and an anxiety—all these things were "torn apart and more or less irreducible to one another." And it is easy to state that they are now technicized, homogenized, and integrated in a new whole, which *is not* the society. No more meaningful social or political organization is possible for this ensemble, every part of which is subordinate to the technologies and linked to other parts by the technologies. "All that reigns is the eternal substitution of homogeneous elements."

In regard to both the social reality and the natural or human reality, technology operates as an enormous abstraction factor. The idea of a "virtual society" is already finding acceptance and crops up in numerous authors. It corresponds to what I analyzed in *The Political Illusion* (politics in the world of images). There is no meaning. There is an abstracting of all activities, all kinds of work, all conflicts, which are located in a present-day reality, that has no depth. For instance, as Baudrillard has noted, in his writing on the consumer society, we are incapable of considering the rationality of the objects we consume. Thus, when watching TV, we are incapable of knowing that this miracle is a long social process of production, which leads to our consumption of images. For technology wipes away the very principle (social) reality. Everything that is social has moved to an abstract level, with the strange phenomenon of an acute awareness of nonreality (for example, the passion for politics) and an unawareness *of reality* (for example, technology). Now this shift of relationship is actually due to technology. It is technology that presents the nonreality which is mistaken for reality (consumer goods or political activity). Technology does this by its own process of distribution, the image. And it is technology that "hides itself" (Of course, this is not deliberate. There is no anthropomorphism here!) behind that luminous play of appearances. This is exactly like certain modern watches which not only hide the *mechanism* under the dial face (as has always been done), but also conceal the numbers and reduce the hands to practically nothing. All this for an aesthetic charge, an extreme ornamentation, or an exquisite design, with the function of the watch itself well-nigh vanishing beneath the decor. This is exactly what is happening today in the relationship between the social reality and our vivid and colored apprehension of a nonreality, which has no other function than to camouflage the mechanism and satisfy us with the "miracle mirage."

But what if we do live in a virtual society, if our attention is thus distracted and captured? What if all the things that used to constitute society are now integrated as separate factors in the technological system and beguiled by technology? If all that is true, then haven't we passed into the stage of the megamachine? Hasn't our society itself turned into a machine pure and simple? That is what N. Wiener thinks (he conceives of society as a cybernetic system). And so does L. Mumford (*The Myth of the Machine*, 1948), though with a totally different connotation. The megamachine is the completely organized and homogenized social system, in which society functions like a machine, with people supposedly as gears. This kind of organization is due to a total coordination, to the continuous growth of order, power, predictability, and, above all, control. The first megamachines were Egyptian and Mesopotamian society, where this organization achieved almost miraculous technological results. The system will reach its most perfect expression with the help of modern technology, in the future of the technological society.

Certain authors hold that the megamachine performs because of the computer. "The diabolatry of the machine is nothing next to the

## TECHNOLOGY AND SOCIETY

conformism of society," says Elgozy. The megamachine functions implacably—and the very meaning of individual liberty has vanished in it. It has the coldness, indifference, and anonymity of a machine. It certainly does not *try* to victimize or alienate man; it simply does so in order to exist. The more order becomes essential to the functioning of the megamachine, the more order engenders order, and the slightest disorder becomes intolerable. Thanks to the media of information and communication, the megamachine also exhibits certain features of a primary society. Each person is known in his totality (which is registered in the national computer). The computer gathers a cluster of previously scattered information about each individual, making the control of society unbearable, especially since this control will be exercised not just by "authorities," but also by the public, the "others," by public opinion. This is so because everything concerning each individual can be diffused and revealed to everyone else by telecommunications.

Thus, the megamachine functions on an abstract level as a social machine and on a totalitarian level by stripping all parts of the machine of their identity.

This primary trait reflects MacLuhan's idea that TV is turning the world into a global village. A fact that is even more acute if it involves not only the ubiquity allowed by TV and the rebirth of mythic thinking, but also the control of each individual by means of information. From this perspective, the technological system ultimately transforms society itself into a technological system. This is a danger (or possibility) tempting many creative writers. But curiously, sociologists can also accept this reduction of society to a machine. No matter how mechanistic or deterministic one may be, it is clear that no society has ever functioned in that way. It is an illusion to believe that Babylonian or Aztec society was a mechanism. This might be said of the institutions, the framework, the form of the society. But the social reality, within and below, was totally different. The very idea that these historical societies were megamachines tends to point out the confusion. For if our society *is* a machine, then the cause is not to be sought in the technological growth of *our* civilization: Yet it is precisely the technological system that could have such an outcome.

I believe, however, that it is highly dangerous to make use of such an apocalyptic vision. It is really quite easy to prove with facts that *our* society is not mechanized. On the one hand, it is full of short circuits, jammings, chaos, and also huge nontechnicized voids; on the other hand, man in this society has not really been mechanized to the point of being just a gear. Michel Crozier rightly points out the importance of interhuman relations in even the most bureaucratic system. *In reality, we must not confuse the technological system and the technological society. The system exists in all its rigor, but it exists within the society, living in and off the society and grafted upon it. There is a duality here exactly as there is between nature and the machine. The machine works because of natural products, but it does not transform nature into a machine. Society too is a "natural product." At a certain level, culture and nature overlap, forming society, in a totality that becomes a nature for man. And into this complex comes a foreign body, intrusive and unreplaceable: the technological system. It does not turn society into a machine.* It fashions society in terms of its necessities; it uses society as an underpinning; it transforms certain of society's structures. But there is always something unpredictable, incoherent, and irreducible in the social body. A society is made up of multiple systems, multiple types, multiple patterns, on different levels. Saying that technology is the determining factor of this society does not mean it is the only factor! Above all, society is made up of people, and the system, in its abstraction, seems to ignore that. It is only at an extreme point that we can view the society and the system as one and the same. But nobody can seriously maintain that this extreme has been reached.

We can thus say that the technological society is one in which a technological system has been installed. But it is not itself that system, and there is tension between the two of them. Not only tension, but perhaps disarray and conflict. And just as the machine causes disturbances and disorders in the natural environment and imperils the ecology, so too the technological system causes disorders, irrationalities, incoherences in the society and challenges the sociological environment.

Of course, if it is wrong to call modern society a megamachine, we still should not forget that some people greatly desire to make it one. Here we are faced with the dilemma posed so magnificently by Kleist in "The Marionette Theater." It is absolute alienation which allows mankind to receive grace—or else infinite consciousness. The latter being the attribute of God alone, man must be reduced to a puppet (and society to a machine) in order to find his original innocence and grace. Kleist does not appear to see *how* man will do that. But we know now. Thus, to achieve total liberty, exemption, and independence from natural as well as moral or social constraints, man must *be* in that state of perfect deindividualization, virtually of absence. The puppet acquires grace in absolute unconsciousness. (But for whom?)

This sums up the argument of certain researchers who do not express themselves in metaphysical terms. Yet that argument underlies and justifies their investigation. That would be the position of the technocrats, who seek to subjugate all social reality to the technological system. We will have to examine this problem later on. But for now, let us discuss two aspects.

One aspect is a very real, concrete, and worked-out project, for which the most serious researchers and politicians have been militating. It was presented in 1972 by the Japan Computer Usage Development Institute in Tokyo, and the goal is a society entirely technicized by the computer. This project would have to be implemented in stages, the first in 1977, the second in 1982. The starting phase involves an experimental urban unit of 100,000. Society is reduced to a certain number of cells (hospitals, schools, factories, offices, revenue agencies, courts of law, etc.) and a certain number of functions (production, development, performance, control, information, etc.). Each of these units is automated (which is not impossible). Man then becomes purely the servant of that totality. Next, all these cells and all these functions are connected through the computer. By now, the decision-making processes are no longer independent. A decision is the obligatory and inevitable result of those multiple connections. To the extent that an analysis could be total, this structure would approximate the famous megamachine. At the moment, there are numerous financial and methodological obstacles. But still, the intention exists.

This intention is quite understandable, for the technicians can have no other aim than to expand their technology, which they are constantly perfecting. But their intention overlaps dangerously with that of the neo-utopians. I have often attacked the neo-utopian trend on various levels.[11] I do not comprehend by what aberration H. Lefebvre can be an antitechnocrat and preach utopia at the same time. Naturally, I know the glorious arguments about how utopia will open up the imagination and grant us a marvelous freedom. But precisely and concretely, I believe that this trend is actually a "new ruse of the devil" to trick us into entering the megamachine. We must remember that all utopians of the past, without a single exception, have presented society exactly as a megamachine. Each utopia has been an exact repetition of an ideal organization, a perfect conjunction between the various parts of the social body. Utopia presents a flawless totalitarian society, which finally assures man of equality, the future, and so on. The perfect organization allowing the squelching of political power. What characterized all these descriptions was that the utopia could not come true.

Today, utopia is presented as wonderfully useful in that it gets us to invent what will be and has actually already been. Certain authors, reducing utopia to its smallest size, declare that man once formulated the utopia of flying, or the utopia of an immediate relationship with someone, or the utopia of seeing things that occur thousands of miles away. And presto! Such utopias came true! Yes indeed, because of technological processes. And we are told: Get thee to utopia, it is the reality of tomorrow. But we now learn how that reality is to be realized. Either it is a wild dream or else it will come true thanks to the progress of the technologies. There is no other horn to the dilemma. Since certain utopias have materialized, we are invited to formulate our utopias. Because, no matter how insane, they are going to establish a new kind of future. In reality, however, either a technology will grab hold of the dream and put it into practice, or else there will merely be smoke without any fire. Hence, the utopias of future societies strike me today as the dreadful seduction to realize my megamachine. The present-day utopians are the "decoys" of the technocrats. And we can rest assured that these technocrats are waiting only for a sign from the intellectual and spiritual elites of the social body to come swooping down in thick droves. The sole utopia is a technological one. And that may be the possibility for making the technological system and the technological society identical. Utopia lies in the technological society, within the horizon of technology. And nowhere else.

# PART ONE
# What Is Technology?

# 1
# TECHNOLOGY AS A CONCEPT

IN my early studies on technology, I employed this term as a concept without explaining it, thereby giving rise to countless misunderstandings. The technologies used in all possible domains, so I felt, had enough common features for us to deduce a general concept. It is common knowledge that, while nobody has ever seen "the dog," we can still find enough common traits in a spaniel, boxer, great dane, pekinese, pincher—despite all the differences—to understand one another perfectly when we use the word "dog." I certainly do not want to get into the quarrel of the universals. Nor will I claim that in some empyrean there is a concrete idea per se of absolute technology. But I do claim that, scientifically, I can construct a phenomenon from the features of, and the interrelations between, the phenomena generally known as "technological" in our society. For this society, in which technology has become dominant, is the first to have the concept of technology. Certain people now declare that "technology" does not exist, and that they know only plural technolog*ies*. Such a notion, however, comes from a shallow sense of realism and is obviously unsystematic.

Technology as a concept allows us to understand a set of phenomena that remain invisible even where technologies are perceptibly manifest. But while the concept may be indispensable for comprehension, it is by no means clear and simple in itself. Nor does it imply the existence of a technological system. We will not recur to the problem of defining technology. But we are going to examine the genesis of this concept in reference to modern reality.

\* \* \*

The terms "technique" and "technology" cover a large number of phenomena and have several meanings. The difficulty is that these meanings refer to various realities: concrete realities (the technology of the internal-combustion engine); objects of scientific study; and finally, strata of diversified technologies in time. Originally, it seems, people spoke of "technique," which, consistent with its etymology, meant a certain manner of doing something, a process or ensemble of processes. Diderot thus speaks of the "technique proper to each painter." But rapidly, as the machine and its industrial application came to dominate, "technique" (and then "technology" in English) began to designate the processes of constructing and exploiting machines. People now more frequently employed the plural. These were then studied by a science called *technologie* in French and *technology* in English. (While English uses "technology" for both the science and its object of study, French distinguishes respectively between *technologie* and *technique*. Trans. note.) This science consists in describing and analyzing these *techniques* (French), i.e., *technologies* (English), in tracing their history and investigating ways of improving them. At the end of the nineteenth century, *the science of technology was divided into five branches,* which is quite indicative of what was then known as *technique* (or *technology*). These five branches were: raw materials; processes and machines bearing upon the home (plus clothes and food); hygiene and health; light and heat; tools and instruments.

Scientists soon distinguished between instruments and energy sources. The classification of technologies was now by: tools and instruments; machines; apparatuses. Tools and instruments are material systems for increasing the efficiency of human action. Notably, they give man access to phenomena with an intensity that is too weak to act directly upon the senses (measuring instruments), or else they multiply the intensity of his efforts. From a technological viewpoint, these tools and instruments have the characteristic of being directly operated by man. Machines are material systems replacing man for actions he cannot perform himself, most often because they require too much energy. Finally, the ambiguous term "apparatus" designates both complex instruments and machines using a small amount of energy. Naturally, each area combines several tools, machines, and instruments in order to perform an operation correctly. Thus, the division of labor multiplies the number of technologies, which themselves produce machines.

Hence, technology was seen no longer as a parceling operation, but as a "set of inanimate or exceptionally animate beings, organized to replace man in performing a set of operations defined by man" (Louis Couffignal, *Théorie de l'efficacité de l'action*). Technology thus has two new features: It no longer relates to just an aspect, an action, but to a whole, a set, an ensemble. It refers above all to machines that tend to replace man. And among these machines, one distinguishes: those that furnish energy; those that utilize energy (power machines replacing man in his processing of material); and those involved in information (operational machines replacing man in his operations of creating, transforming, or transmitting information[1]). On this level, "technology" scarcely refers to industrial operations.

The stages of technology are readily compared to the stages of industrial growth. These stages are dictated by energy production. Observers thus speak of the "first industrial revolution," characterized by the use of coal as a power source, and by the machines built to use coal. Then came a second industrial revolution, characterized by electricity. The third one causes some wavering: the use of atomic energy. But for several years now, people have been speaking of a fourth industrial revolution: the one launched by the computer. It is obvious that we are now switching gears, for this is no longer a change or advance in power sources. The dominant factor is no longer a growth of potential or exploited energy, but rather an apparatus of organization, information, memorization, and preparation for decision-making, to replace man in a huge number of intellectual operations.

We can see that all the above stages are linked to the use of machines and specific technologies. But technology is then viewed as a reality that is independent of more or less improved practices and of machines. Technology as a whole has a general character in relation to individual technologies, but it does not leave the area of machine application. Nevertheless, a new meaning soon appeared. It became more and more obvious that these technologies and machines had vast consequences for human behavior and societal organization. People now began speaking of the "technological society" (Georges Friedmann, *"société technicienne"*). Using "technology" in a wider sense, they began studying the machine not only in itself, but also in its relations to man and society. (We will not examine here this social science of technology studied as the "industrial society.")

Nevertheless, at that time—twenty years ago—the term "technology" was limited to the strict meaning of a scientific study of technological processes *with no reference* to sociological dimensions. For the latter, people spoke of a sociology of the machine or of technology. However, a new concept was already emerging. On the one hand, technology could apparently be defined very broadly in terms of what had implicitly been its overriding feature since its origins: efficiency. People could now say that technology was the ensemble of the absolutely most efficient means at a given moment. This allowed unhooking technology from the machine. For there were so many other technologies than those coupled to machines— for instance, sport technologies. Moreover, this definition had a great advantage. It reminded us that technology was made up of means, all means, but that we could focus only on those regarded as the most efficient at any moment, because that was the very criterion of choice and progress in the technologies. In other words: Wherever there is research and application of new means as a criterion of efficiency, one can say that there is a technology. The latter is not defined by the instruments used or by some area of action (clothing, transportation, etc.). There are perfectly abstract technologies (for example, speed reading). Yet the same word was employed to designate the parcellary, mechanical technologies and technology in that latter sense.

Americans waver among *technics, technique,* and *technology.* They frequently employ "technology" for what the French call *technique* in the general sense that we have just defined, rather than for the science of mechanical *"techniques,"* as in French. But this word did not achieve a varied gamut corresponding to the diversification and complexification of the phenomenon itself. Scholars observed that individual technologies, applied to different domains, react upon one another, which makes it impossible to study them separately. On the other hand, technologies were becoming more and more numerous, gradually encroaching upon the whole field of human activity. They took on a new consistency because of their very number and density. Finally, these two factors were joined by the computer. The data processer is an element of connection, of coordination among a huge number of technologies, just as in itself it is the product of diverse technologies conjoined. People thus came to a new conception of technology, as an environment and as a system. That is to say: The combined technologies, affecting the totality of human actions and life-styles, took on a qualitatively different importance. Technology was no longer an addition of *"techniques."* By combining and universalizing, observers had now given it a kind of autonomy and specificity. This is the point we have reached in the domains of both accomplished and established facts, ergo, of scientific analysis. This analysis is hard enough and risky enough for the social science of technology (the study of its effects on human groups). But it is even more difficult and hazardous for the study of technology as an all-inclusive and all-including system and reality.

Yet when we try to formulate the concept of technology, are we constructing a model? "Concept" does not necessarily mean "model." Today, we know that in many human sciences, the "model" is an ideal emergency exit.[2] Constructing a model enables one to have an irresponsible attitude. After describing a certain sociological phenomenon, one can state, in case of error, that the goal was not to describe a reality, but rather to construct a model "to see how that works." However, people forget that if a model is remote from reality we may see the model working, but its workings will explain nothing. It is exactly like a man who claims he can explain how a painter creates his work. The man takes a puzzle representing a canvas by that painter and starts to piece the puzzle together. He will wind up with the picture, but he will have shown only how a puzzle works and not how an artist paints!

Hence, I do not claim to establish a model. I want to give an account of reality, but on a certain level of abstraction. I will approach Max Weber's ideal type (see *Gesammelte Aufsätze zur Wissenschaftslehre,* 1972) by stressing one or several viewpoints, dwelling on certain phenomena, linking facts that seem isolated, in order to achieve a homogeneous whole. It is not a model because I claim that the whole is truly homogeneous, but cannot be seen as such due to epiphenomena, accidents, and, at the other end of the scale, the incognito aspect of interrelations. Thus, what I am constructing under the name of concept, then system, may look like a model in that we ask at the outset: "Is looking at the facts in this way useful for understanding?" rather than, "Are things really like this?"[3] But we will rapidly leave this stage in order to consider not how the model works, but what its problematics are. That is to say: What is questionable about the model in and of itself. At that point, we will integrate the destructive process of the model in order to give an account of reality. And from there, we will go on to question the very fact that serves as the origin of the model. That will establish the critical relationship between the model and reality, and we will avoid both the rhetorical discourse of a philosophical technology and the easiness of setting up a model with no external problematics.

\* \* \*

In any case, the present concept has the crucial advantage of underlining the specific character of technology and sidestepping the habitual confusions. C. Wright Mills quoting Lionel Robbins, for example (*The Sociological Imagination*, p. 80), rightly says: "It is not an exaggeration to say that, at the present day, one of the main dangers of civilization arises from the inability of minds trained in the natural sciences to perceive the difference between the economic and the technical." These are confusions between technology and science, between technology and the machine, which we have already abundantly talked about. And then there is the even more frequent confusion between technology and economy. The instant one tries to differentiate them, Marxists accuse one of diversionary maneuvers and antirevolutionary idealism! And yet, so long as we fail to study the technological phenomenon beyond its economic implications and the problems of the economic system and class struggle, we are doomed to ignorance of contemporary society (and hence, impotence for any revolutionary action). Economic progress and technization are not synonymous. Technization does not have an economic aspect *from the very outset*. Today, if there really is a (potential and debated) kinship between technological and economic growth, there is no kinship whatsoever between technological growth and economic development, as we shall see.

A good example of the superficial view of the matter is provided by Rocard, ("La Crise de la recherche," *Le Monde*, May 1970). He keeps mixing up technology with its economic use, especially its "capitalist" and De Gaullist use. Since discoveries have an economic end, he says, the only question is whether economic growth "permits satisfying the aspirations of the entire society or only maximizes the profits of a tiny number." The problems (the real problems, of course, and which I do not contest) are those that radically prevent our discerning the structure of our society and that cause insoluble difficulties. For instance, Rocard feels that the capitalist structure hinders a complete utilization of technological discoveries. But he does not explain why the system manages to work rather well in Japan and West Germany.

## TECHNOLOGY AS A CONCEPT

Thus, the first step in elaborating on the concept of technology is, obviously, to isolate it from untold connected phenomena that are not in the realm of technology. Or else, they are—at first sight, inextricable—mixtures of technologies and other factors (political, familial, psychological, ideological, etc.). A *failure to isolate* the concept in order to first consider it in itself will spawn countless mistakes. For example, in the questions we ask ourselves about technology per se.

A good catalogue of wrong questions on technology (wrong simply for lack of rigor) is supplied by the World Council of Churches in a document summing up the many writings that raise these questions.[4] This document actually lists the problems to be studied: the necessity of an environmental policy, the world food problem, the establishment of national and international structures for a more equitable use of technology, city planning, new problems of the oceans and space, the consequences of genetic and biological progress for controlling and improving life, the creation of new consumer needs, a revolution in producing and storing information, the effects of communications technologies on education and on conditioning public opinion. All these questions, none of which is wrong, are raised with no previous study of technology per se.[5] However, if we study facets of the phenomenon but not the phenomenon itself, we must wind up with mistakes and/or platitudes. Remarkably, these experts, in a second chapter, ask about the "politico-economic consequences of technology" without realizing that the first chapter studies only the consequences and not the cause itself. But how can we speak of consequences without first asking: consequences of *what?* The authors act as if everyone knows a priori what technology is. A brash assumption. Which, of course, results in a lot of shallow work by the World Council of Churches. We have to avoid proceeding along such lines. First, we have to analyze the fact itself, which can be done only if we establish a concept, separating technology from its cluster of economico-political factors.

\* \* \*

However, such a procedure does not imply that technology will hereafter be considered in itself, as a self-sufficient entity. That would lead to a further and opposite error. Clearly, one cannot perform an intellectual operation of abstraction and then stop dead. We have to consider things as they are and not carry on about a technology per se, even though that is what countless authors are doing—i.e., describing technology as though man, economy, politics, and society simply did not exist or were still a perfectly malleable clay.

Take D. Rorvik, for instance. His unbelievable books, *Brave New Baby* (1972) and *As Man Becomes Machine* (1971), contain a huge catalogue of what certain advanced technologies are bringing about. And once again, we cannot tell from these descriptions whether they bear upon technologies that are already acquired and mastered, or ongoing experiments whose results are not yet known, or a scientist's hopes of success, or a research project, or the conviction that twenty years from now we'll attain something or other. Rorvik presents: the machine man, the "kibert," the direct link between the brain and the computer; electronic medicine; the generalized use of robots; E.S.B. (electronic stimulation of the brain, which he translates marvelously into electrosex, electromemory, electroeuphoria); A.R.M.S. (a cybernetic system allowing the extension of the senses and of work to thousands of miles away); B.F.T. (bio-feedback training to separate the mind from matter and liberate the body); etc. And Rorvik (like A. Toffler, by the way) offers all these things as the reality of technology in the near and sure future. A lab technician does a few experiments—like putting fifty electrodes in a guinea pig's brain—and that, we are told, is going to be the normal, everyday situation tomorrow. And nobody wonders about the moral and psychological obstacles set up by men, or about the economic difficulties of putting such enterprises to general use, or about the political and sociological problems involved. Everything happens as in a dream world. The great wizard discovers a new technology, his magic wand touches reality, and presto! Everything is transformed.

To be precise, I am not passing judgment on any particular technology, I am simply trying to point out that there is a world of difference between the laboratory discovery of a technology and its universal application. All sorts of discoveries have seemed possible at a given moment, and yet ultimately they did not materialize. Bear in mind all the density of reality. It is not the "dangers" in the growth of those technologies that frighten me, but rather the childishness of the authors who believe that these technologies are already here and that tomorrow's world is today's laboratory. To speak of a machine that lives and thinks, or even reproduces itself is infantile anthropocentrism (Von Neumann). Jean Claude Beaune declares that the machine has a superrationality "testifying to the strength of a creative thought of its own norms, founded on a new world full of noise and senses." But that is pure phantasmagoria. Again, this is precisely a focus on *aspects* of technology (mainly computers); and Beaune is pushing them to an extreme as if they were the reality.

But technology is inevitably part of a world that is not inert. It can develop only in relation to that world. No technology, however autonomous it may be, can develop outside a given economic, political, intellectual context. And if these conditions are not present, then technology will be abortive. Once again, the magicians who tout the machine as the perfect substitute for man, as thinking so much better than man because it can think "outside the tumult of passions" (Beaune), are lapsing into the same error. They are considering an aspect, one facet of the technological phenomenon, but not the technological phenomenon itself.

Only by knowing this phenomenon in its totality can one measure both its newness and its limits. Obviously, if we picture *plural* technologies, next to one another, then we can always imagine their indefinite development. But if we study a system in which the technologies correlate to one another and we perceive that the system is not closed, then we also have to realize that we can neither anthropologize the technologies nor imagine their indefinite development. That is why we have to start by conceptualizing technology and flatly rejecting the hyperbolic and phantasmagorical depictions of tomorrow's society à la Godard's *Alphaville*.

This is a mythological picture of civilization, which is not about to, and indeed never will, come true. Like *2001*, it is as alien as it is both horrible and perfectly reassuring. An author constructs a monstrous and imaginary vision of the world to come, and then he attacks it—which he can do with impunity, since it does not correspond to any social structure or any group. This also plays a part in the development of the system, as we shall see further on; but it is downright false in regard to technology. And whether the mistake is due to overgenerosity, as in Rorvik, or to horror, it comes down to the same thing: this is not technology, this is not "the world of tomorrow."

Ferreting out a concept of technology allows a precise measure of its possibilities by establishing its totality and by placing the technological phenomenon in relation to the context in which it develops. On the other front, it allows us to assert the autonomy of technology and prevents us from falling victim to the equally simplistic optimism of a Charles Reich (*The Greening of America*,

1970) who sees everything as occurring solely on the level of consciousness. To control technology, "it suffices to take hold of controls that no one is holding. We have to fill a void, put an intelligence where none exists. . . ." It's that simple. Once again, a touch of the magic wand, but instead of the explosion of the universal use of advanced technologies, we have a miraculous control by a simple awareness of the entire system. Technology itself produces "Consciousness III," which is that of man as a free and spiritual adult. Hippies everywhere. It "suffices" if the system of values changes, if psychological behavior is transformed, if the way of life is transformed, and poof! Technology has no more power. The triumph of long hair and bell bottoms, proclaims Reich, guarantees our mastership of technology. "For the choice of a lifestyle is an act of transcendence of the machine, an act of independence, a declaration of independence. We are entering a new age of man."

Watch out on the right, watch out on the left. Of course, Rorvik is correct when he underlines the enormous growth of technological potentials and the prodigious gamut of possible uses. But he is wrong when he believes that technology develops within the perfect void of a closed balloon. Reich is correct when he, conversely, emphasizes that nothing can be done without consciousness and that consciousness plays a preponderant role in fashioning the society. But he is wrong when he believes that a change in consciousness is in itself the transformation of the technological system. One man dreams of the perfect malleability of man and society, the other of the perfect malleability of technology. Conceptualizing ought to help us avoid both mistakes. By its intellectual rigor, the concept will prohibit us from going off course. Far from removing us from reality, its very abstraction (if the work is done right) will allow us to take account of all reality and prevent us from forgetting any of the correlations in which the concept is located.

Thus, our primary work does not consist in dillydallying in the field of possibilities, culling an iris here, a heart transplant there, or a lily of the field, a thinking computer. We have to come up with a system that takes into account different elements as well as their being factors of the realities that condition and are conditioned. By working out a concept, we have "to grasp things as they are" and not be swept away uncritically into any random direction in which our hearts happen to carry us!

Under these conditions, we absolutely have to establish the difference between the concept of *technique* and the concept of *technology*. It is a grave error, often made by French intellectuals imitating Anglo-American usage, to speak of *technology* when they really mean *technique*. The former is a discourse on *technique*, a science of *technique*. First of all, it is a discourse on different *techniques* (English, technologies); then an attempt at discursing on *technique* (English, technology) in general, i.e., actually on the concept itself. This, however, is not intended as a study of the procedures of some—say, industrial—operation (That would be the subject of technical courses!); the goal here is a philosophical reflection. Now the latter is actually uncertain only so long as we do not start by determining the very concept of *technique* (English, technology) and the *système technicien* (the technological system). At this point, the logos becomes a kind of abstract dissertation without references. It is all the more interesting in that, according to the customary mania of philosophers, this is a discourse on *technique* (English, technology) per se, in any era, in any environment, as though it were possible to identify Western *technique* (English, technology) before the eighteenth century with present-day *technique* (English, technology).

Simondon directly tackles the technological phenomenon itself, and in these terms he does good work rather than producing a chimerical discourse. In contrast, we have a fine example of empty discourse, using the Anglicism "technology," in Beaune's book *La Technologie* (1972). This effort is adorned with all the pompous rhetoric of structuralism, post-Marxism, and modern linguistics in order to sound deep. It supplies four or five definitions of "technology" without avoiding the simplistic pitfalls (the machine lives and thinks) or the most elementary confusions (we cannot judge the technological phenomena because "the object is indifferent to the phantasms that we bring to bear upon it," etc.). This is an utterly naive labor, which is given a scientific appearance by the rhetorical system. As such, it is quite "technological." A simple discourse about nothing that has been clearly conceptualized.

(In this English version of Ellul's book, the translator, with the author's permission, has gone along with American usage by rendering the French *technique* as "technology." J.N.)

# 2
# TECHNOLOGY AS AN ENVIRONMENT

EVEN when technology is abstract, a procedure, an organization, it is far more of a mediation than an instrument. People generally conceive of technology as a means of action allowing man to do what he was unable to achieve by his own means. That is true, of course. But it is much more important to consider that these "means" are a mediation between man and his natural environment.[1] This mediation can be either passive or active (clothing, dwellings, technological products are screens placed between the body and the surrounding environment). Man has thus created a whole set of mediations all around himself. So long as technologies of traditional societies were sporadic and fragmentary, they represented singular mediations. The overall situation has changed with the multiplication of technologies and the development of the technological phenomenon.[2] Now the character of that mediation is already that of the technological object. As Simondon emphasizes: "Concretization gives the technological object an intermediary place between the natural object and the scientific representation of the abstract," i.e. primitive technological object, which is a far cry from constituting a natural system. It is the translation into matter of a set of scientific notions and principles that are separate from one another. . . . On the other hand, the concrete, i.e. evolved technological object approaches the existential mode of natural objects, it tends towards inner coherence, towards closure of the system of causes and effects; furthermore, it incorporates a part of the natural world, which is involved as a condition of functioning."

It has often been said that work is what makes the human being the mediator between nature and mankind as a species. If this is true, then technological work creates for itself the most immense

## TECHNOLOGY AS AN ENVIRONMENT

set of mediations imaginable because the work is incorporated and lasting:

"Through technological activity, man creates mediations, and these mediations can be detached from the individual who produces them and conceives them. The individual expresses himself in them but does not adhere to them. The machine has a kind of impersonalness, which allows it to become another man's instrument. The human reality that it crystallizes within itself is alienable precisely for being detachable. . . . The technological object, conceived and constructed by man, is not limited to just creating a mediation between man and nature. It is a stable mixture of the human and the natural, it contains the human and the natural, it gives its human content a structure resembling that of natural objects, it can be inserted into the world of natural causes and effects in that human reality. The relation between man and nature is not merely experienced and practiced in an obscure fashion; it takes on a status of stability, of consistency, which makes it a reality having its own laws and its orderly permanence. Technological activity, by putting up the world of technological objects and universalizing the objective mediation between man and nature, reattaches man to nature with a far richer and more definite bond than that of the specific reaction of collective labor."

(Simondon)

All those things are perfectly true. But we have to add that this mediation becomes exclusive of any other. There are no other relationships between man and nature; the whole set of complex and fragile bonds that man has patiently fashioned—poetic, magic, mythical, symbolic bonds—vanishes. There is only the technological mediation, which imposes itself and becomes total. Technology then forms both a continuous screen and a generalized mode of involvement. Technology is in itself not only a means, but a universe of means—in the original sense of *Universum:* both exclusive and total. The same is manifest in the relations *between* individuals or between individuals and the group. Here too, everything becomes technological. Human relations can no longer be left to chance. They are no longer the object of experience, of tradition, of cultural codes, of symbolism. Everything has to be exposed (group dynamism, psychoanalysis, depth psychology), elucidated, then transformed into applicable technological schemata (pedagogy, human relations, etc.). This is done in such a way that each individual adds his construction and also plays the exact role that is expected of him. Only then does he have full gratification for himself, and the others are gratified by his conforming behavior.

The code has become technological. Baudrillard has marvelously described that in respect to communion. Speaking about televised sports, he shows that they have an important function: participation. The participating athlete and the participating spectator each gets what he wants: the athlete, the pleasure of being on the tube; the spectator, the feeling of being part of a whole "in contact." They get what they're after: communion. Or rather that modern, asepticized form of communion: communication, "contact." What distinguishes the consumer society is not the deplored absence of ceremonies. The telecast game is as much of a ceremony as the eucharist or as the sacrifice in primitive society. Now, however, the ceremonial communion does not go through bread and wine which are flesh and blood. It goes through mass media, which are not only the messages, but also the broadcasting devices, the broadcasting network, the broadcasting station, the receiving apparatuses, and of course, the producers and the public.

In other words: *"Communion no longer passes through a symbolic support but through a technological support. It is in those terms that communion is communication."* Baudrillard here puts his finger on the most profound mediating reality of technology: Technology is the support of interhuman communion. But this communion, no longer symbolic, has turned into sheer technological communication. In this way, and because man has entered a single, centralized, and exclusive model of mediation, technology has become a mediator. One can, of course, say that technology has always been that, and that it is only that by its very nature: As a means and an ensemble of means, it is obviously a mediator, an intermediary between man and his ancient environment.[3]

This, however, has three vast consequences. The first is that we are dealing with an autonomous mediation. It is common knowledge that the most important thing is not so much the choice of a value as the possibility of a mediation between the value and the individual or the social body. Technology, as the sole mediator now recognized, actually escapes any system of values. Is there, then, no other mediator to make a choice for or against technology, to find the means of subjugating it? Man? Which man? The one who is already incorporated in the system? How about the state? But the state has already become technological. The people? The nation as a whole? (According to the carefully nurtured myth that the people have to decide on the "great options," and technology has to carry them out!) But the people are half a century behind the reality, and they understand nothing of the real problems that arise! At most, if the popular decisions were applicable, they could halt technological growth, interfere with the system, and provoke a socio-economic regression, which the aforesaid people are in no way ready to accept! Thus, mediation by technology excludes any other, and this allows technology to entirely escape the desired or supposed values.

No doubt, we have the impression that the intermediary of man or of the masses or of public opinion is what brings about each development, each orientation of technology. But let us not forget that we are dealing with a man who is already within the system and on whom the pressure is brought to bear. And this pressure is exerted not only by the existing reality, but also by the foreseeable and expected possibilities.

Technologies now make it possible to shape desire, and public opinion forms on that basis. Yet, in its turn, public opinion exerts pressure in demanding the fulfillment of the desire. A small example: All experts are now unanimous that auto accidents are largely caused by speeding.[4] A very simple measure would appear possible. Car manufacturers might only install engines having limited power. If an engine could not go beyond sixty-five miles an hour, then a large number of the dangers and laws could be done away with. But no one seems to have envisioned this solution. Because as soon as it is *possible* to manufacture engines and cars that can do one hundred twenty miles on the highway, the technological *possibility* exerts a pressure of necessity on opinion. For modern man is situated in *that environment*. And public opinion, in turn, would not allow the manufacturers to curb the speed of their engines or prevent a possibility from coming true. One may therefore believe that the pressure of consensus is what mediates and controls. In reality, it plays that part only to the extent that it is preformed, adapted, and obedient to any technological possibility. But it has no more independence or specificity.

The second consequence: The mediation by technology is essentially sterile and sterilizing, contrary to all previous systems of mediation, which were plurivocal, equivocal, unstable in their applications, and also deeply rooted in a rich and creative unconscious. Technology, on the other hand, is univocal, superficial, but stable. It involves clear and orderly mediation, but without playing or evoking, without remembering or projecting. It is a truly efficient medium, and it has imposed itself in lieu of poetic mediations. It sterilizes all around itself anything that could disturb that rigor. It gives man a sterile universe with neither germs nor microbes.

Finally, the third consequence: the relation between technology and man is nonmediated. The social or individual consciousness today is formed directly by the presence of technology, by man's immersion in that environment, without the mediation of thought, for which technology would only be an object, without the mediation of culture. The relation to technology is immediate, which does not mean that consciousness has *now* become the simple reflection of the technological environment. That is what, say, MacLuhan means with his celebrated formula: "The medium is the message." The message that man is trying to transmit has become the pure reflection of the technological system, of technological objects, of images and discourses which can only be technological images and discourses on technology. For the system permeates the totality of experience and social practice.[5] "The focus on the technological object, a passive focus, attentive only to the functioning, interested only in the structure, fascinated by this spectacle without a backdrop, fully absorbed in its transparent substance, that focus becomes the prototype of the social act." Thus the mediating technological system becomes the universal mediator, excluding any other mediation but its own.[6] That is the highest degree of its autonomy. Mediatization by technology is fundamental to understanding modern society. Not only does technology mediate between man and the natural environment and, to a second degree, between man and the technological environment; but it also mediates between men. People are more and more in contact with one another because of technological instruments (the telephone) and psychological technologies (pedagogy, human relations, group dynamism). But also, each person enters into contact with humankind, the totality of men, through technological devices (TV, radio, etc.), launching the reign of what has been dubbed long-term relations. These are qualitatively different from short-term relations, which are nonmediated (or mediated by highly ineffective traditional cultural approaches). This technological mediatization of human relations produces a phenomenon that never stops amazing us: the growing sense of individual solitude in a world of universalized communications.

Having become a *universum* of means and media, technology is in fact the environment of man. These mediations are so generalized, extended, multiplied, that they have come to make up a new universe; we have witnessed the emergence of the "technological environment." This means that man has stopped existing primarily in his "natural" environment (made up by what is vulgarly called "nature": countryside, forests, mountains, ocean, etc.). He now is situated in a new, artificial environment. He no longer lives in touch with the realities of the earth and the water, but with the realities of the instruments and objects forming the *totality* of his environment.[7] He is now in an environment made of asphalt, iron, cement, glass, plastic, and so on. Unless he is an aviator or sailor or on a mountain excursion during a period of leisure, he no longer has to know the signs of coming weather. Instead, he has an essential need to know the meanings of traffic signals. And even the problem of weather forecasting is no longer taken care of by a direct knowledge of the sky, the wind, etc., but by radio and TV weathermen. A person deals with the natural elements only through a set of technologies which is so complete that he is actually dealing with those technologies themselves. The natural environment itself disappears. We obviously have to make a comparison with the city, an essential product of technology. In the city, man perceives the natural elements only accidentally (parks, sidewalk trees). Nothing spontaneously natural is left here. And outside nature is reserved for spare time, relaxation, etc., given the decreasing importance of agriculture and the decline in the farming population.

However, the substitution of the technological environment for the natural environment cannot be reduced to the phenomenon of urbanization. Work also produces the same rupture. The worker, for instance, no longer knows anything about the material he is working on. He only has to know the machines performing the necessary operations.

And then soon, there is a second abstraction with automation. We can take all sectors of life and we will see the same trend everywhere. Children are brought up for this environment. A child does not have to know anything about the elements of nature, he has to know about factories and how to cross the street. He is technologically prepared to ply a trade in the technology. Technology is the living environment, not only because it excludes any direct relationship to the natural elements or modifies those that exist (water, air), not only because man's environment is now made up solely of technological objects; but because technology infringes directly upon man's life, exacting adaptations like those once demanded by the natural environment.

The world in which man lives is that of his mechanical environment. This brings both a knowledge of that environment and an overall behavior relative to that environment. Man no longer seeks to know the natural environment as such.

And that is why the technological mind is radically different from the savage mind. The thinking process is most likely the same, but it applies to a different area, which necessarily results in a certain mode. The mode of savage thinking was in accord and in harmony with the natural environment. When man finds himself in an environment that is becoming exclusively technological, the mode of savage thinking, which survives as such in man, becomes fairly useless. The savage mind is determined by the natural environment. Its application point is the natural environment. It shapes that environment by establishing the relationship between the human environment and the natural environment. However, it is the natural environment that serves not only as an environment but even more so as an interpreter for the relationship of man to himself and of men to one another. Substituting the technological environment for the natural environment produces a change in those relationships. A schism occurs among men, a splintering of natural groups, formal communication replaces communion, and the technological environment then serves as interpreter for the (false) relationships of men.

For if we admit—and I willingly do so—that the savage mind is a constitutive part of "human nature," then the fact that it exists in an inadequate environment commits men not to community but to all kinds of schisms. This is particularly obvious in the difficulty or impossibility of symbolizing. One of modern man's greatest losses is the faculty of symbolizing. This faculty did and could function only in relation to the natural environment. Symbolization, which helped man to survive in a hostile world, has become inadequate for the technological environment, in which it has no use. Modern man is torn apart: Symbolization remains so profoundly inscribed in him after millenia that it cannot be annulled. But all in all, it has been rendered gratuitous, ineffective. It is even blocked because the environment of man today is utterly unsusceptible to the necessity of that process. The results are: escape symbolization, as in modern art; artificial symbolization (bearing upon technology but perfectly useless and meaningless, as we shall see later on). The approach to, the grasp, interpretation, and control of, the technological environment cannot take place through symbolization. As for the natural environment, symbolization is made perfectly meaningless here by the dominance of utilitarian technology.

Our knowledge concerns an abstraction of the natural environment, which is grasped through finer and finer technologies. But the *living environment* is the mechanical and technological environment, which is studied directly as such. We would, *for instance*, be therefore dealing with the theory of vibrations and shocks as a total explanation for the living environment.

This kind of study concerns not only a mechanical resource that the engineer has to utilize in his work, but the whole of the human environment. And there is no way of thus analyzing the human environment than by starting with the technological environment. Mechanics in itself constitutes an environment, and it, in turn, is merely a part (a tiny part) of the technological environment. Man now has to study his surroundings exactly as "primitive" man had to "study" his natural surroundings. First of all, in order to survive in them and then in order to try and master them and get as much out of them as possible. When we are dealing with an environment that is intermediary between the natural and the technological environment, namely the urban milieu, we have only one thought in mind: to transfer it into a purely technological environment.

The urban milieu preserves a few aspects of the natural environment: a certain spontaneity, an incoherence in regard to man, a luxuriance, a diversity, an irrationality. Like the natural surroundings, the urban environment is both close and alien to man. Formed uniquely out of technological products, it is, nevertheless, not the technological environment per se, because its development was anarchic and not technological. Yet that is exactly what makes us so ill at ease. It does not have the rigor, the simplicity, the rationality of technologies. Man has introduced his disorder here, he has turned these surroundings into his own thing. The streets are dirty and crowded, there are mysterious nooks, there is wasted space, the lines are not clean, and nothing is functional.

This is not just the "conflict" between medieval towns and automobile traffic. It is, far more deeply, the product of traditional technologies, a product that man has humanized and that fails to satisfy our impetuous desire for subjecting everything to exact technologies. The Swedes have managed to do so. By dint of rigorous planning and an efficient system of public transport, they have succeeded in renovating the center of Stockholm and creating new suburban towns out of nothing. They have achieved a near-perfect technization of the urban texture, and thus, of course, they have produced an *agreeable* milieu.

Not only is the technological rationality satisfied. But the latter can *also* be agreeable if correctly employed. We now realize that people need so and so many places of relaxation, so and so many square yards of green space, so and so many socio-cultural appurtenances, etc. And yet Stockholm is tinged with a certain anxiety. As though people were wondering what is to come once this perfection is attained. And then what? What is there beyond paradise?

Urbanism remains a problem even when everything has been worked out. Is this "man's eternal dissatisfaction" or the difficulty that a still primitive man has in adjusting to an environment that is utterly technicized, though agreeable? We cannot answer this question today. Nevertheless, it is true that now, as modern men, we are called upon not to employ technologies, but to *live* with and among them. Rorvik can, assuredly, describe the idyllic marriage of man and robot. But the problem is more subtle. Our adaptations to natural realities, going back to remote ages, have now become useless. What good is knowing how to tell a mushroom from a toadstool or how to steal up to a deer?

We have to adjust to a new set of realities. We have to train new reflexes, learn technologies for using the brain, for appreciating art (itself an expression of the technological society), for establishing human relations through the intermediary of technologies. The technological environment is no longer a set of resources that we sometimes use (for work or distraction). It is now a coherent ensemble which "corsets" us on all sides, which encroaches upon us, and which we can no longer do without. It is now our one and only living environment.

\* \* \*

Nonetheless, we have to avoid a misunderstanding. People habitually speak of an artificial environment made up of *objects*. For several years now, they have belabored the point of the invasion of the objects. Georges Perec's *Les Choses* is significant. We live in an object universe. And Baudrillard has even made a system of these objects. That universal presence, that need to make up for that existential fault by owning a lot of things, that process leading to the reification of man, which I myself have studied—all those things certainly exist. But we have also noticed that these objects are not lasting and are made to be thrown away. These objects do not exist by themselves, they replace one another in rapid succession. They are totally valueless; they have an obvious momentary luster when acquired; then they stop being truly useful, pleasant, familiar, they are no longer our companions. They are really made, in full use, to be destroyed and cast away.

The invasion by the objects is accompanied by the scorn for those very same objects. These two facts must be viewed together. There is not a proliferation on one side and, on the other side, an appended remark: the replacement. In point of fact, things are made to be destroyed, bought to be discarded, multiplied in order to be eliminated. Objects are the object of our profound scorn.

But why is that? In reality, these objects have no value or importance whatsoever, they exist only as products of the technological mechanism. What characterizes this society is not the object but the means. It is not the invasion by the objects, but the multiplication of means *ad infinitum*. Modern art bears fine witness to that structural reality. This is profoundly corroborated by the fact that it ultimately makes no difference what technology bears upon, because technology allows anything to be done. And if there is a proliferation of objects, it is not a phenomenon in itself nor a response to a human desire, but rather it is the direct effect of applying technological means. Only the means are glorified.

Products are not valued very highly. We need only consider the communist goal. An equal sharing of products and incomes is not at all satisfying. The real point is to control the instruments of production. The stakes are not greater consumer power but ownership of the technology. Of course, the Leninists are ignorant of any correct analysis of the technological society; and in formulating their demand, they do not realize what they are doing; but they are spontaneously obeying the scale of real values. And if we regard objects as the reality surrounding us, then we have to watch out for the more and more widely stated belief that the object ultimately does not exist—anymore than the subject. The sharp traditional distinction is vanishing. For the sake of what? Processes of involvement, structures of functioning. We will have to show elsewhere that structuralism is not a creative way of thinking, but the simple product of the primacy of the means. How "it" works. But this is exclusively technology. This is the universe dominated by technologism.

However, there is one very interesting thing about this philosophical trend: It reveals that, in order to give elbow room and free play to the superordinated activity of the (technological) means, the subject must not exist: the subject must only obey the means. However, the object must not exist either: the object is merely an unimportant product of the workings of the technologies. Which is exactly what that philosophy states. We thus reach the decisive conclusion that our universe is not a universe of objects, that it is not a system of objects, but a universe of means and a technological system.

\* \* \*

The fact that the technological environment has become our living environment obviously entails a certain number of modifications in the traditional environments within which human history has unfolded. Let us use the schematic terms, *nature* and *society*.

Nature, now technicized, and society, now technological, are no longer what they have always been. In fact, this change may be viewed as the final question of our study; but at the outset, we have to take a few quick looks. It is probably unnecessary to stress the action of modern technology on the natural surroundings, on that nature which is itself a product of human work, albeit with soft technologies and without involving an endless control. We need merely point out the admirable studies by B. Charbonneau in particular (*Le Jardin de Babylone, Tristes campagnes*). More abstractly, however, we have to understand that the new environment acts by penetrating and bursting the older ones. The old (natural) environment is not really abandoned in favor of the new (technological) one. Rather, the new one permeates the old one, engulfs it, utilizes it, but in order to become the phagocyte, and disintegrates it—like a cancerous tissue proliferating in an earlier noncancerous one. The simplest visual example is the way the city world encroaches upon rural areas through the spread of the suburbs. The technological environment could not exist if it did not find its support and resources in the natural world (nature *and* society). But it eliminates the natural as a milieu, supplanting it while wasting and exhausting it.

Technology can become an environment only if the old environment stops being one. But that implies destructuring it as an environment and exploiting it to such an extreme that nothing is left of it. In other words: The well-known "depletion" of natural resources (which we shall come back to later) results not only from abuse by the technologies, but also from the very establishment of technology as man's new milieu.

Technology acts upon these environments first by dividing and fragmenting the natural and cultural realities. The process of technological encroachment upon reality always consists in breaking up reality into malleable fragmentary units. This breakup corresponds to the scientific discovery of discontinuity: "Scientists have discovered separable units (atoms, particles, phonemes, chromosomes) in the heart of temporality. . . . This investigation of the

## TECHNOLOGY AS AN ENVIRONMENT

discontinuous is reaching through all areas. . . . Things that change, things that seem to come into being, are defined by an arrangement of elementary units."[8]

This analysis reduces all motion to elements and a motionless whole. Machines operate on those givens. But science's reduction of reality to discontinuity is transposed by technology. Reality is broken up into elements that are actually (and not theoretically) separated. Thus, each element can be used by itself. It can be rearranged and recombined, it can be quantified and classified in any way. But here we are dealing with both a new system (technological) and the concrete reality in which man is forced to live.

Technology reduces a whole to simple units by analyzing it and generally compartmentalizing it. The Taylor work method is a model example. Craftsmanship was once a complex ensemble of undivided gestures and operations; it expressed the laboring individual and it produced a complete whole, a "work." The division of labor and then Taylorization brought greater efficiency and interchangeability, but at the price of splintering and dividing work into perfect and indivisible gestural units. The work gesture was totally separated from the worker's person and existed on its own. This led to fragmenting the primary datum in all domains. Next, technology took up these utterly simplified elements in order to reconstitute a new whole, a new synthesis, integrating the natural factors, which were previously disintegrated.

But this technological whole is not at all "gratifying" for man (perhaps because he remains traditional). Man still feels as if he were living in a splintered universe. A splintered society (Even though it is more thoroughly unified than ever!), a splintered, incoherent life. The wholes established by technology do not make us feel complete or satisfied; they are still experienced as splintered wholes. Here and there, man recognizes and greets a fragment of his former universe, integrated in a functional but alien and anonymous whole, in which he nevertheless must live. There is no other. Against that feeling of splintering, modern man feels a keen desire for all-inclusiveness, for synthesis. But, alas, any synthesis produced by anything but technology fails and comes to naught. There is no possible *archê*, nor any return to earth.

Man is dissatisfied for being man; and this dissatisfaction, which we know up to this point, cannot be avoided. For in regard to all the environments that technology invades (and it now invades all of them), it is inevitably *simplifying, reductive, operational, instru-*

*mental,* and *rearranging.* It reduces all that was natural to the fragment of a manageable object. And anything that cannot be thus managed, manipulated, utilized, is rejected and discarded as worthless. On the huge debit side of possibilities, value is placed only on things that can be utilized. Anything else, which for the moment is not yet the object of technology, is abandoned to contingency and chance in a technological society.

We thus have the double aspect of simplification and reduction of all reality by all technology. On the one hand, we have a rigorous system that performs without fail; on the other hand, a terrain that we consider unknown, absurd, "having destroyed in advance the values that were able to give meaning to freedom." Thus, in the complex tissue of (social and human) reality, technology cuts out what can constitute an environment, but neutralizes and designifies anything it does not keep. However, since the technological system is essentially dynamic (far more so than the ecosystem), technology tends, blindly, to replace the totality of what formed the natural ecosystem. Technology keeps conquering more and more, assimilating and reorganizing endlessly. Ultimately, the "ideal" for this new environment is to exist to such a degree that nothing else exists. Such, basically, is the dream of authors like Rorvik.

But there's a rub. The old environment has not totally disappeared. We still have air and water. And even man cannot do without them as yet. This is essentially what causes the irrationality and the system crisis as we see it. For the moment, let us remember that there has been a decisive reversal. Man once lived in a natural environment, using technical instruments to get along better in it, protect himself against it, and make use of it. Now, man lives in a technological environment, and the old natural world supplies only his space and his raw materials. Ultimately, the technological environment thus presumes to replace *all* of the natural environment, performing all of its functions.

But obviously, we will never reach the old complexity of the natural environment (a complexity that we discover more and more as we destroy it). We cannot reach it because technology simplifies. We still have to ask whether that complexity was necessary to human life. (We will study this topic later.) But there is no imitation, no reproduction of that natural environment. There is only a creation of a new environment, even though in many cases we are forced to replace natural mechanisms, which turn out to be indispensable. Thus we keep introducing more and more exterior regulations. One of the fundamental laws of ecology is that we can achieve stability through ever-growing complexity. A complexity of modifications and exchanges in the environment, which allow a diversified adaptation. When we replace a complex natural mechanism with a simple technological mechanism, we make the ecosystem "more vulnerable and less adaptable."

Now this solution by the technological environment (simultaneously the condition for its expansion) applies to both the natural and the social environment. (In the social milieu, the complex relations of a traditional society are replaced by the rationalized and simplified relations of a bureaucracy—in the technological and positive sense of the word.) This environment thus has features linked to the efficiency of technology. But they are dangerous—at least to the extent that we do not exactly know the complexities of the ecosystem (reduced to a supporting role) that we are destroying. We discover them by the consequences of their disappearance.

Needless to say, this environment is totally artificial (which is not a criticism; the natural does not have an eminent and normative value for me). Each factor in this environment results not from the combinative creation of a living whole, but from an addition of processes that can be isolated and combined as artificially as they were created, ex post facto. Each factor can be examined, measured, isolated from the rest because *we* establish the connection; and we can test the result.

The technological environment is in fact characterized by the growth of abstraction and controls. It is obvious that in such conditions, the technological environment scarcely favors spontaneity, creativity. Nor can it know living rhythms (which are obviously tied to the natural environment[9]). We will come upon this question again.

The artificiality means essentially that only artifacts can enter this environment and that man can relate only to them. Anything else cannot be part of the environment, it would not harmonize, which is perfectly intolerable in the technological environment. There is no way to picture a car engine with a little grass or some flowers. Such additions may be a charming fantasy, of course; but they are incongruous.

Without claiming that the technological environment is equivalent to an engine, the comparison is a good one. Only the artifact can enter this environment, for it is made in such a way as to fit in exactly. It is "made for." Which cannot be said of any of the natural elements. Hence, the artificialness of the technological environment causes it to be absolutely exclusive.

And this is also translated into the economic and social forms. Observers, for instance, emphasize that statics have disappeared and been replaced by dynamics. Some, like J. Leclercq (*La Révolution de l'homme au Vingtième Siècle*), even dwell quite triumphantly on this fact. Property (capital) is losing its importance to know-how. Raw material is becoming secondary to the product. The stress must be placed on action and not on passivity—just as man's isolation, triggering stagnation, has given way to the worldwide relationship, socialness, community, public services.

In reality, all these things, which are accurately pointed out, are the visible social signs of a passage from a natural to a technological environment. It used to be nature that imposed its evolutionary rhythm upon us. Now it is technology. It used to be nature that determined certain social structures (Bodin's and Montesquieu's famous theory of climates). Now it is technology. It used to be nature that meted out the raw materials. Now the crux is the technological processing. It used to be nature that required man to establish fixed laws of relations between objects and himself (property). Now, the objects, emerging from a constantly renewing technological action, are no longer so important. What counts is know-how, which enables us to fit in precisely and find our places in the technological environment.

This technological environment forces us to consider everything a technological problem and, at the same time, to lock ourselves up in, enclose ourselves in, an environment that has become a system.

Let us take the first aspect. We now have a certain frame of mind, a certain way of looking at situations. We automatically regard every issue, every situation in terms of some technology. We are disabled when we have no technology to deal with some administrative or psychological matter. We have to reduce a situation to technological terms so that it truly becomes a technological problem. A typical (though anecdotal) example: Madame P. Sartin writes an article in *Le Monde* (April 1973): "Woman's Status in Our Society: A Technological Problem." The contents of the article do not matter. It is the title that is highly significant in linking the two concepts, status and technology. A person's status in society, a complex, ambiguous problem tied to infinite variables, is suddenly boiled down to a technological problem. Study the problems of the woman's condition with some technicians, modify a few factors, and you will change her status—that is to say, both the opinion about women and their opinion about themselves, the *experienced* social hierarchy, the metaphysics of love and of the complementary opposition of the sexes, etc.

No! It's all a dream. There are, indeed, a few technological issues in that question: the woman's dilemma of home vs. a job, the use of psychological knowledge, and so on. And yet the woman's status is not a technological one! But Madame Sartin is typical in being convinced that it *is*. I could cite a hundred analogous examples showing to what degree we *think* we are living in a technological environment.

On the other hand, it is quite true that the more technological factors we get involved with *in fact,* the more the problems raised are *really* technological problems. There is thus an actual growth of technological problems, which makes us infer that all problems are technological. The further we advance, the more vulnerable we become. We depend more and more on systems. The natural mechanisms tend to get out of order and have to be replaced by technological mechanisms. Hitherto, any difficulties were of a natural order; but with the mechanism of replacement, they become technological. When we can no longer have drinking water furnished by nature, our water supply will depend on factories that purify polluted water or desalt ocean water. Under such conditions, a water shortage will be due not to a climatic drought but to a breakdown at a plant. We can generalize this example. The technological environment makes problems and difficulties technological. Though not all so far.

Finally, there is a trend toward a genuine enclosure in this environment. And this strikes me as particularly important in language. Linguistic studies (and not just structuralism) tend more and more to reduce human language to a certain number of structures, functions, and mechanisms giving us the impression that we now understand this strange and mysterious phenomenon better than before. But what modern linguistics really does is to reduce language in such a way as to make it fit neatly into this technological universe, trimmed down to an indispensable communication for the creation of the system. Language is losing its mystery, its magic, its incomprehensibility. It no longer expresses dreams. Or rather, by being technologically deciphered, language becomes a way of bringing dreams, inspirations, aspirations, and ecstasies into the technological environment. Today, it is out of place to make fun of the many hermetic jargons emerging everywhere. This use of bizarre words ("perfect a praxeological approach," "optimize decisions," "explore qualitative fields of action," "parameterize future possibilities," etc.) is a desperate effort to grasp the new "technological reality" by means of language. It is intellectual hypocrisy to mock an attempt at fitting language to this environment. But this striving is innocent. The true aggression is the technization of language. For at this moment, *everything* is locked up in the technological environment. When speech is a serf, everything is a serf. Language is the ultimate outlet, the ultimate questioning, even if it is reduced to a shriek. But the "it" and the "one" who are speaking tell us that the technological lid has clamped down, and that this universe is closed. Our modern linguists are heatedly working toward that end.

At this point, we ought to go into Tzvetan Todorov (*Theories of the Symbol*, 1977). According to Todorov, the romantic crisis was a total upheaval. The classical conception of identity, of the unity of the world and language, involved an imitative behavior (mimesis). This was followed by the image of a diversity, an uncertainty (melodrama instead of tragedy), illuminating the difference, with the whole thing resting on the concept of production. How can we fail to see the aesthetic, spiritual, and image-fraught expression here of the passage to technology and to the indefiniteness of technological production.

# 3

# TECHNOLOGY AS A DETERMINING FACTOR[1]

THE sociologists, like the historians, of the modern schools no longer accept the causal in sociology or history. It is impossible to determine a direct and univocal causality. Phenomena determine each other mutually, we can describe interactions, establish correlations, analyze systems, make a phenomenon the factor of a whole, uncover differential structures. But it is impossible to say that one fact induces another, etc. We generally accept the idea of the factor. Nevertheless, the Marxist sociologists reject that notion, viewing it as characteristic of bourgeois agnosticism. They feel that so long as we maintain reciprocal interactions, a sociological analysis requires the schema of determining and determined phenomena (with the latter, incidentally, able to become determinants in their turn).

It seems to me that the best method would be to take both attitudes into account. On the one hand, it is true that we can hardly speak of causality in sociology. Contrary to the exact sciences, we cannot isolate a phenomenon, examine it in a pure state, experiment, and repeat the exact conditions of the experiment. But obviously, if we never establish a relationship between the determinant and the determined, we will be limited to infinite and indefinite descriptions that are meaningless and hence incapable of explaining the "how" (without even claiming to seek an answer to the "why").

On the other hand, if we go by the Marxist method, we have a "pattern" prior to any analysis; we know in advance what is the determinant and what the determined. The explanatory schema has been established once and for all (even if rendered flexible, as Plekhanov once did and Althusser is now doing). But for that very reason, we cannot be certain of grasping new structures, new types of relationships that differ from those analyzed by Marx. Hence, I believe that we have to try both to consider phenomena in their newness, their singularity, and to find the determining relationships between them by preserving the notion of the factor, which is the only acceptable notion.

If I study a sociological phenomenon in present-day Western society, if I analyze its structure, its relations to other structures, as accurately as possible, I can obviously discover a large number of determining factors. If, for instance, I peruse the culture of juvenile gangs, I am obliged to consider the home background, the moral development, the habitat, the consumption of multiple goods and advertising, the distractions, the sexual precociousness, etc. All these factors are involved and form the general context for juvenile gangs. It is almost impossible to pinpoint *one* determining factor among them or even isolate two or three. It is ultimately their combination that offers a more or less approximate explanation.

Let me instead consider *one* sociological phenomenon in its *evolution* instead of taking it at a given moment as a static datum. Among all the factors making up its context, I can perceive those that have evolved beforehand and whose change has come first. And I can prudently try to establish a correlation between those two successive changes. I will thus zero in a bit on the question while bearing in mind that there is always plenty of uncertainty, for it is very hard to analyze the context fully. The study of an evolving phenomenon can bring out the factor, which the static analysis has not revealed.

Let us scrutinize what can be called a "problem," i.e., a sociological phenomenon that, because of its development, arouses intense positive or negative responses from individuals, creating difficulties in adjustment and anxieties. These problems may be more or less vast, relatively individual (the automation of a workshop as a problem for the workers), or universal (the bureaucratization of society). We can see that the determining factors are less numerous and comparatively easier to isolate in a "problem" than in a simple, neutral phenomenon. We are actually bringing in the dimension of "how the phenomenon is experienced." This seems to complicate matters because we are considering a new kind of factor, a nonobjective one. In reality, however, that dimension makes our approach easier, for the knowledge of the opinion seems relatively assured. The involvement of the "experience" factor gives the others a certain coefficient of importance, which allows us to classify them.

If, now, instead of considering one phenomenon or problem, I examine several belonging to the same overall society, what will happen? To the extent that they actually belong to one and the same society, they are bound to be in relation to one another. Of course, each is situated within a certain constellation of factors. But if I view these phenomena together, I notice that certain factors are peculiar to that constellation and do not bear upon the neighboring problems. In contrast, other factors are common to several phenomena or problems. Needless to say, the wider the scope of my research—i.e., the more phenomena and problems that I investigate in an overall given society—the further the number of factors common to them all will diminish.

But we must then ask a twofold question. Are the factors that I preserve determinant in each case? Are not the determinant factors that I examine so general as to become meaningless? (For instance, one can certainly explain all present-day sociological phenomena by population growth, but this is too general.) Do not those determinant factors come into play only as "a remote cause," to the second or third degree, thereby no longer having an explanatory character?

We therefore must be keenly attentive to the closeness of the relationship and proceed to the critique of the factor being investigated. There is obviously great danger in attempting to boil the multiple phenomena or problems of a whole society down to a single determinant factor. And that is the difficulty experienced by Marx's followers. Nevertheless, in an ensemble of factors that are taken as explanatory, it is not impossible to discern one that is more effective, more constraining. If, in the evolution of several phenomena, if, in the givens of several problems, we keep finding that same element, we have to accept it as determinant (and perhaps even assign it a coefficient of power that does not appear at first sight). If this factor allows us to take into account a large number of data in the society being examined, and if it permits us to understand the correlations and differential structures of those data, then we have to admit that this factor has a "strategic" place and an exceptional role. We thus have the two criteria that allow us to evaluate the importance of a factor.

It is obvious that in an entire society we cannot cleave to the "punctiform" fixation of a huge number of data. We must try to account for their existence and trace their relationships. If one factor allows us to account for a larger number of ascertained data, it is bound to be more important and has to be taken as more determinant than another factor accounting for only a small number of data. The same holds for a factor that lets us explain a very large number of relationships. But this presumes our regarding the social data as data of relation and attempting to consider the large number of possible relations, which is not always the case.

It goes without saying, incidentally, that such work entails the great danger of "forcing" data. And that too is something we often note in the Marxist sociologists. The instant we think we have a factor determining a very large number of data and relations, we are tempted to ignore those data that are contrary or on which our factor does not act. Even more, we are tempted to modify the data in order to insert them into our explanatory schema. Hence, the first rule is to admit that once a datum has been defined in itself, it must not be altered by any endeavor to relate it to what has been established as the determining factor of other phenomena.

We will conclude these reflections on method with a final remark. If we look at the (sociologically) major problems of our whole society (Western/American, 1970) we will notice that most of them are posed in such a way that they appear to be made up of mutually contradictory givens. It is this truly perplexing feature that generally allows contradictory positions to be taken on them. In French or American society, we find, for instance, serious authors claiming that citizens are being depoliticized, and other, no less precise authors claiming that citizens are being politicized. In reality, the problem of the relationship between the citizen and the ruling power must be posed in terms of "politicizing/depoliticizing." It is not an "either/or," but a complex of phenomena, which are apparently contradictory although correlative.

A further example. In our Western society, a few sociologists speak of the "death of ideologies," while others show that ideology has a growing place and that everything is done and experienced in terms of ideologies. Here, once again, the problem must be posed as a complex of "the correlative death and growth of ideologies."

And of course, the more inclusive the problem, the more important the contradictory or ambivalent character of the phenomenon. The point is not to seek multiple, diverse, and inverse causes for each aspect. The point is not to say, on the one side, there is a depoliticization affecting such and such an area and having such and such a cause; and on the other side, there is a politicization afecting some other area and having some other causes. This splitting of the phenomenon destroys its specificity. The important thing is to investigate whether there is a factor determining the inner contradiction of the phenomenon. If we find such a factor explaining the two contrary givens of one and the same phenomenon, then chances are that this factor is truly determinant, and we will also safeguard the unity, the specificity, and the intelligibility of the phenomenon under observation.

These few explanations were indispensable. It was actually by applying this method that I came to conclude that in the sociopolitical problems of Western society as a whole, the main if not single determinant factor is the technological system. This wording will instantly provoke contradictions. Yet it is a perfectly evident and admitted truth to say that "research" (obviously what is known as "research and development") is the youth and future of societies. A country that abandons research . . . will be stricken with a mortal sickness. . . . Limiting research makes it patent that the very brain of society is *sick*, that its hope for survival is stricken" (Chombart de Lauwe). If research is so important, it is because it leads to technology and not to pure intellectual satisfaction. These current formulas point out that technology is the determinant factor in our society. I will examine a few problems of our society to justify my statement.

The demonstration could be regarded as complete only if I presented this work for *all* major problems totted up in our society. But that is obviously impossible.[2]

\* \* \*

The problem of Statism is assuredly a major and characteristic phenomenon in our society. But it presents a double and apparently contradictory aspect. On the one side, we are dealing with a growth of the state; on the other side, with a decrease of the political function. The growth of the state can be analyzed as a growth of function, organism, and concentration.

It is easy to see how greatly the functions and competencies of a modern state keep increasing nonstop. It does not suffice to quote the formula about our passing from the liberal state of the nineteenth century to the welfare state of the twentieth century. Actually, during the past half century, the state has taken over education, welfare, economic life, transportation, technological growth, scientific research, artistic development, health, and population. And it is now moving toward a function of sociological structuring (national development) and psychological structuring (public relations). This simple enumeration points out that the present-day state has nothing in common with the state of the eighteenth or nineteenth centuries. The organism of the state has augmented along with its functions and areas of intervention. The point, however, is not so much the number or importance of its services as their complexity. In a word, each activity has become specialized, the connections between the parts of the organism are getting finer and finer, more and more numerous, and often questionable. In this multiplicity of services, which are more and more fragmented, new coordination services have to be created. This leads to a kind of second-degree administration, charged with administering the primary administration.

At the same time, we are witnessing a centralization movement that is easily conceived. The more complex the body, the more the whole must be tied to one head. There is much debate about this centralizing. In reality, all the so-called decentralization efforts merely produce deconcentration, which actually intensifies the centralization. These three movements are all the more important to emphasize because they are taking place not only in traditionally centralized countries like France, but also in countries traditionally decentralized like the United States, and where the state was greatly distrusted. Yet, since 1936, the United States government has been increasing its jurisdiction and centralizing its powers.

It would seem that, as a result, the function of the state, the political function, has been growing at the same time. But, on the contrary, we are witnessing the diminishing importance of that function, despite certain appearances that remain trditional. This decrease can be observed on two levels: that of the citizen and that of the politician. The citizen, as an individual, is less and less capable of an opinion on the real problems a modern state has to cope with. He has fewer and fewer possibilities of expressing his opinion or truly affecting politics. Elections, those temporary expressions of opinion, and even referendums have little influence on the workings of politics. The citizen must, in any event, be incorporated in a vaster body—a party, trade union, etc.—which will act as a lobby, a pressure group, a representation of interests far more than opinions. And in these groups, the individual has very little weight vis-à-vis opinion leaders or specialists. But even more, we have to realize that the individual has practically no means of defense against or pressure upon what has become by far the most important part of government action, the administrative function in the widest sense. In reality, the citizen can do nothing about administrative decision. We can thus say that the more important the state becomes, the less important the citizen (the theoretical bearer of political sovereignty).

Remarkably, the same is true of the traditional politician; the congressman, senator, even the government minister, have less and less real power. Modern analyses of decision-making show that, on the one hand, the politician's role in this process is greatly reduced, and that, on the other hand, the true "place of decision" is often not the minister's office or the National Assembly. The famous distinction between "major orientations" and "current decisions or their application" assigns the former to politics and politicians and the latter to administrations. But that is a myth. The politician has less and less autonomy, if in no other way, then at least by being far more determined by earlier decisions when he makes a decision now. For example, in 1900, it was quite easy to reverse alliances. But in 1960, it is almost impossible to throw over an economic plan being carried out; and the plan that follows is inevitably conditioned by the previous one. The margin of political option is indeed very narrow.

I will not dwell on the politician's lack of competence: that is too facile an argument. But the enormity, the complexity of issues make the politican highly dependent on research departments, on experts who assemble dossiers. And once the prepared decision has been submitted by the politician, it escapes him, and the agencies take care of implementing it. And we know that today everything depends on implementation. The politician has a façade role, he provides the showy front; and he also assumes responsibility for a matter of which he has only very shallow knowledge.[3]

What is the source of this double phenomenon? I believe that the reason for the system is technological growth. On the one hand, if the state is expanding its jurisdiction, then this is not the result of doctrines (interventionist, socialist, etc.), but rather of a kind of necessity deriving from technology itself. All areas of life are becoming more and more technicized. In proportion, actions are becoming more complex, more intervolved (precisely because of extreme specialization), and more efficient. This means that their effects are vaster and more remote while their realization implies the use of costlier apparatuses and a sort of mobilization of all forces. In all the technicized activities, a programming is now necessary. And this programming must have a national, often an international, framework. Hence, only the state organism is able to carry out this coordinating and programming, just as it alone is capable of mobilizing all the resources of a nation to apply one or several technologies; just as it alone is in a position to measure, and take upon itself, the long-term effects of such a technology. We could go into detail here and cite countless examples to show that in modern society it is always because of technology that the jurisdiction of the state keeps expanding.

As for the growth of the state organism, one may be tempted to view it as a simple consequence of the increased jurisdiction, and to say: "The more things the state has to do, the more services it has to create and the more functionaries it has to appoint." Naturally, that is an exact aspect of the problem, but it is only an aspect. Here too, there is a direct influence of technology on the growth and complexity of the state organism. We can already note an influence whose ultimate consequences we do not yet know: the use of all kinds of electronic machines in office work. In any case, this use is bound to transform bureaucratic structures, bringing a new analysis of tasks and hence a new legal analysis of administrative functions. But the thing that changes the state organism even more is the use of organization technologies. Here we are dealing with an imperative of efficiency that is, of course, bound to the growth of functions. We can no longer work with a bureaucracy comparable to the one that Courteline made fun of. A new bureaucracy is emerging, more rigorous, more exact, but also less picturesque and less "human." These two movements are taking place together, and if there is, say, an effort towards deconcentration, the reasons are not ideological or humanistic; the goal is to attain the maximum efficiency of an administrative organism.

And, vice versa, it is the action of technology that devaluates the political function, the role of the citizen and of the politician. The citizen is grappling with problems that are mostly technological. For the things the state has to decide on are most frequently technological (and more and more seldom purely "political"). It is not the citizen who may decide even the great aspects of an economic plan, for those aspects really depend on data established by technicians. Those aspects are located in a "bracket" that the technician fixes and they have consequences that the citizen is incapable of evaluating. Furthermore, a different sort of technology is transforming the condition and possible participation of the citizen: namely, the technologies of information and psychological control. I have shown elsewhere (*Propaganda,* 1965) that a modern state, though democratic, absolutely cannot forgo a certain psychological action tending to "form an opinion" and that, moreover, the citizen, drowning in floods of information, wants problems to be simplified, clarified, and explained—that is, he desires a propaganda to facilitate his political choices. Certain politologists therefore tend to say that the citizen's only role is to choose a "ruling team" (in terms of likings, of human qualities, and not in terms of ideology).

But it is here that the politician's role is devaluated, a process also caused by the technization of society. In point of fact, the politician can exercise no control in the multiplicity of services. He depends entirely on three kinds of people: experts, technicians, and administrators (themselves technicians, of organizing and implementing). These people alone have the knowledge and the means of action. To be sure, the politician does have a way out. He can stop being a politician in the old sense of the term; he can specialize very rigorously in an issue and become a technician in that issue. (Keeping in mind that today one can no longer be a technician of economy, but only of a small sector of economy!)

Does that imply the emergence of a technocracy? Absolutely not in the sense of a political power directly exercised by technicians, and not in the sense of the technicians' desire to exercise power. The latter aspect is practically without interest. There are very few technicians who wish to have political power. As for the former aspect, it is still part of a traditional analysis of the state: people see a technician sitting in the government minister's chair. But under the influence of technology, it is the entire state that is modified. One can say that there will soon be no more (and indeed less and less) political power (with all its contents: ideology, authority, the power of man over man, etc.). We are watching the birth of a technological state, which is anything but a technocracy; this new state has chiefly technological functions, a technological organization, and a rationalized system of decision-making.

That is the first—very summarily analyzed—example of the situation of technology as a determinant factor.

\* \* \*

My second example is taken from a completely different sector. I want to discuss the major phenomenon of population growth as tied to production growth. It is hard to attribute a "cause" to population growth, for historians know that a sudden increase of population occurs at certain periods without our being able to pinpoint any exact causes. In particular, we cannot resolve the following problem: Is population growth the cause or the result of economic growth? Either side can be argued. In all likelihood, the two phenomena give rise to one another. Nevertheless, at the present time, the determining factor of production growth is indisputably the technological development. This point would be difficult to contest.

But, less obviously, it would seem that in various areas, technology has contributed very greatly to population increase. These areas are the technologies of medicine, hygiene, ground drainage, plus the improved standard of living and the creation of better adapted life-styles, which together allow, if not trigger, a rise in population. Technology wipes out the ancient regulators—infant mortality, famine, etc.—and we no longer believe what was a certain truth twenty years ago: namely, that the rise in the overall living standard and the wealth of food automatically cause a drop in the birth rate. The baby boom in the United States contradicts that earlier assumption. It is certain that at a rather low level, the greater possibilities of consumption already bring a surge of procreation. Without forcing things, I feel we can say that technology may not be *the* determining factor but *a* major determining factor in the two linked phenomena. We could then legitimately conclude that if the two phenomena are linked and have a major determining factor, the growth must occur in a harmonious way.

That is to say, the production technologies allow a consumption of goods corresponding to the population growth. There might not be an exact correspondence; perhaps in some cases, the population curve would tend to exceed the production curve—or vice versa. There might also be differences in production, a wider and wider range of objects produced, so that not all the needs of the increased population would be exactly filled. But on the whole, the discrepancies could be ironed out, and we would note a balanced expansion. Yet we do not note any such thing. Far from it. We see that production growth is not adapted to the consumer needs of a greater population. It would even appear that we can speak of a growing divergence between the two curves. The population is rising a bit faster in absolute numbers in areas where production remains practically stagnant (just barely improved to allow the surge of procreation). Conversely, consumption is rising very swiftly in countries with middling population growth. Because of that double movement, the gap between the haves and the have-nots is widening ceaselessly.

It is this widening gap that I wish to consider as a problem here. Hitherto, we have been faced with manifestly simplistic diagnoses and therapies. Some observers start with the fact that 3,200 calories a day are necessary for survival and that Western man consumes 3,800 or 4,000. Hence, we are told, cut down on your consumption and ship the rest to the poor countries. There is enough to considerably improve the situation of the undernourished by a more equitable redistribution of wealth. Morally, of course, it would be a praiseworthy act of justice, the distribution of agricultural surpluses would be legitimate. But this is no solution; first of all, because the extra food of rich countries would be of very little help to the others; and then because such a procedure would maintain a situation of people on welfare. It cannot be said that the problem is simply one of distribution and that the obstacle lies in national egotism or a lack of generosity.

Far more serious is the attitude that the technologically over-equipped countries are mishandling their output possibilities, and manufacturing superfluous or useless goods to the detriment of fundamentals. If the power of American and European production were reoriented toward indispensable consumer goods—food, clothing, basic tools—we could assuredly fulfill the demands of a growing world population for quite a long time. Instead, industry is developing far more rapidly in the areas of tape recorders or electric razors. This, supposedly, shows a bad trend in the use of technological power, which ignores the real needs around the world. The situation is accentuated even more strongly by the use of an increasing quantity of manpower for unproductive tasks. The goal should not be shorter working hours or a growth in tertiary activities, but rather the application of all the work forces to that essential production for the sake of the rising population. This thesis is forwarded very often and has every semblance of a rational analysis. Unhappily, I feel that it rests on a dubious presupposition and a dearth of overall vision in the technological society. The presupposition is the belief in a totally fluid adaptability of production forces and technological possibilities.

"It suffices to decide" that we must produce more grain, more meat, etc.—with the conviction that if we do not make such a decision, the reasons are unwillingness, the capitalist structure of the economy, which is interested in the branches of production assuring the greatest profit. I believe that this is now inexact, and the presupposition strikes me as being based on an analytical error. The orientation of technological progress and its possibilities of application are extremely rigid.

The first fact to take into account (well known and barely discussed) is that technological progress cannot occur everywhere at the same time. There are privileged points of technological progress; and, as we shall see, they depend essentially on previous technological progress, with the speed of technological growth tending toward a geometric progression. Thus, we cannot hope to perform a technological leap in the underdeveloped countries, starting with nothing. Brief as the phases may be, we have to admit that two centuries of technological progress in the Western world cannot be boiled down to five or ten years in Africa or Asia! Hence, the autonomous help to be expected from those countries in solving the problem of "population and consumption" will be slow and feeble. We certainly have to await a good deal from the highly technological countries.

But that is the problem! Can we simply apply that technological power to that type of consumption? The thing that people are unaware of is that such a powerful technological progress creates a new universe. Now the usual hypothesis is, in a word, that we are dealing with a society that is traditional but that has an extraordinary productive power, and with a human being who is always identical but also a privileged consumer. If this were so, we could certainly tell this human being to consume less and this society to produce only the necessities for all people.

Unfortunately, the hypothesis is wrong. The massive development of technology triggers a certain number of changes in the individual (especially by creating new needs that are in no way false or artificial) and in the society, which cannot maintain the same structures. Consider these two facts. Man cannot live and work in a technological society unless he receives a certain number of complementary satisfactions allowing him to overcome the drawbacks. Spare-time activities, distractions, their organization, are not superfluous; they cannot be done away with for the sake of something more useful; they do not represent a true rise in the standard of living. They are thoroughly indispensable in making up for the uninteresting work, the deculturation caused by specialization, the nervous tension due to the excessive speed of all operations, the acceleration of progress requiring difficult readjustment. All these things, which are brought on by technological development, can be tolerated only if man finds a new level of compensations. Likewise, the diversity of food, the increased consumption of nitrogenous foods and glucoses are not a gluttonous overload but a compensatory response to the nervous expenditure caused by this technicized life.

We cannot ask a man absorbed in technological activities and an urban milieu to follow a uniform and mainly vegetarian diet. Physiologically, he would be unable to do so. Gadgets are indispensable for coping with a society that is more and more impersonal; remedies are necessary for adjusting. In sum, the tendency of productive strength toward these products, which are regarded as luxurious or superfluous, comes far less from a capitalist profit drive or the public's abnormal, immoderate desires. The true causes are needs that are strongly felt by people living in a technicized environment; and they simply could not continue living there if these needs were not satisfied.

It seems that the more production rises, the more our society becomes technicized, and the more these needs grow in number and quality. Thus, productive strength is increasingly oriented toward satisfying these needs. But if there were no response to these needs (we should not have any illusions), it would not follow that productive strength could be applied to something else, something more useful. It would mean that productive strength would be blocked by a human impossibility of adapting to this sort of life. There would even, I think, be a risk of regression. Motives of capitalist cupidity play only a flimsy role in deciding upon useless productions. As the Soviet Union industrializes and becomes a technological country in its turn, the same articles are produced, corresponding to the same attitudes toward life. Men are not free to opt for a useful production; and the more production increases, the more it grows in secondary factors. But the needs to which it responds are futile only in appearance. They are actually irrepressible, even though they are created by the artificial environment in which man is obliged to live. The more the technological universe expresses itself in intense and continuous noise, the greater the need for silence, the more research and money must be applied to creating silence. The same holds true for the pollution of air or water. But here we are faced with problems that have to be solved not only by new productions, but also by services and organizations.

We thus come to a second aspect that must be delved into. It is common knowledge that technological development brings a growth of "tertiary activities." But this seems like an application of forces to activities that are not immediately useful, say, for the whole of humanity. Here too, could not advanced societies (as is sometimes proposed) do away with a few services in order to apply the full momentum to useful production? This too is impossible.

For, in order to be technicized, a society must create a whole set of organizations permitting the development of technologies. It is impossible to simply "graft" a certain technological power on a "natural" society. A growth of production technologies requires a transportation network, organization facilities, distribution machinery, etc. (We know, for instance, that the food shipped to India by various nations reaches the points of raging famine only with great difficulty because of the lack of transportation. The excellent harvest of 1968 was partially wasted in India for that very reason.) The vaster and better the mechanism of production, the more complex and numerous the services of organization become. It thus appears that the forces of society are utilized in nonproductive fields. But in reality, the productive fields themselves can increase and improve only because of, and on the basis of, those organizations, those services, those agencies which represent sheer, nonprofitable expenditures, yet without which nothing could function. It may seem absurd to create psychological services everywhere and to study workers' problems in that light. But actually, the worker will cease to be a producer adjusted to his new technological equipment if he is not enframed and supported by such facilities.

Moreover, we would be tempted to say that now, in a technological society, all progress in the area of production (industrial or industrial-agricultural) is impossible without there first existing an enormous organization, of an active administrative type, which authorizes this progress and integrates it, unruffled, in the overall structure. We would like to maintain at this point that the growth of tertiary activities (a well-known established fact) has two consequences.

First, in the Marxist interpretation, the forces of production are called the infrastructure, and everything else—state, law, etc.—is a superstructure. However, I submit that in our technological society, the forces of production are no longer the infrastructure. They have become a superstructure. That is to say, they can develop and keep advancing only if there is a social infrastructure of organization capable of both producing the research indispensable to such progress and receiving this progress into the social body. The mechanism of production is now conditioned by services. It is no longer the interior of the technological world, the determining factor.

As a second consequence, one could very cautiously cite a new aspect of the law of diminishing returns. We know that this law was

## TECHNOLOGY AS A DETERMINING FACTOR

formulated for agricultural output and is today judged incorrect. But it can, I feel, now be applied to industrial production. Let us say schematically that when technology is first applied to industrial output, the growth is in direct proportion to the technological progress. But the more this output increases, the more it requires a framework of multiple services. The technological progress then encompasses vaster and more complex ensembles, and only part of that progress can be directly applied to production. As we advance, the part applied to production diminishes proportionally. In other words, an increased output of useful goods requires greater technological strength applied to sectors that are not directly useful. Hence, the growth in production of useful goods tends to keep declining at a constant progression within a technological system. Of course, this notion of decreasing useful returns is valid only under two conditions: if we look at overall production, and if the country being studied is highly technicized. This phenomenon can be observed only at a very high production level.

However, we started with the idea that at the moment, it would have to be the highly technicized countries that assure the survival of the others. Yet this seems unrealizable. We simply cannot say that there is ultimately a choice to be made between producing grain and producing gadgets. At first sight, it appears to be an obvious fact. But this "fact" is based on an erroneous analysis of what a technological society really is. People habitually argue as if all kinds of societies were subject to the same criteria of judgement, showing comparable structures and the same process of development: a natural society (for instance, African or medieval European society), an industrial society (for instance, Europe in the eighteenth and early nineteenth centuries), and a technological society. It is likewise assumed that human needs have remained identical throughout those various types of societies. But that is far from the truth. A structural analysis reveals differences that are not merely quantitative but indeed qualitative, so that almost no comparisons are possible between those three types of societies. Concepts applicable to one are not applicable to another. There is no common yardstick. This explains the failure of China's industrial "great leap forward," which was based on the village blast furnace. Such differences in the nature of the societal types are determined by the growing complexity of the technological phenomenon, which must be considered as a whole, and not by detached pieces that can be used individually without the others.

Beyond a certain degree of technization, we pass from a society determined by natural factors to a society determined by technological factors. Now in the latter society, there are changes in its structure and in human needs and attitudes. It is therefore impossible to argue without taking heed of those changes. Yet people ignore them when they claim to solve the problem of the survival of excess population by drawing on the productive capacity of modern technology. The change is, in reality, impossible. There is no parallel between growth in population and growth in productivity of goods needed for survival. Thus, the problem is raised because of the specific feature of technological growth. It is technology that appears as the determining factor, in respect not only to the two terms considered separately, but also to the problem itself, in its formulation as a problem stemming from a contradiction. I am not saying that aid to underdeveloped countries is impossible. But it must be handled differently than in political passion.

\* \* \*

We have, in sum, chosen, not quite arbitrarily, as examples, two sociological phenomena that are the most massive in our era and have considerable scope. We have stated that their internal structures are marked by a set of fundamental contradictions, which seem difficult to explain. But both cases have a factor that appears to play a large part in the development of the fact itself and in the establishment of the contradictions that point it out. We have recognized that this factor is technological development, in very different fields of the application of technology. Of course, each of the phenomena observed has other constituent elements, perhaps as important as technology for each of them. But in neither case do these elements seem capable of explaining the contradictions in the system. And above all, we do not find the same elements from system to system. Whereas we do find the technological factor everywhere.

The technological factor can thus, it seems, be called the determining factor, even if a nonsignificant and nondifferential analysis of a sociological phenomenon (a quantitative analysis, for instance) does not allow us to grasp technology as the most important factor.

\* \* \*

However, I know to what extent the theory of the determining factor has been criticized.[4] I will therefore have to specify what I mean. This theory is often reproached for artificially isolating several factors in order to give one a preference. Yet nobody is saying there is *one cause*. Rather, among the countless factors operating within a society, one factor, at a given moment, appears more decisive than the rest. This factor, in turn, has numerous sources—socio-intellectual, ideological, political, etc. But all of Hamon's criticism merely reveals that the technological factor is not independent of the "episteme," of economy, etc. He never shows that the technological factor *is not* ultimately the determining factor for everything else (since it too was determined). For what determines it pushes it along, as it were, transforming it precisely into a determining factor.

We have to avoid generalizing. I am by no means saying that technology has always, and in all societies, been the determining factor (this is the kind of generalization that I rebuke in Marx). What I mean is that in our Western world (and we can generalize for the past twenty years), technology is the determining factor. Most authors who criticize fail to see the new character of the situation in our society; hence, the historical experience concerning the existence or unreality of the present determining factor is incommensurable. It seems to me that one comes closest to reality in speaking of a determining factor when it evokes a fact, a situation, and when it not so much creates the fact, as gives it a form, pushing it to the front of the stage, into the limelight of human attention (with the determining factor itself remaining in the darkness), and integrating it in other social factors. That is a work of catalysis far removed from creation *ex nihilo*. To that extent, the theory of the determining factor strikes me as correct; and in our time, this factor is technology.

We must also ask ourselves what that factor determines, and we are tempted to draw up an inventory. If technology really constitutes an environment, one might be tempted to say that it determines everything. But no. That would be making the same mistake as Toffler, who claims we are entering an era of total and constant change, which is a bit juvenile. One could try taking stock, like B. Cazes in his excellent synthesis ("Vraies et fausses mutations," *Contrepoint*, 1971). Constants persist, "structural certainties" (Jouvenel), and Cazes feels, for instance, that the course of science, the political function, and the developmental laws of human beings are permanent necessities that never change. Nonetheless, if we retain what I defined as the determining factor, I will say that nowadays technology gives a different form to both the course of science and the political function and is bringing new integrations of those constants. Furthermore, Cazes insists on the destructuring impact of technology on all social, moral, and generally human realities, the acquired structures, the intellectual compartmentalizations, the social roles, etc. But if this challenge to the roles goes so far as to impugn the role division between man and woman, young and adult, specialists and nonspecialists, teachers and pupils, insane and sane, etc., then I feel we can say that technology, with such a destructuring effect, certainly has the character of a determining factor. On the other hand, we should not trace *everything* back to technology either. And, like Cazes, we must carefully distinguish between real, false, and apparent changes.

\* \* \*

We can, by using a far less complex method, show to what extent technology is a determining factor. Technological growth has a certain number of consequences on which all authors, whether for or against technology, are ready to agree. One group will cite these facts to prove the excellence of technology, the other, to demonstrate its danger. But all that is mere coloring. Everyone concurs about the basis itself. And we are faced with a rather impressive set of undenied consequences. It is almost impossible to list them all. We can only give a sketchy idea of them—while stressing that this is no return to the method of the "authorities." It is not *opinions* that are the issue here, but facts on which agreement is implicitly established. As a whole, technology is viewed as radically modifying both human relations and the ideological schemata or the qualities of man himself. It is useless going back to William H. Whyte and *The Organization Man*, which many people will find too partisan. But we know G. Friedmann's synthesis (*Sept essais sur l'homme et la technique*), which shows to what degree man is transformed even physiologically by living in a technological environment. Friedmann pursues this theme in *La Puissance et la sagesse* (1970) in regard to mental illness, discussing the consequences posited by psychiatrists: a rise in psychoses, depressive states, anxieties, and maladjustments. Observers, it seems to me, are quite unanimous in blaming a large number of these phenomena on the existence imposed upon man by the technological environment.

And we are basically back to what Charles Reich (*The Greening of America*, 1970), described as "Consciousness II." His portrait of man as integrated in the technological system may be rather easily accepted to the extent that he criticizes the man of yesterday, let us say, of "industrial capitalism." The utterly classical portrait, banal, drawn in broad strokes, resembles everything that has been said about the psychology and values of that man. It all seems to correspond to a certain reality when taken on that assuredly low but not inaccurate level. Nonetheless, we must also remember that for Reich, Consciousness III (quite positive in his eyes) likewise derives from the technological process. For, if he asserts that the revolution is produced by "consciousness," he simultaneously shows that this "consciousness" is generated by technology itself.

These sketches take up both the novels of the period (1930–1960) and famous studies like *The Lonely Crowd* or even *White Collar*. What seems to characterize man in his technological environment even more profoundly is the growth of the will to power. In my previous studies, I have tried to show that technology is a realization, hence an achievement, hence an increase, of the spirit of power, which led to a polarization of man in respect to power. This is brilliantly taken up and demonstrated by Bertrand de Jouvenel (*Arcadie*) when he meticulously studies the fact that modern wealth is the expression of the will to power. (Technological progress is essentially a manifestation of human power, a chance for man to admire himself. The development of power was the goal, with greater comfort as a by-product.) Likewise, technological progress, for man, is a variant of the spirit of conquest, which is both satisfied and reinforced by technology. This spirit of conquest causes the division of man into producer and consumer and his obedience to the imperative of efficiency. What is interesting in Jouvenel's study is not only his demonstration of the consequences of these well-known phenomena but also his insertion of them into economic theory.

Be that as it may, this first group of simple findings points out a formidable change in the human being. Naturally, this cannot fail to have repercussions on what we call culture. And indeed, the technological impact transforms culture as well. Whether it is the appearance of so-called mass culture; or the change in human relations because of multiplied communications, which transform brief relations into long-term ones (Ricoeur); or even a changed atmosphere in the world because of the dynamics of information—whichever point is observed, we are witnessing a well-known change of that culture. Because of the technological demand, "general culture [i.e., general education] is a paper wrapping and its acquisition a mere pastime."[5] This insipid and unimportant general education must be replaced by a technical education, with permanent training, for instance. But it is the very concept of culture that is modified, and not just its substance, its practice, or the ways it is acquired. "Every time the words *general* or *educational* crop up, they are instantly followed by comments that they mean an adjustment to technological progress, a better knowledge of economic mechanisms, or the improvement of know-how."[6] A good panorama of this evolution was presented by J. Gritti (*Culture et techniques de masse*, 1967), especially with an attempt at analyzing "dialectical pairs": education/specialization, tradition/modernity, encyclopedism/assimilation, gratuity/efficiency, effort/pleasure, word/image, etc.

Similarly, Baudrillard shows to what extent the culture and education issuing from technology are the absolute reverse of the culture conceived as: (1) the heritage of works, thoughts, traditions; (2) the continuous dimension of theoretical and critical reflection, critical transcendence and symbolic function.

Both aspects are likewise negated by the cyclical subculture (made up of obsolescent cultural ingredients and signs) and by the cultural topicality. We can see that the problem of cultural consumption is linked to neither the cultural contents properly speaking nor the cultural public. The crucial thing is that culture is no longer meant to endure. It is the rapid progression of technology that condemns culture to being the opposite of what it has always been; now it is the immediate consumption of a technological product without substance. As Baudrillard rightly notes, there is ultimately no difference between mass culture (which devises contents) and avant-garde creation (which manipulates forms). Both are determined by the functional imperative of technology that everything must always be up to date.

Once again, the point here is not to evaluate what is good, but to establish that the very fact of technology has wrought a transformation, far more than a modification, in the cultural whole. This is not what the French traditionally refer to as *"culture générale"* (general education); but rather what is covered by the term *general culture* in English. We can cite several examples.

Thus, the fact—probably essential in this area—is the transformation of a hierarchical society into an egalitarian one. Traditional society, *all* traditional societies, are hierarchical. And when L. Dumont labels man *Homo hierarchicus*, he is designating a characteristic that is at least as essential as that of *Homo faber.* There have never been any egalitarian societies, and hierarchy was part of the general-cultural universe. Only a few ineffective utopians could pretend to build an egalitarian society. But, contrary to what moderns may believe, they were not expressing any basic popular demand. The rare egalitarian movements (the Levellers, for instance), envisioned no real equality, but rather a conquest of power for themselves! Since the eighteenth century, not only has the idea of equality become general, but, even more, it it taken as an established fact, and its realization seems possible.

And all this is a direct result of technological growth. Technology cannot put up with irrational discriminations or social structures based on beliefs.[7] All inequality, all discrimination (e.g., racial), all particularism, are condemned by technology, for it reduces everything to commensurable and rational factors. A complete statistical equality for any adequate dimension and any identifiable group— such is the goal of a society having technology as its chief factor. And this corresponds to the process of specialization. If everything is specialized, if all specialties are equally technological, equally necessary from a technological point of view, how could we help but have equality? In fact, we can resolutely say that the demand for equality (as found in Marx, for instance) is nothing but the ideological product of the unlimited use of technology.

A further "cultural value" was likewise greatly modified by technology: to wit, property. Despite Marxist orthodoxy, which is once again forced to deny reality, we can certify a change in property. The fact that the organization is now the main condition of production has transformed the nature of wealth and private property. "Organizations" do not belong to the "capitalist." What used to constitute property has *split up* into several things: the rights of stockholders to share in profits; the management's power to establish guidelines; the rights of employees to status and security; the right of government regulation, etc. New forms of wealth have replaced what used to be "capital": a job, retirement rights, a management or concession license, social security, hospitalization under a doctor's care. Those are the new forms of wealth representing *relations* to organizations. What counts is not so much the money that an individual *possesses*, but rather the money that he can spend. And this depends on his technological capacity and his "status." He is an engineer at Renault, a doctor of political economy, etc., so that status unites the condition of people in a socialist and in a capitalist society. Property is transformed into relations. Such is the new property based on the "technological capacity," which guarantees status. The link attaching present-day man to this status is as strong as the one that used to attach man to property. And consequently, decisions are made not by those who have the capital, but by a combination of those who have the status relating to a decision. It is to this degree that joint management by all participants is sure to come about, but that, conversely, self-management by the workers at the bottom is a dangerous utopia!

Finally, in this quick survey of the well-known changes brought on by technology, we have to cite the one that has been most studied: the change in work. It is obvious that this is where technology began its general modification of society. It is also what appeared as most immediately evident. The reader can therefore consult the many investigations of this subject during the past half century. We shall merely add two new remarks.

First of all, as we have already said, observers habitually declare that a modern man has to be ready, because of the technologies, to "change his profession two or three times" in his life. But according to Montmollin's very judicious comment: *There are no more professions*, there are only *jobs* or activities. "It is wrong to say that nowadays a worker has to change trades two or three times during his life. He does not change his trade, he does not have one. He therefore has to keep readjusting almost permanently. The most important measure to be taken in 1980 in the retraining of workers is to abolish the very idea of retraining. We would have to be so accustomed to training in industry that we should not think in terms of training and *re*training, but only of training and more training."[8]

However, contrary to what is often asserted, work is far from having lost its "laboriousness" because of technology. Quite the opposite. It seems that even after the era of the machine (whose effects on man are common knowledge) work has actually become even *more* laborious, more draining than before. The transition to fully automated work, to the push-button factory, is still rare and slow. And this is not due to capitalism; the rate is no faster in socialist countries. It is not profit-seeking that blocks this development but the gigantic change demanded by automation, and it is not easy to put through in all areas. In reality, for most workers, technological growth brings harder and more exhausting work (speeds, for instance, demanded not by the capitalist but by technology and the service owed to the machine). We are intoxicated with the idea of leisure and universal automation. But for a long time, we will be stuck with work, we will be wasted and

## TECHNOLOGY AS A DETERMINING FACTOR

alienated. Alienation, though, is no longer capitalistic, it is now technological.

On all these points,[9] all observers agree that an immense transformation has been wrought by technology alone. In other words, the *entirety* of human relations, both interindividual and overall, has been modified. How, then, can we fail to believe that technology is really the "determining factor"?

\* \* \*

In this survey, we cannot omit citing the role of the computer—without overestimating it and, above all, without assuming that it now applies to everything or that all its potentials will be realized. Nevertheless, we must emphasize to what extent this area of technology can be determining.

One technology, writing and printing, gave birth to a civilization. Another technology, namely television, has, as Marshall MacLuhan shows, changed the field of the brain. Still another, the computer, has carried us from the civilization of experience to the civilization of knowledge.

Printing allowed the gigantic accumulation of a mass of information that was mostly unusable because it could not be grasped by individual intelligence. Printing gave us an excellent collective memory, but the individual memory was not up to its mark; the information of the collective memory was dormant.

The computer is now the relay between that collective memory and its utilization by man. The electronic brain plays the role of the individual memory and makes the acquired information usable. At the same time, it was correctly pointed out (by R. Lattès) that, hitherto, man devoted all his efforts to solving the problems that came up or else he posed problems that, as he knew in advance, the human brain could solve (a highly limited number of variables). Now, the computer lets us pass to the stage of reflecting *on* problems, with the possibility of posing them as complexly as we like. And we must note the strange feature of "coincidences": the computer "appeared" when information (stored, written) became unusable.

This reflection *on* the problems has, let us say, existed for half a century already. I am quite familiar with it in historiography, for instance. Writing history is no longer the result of archival research but an elaboration of more and more complex problems. And the "appearance" of the computer corresponds exactly to that reflection which has no way out.

The computer is not exactly the creative factor of newness; it is itself the novelty allowing creation to concretize. Hence, it is the determining factor on a collective and concrete level. With the computer, knowledge becomes a force of production, a decisive power in politics, though to the degree that all the economic and technological factors cohere in a rationally grasped whole.

The computer faces us squarely with the contradiction already announced throughout the technological movement and brought to its complete rigor—between the rational (problems posed because of the computer and the answers given) and the irrational (human attitudes and tendencies). The computer glaringly exposes anything irrational in a human decision, showing that a choice considered reasonable is actually emotional. It does not follow that this is translation into an absolute rationality; but plainly, this conflict introduces man into a cultural universe that is different from anything he has ever known before. Man's central, his—I might say—metaphysical problem is no longer the existence of God and his own existence in terms of that sacred mystery. The problem is now the conflict between that absolute rationality and what has hitherto constituted his person. That is the pivot of all present-day reflection, and, for a long time, it will remain the only philosophical issue.

In this way, the computer is nothing but, and nothing more than, technology. Yet it performs what was virtually the action of the technological whole, it brings it to its bare perfection; it makes it obvious. Technology contained in itself that complete transformation of the relationship to reality. Baudrillard (*La Société de consommation*) did an excellent job of showing this. It is remarkable to think that technology, which is often accused of "materializing" man, of chaining him to the material environment (and which does indeed center everything on activity in the material), de-realizes everything, transforms everything into a "sign-of-nothing-to-consume. . . . Nature has been rediscovered in the guise of a rustic sample, framed by the immense urban tissue, gridded and honeycombed in the form of open spaces, nature preserves, or as backdrops to weekend cottages. This rediscovery is actually a recycling of nature. That is to say, nature is no longer an original, specific presence, in symbolic opposition to the culture, but a model of simulation, *a digest of signs of nature* put back into circulation." Moreover: "The closer one gets to the document of truth, to the direct experience, the more one hunts down reality with color, relief, etc., the more the real absence of the world looms from technological perfection to technological perfection."

Technology, as a mediator and as the new environment, makes every reality other than itself abstract, remote, and devoid of content. In this gigantic transformation, how can we help but attribute once again the role of determining factor to technology?

# 4

# TECHNOLOGY AS A SYSTEM

## GENERAL IDEA

Today, numerous conceptions of "system" exist.[1] Most authors start with the object to be studied and define the system in terms of that object. Deutsch (quoted by Hamon) calls a system "an ensemble of parts or subsystems which interact in such a way that the components tend to change slowly enough to be provisionally treated as constants. These slowly changing parts can be called structures—if the exchanges occurring in their mutual relationships prove to be oriented towards maintaining or reproducing systems, they can be called functions." Hamon specifies a set of rational elements, whose evolution is characterized mainly by feedback. But he points out that this is the feedback of the whole on the parts, which assures the autonomy of the system in the whole of reality. Thus, the system is not a collection of objects placed side by side, nor a nonspecific aggregate. Many authors overlabor "feedback" as the true "key" to the system.

In contrast, Henri Lefebvre stresses only the difference between the whole and the sum of the parts: "A system is a set of relationships that adds something to the sum of the diverse elements. That is why we can speak of the principle of the isomorphism of the system. Very different elements can have homologous energy laws; in other words, a system is a totality having its own laws of structure. And in this way, aggregates always appear as subordinates."

However, Lefebvre draws the contestable idea that a system evolves purely in terms of its own internal logic. And for Meadows (in *The Rome Report*): "The structure of any system—i.e. the relations between elements, numerous, forming interlocking loops, and sometimes with effects that are staggered in time—is as important in the evolution of the system as the nature of each individual element making it up."

Finally, there is Talcott Parsons's definition (*The Social System*, 1951): Two or more entities make up a system if they are linked in such a way that a change of state in the first is followed by a change of state in the other(s), which, in turn, is followed by a new change in the first. This definition certainly characterizes an aspect of the technological system, but it is really too vague. In any case, the facet of Parsons's thinking that applies especially well to the technological system is the idea that a system is inevitably both integrating and integrated (or rather a "structural organization of the interaction between units"). It involves a model, an equilibrium, a system of control.

I would like to single out several features in Parsons. The system is a set of elements interrelating in such a way that any evolution of one triggers a revolution of the whole, and any modification of the whole has repercussions on each element. Thus, quite plainly, we are by no means dealing with isolated objects, but rather with a network of interrelations. It is also obvious that the factors making up the system are not identical in nature. There are, for instance, quantitative and nonquantitative elements. Finally, it is certain that the individual factors do not all change at the same rate; the system has its specific process and speed of change in relation to the parts. Just as it has its special laws of development and transformation.

The second feature that I would like to emphasize is the following: The elements composing the system have a sort of preferential disposition to combine among themselves rather than with outside factors. The economic system implies a preferential relationship, which involves both a tendency to change for internal reasons and a resistance to external influences.

The third feature is obviously that a system able to be grasped at a moment of its composition is nevertheless dynamic. The interrelations between the parts are not of the same type as those between the parts of an engine, which do act upon one another and in terms of one another, but always keep repeating the same action. In a system, the acting factors *modify* the other elements, and the action is not repetitive but constantly innovative. The interrelations create an evolution. The system never coagulates—albeit remaining a system and recognizably System X, even after many evolutions.

The fourth feature is that a system existing as a totality can enter into relationships with other systems, other totalities.

Finally, it is common knowledge that one of the essential traits of a system is the feedback, or rather the "feedback structures," which do not, however, make up the system itself.

A system is thus characterized by two elements. On the one hand, the interrelations between the principle and significant elements of the whole (which, incidentally, can thus *never* be tested, all things being equal); on the other hand, its organic relationship to the outside: a system in the social sciences is necessarily open. It can never be considered in itself to the exclusion of any other relationship.

If I choose the term "system" to describe technology in present-day society, it is certainly not because the word is fashionable now, but because I feel that it fits technology. It is an indispensable tool for understanding what is meant by "technology," while disregarding the spectacular, the curious, the epiphenomena that make observation impossible. Take medicine. Once (especially in the past) doctors described ideal models of diseases, but each concrete case of typhus did not show *all* the hallmarks listed in books as belonging to *the* abstract disease and ending with paroxysm and death. Yet if the physician had not had that schema of the abstract disease, which was obtained by eliminating all secondary elements of chance, he would never have been able to tell that a set of symptoms corresponded to typhus. The system thus involves a choice of symptoms, factors, an analysis of their relationships. But this is not a mere intellectual construction. There is quite definitely such a thing as a system—just as there was a disease expressed in a correlation between the systems that could be grouped and labeled.

Technology has now become so specific that we have to consider it in itself and as a system.[2]

By speaking of the technological system, I propose to take account of an important part of reality. This is no simple hypothesis of an aleatory development; I am not extrapolating from a curve while singling out quantitative data from the past in a particular sector. At the moment, technology, in its qualitative and quantitative aspects, has developed in such a way that we can conceive its "normal" development. There is a logic which *makes* the system. Consequently, I propose to take reality into account by analyzing this system and its evolution. But obviously, I cannot do so with full certainty, for the technological system is not completed. It is not closed, it is not a system evolving by its own unique internal logic. Thus, it includes not only a large margin of chance but also a large portion of probability. It is no use forecasting technological "inventions" (in 1990, we'll have this and that, etc.), for prophecies can be made only after an overall study of the system as such, not by totting up countless innovations and applications. Finally, to the extent that it is not "repetitive," the technological system, while giving us only one case to study, is more difficult than physical, ecological systems, etc., which have repeated cycles that can be observed.[3]

The technological system is formed by the existence of the technological phenomenon and by technological advance. I am using "technological phenomenon" in the sense that I gave it in *The Technological Society*, distinguishing it from technological operation, which has always existed throughout history.[4]

The technological phenomenon has been specific to Western civilization since the eighteenth century.[5] It is characterized by consciousness, criticalness, rationality.[6] I will not come back to that. But the technological phenomenon does not suffice per se to make up the system; in fact, it can be regarded as essentially static. One may be tempted to take the phenomenon as such, and, that being the case, to consider and analyze it.[7] In so doing, one would not only be making the habitual error of this kind of "cut" at a given moment. One would also miss the system itself, which, as a system, is evolutionary. But I have to make myself clear. I do not mean that objects or the technological system are evolving. That goes without saying. It is an obvious fact, and it does not add anything. Everyone knows that the automobiles of 1970 are not those of 1930. But that does not make the technological object or, more generally, the phenomenon any different from any pebble. We have said that the technological system is made up of the phenomenon and of progression. The latter is not the modification or evolution of the object. Yet we are always tempted to think it is those things. "Everything flows," time goes by; hence, the object changes. One might almost say that evolution depends on that passing of time, a kind of force exterior to the object, a river bathing it and carrying it away.

But with technology, we are dealing with a totally different reality. For it is technology that works its own change. It has what Jouvenel calls "a permanent revolution of processes." Progression is a part of the object itself; it is constitutive to the object. As we have said, there is no technology without progression. Technological progress is not evolving technology, it is not technological objects that change because they are improved, it is not an adding-up of influences on those machines or those organizations that impels them to adjust. Technology has as a specific given, the feature that it requires its own transformation for itself. From the very instant that it existed in its modern reality, it produced the phenomenon of progression. The progress with which we are imbued and whose ideology inspires all our judgments is a direct result of technology. It is not "technology progressing," it is a new and independent reality; it is the conjunction of the technological phenomenon and technological progress that *constitutes the technological system*. Hence, there are traits, regulations, "laws" (if one can still phrase it thus) in both. Technological progress takes place in a certain way and offers pecularities distinguishing it from other types of evolution. Economic growth or cultural development does not happen along the same lines as technological progression. Therefore, the technological system is characterized by a set of specific traits that distinguish it from other verifiable systems.[8]

As for the singularity of this system, it reveals itself in the very circumstance that a technological factor always preferentially joins with another technological factor. An "attraction" exists between them, and it is clearly due not to the "nature" of either factor but to their belonging to the same system. Hence, the associations with external factors, depending on other systems—political, economic, ideological—are certainly not excluded, but they are always secondary.

Of course, in employing the word *system*, I do not mean that technology is alien to the other environments—political, economic, etc. Technology is not a closed system. But it is a system in that each technological factor (a certain machine, for instance), is first linked to, connected with, dependent on, the ensemble of other technological factors before it relates to nontechnological elements. Or rather, to the extent that technology has become an environment, each technological factor is situated in that environment and constitutes it by subsisting on it.

There is a system just as one can say that cancer is a system. There is a similar mode of action in all the points at which the cancer manifests itself in the organism; there is a proliferation of a new tissue in regard to the old tissue, and there is a relationship between the metastases. A cancer within another living system is itself an organism—but incapable of surviving on its own. The same holds true for the technological system. On the one side, it can appear, develop, exist only to the extent that it integrates into a social body existing apart from it. One cannot conceive of technology like "nature," as able to live on its own. Social nature is preexistent to the technological system, which finds its integration, its possibilities, its support in social nature. Yet on the other side, the growth of technology does not leave the social body intact, nor does it allow its various elements to develop by and of themselves. For instance, there is no family per se, which, thanks to technology, would change as a family and find a new familial equilibrium. In reality, the technological impact challenges the totality of the family as a fact, the family is no longer a sociological reality attached to the body social in order to depend above all on the technological system. The family has now become the "family-in-the-technological-environment."[9]

What is more, each technological factor is not first bound up with some group, some economic or social phenomenon; it is primarily integrated into the technological system. Hence, the mechanization of office work. The current idea is that the government/administration/offices complex remains dominant; and technology is integrating into it. An extra technological element is added to the bureaucratic organization, integrated into the administrative mechanism and attached to this activity.

Such a view of things obviously leads to regarding technology as put together out of disparate bits and pieces, with random and uncertain relations between them. Yet the opposite is true. Each technological element is associated with all the others preferentially. And when mechanization is introduced into offices, it is a kind of spearhead launched in that direction by the technological system. Administration is then modified; above all, it loses its determining character, and is now determined by the new apparatus. Unity is achieved not so much in the earlier framework (government/administration), but by means of the correlations between the diverse technologies. Thus there are no scattered technological factors, integrated into various social, political, economic contexts, which have their organizational principles, their unity, etc. Quite the reverse. There is a technological system having various modalities of intervention and attaching to itself every fragment of the human or social reality, which operation, moreover, removes that fragment from the tissue it was a part of. Hence, every technological factor, associated with the others, forms a more or less coherent and doubtlessly rigorous whole (the coherence is internal but not necessarily evident).

## DEFINING THE SYSTEM

We will have to show at length in what way technology is a system and how that system functions; but in this paragraph, we can offer a general justification of this undertaking.

Total technization occurs when every aspect of human life is subjected to control and manipulation, to experimentation and observation, so that a demonstrable efficiency is achieved everywhere.[10] The system is revealed in the change (a technological, social change, mobility, adjustment, etc., a necessary change for continuously solving the problems raised more and more swiftly by the very existence of technology), owing to the interdependence of all the components, owing to the totality and, finally, the stability attained. This last point is particularly essential. "Detechnicization" is impossible. The scope of the system is such that we cannot hope to go back. If we attempted a detechnicization, we would be like primitive forest-dwellers setting fire to their native environment. These four traits of technology offer a first glimpse of what may be called the system from an overall vantage point.

However, Simondon has shown that the technological object requires a separate treatment to be understood and for the whole to be grasped. The problem posed by Simondon, namely the specific knowledge of the technological object, shows that there is a system from which that object cannot be divorced. The technological object must be taken in the totality of its relations and genetically. According to Simondon, the mode of existence of technological objects is definite because it proceeds from a genesis. But this genesis creates not only objects. It creates, first, a "technological reality," then a general technicity:

> It is the ensemble, the interconnection [of technologies] that makes this both natural and human polytechnical universe. . . . In existence, for the natural world and for the human world, the technologies are not separated. However, for technological thinking, they are virtually separated, because there does not exist a thinking developed highly enough to permit theorizing about this technical network of concrete ensembles. . . . Beyond technical determinations and norms, we would have to discover polytechnical and technological determinations and norms. There exists a world of the plurality of technologies, with its own peculiar structures.

Simondon considers this the true task of philosophy. It strikes us that the philosopher (in general, for Simondon manages to demonstrate the opposite) is rather ill-equipped to proceed toward this

## TECHNOLOGY AS A SYSTEM

discovery. In reality, the discovery would be of an artificial universe to be taken on its own terms, in its own specificity.

"The technological object, becoming detachable, can be grouped with other technological objects according to such and such an arrangement: the technological world offers an indefinite availability of groupings and connections. . . . Constructing a technological object means preparing an availability: the industrial grouping is not the only one to be realized with technological objects—we can also realize nonproductive groupings, whose goal is to attach man to nature through a regulated concatenation of organized mediations, to create a coupling between human thought and nature. The technological world intervenes here as a system of convertibility."

Thus, this technological system exists not only by its intrinsic relationship, but also because the objects to which the technologies are applied are systems themselves. "Nature," "Society." Since "Nature" and "Society" have existed as systems (the ecosystem, for instance), technology, applied to separated, specified, differentiated aspects of the one and then of the other, has finally covered them in their entirety. But these parceling operations (the correspondence of a technology to, or the creation of a technological object for, a certain natural need, a certain natural challenge, had an interrelationship, owing not to their technological qualification at the outset, but to their application to systems. It was only gradually, with the acquisition of second- and third-degree technologies, that technology, constituted as a veritable continuous tissue, then as an environment, became, in turn, a system in itself, independent of its objects. At that moment, the technologies became coherent with respect to one another, they were organized in terms of one another. The elements, the technological factors, were not simply juxtaposed, they combined with one another. An ensemble was established: of "solidarities," connections, coordination among all the objects, methods, etc., of technology.

We must, however, pinpoint something here. When I speak of a system, I do not mean that I am constructing a system intended for descriptive and operational analysis and based on simulation by a data-processing model. I could say that, to a certain extent, I am applying systemic analysis to a concrete ensemble. But rather, I believe I can establish that the technological phenomena have combined in such a way as to now present the characteristics of a truly existing system. The goal is not to formalize in terms of a computer processing but rather to establish a certain reality (by no means every reality), which allows setting up the theory.

Indeed, one thing struck me very sharply. The formalized systems I investigated were all very weak conceptually and very poor in understanding facts, all of which rendered them utterly inadequate. The operations issuing thence, perfect as they may be on a mathematical level, therefore made little sense! It seems to me that the limit of application depends on the size of the object. I feel that this method is applicable to precise and relatively limited objects—an organization or an ensemble of organizations, with the study of the pertinent system of information and system of decision.[11] But I feel just as strongly that this is impossible for an entire society, for Western economy as a whole, or, for, say, the general politics of Europe. At most, the formalization into a system here could best reveal what is not possible as interpretation. In this book, however, I tend far more to share Parsons's outlook in his *The Social System*.

\* \* \*

But we have to face a serious criticism. How can we deal with technology as though it had a kind of existence in itself? How can we analyze a technological system as a sort of clock running all by itself? Technology exists only because there are human beings participating in it, making it function, inventing, choosing. To claim we can examine technology without regarding the chance elements, the irregularities produced by man, means proceeding to an illegitimate and, moreover, impossible abstraction. The technological system is purely imaginary, we never see it. What we see, what we encounter, are men using the instruments. Ultimately, technology does not exist. There are products, there are machines, there are methods . . . But it is artificial to view them together. Lefebvre wants to show that there are *plural* technologies, diverse, mutually unrelated, and *plural* technological objects, scattered, dispersed, with very divergent finalities, and never concerning the same environments. There is thus a collection, an addition, but no system.

I realize that by analyzing the technological system as an object in itself, without considering mankind or groups, I am going counter to one of the chief trends in present-day sociology. Weber is reproached for studying bureaucy as a system, setting forth its traits and operating laws. His detractors point out that it is the officials, the clerks that count, and that, ultimately, no concrete investigation reveals any of the laws and principles forwarded by Weber. Instead, we find human relationships, actions and reactions of groups and individuals, "dysfunctions," choices, and initiatives.

That, and nothing else, is the verifiable reality of an administration. That is man in relation to what is known as *technology;* it is he who, in the final analysis, is called upon to act and to choose. Even if there *is* a certain reality of technology, it is erroneous to claim we can analyze it by disregarding the human presence.[12] And yet, although I am familiar with this objection and acknowledge its full accuracy, such an analysis is precisely what I have attempted here. And my reasons are twofold.

First of all, to say that one "sees" only separate technological objects which do not form a system is (with all due respect) a limited attitude. When man, looking at the things of nature, finds only separate objects—clouds and grass, pebbles and water, etc.— all of them scattered and unrelated, one cannot call this a very satisfying intellectual position. We know that from his very origins, man has tried to establish a system of nature. He has striven for both a system of relations, and an explanatory system. He has often gone awry, with magical or metaphysical explanations and correspondences; but each time, one system replaced another, until he formulated a system of rational relationships that are called scientific. This is precisely the same labor that we have attempted here. We do not claim that our description of the technological system is scientific or decisive, but only that this is an indispensable first step, without which nothing can be done toward comprehending man's new universe.

Furthermore, when omitting human dysfunctions, my attitude is simply that of the scientist who assumes "all things being equal," whereas we know very well that such a situation will never exist. Likewise, we know very well that in chemistry and physics, the analysis of a phenomenon must perforce disregard certain conditions. One comes to a law, but when one tries to experiment, the experiment never exactly supplies what was foreseen, because the disregarded factors are not absent in reality. Yet if researchers did not proceed in this way no science would be possible. To discern the phenomenon itself, to know its regularities, we have to detach it artificially from variables, hazards, accidental disturbances. If we realize that these variables are nevertheless always present in reality, we need only reintegrate them and consider, on the basis of the first analysis, the modifications thus occurring in the phenomenon.

What is well known for the so-called exact sciences must also be applied to the social sciences. Marx's attitude toward political economy strikes me as exemplary. Those whom he called the economists (i.e., the "classic" ones, the liberals, the founders of economic science) had indeed disregarded the human factor. Marx did not say that they were wrong or that their analysis of economy was therefore inaccurate. On the contrary, he ceaselessly used their analysis, and he looked upon their results as scientifically correct. But he *then* asserted that it is impossible to leave out the human factor from the economic milieu, and that we must see what its reinsertion will bring about. Even more, he drew conclusions about the economic reality because it was *possible* to study it scientifically by eliminating the human factor; and he went on to a critique of political economy based on the very data supplied by the classical economists. Their previous work was indispensable.

The same holds true for Weber and bureaucracy. The study of dysfunctions and the analysis of employee behavior is impossible without Weber's schematic construction. It would be wrong to say that bureaucracy *is* (exclusively) the system taken apart by Weber. But it is just as wrong to say that bureaucracy is (exclusively) an ensemble of human relations, pressures, interests, etc. These have meaning or even a possibility of existence only to the extent that this ensemble is situated *in,* and in terms of, this objective system.

What would those human relations mean if one did not know in advance that they are integrated in an ensemble of regulations, examinations, hierarchies, jurisdictions that are objectively established and that one must first become familiar with and determine, before knowing what, in this context, is the reality experienced by human beings. One should not protest that there is no reality but what is *experienced,* that only the "accepted as," the "understood as" are what count, with nothing existing beyond that experience. This is certainly accurate. But for such an experience to exist, there must be a reality outside that experience. I refuse to get entangled in philosophical debate, I am only saying that the official can "experience" the civil service examination as . . . But the fact that the examination is laid down by a law giving it its reality, that there are rules of application, a designated jury, etc.—well, this ensemble exists, not so much prior to the experience, nor as the occasion of the experience, but by itself. Of course, it is experienced only through a series of personal or collective experiences and perceptions. But it cannot be reduced to that, for if these laws and rules did not exist, there would be no experiences or perceptions. And it is not useless to know what the object is.

In other words, by studying the technological system, I appear to be disregarding man. But in fact, I am showing the canvas on which action, refusal, angst, approval, perception, etc., take place. And without knowing that canvas, I could not understand those experiences and perceptions.

Thus, I propose to furnish not so much the reality as a certain given that is indispensable for knowing this reality. To be sure, these matters have no objective reality independent of man's experience; but what man experiences does not boil down to his subjectivity. We have to bear in mind the rules imposed upon him, the obstacles he comes up against, etc. It is only if I know the *wording* of the law that I can understand a specific interpretation, a specific behavior of obeying or flouting. Thus, in describing the system, I do not exclude the initiatives and choices of individuals, but only the possibility that everything boils down to them. I do not offer "what takes place," "what is," but what man modifies, accelerates, disturbs, etc.

Nonetheless, there is a further error to be avoided here. We should not believe that if technology is considered in this way, it is an object, or that, in relation to technology, man is a subject. Yet that is what we hear all the time. After all, technology merely supplies things, and man does whatever he likes with them. Thus, everything depends on their good or bad use . . . Remarkably, moreover, the very same people declare that the technological system does not exist as such and that there are only technological objects. In point of fact, however, those objects are not scattered and unrelated, they are included in a system. Furthermore, man, who is to act upon this system, who is to use these technological objects, is not a man per se, an absolute subject either. He himself is incorporated in a technological society.

We have to zero in on this current opinion. First of all, it belongs to the "man in the street," who, of course, does not perceive a technological ensemble; he thinks he is dealing with his car, his TV, his modern accounting register, the IBM machine, and the airplane. Separate elements, distinct uses, an absence of reflection on their coherence and continuity. But this attitude results just as much from specialization. Each sector develops independently of the others (in appearance). Each of us is immersed in a separate technological domain. Each man knows his professional technology, and only that. He is aware (theoretically) that other technologies exist side by side with his, but he does not see the inner coherence of the sectors, and he can dream about all those vast and free fields which are ruled by independence and imagination—his own field being that of rigor, efficiency, and enslavement. Last but not least, among intellectuals, this attitude results from a systematic refusal to consider this reality: If technology is truly a system, then freedom of thought is a mere decoy, man's sovereignty is threatened, etc.; and since this cannot be, then technology cannot possibly be a system.

This panicky reflex dominates most intellectual judgments on the nonexistence of technology per se. It is really so convenient and so reassuring to consider only completely unrelated devices, objects, methods. One can then imagine sovereign man throning in this collection and acting upon it in full independence. All technological elements come from him, have no existence outside of him, and return to him; in short, man gives them their coherence. For there is great reluctance to admit that a specific organization of technology exists, relatively independent of man, a sort of schematizing of life by technology. This reluctance is manifest in the following: romantic reactions, (which explains a whole portion of modern literature); the intellectual impugnment of this possibility; and the elaboration of false concepts to account for our society, to attest that ultimately nothing has changed, man is still man, society is still society, nature is still nature. Society is still formally and substantially the same—i.e., nothing has essentially changed in two centuries. Of course, there is speed, urbanization, and so on, but . . .

At bottom, those intellectuals maintain the image of an intact society (and an intact human being): a society whose structures are comparable to those of the past (not the same, to be sure), whose groups, culture, work are subject to the same principles and the same analyses (though we perceive the differences, to be sure). Society (the same old society) is thought of as consisting, still, of classes (with similar class relationships) and obeying the same old dialectics . . . In other words, there is a permanent reality undergoing surface modifications, the reality of man for some, the reality of society for others, the reality of classes; and this reality is joined by an ensemble of processes, objects, work methods, machines, which certainly change one or two aspects of the society, but ultimately integrate into it, *add* to it. This image recurs endlessly, even among the most "forward-looking" people—the image of a modern society, which, in short, is merely the traditional society *plus* technologies. Naturally, it is not put in that way, but the type of analysis presented shows that such is the (hidden) assumption. And that is exactly what Lefebvre assumes in the statement quoted above. It is very hard to accept that we live in a society having no

## TECHNOLOGY AS A SYSTEM

common measure with earlier societies, and that the experiences and thoughts of our ancestors are no longer of any use to us.

Far more interesting and attractive is the phenomenon known as "rapid change", a term widely used in Christian studies, the World Council of Churches, etc. This notion is wrong—from two points of view.

First of all, this term focuses on the rapidity of change in a previously known factor, e.g., the family. There is a state $a$, a state $b$, a state $c$ of the family, and we are told that the present transition from state $b$ to $c$ is far swifter than the earlier transition from $a$ to $b$. But this problem is quite secondary. The issue is much less the rapid evolution of old elements than the appearance of a structure and an ensemble of radically new functions. From a moral or humanist point of view, we must certainly deal with the concrete fate of the individuals and groups affected by rapid change. But so long as we consider the latter first, we doom ourselves to understanding nothing of that issue. We have to regard not so much the change of older frameworks as the appearance of a new environment, we have to highlight not so much the urban transformation as man's situation in the technological structures.

The second aspect of the same error crops up when we consider the origin of the concept of rapid change, which results from a particularly strong impression of some striking event: "People produce more, people go faster, etc." "Rapid change" concerns the spectacle aspect of our society. It implies that we do not stick to the purely factual event. On the contrary, the essential thing is to focus on the overall mutation resulting from the appearance of the technological system. The instant one actually grasps what that means, the sensational discoveries lose much of their interest. Walking on the moon is no longer an event, it is a reasonable and normal consequence of what already exists. We can then say that once the technological system becomes the structure of our society, we can no longer speak of "rapid change," but rather of normal, foreseeable, and almost unilinear consequences of the previous mutation. That is why we find it necessary to reject the concept of "rapid change," which is a red herring.

The technological system is a qualitatively different phenomenon from an addition of multiple technologies and objects. We cannot absolutely understand them if we consider them separately or isolate one field of action from technology; we have to study them inside of, and in terms of, the overall technological system. How could we evaluate the influence of rapid communications if we separate them from the methods of modern work, the forms of housing, the technologies of government and administration, the demands of production and distribution, etc.?

The mere act of isolating one aspect completely falsifies the issue as a whole. To understand the technological phenomenon, to analyze its sociology, the first condition is to regard it as a whole, in its unity. So long as we look at the technologies separately, we can certainly study each one's formation, its specific methods, its particular influences; but that sheds no light for us on the society in which we live or on the reality of the technological milieu. We would therefore have a false view of not only the whole, but also every particular technology; for each one can be truly comprehended only in its relationship to the others. To what extent does that one technology spark the development of other technologies; to what extent is it based on other technologies, etc.? This is a decisive methodological problem. We have to study the technological system in itself; and it is only this approach that makes it possible to study the different technologies.

That leads to rejecting what I will call "abstract empiricism" (already abundantly criticized by Sorokin and Mills): i.e., the attitude of abstracting one aspect, retaining only that, and sticking to the most immediate reality as the object of study, applying exact methods to it. Obviously, the mathematical method, statistics, surveys, can be useful only for limited and quite subordinate facets; and such an investigation should certainly be launched. But when it is done, we ought to know that it is neither the faithful report nor the exact interpretation of the whole, that it must not claim any privileged or preeminent explanatory position. If it is not part of an analysis of the overall reality, of a description of the general correlations, it will mislead anyone who trusts the results, for it lacks the essential: the interactions.

\* \* \*

Having said that, we can attempt a quick first view of this system by naming certain of its aspects.

The first aspect of the system is obviously its specificity. Technologies are not comparable to anything else. That which is not a technology has no point in common with what which *is*. And they possess, among themselves, similar characteristics; one can find traits common to all technologies. But we have to go further. All the parts are correlated, a correlation accentuated by the technicizing of information. The consequences are twofold. First of all, one cannot modify a technology without causing repercussions and modifications in a huge number of other objects or methods. Secondly, the combinations of technologies produce technological effects, engendering new objects or new methods. And these combinations take place necessarily, inevitably. But beyond that, the technological world, like any system, has a certain tendency to regulate itself, i.e., to constitute an order of development and functioning which makes technology engender both its own accelerators and its own brakes. Nevertheless, as we shall see, this aspect is the most uncertain. The system thus seems highly independent of man (just as the natural environment used to be).

This system exists basically not because a mechanical relationship has established itself between the different factors (by no means should we imagine the technological system like the different parts of a clockwork); but because we have a denser and denser ensemble of information relationships. We already know this on the level of our own interpretation. Information theory, which is all the rage nowadays, is an "interscientific technology . . . that allows us both to systematize scientific concepts and schematize diverse technologies." Information theory is not a new science, nor a technology among technologies. It has developed because the technological system exists as a system by dint of the relationships of information. It is neither a chance thing nor a brilliant human discovery. It is a response to man's need to understand the new universe. Information theory is a mediating thought among the various technologies (but also among the various sciences, and between the sciences and the technologies). "It comes into play as a science of technologies and a technology of sciences."

But if that is so, if information theory now appears to be a means of finally penetrating that system, then it is because information has done its share in structuring the system itself. The various technologies have unified into a system by dint of the information transmitted from one to another and utilized technologically in each sector. One can fittingly apply Norbert Wiener's statement (*Cybernetics*) to the technological system: "Just as the amount of information of a system measures its degree of organization, so too the entropy of a system measures its degree of disorganization."

Once every technological object or method no longer had just the function of doing the exact task it was created for, but also acted as a transmitter of information; once every technological object or method started not only to function as such, but also to register the information transmitted by the whole technological environment (aside from what comes from the natural environment); and finally, once everyone took all that information into account—that was the point at which there was a system.

It is not only the emergence of information theory which forces us to note this, but also the multiplication of devices transmitting information and of information technologies. The technological system has thus become a demander in these areas. The more technology develops, the further the labors of information increase as a condition of that development. Material output and the movements of physical objects have become less important than these nonmaterial activities. The information explosion was necessary for the creation of the system; it is not a mere accidental product of our capacity to produce information. The moment the system tends to organize itself, the demand for information becomes explicit; that is to say, a new informational sector appears, which is itself made up of technologies whose sole specific feature is to produce, transmit, and gather information. At present, ninety percent of this information is produced by technologies of action and intervention, and its purpose is to allow other technological sectors to improve or adjust.

Thus, what we have is an intertechnological relationship, the emergence of an ensemble of mediations; and that is what constitutes technology into a system. It is not just a matter of (though this *is* important) communicating, and reading about, scientific discoveries, innovations, (the international grid of information that will integrate the present-day electronic data banks, for instance). Far more significant is the permanent relation, on a concrete, often very humble level, between *everything that is performed* and *everything that could be performed* in the neighboring operational areas. Scientific information has always been highly attractive and unsettling, but it is not the center of our world; it is the permanent movement of thousands of bits of operational data from one technological sector to another. Now this movement has been decisively facilitated by the appearance of computers. And it is in this context that we must ask about the new technological ensemble, thanks to which the technological system is *completing* the process of constituting itself.

The importance of the computer is obviously tied to the fact that the further we advance, the more significant a part of our world information becomes (this is already a platitude). We are no longer

## TECHNOLOGY AS A SYSTEM

a society dominated by the imperative of production; now, we are ruled by the transmission, circulation, reception, and interpretion of multiple information. And that is exactly how the system is completing its constitution. The parts are not coordinated or even connected with one another; they are not materially linked. But each part is a receiver of information, and the system is held together by the network of endlessly renewed information. What makes it flexible and ungraspable at a given moment is that one can never draw up any sort of "inventory of the system," because that would mean coagulating the information, hence negating the system itself.

\* \* \*

The computer is an enigma. Not in its making or its usage, but because man appears incapable of foreseeing anything about the computer's influence on society and humanity. We have most likely never dealt with such an ambiguous apparatus, an instrument that seems to contain the best and the worst, and, above all, a device whose true potentials we are unable to scrutinize. Naturally, we know what a computer can be employed for directly. There is no need to run through its possible uses here. This is not part of our investigation. I will merely recall a few acknowledged facts.

The machine does not do everything. Man must first: define the goal, the objective to be attained (on condition that it can be evaluated quantitatively); decide on a program to put into the machine's memory and translate the program into a language that the computer can understand; and gather the specific data of the problem to be solved. The machine performs the operations and presents the results, but it is man who decides what he will do with the results. The machine cannot (in theory—we will see the discussion below) surpass its own limits or take initiatives; it functions according to rules that are defined in advance. By using the computer, man, admittedly, can pass along inferior, automatic tasks (and it is inferred that he can therefore devote himself to the superior tasks of inventing, of conceiving programs). But we can stop here in this recollection of platitudes.

Instantly, we are confronted with the apparently insoluble questions, and extreme controversy among researchers. And it is this division, in which I find it impossible to discern a reason for choosing one stance over another, that strikes me as attesting the true unknowability of the computer—on the simplest level. Will the computer cause unemployment? For some, this is indisputable, since whole job categories are going to be brutally displaced. One computer doing the work of fifty or a hundred men. But then again, building, maintaining, and programming these machines will require considerable manpower. A program taking only a few seconds to be answered will necessitate months of elaboration by a team of workers.

But between those two outlooks, we are absolutely unable to arrive at any choice, for we have no concrete experience. One can merely put forward that all technological progress brings unemployment and some jobs to make up for it, although these new jobs will not be taken by the people who are thrown out of work. What does seem certain is that the computer will accentuate the predominance of technicians, highly qualified employees and the young—and it will make the skills of old and unretrainable employees useless at a faster and faster clip.

Another insoluble problem crops up. Is the computer going to bring about centralization, or will it permit decentralization?[13] The computer accelerates decision-making and modifies the areas of centralization and decentralization. The centralization of means, the coordination of decision-making power in one point, the coherence of decisions, which postulates centralization: the integrated processing allows analyzing the procedure of decision-making in its coherence. Storage procedures permit centralizing all the useful facts at one single point. Hence, one can perfectly visualize a single center of "political" power. The data banks award a decisive superiority to the group that runs them—it could discuss an economic plan drawn up by the authorities, on the basis of millions of facts that the group alone would know and that would be processed by computers that the group alone would possess.

But in contrast, other authors state that the computer is a marvelous instrument for decentralizing. Open the data banks to everyone, and everyone will be able to discuss politics with means hitherto unknown. The centralization of decision-making is necessary only to the extent that coordination and impetus demand it. In all other cases, the centralization of data processing can combine with a decentralization of decision-making. Decentralization is not only possible but facilitated: the computer relieves the decentralized collectivities of all-absorbing tasks and increases their decision-making power by augmenting their means of information—data processing coordinates (and hence reinforces) the decentralized system, which, moreover, will soon be made necessary by the congestion of the center.[14]

The consoling thing in such a discussion is that once again we seem to be dealing in everything and for everything, with a simple orientation of man himself. Hence, whether the data banks are opened up for everyone or kept shut and reserved for only a few is a simple matter of human decision. *If* man wants, the data-processing system can be an instrument of dictatorship or democracy. Alas, as we shall see, it is not all that simple.

Let us discuss one final question, the most central, and apparently insoluble: the limits of the computer, or even the total replacement of man. Will the computer remain a simple inert instrument, which man can do with as he pleases, or will the robot seize its autonomy and replace man? This would be an evolution which Leroi Gourhan interprets as man creating endlessly outside of himself something that acts in his stead and thus makes human action useless. With the computer, we are reaching the final stage of that replacement; man's mind is becoming unnecessary. Technology is a process of exteriorizing human capacities. And the final step has been taken. Man is faced with another being capable of doing everything that man used to do, but with greater speed, accuracy, etc.

The presentation in Rorvik's book is characteristic. Evolution, he says, passes from the amoeba to man through progressive animal mutations, then from man to the computer, which is simply a final stage of evolution. However, the computer must replace man as the "king of creation." The machine is intelligent. There is no limit to its intelligence. And in visions that he wants to present as scientific, Rorvik describes all the possibilities of the computer: total automation of factories, the computer's aptitude for learning spontaneously, for programming itself; computers have personalities, they have mental crises, they feel friendship, dislike, affection, they can do very flexible tasks; they can create music or poetry, teach, deduce, direct a psychoanalysis, treat an illness. As for the machines that can translate, pass legal judgments, read and use any text, etc., Rorvik feels that they already exist. And in support of his opinion, he cites hundreds of statements by experts (without, however, giving any exact references)!

Countless examples of such fantasies turn up in Elgozy (*Le Désordinateur*). This interpretation of the phenomenon is practically rubber-stamped by Beaune: "The machine lives and thinks."

(He too envisages a close symbiosis between the computer and man, taking into account the computer's ultimate autonomy.) "The machine thoroughly explores the attributes characterizing those two functions. But it lives and thinks *in its own fashion*, filling the classical conceptual framework with new potentialities and autonomous meanings. . . . This affirms the power of a creative thinking of its own norms, literally establishing a new world full of noise and sense. . . . Human behavior, such as voluntary mobility, the mnemonic process, evaluating a random situation, are favorably simulated by those apparatuses . . . and mechanically explained. . . . These apparatuses no longer mimic life and thought, they actually live and think, faster and better than man in the silence of passions and feelings that . . . prevent us from living."

It is clear that Beaune was deeply impressed by John von Neumann's celebrated opus, *The General and Logical Theory of Automata in the World of Mathematics* (IV, 1956), from which he quotes the part about the robot's ability to reproduce itself. Neumann shows how a self-reproducing system can (theoretically!) exist. A reproduction that, moreover, would be totally lucid and self-aware, the opposite of biological reproduction, which always partially involves contingency. Neumann shows how, in the system he describes, an instruction will function as a father, the copying mechanism will perform the basic act of reproduction (duplication of genetic material), and one of the subsystems in the ensemble will even introduce arbitrary changes.

Nevertheless, without going into an overall critique, I am obliged to state that throughout Neumann's description, there is a mysterious "one," who supplies programs, instructions, who puts automaton A in contact with automaton B, etc. In other words, so that the computer may be capable of a "self-reproduction," it must be programmed to that end. And thus, I do not see the idea of *self-reproduction* anywhere. But still, Beaune will not hesitate to speak of the "initiative" of the computer, of an artificial model of human thought, of an "electronic brain," which links up with Couffignal's "*Machine à penser*" (thinking machine).

In regard to this entire trend, I would like to point out that *all* the works giving the computer the power of identifying with man, only better, and a sort of total possibility, are *old* (one exception, however, is W. Skyvington's *Machina Sapiens*, 1976). There are no recent works, aside from writings that are totally secondhand.[15] Now it is well known that right up to about 1963, there was infatuation and enthusiasm among the specialists. Anything was possible thanks to the computer. For the last ten years, however, we have had a period of wavering criticism, uncertainty. It must be said that one cannot be sure of what is actually gained thanks to the computer. Some people assert that medical diagnosis is already being applied with success; others, on the contrary, maintain that all the present-day attempts are disappointing. The translating machine? It exists and is being used. But we are told by Elgozy, Vacca, and even Moles that it is a complete flop. The machine furnishes "translations" that are perfectly unintelligible, just as the teaching machines or chess-playing machines are still in the realm of fancy.

As for demonstrating theorems, these theorems were all known; the computer has not advanced mathematics by even one jot. Regarding the possibility of having the computer "learn" autonomously and on the basis of its previous experience, it is, as Vacca says, a matter of definitions. One can program computers to react to signals from the outer world and to put those signals to their own use. The computer can work out statistics on the behavior of the surrounding milieu and, in terms of results, orient the apparatuses that are placed under its control. But there is no way that the computer can furnish an optimal reaction to events that were not foreseen by the programmer.[16]

Quite plainly, the tales about the computer feeling pleasure, affection, and what not are stupid. The word *psychosis* pops up when the machine goes out of order, and the word *love* when the machine responds better to its habitual programmer (who quite simply knows its possibilities better). Is there even a shadow of resemblance between the machine and the brain, between the mechanism and the mind? It is quite fundamental to realize first that the functioning of the human brain is essentially *of a nonformal type*.[17] By a route which is in no wise comparable to thinking, the computer can achieve a certain number of results that man achieves with the mind; but in human thinking, there is always a share of surprise and unpredictability, which are inaccessible to the computer. Furthermore, the human world is not an exclusively rational world. It is just marvelous to hear someone peacefully declare that passions and feelings prevent us from living! I would rather not discuss it. However, for a still undetermined time, we are going to be creatures of passion, suffering, joy, hope, despair. Hence, the decisions we have to make cannot disregard that fact. They must include factors strictly inaccessible to the computer. Man must reach decisions, albeit with incomplete information; and even if he has complete information, he has to add irrational factors. To decide about a war, who can measure in advance a panic affecting an entire population and blocking the army, like France in 1940!

A decision reached by man is never (not because of his incapacity, incompetence, inadequacy) the *solution* to a *problem* (which the computer is able to supply). A human decision is the breaking of a Gordian knot (which the computer is unable to dò). The logical process is merely one part of decision-making, because the world in which a decision is to be integrated is itself not rational. Hence, one cannot imagine a perfection of the computer, which is able to do anything and ultimately will replace man. Likewise, Elgozy can accurately say that "the intrinsic feature of the human mind is not making calculations but knowing that it is making calculations and knowing what they signify." And this is something the computer will never achieve!

In these conditions, what is the true role of the computer outside the parcellary functions that are often described (gathering, storing, transmitting data) and the equally parcellary application areas? In reality, it is *the computer that allows the technological system to definitively establish itself as a system*. First of all, it is the computer that allows the large subsystems to organize. For example, the urban system can close itself up only because of the urban data banks (census results, building permits granted, housing already built or under construction, water, telephone, power, transportation, and other networks). Likewise, the air-communication system can function only due to computers, given the complexity, the very rapidly growing number of problems sparked by the multiplication of transportation combined with the technological progress in those areas (it is not only the oft-mentioned booking of seats, but also, for instance, the permanent relationship of each airplane, at every moment, to a huge number of control centers on the ground). The computer also makes possible the large accounting units, that is, the infrastructure for an unlimited growth of economic and even administrative organizations. Would it help to recall the importance of the computer as a memory for scientific work? It is the only solution for preventing the researcher and the intellectual from being swamped by documentation. The major part of a scientist's time goes for bibliographical research (the present world has over one hundred thousand purely bibliographical works, all listed in a second-degree bibliography, the *World Bibliography of Bibliographies*). In other words, it is the computer that

## TECHNOLOGY AS A SYSTEM

will allow the scientific subsystem to finally organize itself efficiently by that very use as well as by registering discoveries, innovations, inventions, etc. And only the computer will permit adapting administrative subsystems, public utilities, businesses, etc. to the population growth.

But of course, we must, in any event, remember that the computer can operate only on very great numbers. It is ridiculous using it largely, as is the case, for medium-sized businesses or for a small institute with a tiny staff of researchers. Most computers that I know of are underemployed by groups who fail to realize, as Font and Quiniou so well put it, that "the computer is a bulldozer, and using it to dig in a garden is inconceivable." One has no grasp of what a computer really is if one thinks of it as doing a bookkeeper's job more swiftly.

Sfez has clearly shown that, for example, the entire administrative system would have to be modified in terms of such equipment. In the administrative subsystem, it is a factor of knowledge and education (a demand that the administrators rigorously conceptualize the problems facing them), but it disturbs the relationships of authority. Politico-administrative decision-making changes its character. The programmer becomes the head of the administrative apparatus. The decision-maker is forced to enter into a dialogue and can no longer maintain his status on a legal and hierarchic basis. A total contradiction exists between the rigid status of the officials and the fluidity of the data-processing sector. The implementation personnel will tend to disappear. The supervisory personnel's task will consist of relations with the public, and forecasting or research.

From a structural point of view, the computer transforms the administrative services from parallel to integrated administration. (For instance, the personnel salaries, previously taken care of by each ministry for its staff, will henceforth be administered by a single machine belonging to a separate and independent agency. Likewise, there will be an integrated administration of information for all agencies. Moreover, the computer is transforming the procedures and structures of administrative controls (by doing away with most of them). It is unifying procedures and concatenating administrative decisions with one another. But this perforce involves new powers of administration (the risk of knowing everything about all the individuals in a nation; each person will have his dossier containing all the information on him).

Finally, computers allow us to organize subsystems by establishing connections and relations *among* the various parts of that whole. It is obvious that, hitherto, speaking about "administration" has been an intellectual abstraction. Concretely, there are, in fact, multiple administrations, mutually alien, competitive, guarding their secrets, etc. But this will no longer be possible with the computer. Either it will not be used; or, if it *is* used, people will have to connect the various networks of data and of preparation for administrative decision-making. The point is not so much to link them, as by a sort of interministerial committee, but rather to integrate them.

Everything that we have just sketchily reviewed, and that was excellently analyzed by Sfez, shows that the computer has everywhere the function of integrating the parts of the *technological* subsystems. (For it can validly be employed only where human activities are technological; otherwise, the area is too vague. Naturally, one can get a computer to paint a picture, but, strictly speaking, this is of no interest aside from curiosity.) And when, like Moles, one puts the computer into the cultural sector, this either is folklore or signifies the total technicization of the cultural world and its transformation into a technological subsystem. (We will study this particular problem when we investigate art in the technological society.) The computer can process only technological data, for they are the only decipherable and the only profitable data. That is why it still has a long way to go before entering fully into pure scientific use (which is not profitable despite the celebrated formula of "research and development"). Nor can the computer enter profitable activities that cannot be reduced to technologies, because they would not be mathematizable. Hence, the computer operates in terms of, and for, subsystems that are technological or that it forces to become technological. There is no other possibility.

Yet this integration is all the more powerful in that, naturally, the computer does not remain a solitary crag. The parallel advancement of the various communications technologies is obsolete. Data processing, television, telecommunications get together on more and more projects, which constitute veritable electronic systems of communication, associating audiovisual broadcasting- and- receiving devices, handling capacity, storage capacity and long-distance transmitting mechanisms. Instead of computers, television circuits, or telephone networks, we should henceforth speak of electronic communications systems. This specific organism is now the new

## TECHNOLOGY AS A SYSTEM

relationship of the technological subsystems, and is allowed by the foundation of the technological system as a whole.

But we should not give in to euphoria, as the Diebold Research Program says (1971). Far from simplifying technology or business, the computer has increased their complexity, forcing a series of constantly changing restraints upon researchers and managers. Integrating an ensemble into a smoothly working system turned out to be much harder than anyone thought or than the computer manufacturers themselves imagined.

Thus, there are incredible difficulties, and no one even knows whether they can be overcome; incredible changes in all existing structures and procedures. So that, as Vacca perfectly emphasizes, "people often prefer sticking to the simplistic use of the computer, on the lowest level." If the sequential project, the structure and the logic of the system in question have not been satisfactorily defined, if the problems raised by its possible congestion have not been studied, then no appreciable advantage is to be gained from using a computer. If one sets up a computer (and we have seen that this is nothing as yet) without first analyzing the system, one ultimately transfers the strategies and structures of the simplest possible system into the programs of the computer in order not to risk a large-scale failure: "Thus, there are systems in which a certain number of processes are run by a computer and which, for that reason alone, are considered modern and efficient, whereas they actually offer highly modest and uninteresting benefits," says Elgozy. Using a computer is not enough to make us modern.

This leads to an essential discovery. It is utterly vain and futile to speak of the computer as a unity. We have just seen the necessary connection between the computer and telecommunications. But even more, the processes of swift calculating, memory dimension, etc., are quite uninteresting. To consider *one* computer is to stay on the mental level of the gawker at the county fair who goes to see the basket case or the bearded lady. The computer is not a gadget to do things better and faster. Computers are the correlation factor in the technological system. Until now, the large technological ensembles have had few interrelations. Twenty-five years ago, there was no way to speak of the technological system, because all that could be ascertained was a growth of technology is all areas of human activity. It was an anarchic growth, however; these areas were still kept specific by the traditional division of operations performed by man, and there was no relationship between them. People did look for the technological means to relate them, but they never managed to think of anything but an institutional-type organization, because they knew only of an institutional method to create procedures and connections among various agencies and separate areas of activity. Hence, what we had was a procedure of external framing and rigid "fastening"; and that was what kept the technological subsystems from developing in relation to one another.

Data processing solves the problem. Thanks to the computer, there emerged a sort of internal systematics of the technological ensemble, expressing itself by, and operating on, the level of information. It is through reciprocal total and integrated information that the subsystems are coordinated. This is something that no man, no human group, no constitution was able to do. The further technicization advanced, the more the technological sectors tended to become independent, autonomous, and incoherent. Only the computer can deal with this. But it is quite obvious that it cannot be *one* computer. It has to be an ensemble of computers working interrelatedly at all communication points of the system. This ensemble becomes the subsystem of connections between the different technological subsystems.

It is (without abusing the simile) like a nervous system of the technological ensemble—so long as we avoid any comparison to *the composition* or *operation* of the animal nervous system (there are so many cells in the animal brain and so many elements in an electronic storage—a perfectly stupid parallel). The simile works on the level of the fixed functions that are the same. The computer ensemble plays the part of a nervous system in the technological order; all other comparisons are uninteresting, they are childish outbursts or halfbaked knowledge.

However, the function we are dealing with is so purely technological that man is truly incompetent. Only the technically most perfect and most powerful apparatus could do the job. Thus, the computer performs a task *inaccessible* to man! And thus, there is no rivalry between them. The ideology that sees the robot as a servant or rebel, or the computer as ultimately replacing man in the evolution of creatures, is a bunch of fancies proving that the people who talk about the computer haven't the foggiest notion of what a computer is, and approach it through anthropomorphism. It is not enough to say that the computer can do this or that. All this talk is nonsense. The sole function of the data-processing ensemble is to allow a junction, a flexible, informal, purely technological, immediate, and universal junction of the technological subsystems. Hence, we have a new ensemble of new functions, from which man is excluded—not by competition, but because no one has so far performed those functions. This does not, of course, imply that the computer eludes man; but rather, a strictly nonhuman ensemble is establishing itself.

When the parcellary technicization of tasks occurred, we gradually took on dimensions (e.g., of production) that required new organization. Man still knew how to manage that. Large-scale organization was made possible by the technologies of organization. But with the technicization of all activities and with the growth of all technologies, we are at present faced with a blockage, a state of disorder, because the things now taking place, in quantity, complexity, and speed, are no longer of a human dimension. No organization can operate satisfactorily anymore. The computer phenomenon has appeared at precisely this bottleneck.

Yet so far, man has failed to see what this phenomenon demands or allows. It is the technological order, proceeding by more information and letting the technological subsystems adapt as a result of that information, which emanates from what has become the new environment. The ensemble of the operation takes place strictly above our heads, even if man programs a computer, and then another computer, and still another. For this is no longer where the problem lies. Either we are going to keep using computers as calculating machines, in which case we can say that they are useless, and all the criticism by Elgozy, Vacca, and Quiniou is accurate, and we can poke fun at those machines. Or else the technological system is powerful enough to impose that veritable and *unique* service of the data-processing complex; and we will then witness the concrete establishing of the technological system, as made possible by correlation and integration. A system in which we will see the internalization and reciprocal integration of technological functions, as well as the creation of a virtual universe (virtual because it is totally made up of communications), possessing its own dynamics. The technological system will then be complete. It is not complete as yet. But the complex of computers makes this possible. If one wishes to *understand* what the computer is (and not describe data-processing technologies, or list parcellary possibilities), then one can reach such understanding *exclusively* from that perspective.

Hence, we have to examine the totality of data processing (and not one computer) in its relationship to the overall technological system (and not to man). Any other approach is superficial and condemns man to never understanding his own invention.

In point of fact, the computer places us in a radically new situation, of which the seemingly magical applications of that apparatus can give us only a false idea. The computer creates a new reality. The transcription, the perfect transposition taking place through it will devalue any ascertainable reality—always uncertain, fragmentary, subjective—for the sake of an overall grasp, that is numerical, objective, synthesized, and imposes itself upon us as the only effective reality.

Now this comes not only from the impressive efficiency of the apparatus, but also from our own gradually acquired disposition. For instance, we are getting more and more accustomed to the idea that what we consider reality (even tangible reality) is, in fact, nothing but the projection, on a cultural pattern, of a reality that we will never grasp in itself. Everything we know is the effect of a cultural training that makes us see or hear certain things, which, incidentally, have no objectivity. We are at present living in that uncertain universe. But along comes a rigorously objective and neutral organism and offers us a transposition which seems certain because it is mathematical. How can we help but believe that this image is resolutely true. The computer (even if programmed by someone in a definite culture) is not a tributary to our cultural clouds. And the other mental pole that helps us to enter this computer reality is, of course, our habit of translating the world in which we live into numbers, or even viewing it in terms that are infinitely huge (the galaxies) or infinitely small.

It is probably the latter element that is the more decisive. When told that the wood we touch is made of empty spaces and atoms whirling at unbelievable speeds, when told that all our solid environment is actually menaced by antimatter, that energy and mass are interchangeable, we insert ourselves into an abstract universe, the reality surrounding us is neither meaningful nor assured, and all we can be certain about is numbers, for they at least are independent and autonomous.

Hence, we are ready to lend reality to the universe manufactured by the computer, a universe that is both numerical, synthetic, nearly all-inclusive, and indisputable. We are no longer capable of relativizing it; the view that the computer gives us of the world we are in strikes us as more true than the reality we live in. Over there, at least, we hold something indisputable and we refuse to see its purely fictive and figurative character. We will plunge into a new chasm if we start imagining that "somebody" could have falsified any of the data calculated by the computer, could have modified the program unbeknownst to us. Whatever the hazard, the result is deemed good. And how can we prove that the computer is wrong? For even if we point out one of those errors that can be easily made fun of, it does not challenge the overall fact that the numerical universe of the computer is gradually becoming the universe that is regarded as the reality we are integrated in.[18]

As for the mutation of reasoning, of man's thinking, a change which all this implies, I cannot now take up the specific conflict between image and word, which we will come to later. But I should perhaps note an interesting point. To the extent that there will be a more than complete integration between man and computer, we must understand that this integration will exclude dialectical thinking, dialectical reasoning, and dialectical apprehension of reality. The computer is fundamentally nondialectical, it is based on the exclusive principle of noncontradiction. With the binary system, a choice must be made, it is constantly *yes* or *no*. One cannot launch into a thinking that is evolutive and embraces opposites. Such thinking can, plainly, *make use of* the computer's data, but it is necessarily led by the computer to choices. And there is no maximum use of the computer; it will remain underemployed. If the instrument must be employed to its full capacity, then dialectical thinking becomes impossible. We have to admit that the computer is both Manichaean, repetitive, and noncomprehensive. Now after prolonged dealings with this marvelous apparatus, how can we help but get involved again in that mode of thinking? Man is only all too spontaneously given to it! And dialectical thinking will be done away with by a complicity between man and the apparatus.

\* \* \*

Thus, the existence of the system considerably transforms the judgments we can make of the facts, the parcellary technological discoveries. Indeed, we are convinced that, when presented with a new factor, we are free to choose, to adopt or reject it. We try to appreciate the "pill," the car, the spaceship, marketing, video . . . And we note that each new element brought by technology could be an extra element of freedom (but also, of course, an element of dictatorship). What a constantly renewed choice! Unhappily, this choice is *never* offered, because each new technological element is merely one more brick in the entire edifice, a cog in a machine, coming just in time to perform a function never before carried out, to fill a space that, we now realize, was a gap. The system magnetically attracts that technological unity to come and make up the deficiency, and that attraction, in advance, gives that apparatus, that method, a clear, precise, exact, and limited function, from which it is impossible to depart. And in the face of that attraction, the scant freedom of man is neither far-reaching nor effective.

Thus, it is perfectly futile to claim that when the computer is applied to the political dimension, it can become an organism of decentralizing, diffusing, of individual scaling of all information, of facilitating political controls. All that is a utopia, meant simply to reassure us and thereby allow the data-processing system to establish itself. We are dealing here with a factor of paramount importance. Man simply refuses to see the process, and by posing the question in metaphysical and absolute terms, he convinces himself that everything is still possible, that from the standpoint of Sirius, the new technological factor is liberating. Thus appeased, he then lets the mechanism progress, and *afterwards*, when he sees the result, he can say: "But that wasn't at all what we envisaged, anticipated, etc." The harm is done. The optimism of the liberating pill or the democratizing computer is a mere operation of unintentional anesthetizing.

*If* it weren't for a political system centralizing everywhere (including China!), *if* it weren't for the class of technicians holding power, *if* it weren't for a technological system arranged in a precise way, if, in other words, the computer appeared in a desert at point zero of a society, then it could be a factor of individual progress. But none of these conditions obtains. The computer has entered a perfectly oriented system. It will not, by itself, bring any democratizing or decentralizing; on the contrary, it will accentuate the opposite trends. Alan F. Westin (*Privacy and Freedom,* 1967) has perfectly analyzed the effects of the computer on freedom. The countless dossiers assembled by the individual bureaucracies for their own use can now be gathered in one central computer. All the information on each individual can be united, with a luxury of detail that we can scarcely picture (all legal infractions, all medical operations, all bank transactions, etc.).

Confronted with this, people are suggesting legal regulation of the use of these files, legislation to respect privacy, etc. In other words, all they have come up with is a set of utterly antiquated defenses: the law—which was helpless against the authoritarian state. Moreover, these judicial means, provided by the administration, will be controlled by the state. That is, the only thing the protection of privacy will hinder is the interference by one individual in the life of another. But how can we believe that the authorities who control the apparatus and its use will themselves obey the same prohibition? They will always be in a position to decide whether or not to employ this gigantic system of control. *Quis custodiet custodem?* It has been proposed that the guardian be the people. But in that case, the central computer would have to be made available to individuals—who would then be able to use it against other individuals. There is no way out. There is no chance that judicial supervision of the computer can be useful. If the central government is honest, respectful of individuals, decentralizing, democratic, and above all, if it is not forced to defend itself (e.g., against revolutionaries), then we do not need any law. The government will not utilize this instrument of matchless power. Otherwise, the government will bypass the legal restrictions and enter the area of pure de facto interference. There is no protection. And the computer is moving in the direction already established by the ensemble of the system.[19]

In other words, this view of technology as a system leads to an essential conclusion. It is absolutely useless to regard one technology or one technological effect separately; it makes no sense at all. Anybody doing that has simply no understanding of what technology is all about, and he will find lots of cheap consolations. And that is the most common error I find in practically all writings on technology. The authors wonder if we can change the use of the automobile, or if TV has a bad effect, etc. But this is meaningless. Because TV, for instance, exists only in terms of a technological universe, as an indispensable distraction for people living in this universe and as an expression of this universe. It is not "raw" or "cultural" per se because it quite simply does not exist in and of itself! It is TV *plus* all the rest of the technological actions! To my knowledge, no author has escaped this convenient parcelling. And naturally, if one focuses on the harmful effects of some aspect of the system, one can easily demonstrate that we can overcome them and redirect the apparatus causing them. But those harmful effects do not exist per se! That is why all the "solutions" proposed by specialized books are anything but solutions.

## FEATURES OF THE SYSTEM

The first feature—so obvious that we will not dwell on it—is that the system itself is composed of subsystems: rail, postal, telephone, and air systems, a production and distribution system for electric power, industrial processes of automated production, an urban system, a military defense system, etc. These subsystems were organized without long-term planning; they were organized, adapted, and modified step by step, in response to demands made by, e.g., the growth in size of these subsystems and the gradually emerging relationships to the other subsystems. Sometimes, people have tried to thoroughly reorganize such an ensemble from square one; but, it must be noted, such attempts work less and less because each ensemble is now tied up with, and conditioned by the others. Each one keeps losing its flexibility, as it turns out more and more to be a mere subsystem of the overall technological system.

Nothing can be done about them spontaneously. These large subsystems have become so complex that everything has to pass through an analysis of the objectives, the structure, the flow of information from the ensemble. This analysis requires that the objectives be redefined in a formal and mathematizable way, that the logic of the ensemble be made clear (decisions on what must happen to each element in each situation it may go through during a process of complete functioning). In other words, we must establish what we would like to see happen in all the possible eventualities of every telephone call, every train, every aircraft, etc., and their history must be determined and controlled by the system. Once the functions of each subsystem have been defined in detail, we still have to define the structure (e.g., problems of centralization/decentralization) and the internal controls. We must therefore be cognizant that the technological system is neither abstract nor theoretical, it is merely the result of the interrelationship between these multiple subsystems, and it functions only to the extent that each of these subsystems functions and that their interrelationship is correct. If a short-circuit occurs among them, or if something goes wrong within any subsystem, then the entire ensemble is blocked. This is what leads Vacca to his theory on the fragility of the great technological ensembles.

The second feature of the overall system is its flexibility. What we have just said would make it appear enormously rigid, and indeed, the imperatives are more and more numerous and demanding. But it seems that while this may be true for each subsystem, the ensemble per se tends to function more flexibly, and the strength and stability of technology reside in that ability to adapt. This is an apparent contradiction, resulting from different levels of analysis, which produces the conflict between the two interpretations. No doubt, M. Crozier is right when he maintains (*The Stalled Society*) that the great modern organizations seem to be evolving solely toward oppressiveness: "The constant improvement in forecasting methods allows a greater exercise of tolerance in the application of rules. The organization can operate with a lower degree of conformity. Knowledge permits limiting the constraint, since one can forecast without taking recourse to constraint in order to assure the accuracy of forecasts . . . etc." But one can say that the better adapted man is, the more tolerant and liberal the system can act toward him. The more he conforms, the less constraint has to be used. Now the technological system produces more and more efficient mechanisms to bring about conformity. It can offer a huge measure of independence so long as human action does not challenge the system.

The system tends to be more and more abstract and to establish itself at a second or third degree. Hence, the primary and superficial conformisms may disappear—man seems to acquire far greater freedom. He can listen to the music he likes, dress as he likes, take on completely aberrant religious beliefs or moral attitudes; none of these things challenge the technological system. The technologies even produce the means of these diversifications for man. But these diversifications exist only to the extent that the technologies function, and the latter function only to the extent that the technological system keeps improving.

It is a mistake made by many thinkers, like Charles Reich or Onimus, to see increased liberty here[20] or a challenge to the system by free behaviors or the emergence of a new phenomenon independent of technology. In reality, these motions of independence are strictly dependent; but technology leaves zones of indifference that keep getting wider as technology gets more self-assured. It is clear that social conformities are all the less apparently intense in that the technological conformities have become interiorized and are no longer obvious—for the social structure has become more technological. Conformity to technology is now the true social conformity. The technological system omits from its scope things that used to be the object of great concern by society (e.g., the identity of moral conducts). That is why we have to avoid posing the present-day problems in classical moral terms. For instance, to talk of liberty or responsibility in the technological system is meaningless. Those are moral terms that are incapable of taking man's actual situation into account. It is, however, true that the technological system appears to give man a larger choice of possibilities—but exclusively within this technological range, and on condition that the choices bear upon technological objects and that this independence employs the technological instruments, i.e., expresses approval.

The flexibility we are discussing concerns not only the apparent independence of man; it is also, and quite concretely this time, a feature of the system with respect to the subsystems. The subsystems have an independence that often causes them to be considered in themselves, i.e., as having their own existence unrelated to technology, their own originality, hence origin, and their own laws of functioning with no reference to technology. This is held to be true of culture or religion or organization, etc., whereas all these things have become part of the technological system, with a very large flexibility in their relations.

People who thus consider the autonomy of the subsystems have often made the mistake of finding (or hoping to find) a remedy for technology in those subsystems. I have shown elsewhere that organization is not a remedy for technology but a further step in building the technological system. For a good example of this seeming independence of subsystems, one can look at S. Charbonneau's study, *"Régionalisme et société technicienne" (Cahiers du Boucau*, 1973). Regionalist theories all have the same function: to refine or justify the reductive dynamics of differences. Regionalism is a product of the technological society, despite the contrary appearances, which make technology out to be always centralizing. Technology can also be decentralizing so long as the decentralized factor is more strongly integrated into the system itself. In this way, regionalism can be an aspect of technocracy, although presenting itself as an application of liberalism. That is why the discussion about and referendum on regionalism in France during these past few years have no importance whatsoever. The regional reform will be a seeming gain of autonomy, permitting greater technological strides. Such administration is more in keeping with technological growth than authoritarian centralism, which is now obsolete. The more complex and total the technological system gets, the more it has to be flexible (this is quite clear). A large number of disorders that we presently ascertain derive from rigidities in the system. No chaos is provoked by technology. There is still a rigid centralized organization, which can only cause incoherences, given the size. But, as we have seen, technology has the apparatus for allowing the flexibility of the whole—namely, the computer. The computer permits the shift from a formal and institutional organization to a relationship by means of information and the dynamic structure according to flows of information. Flexibility also allows keeping cultural diversities where centralization has not yet taken place. To be sure, there is still a Khmer or a Sahelian culture; those are survivals fully tolerated by technology, but classified by it as leftovers from the past, folklore, the living museum of the anthropologist. Those cultures are a semblance covering the reality of a ubiquitously similar technological system (but with different degrees of advancement). And when there is a risk of conflict, the local culture disappears—for example, in a war, when technology presents its most brutal and ruthless side. In general, however, technology is flexible enough to carefully adapt to local conditions. I have already shown this in my previous book. Hence, let us say that the cultural diversities bear witness to the flexibility of the system, but do not prove that the human realities are outside it.

The same is true of time. Richta is perfectly correct in emphasizing that the basic feature of technological growth is the economy of time. It acts upon time, it produces time to the detriment—one could say—of space. It creates time for man while reducing space. Hence the gratuitous and purely utopian character of Lefebvre's thesis that the important thing now is to create space. Heading in this direction, one can only go astray in the slough of unreal discourse.

On the other hand, Richta sees clearly when he writes: "The economy of time is presumed to become the adequate economic form of the scientific and technological revolution at a certain degree of development" (*Civilization at the Crossroads*, 1969). And he tries to draw from this principle a new economic rationality, which differs from all the other types known. But the problem is that this economy of time cannot be ascertained in an industrialist system and is meaningless if it boils down to leisure. It makes sense only in respect to the technological system itself, i.e., as Richta shows, if the economized time ultimately serves for an improved training of men to work toward technological and scientific development *in an integrated culture*.

A third feature, and an utterly essential one, is that the technological system itself elaborates its own processes of adaptation, compensation, and facilitation. Let us consider, in fact, that, speaking very generally, the processes of adaptation are technologies. Whenever technology creates, say, desperate social situations because of the complexity, the demands (which make countless young, old, and semi-capable people powerless and marginal, etc.), the free motion of technologies—it instantly establishes a social service, technologies of prevention, adaptation, readjustment, etc. These are actually technologies and hence represent the system, being meant to facilitate life in this inhuman universe. Thus, an ensemble of reparation technologies is formed.[21]

Because of these technologies, man can succeed in having a pleasant and livable life. But this is nothing more than substituting an artificial system and a technological fatefulness for the old natural system and the fatefulness of the gods. There is no retort, no original invention by man: In reality, the facilitation is always produced by technology itself. It is technology that furnishes gadgets, television, travel, to make up for a colorless, adventureless, routine existence. Likewise, the mass production of wretched science-fiction books or movies like *Alphaville, 2001, Fahrenheit 451* is a mechanism for adapting, for adjusting to the technological society as it really is. We are shown a horrible, unacceptable model, which we forcefully reject; but it is *not* technology, it is an *imaginative* treatment of what technology could be! And in our refusal, our rejection, our condemnation of *this*, we think we have waved off technology; hence, we must be lucid and vigilant beings, we are rid of our anxiety. Technology (*this* technology!) will not seize control of us. We are very cognizant, and we will not be gotten the better of. Now this facilitates the acceptance of real technology, which is neither wicked, visible, nor appalling, but utterly gentle and benign.

Since technology is nothing like what it has been shown to be, it strikes us as perfectly acceptable and reassuring. We take refuge in the real technological society in order to escape the fiction that was presented as the true technology. This is why I am resolutely hostile to all these antitechnological novels and films. They are never anything but that old military trick: You simulate a massive attack, with trumpets and lights, so as to divert the attention of the men defending the citadel, while the real operation (digging up a mine, for instance) takes place somewhere else and in a very different way.

Countless other adaptation processes appear, and we may say that the entire phenomenon of Charles Reich's Consciousness III is nothing but a method of adjusting *to the new stage* of the technological society. Consciousness II was adapting to the industrial technological society, Consciousness III to the technological society of the computer. Nothing more, because Consciousness III brings no reversal of the social process; on the contrary, it is bound up with the most modern production. Reich is ecstatic because engineers sport bell-bottoms and long hair. The important thing for me is that as engineers they are still doing their engineering work exactly as they did before, and, hence, they directly make this technological society continue and progress. The rest is childish, a pitiful affirmation of "personality."

When faced with difficulties of human adjustment, the technological system produces satisfactions and compensations facilitating the growth and functioning of the system. Likewise, it now presents demands which can appear as possibilities for personality development. Crozier, in *The Stalled Society*, very accurately points out that, in order to cope with technological growth, there will have to be more invention, creation, nonconformity, and challenge. Creativity and nonconformity are fundamental values in the technological society; indeed, for its progress, this society requires not passiveness but an enthusiastic approval of change. It is technology that demands an assault on the old values, on morals and traditional ethics. The challenger opens the way for technological strides. Creativity is called upon, because whenever technology advances, forms of life that are possible in technology must be invented.

But it is wrong to believe that there is true creativity (this relates only to technology), true nonconformity (it expresses merely a conformity to the deeper and stronger reality). When I speak of conformism and Crozier of nonconformism, we are simply not on the same level of analysis. It is certain that by progressing nonstop, technology challenges the old structures and values, and incites man to create whatever allows him to live in this environment. But this is never anything but conformity; and creativity will produce the countless gadgets. Those bell-bottoms so dear to the heart of Charles Reich are an essential product of this adaptable creativity.

Likewise, an altruistic ideology will see the light of day (neo-Christianism for others, or the ideology of socialism with a human face). The more truly oppressive the system gets, the more man has to compensate by affirming his independence. The more destructive the system gets toward human relations, the more man has to aver himself an altruist—which Baudrillard is perfectly correct in labeling a "social lubrication." Once this altruism leaves the verbal and institutionalized domain, it will itself become very quickly technicized. One should not view the technological system as manufacturing human robots. On the contrary, it develops those things on which we make our humanity most strongly dependent: diversity, altruism, nonconformity. But they are perfectly *integrated* into the system itself. That is to say, they function for the benefit of the system, supplying it with new nourishment and making one another materialize thanks to what the system furnishes.

Thus, the need for play, which is discovered to be so fundamental to a human being, is put to use by the technological system. Man has a wonderful time playing with all the machines at his disposal—and this playing will be so much more exciting, because of technicity. Thus, similarly, the technological system has allowed man to rediscover the refined techniques of sexual play—which, however, are nothing but technologies.

I realize I may be asked: "But if man can develop all his potentials through technology, what more do you want?" A tough question to answer. How can we point out that highly technicized sex is not love? That playing with complex or fascinating apparatuses is not equivalent to a child's playing with bits of wood? That the nature reconstituted by technology is not nature? That functionalized nonconformity is not existential? In other words, that all those things make us live in a universe of facticity, illusion, and make-believe. I always come back to the example of the Nazi soldier (at the start of the war). He was trained for individual initiative, for nonservility toward commanders, for the capacity to take over an enterprise himself, and he therefore seemed the opposite of the mechanized soldier, who is at his sergeant's beck and call. But this freedom existed only *within* the army (he was not free to desert!); it was meant to turn out better fighters, *within* the Nazi ideology, and it was achieved by extreme psychological manipulation. Such is the "creativity," the "nonconformity" of man inside the technological society. They are now necessary conditions for the development of the system; nothing more. The essential here has been said by B. Charbonneau (*Le Chaos et le système*): "The cog is the antithesis of the human person; the latter is a universe turned toward the Universe, the former an inert piece that only an outer force can situate in the ensemble."

For we are not just dealing with man's absorption into technology. The system has been able to develop all the better in that technology has been assimilated by and to groups that have identified with it. People would have realized the danger more quickly if the professional organisms in charge of technologies had understood what was happening, if they had managed to "reflect" on what they were doing. In contrast, however, for reasons of both ideology (beliefs, etc.) and personal interest (success, money), they fully identified with technology. And it was even the strength of these groups of technicians that allowed the predominance of technology and its organization into a system.

It was also the stranglehold of these groups on society that blocked the first intellectuals aware of the danger. I am thinking of the mathematician Cournot, who (in his *Considérations sur la marche des idées et des événements dans les Temps Modernes*, 1872) was probably the first to understand and expose the vast danger of not only mechanization but technology as well. A good deal later, Adams (*The Degradation of Democratic Dogma*, 1919) saw the consequences of technology with an extreme lucidity. The voices of these scientists were muffled by the existence of the "pressure group" of technicians and scientists—which Galbraith clarified in *The New Industrial State;* the group of technicians is perfectly integrated into the technological system and acts as a relay between technology and society. Kuhn took up and deepened these ideas for science by showing that science exists only because of a sociological group of scientists, who provide its tendency and its clarification. The identification of the scientist with science is accompanied by the identification of science with the scientist. And the defense of the technological system occurs when technology is defended by a social group that defends itself by defending technology, which is the group's raison d'être, justification, livelihood, its way of gaining prestige, etc.

One of the compensatory processes is the development of language. It is absolutely essential to understand that in this proliferation of things that invade him because of technology, man reacts by throwing himself toward the verbal universe. And the word becomes all the more important as things become more overwhelming. We find the same verbal magianism in the past, when man was in the midst of a nature that he did not control. Holding the word that represented the thing was having power over the thing. Thus today, since he no longer controls the technological universe, man has abandoned his rationality and gone back to the magic of the word in the face of, and upon, the technological thing. But though the use may be the same, there has to be a difference because of context. Language has to take on an objectivity permitting it to correspond to the objectivity of the technological system (now this is certainly magianism, for verbal magic too was the objectivation of the *formula* so that it might act upon the objectivity of the natural environment). The "one," the "it," the field (all Lacanism, etc.) is purely and simply magianism—just as incidentally, the style of Lacan, and of so many other writers, is—very significantly—sheer incantation. It is a *mechanical* expression of the compensatory reaction by the technological system. But on the other hand, language must itself be integrated into the system in order to play its role. Hence, the structuralist studies of language, which are precisely characteristic of that technicization; hence, likewise, the trend toward viewing the text as an entity in itself, an object. And the orientation toward focusing on *how* one says something rather than on *what* one says, in order to demonstrate technologically. Here, Roland Barthes is very directly one of the reducers of language to its function of compensating for the technological system.

The technological system produces its own compensations, it reproduces its conditions for existing and developing; the qualities of man are part of it. This is simply a way of removing an obstacle to development and reducing the contradictions. For the system obeys a law, the law of the indefinite evolution of technology. The system cannot stabilize (contrary to the image that certain people have of it); it includes within itself its own expansion. It is a permanently expanding system. But this expansion therefore keeps challenging both the adaptation of man (and of institutions and society—to which we will return) and the very structure of the system itself. However, technology is a flexible ensemble that tends to endlessly reproduce its own reorganization. Otherwise, it would not be technology. A bit like a doll with a lead base, you can push it down and rock it, but it always regains its balance, *though in a different place from before.*

Thus, technology contains within itself its own processes of reorganization, for it is precisely a technological organization. Any challenge to, any disturbance in the system is nothing but a provocation, a solicitation to have new technologies, new organizations, new procedures established, each time integrating a larger amount of data (its quantity unlimited thanks to the computer). And this does not take place against man or to control or dominate him. The system has no intention and no objective. It merely rolls along. And its servants are quite convinced that they are working for the good of man. They are inspired by the best intentions. Which

# TECHNOLOGY AS A SYSTEM

makes the technological system more and more humanized. But through the absorption of the human into technology. Any other process is unthinkable.[22]

## THE ABSENCE OF FEEDBACK

We have just said that technology produces, for man's benefit, *compensations* for harmful effects, that it produces *facilitations* for itself, and that it can change character (decentralization). Yet it appears more and more that this system does not have one of the characteristics generally regarded as essential for a system: feedback, i.e., the mechanism intervening when an ensemble, a system in movement, makes a mistake, and rectifying that error, but acting at the source, at the origin of the movement. There is no "reparation" of the mistake in its functioning; the movement is taken back to its origin, modifying a given in the system. Feedback exists not only in mechanical, artificial systems, but also in biological or ecological systems. It involves a checking of the results, followed by a rectification of the process when the checked results are injurious or unsatisfactory.

Now the technological system does not tend to modify itself when it develops nuisances or obstructions, etc. This system is given to pure growth; hence it causes the increase of irrationalities. Also, it is clumsy and lacks fluidity. When disorders and irrationalities are noted, they bring nothing but compensatory processes. The system continues to develop along its own line. The rigidities themselves are very slow: not only by a mechanical effect as in population but also by the appearance of necessity in the technological operation. When we see that the housing built according to the most economical technological standards is disastrous from a sociological or psychological standpoint, we nevertheless go with the momentum, we cannot turn back. The same kind of housing has been put up for twenty years now because it is impossible to take the technological issue back to square one with the enormous complex of decisions, devices, etc. Likewise, when an operation is launched, it *has* to be pushed to its end, even when we realize how disastrous it is. On two very different levels, take from among a thousand examples, the Concorde, and the garbage incinerating factory at Pau.

In reality, for a system on so vast a scale to have a self-regulating behavior, its reactions would have to be based on a *model* of its relations with the environment which gives it continuous instructions. We find such a model in the traditional societies with, for instance, the view of the world accepted by all members of that society, its religion, its *Weltanschauung*, its traditional laws, etc. But the technological system does not have such a system because of its absolute domination over the environment. It evolves by its own logic.

Yet we should not go so far as to believe that technology cannot resolve the difficulties it creates; we have to distinguish, as J. Boli-Bennet does, between microproblems and macroproblems. Here, by way of example, is his list: job-related difficulties (work, free time, unemployment), the subordination and "alienation" of workers (the transition from capitalism to socialism), pollution, population growth. Those are a certain number of problems caused by technology, and which it could probably solve (I will not join him in labeling them *micro*problems, for they are tremendous!). We shall see that technological progression is due to coping with those difficulties.

And, to the extent that technology is also an ideology, it leads, as J. Habermas shows, to replacing purely practical issues with technological problems (but on condition that we take "practical" in Habermas's sense); the state, for instance, shifts from politics to administrative and technological management.

However, there are other problems, which have no chance, no likelihood of a technological solution. Take for instance: the totalitarian character of the system, the indefinite complexification, the reconstitution of the destroyed human environment, the search for the quality of life, the tendency toward dislocation caused by the disappearance of qualitative controls, the reckoning of costs (the external economic costs), the denaturalization of man with the disappearance of natural rhythms, of spontaneity, of creativity, the incapacity for moral judgment because of power. Those are insoluble problems, because, in order to deal with them, it is not enough to overcome drawbacks, to remove a present-day difficulty, to find a way of counteracting a danger; we would have to be able to go back to the source of the technological process to modify the totality of the functioning and the organization.

The first category of problems that impels the evolution and expansion of the system is a type that can be put in technological terms, in view of the now existing technologies. That is, these problems are solved *in a linear fashion* by the very progress of technology.[23] It suffices to let the present combination of elements

## TECHNOLOGY AS A SYSTEM

function in order to get answers to the questions more or less shortly. Whereas in the other cases, we have to make a "loop," i.e., double back to the source of the process in order to introduce new information there. But the difficulty is that we are working with the communication of external data. Once again, there is so much talk these days about communication, because in the technological system, communication is essential. We saw earlier that communication is what allows the system to establish itself as such; and now, an impossibility of communication prevents feedback. Feedback is never anything but a matter of communication, albeit the communication of external data. P. Kieff (*Blueprint for Survival*, p. 57) remarks that technology is devoid of internal regulations: "It is in its principle even an abolition of internal limits; if anything is possible, technology will do it.... Technology has no internal regulations that can organize inner life. It has nothing to do with inner life except to abolish it. Once reduced to an intellectual model equivalent to the technological model itself, the repression by the forces of technology will inevitably have a tyrannical character... the response would be the reconstitution of a deep-seated ethics, which would itself contain its own organs of command." And Goldsmith (in the same book) makes the same statement: "The natural phenomena are capable of self-regulation, those that create technology ought to be regulated from the outside. ... When one has used chemical fertilizers, one is doomed to continue, when one has undertaken to get rid of malaria with DDT, one is forced to keep using it year after year ... if the cleanliness of our waterways depends on purification plants, etc., we are obliged to keep these installations running." In other words, there is no internal control of results, no internal mechanism of regulation, for these results are felt on levels and in areas that are nontechnological. The technological system does not function in a void, but in a society and in a human and "natural" environment.

Thus, there are two difficulties. One is to ascertain the qualitative effects of technology in those areas; but that is not in the province of technology. There is a whole set of phenomena that elude all measuring instruments and even the technological imagination itself. But on the other hand, once those phenomena are registered, they have to be reintroduced at the origin of the process. Now we have seen that the electronic complex could register a large amount of this data (but not all) and perform this work of reinserting new information. But the junction between the data-processing complex and the rest of the technological system does not come about by some kind of intrinsic growth, by some technological self-development. We are dealing here with an innovation in the technological system: this junction is possible only through human mediation. The computer cannot by itself enter into a relationship with such a sector of technology; it is man who must establish the connection.

Of course, what I am saying will not surprise those who have stuck to the ancestral and antediluvian idea that technology is a tool, which man uses as he pleases. The *entire* technological drama at the moment is heading toward a situation in which technology, having conquered its autonomy and functioning by self-augmentation, could not, on the contrary, have feedback except by outer pressure. Feedback is made *possible* by the data-processing complex, but the relationship has to be mediated by a nontechnological element—which runs counter to autonomy and is perfectly unacceptable.

It is not only the relationship that depends on man, it is also the reception of this data and its transformation into programs. Hence, the feedback of the technological system necessarily passes through the awareness of the major effects of technology, an awareness reached by man who is integrated in the system. Hence, it could not be enough for man to act with his good sentiments, his moral or humanist ideas, his political convictions, his principles.[24] We cannot appeal to amenity or humility. All this presupposes that man can act directly on the consequences of technology. It is obvious that for those who believe that there are only isolated technological apparatuses, man being master of each, this whole problem of feedback is never raised. All man has to do is wish to change a certain use, and everything will docilely be modified.

But we have seen that nothing can now justify this universal royal reign of man. It is not enough for man to have created an apparatus or to know everything about it in order for all the effects of the apparatus to be perfectly clear to him. We have passed into a phase of technological organization in which man should not interfere. But he cannot help interfering, because of that absence of internal regulations, due not to a deficiency in the technological system itself, but to the fact that it functions only by intro-information (data on itself) and never by extro-information. Thus, the true problems are on the inside of the system.

That is the bottleneck of our situation. The issue is not to "make ourselves the masters" of technology. Which, strictly speaking, is meaningless. Nor to have an extra soul. We must be able to integrate into the technological system the qualitative external data capable of modifying the process at its origin. That is where the conflict is located and not, according to stupid images, in a rivalry between the robot computer and man dispossessed of his brain! We will study this problem in detail in the last part.

PART TWO

# The Characteristics of The Technological Phenomenon

# 5
# AUTONOMY

SIMONDON has strikingly demonstrated the autonomous character of technology with what he calls "concretization," i.e., the existence of a concrete schema of organizational invention that remains underlying and stable through all the ups and downs and changes of the technological object. Hence, "concretization-adaptation is a process conditioning the birth of a milieu instead of being conditioned by an already given milieu: it is conditioned by a milieu that exists only virtually before the invention. . . . But this concretizing invention produces a technogeographic milieu, which is a condition for the functioning of the technological object: thus, the technological object is its own condition as well as the condition for the existence of this mixed technological and geographic milieu." The autonomy of the technological object itself could not be better demonstrated than by the highly concrete examples he offers.[1]

The most elementary form of this autonomy is that of the machine in regard to the environment. As Ben B. Seligman (*A Most Notorious Victory*, 1966) notes, the machine seems to acquire a certain independence and function in itself. And he promptly generalizes: To be sure, one may speak of an interdependence between technology and its environment, but it is nevertheless technology that now dominates its environment.

An autonomous technology. This means that technology ultimately depends only on itself, it maps its own route, it is a prime and not a secondary factor, it must be regarded as an "organism" tending toward closure and self-determination: it is an end in itself. Autonomy is the very condition of technological development. This autonomy corresponds precisely to what J. Baudrillard (*Le Système des objets*) sees under the name of *functionality* when he says that "*functional* qualifies not what is adapted to an end but rather what is adapted to an order or a system." Each technological element is first adapted to the technological system, and it is in respect to this system that the element has its true functionality, far more so than in respect to a human need or a social order. And Baudrillard presents numerous examples of this autonomy, which transforms everything covered by technology into technological objects *before* being anything else: "The entire kitchen loses its culinary function and becomes a functional laboratory . . . an elision of prime functions for the sake of secondary functions of calculation and relation, an elision of impulses for the sake of culturality . . . a passage from a gestural universe of work to a gestural universe of control. . . . The simplest mechanism elliptically replaces a sum of gestures, it becomes independent of the operator as of the material to be operated on."

Performing this function, technology endures no judgment from the outside nor any restraint. It presents itself as an intrinsic necessity. Let us recall a rather typical statement among a thousand. Professor L. Sedov, president of the Permanent Commission for the Coordination of Interplanetary Research in the USSR, has declared that no matter what difficulties or objections crop up, nothing could halt space research. "I feel that there are no forces capable today of stopping the historical processes" (October 1963). This remarkable declaration can apply to all technology. The technological system, embodied, of course, in the technicians, admits no other law, no other rule, than the technological law and rule visualized in itself and in regard to itself.[2] I have discussed this phenomenon at length elsewhere. I will not dwell upon it here.[3]

However, we must know more about this autonomy. First of all, it is the notions or hopes that are modified by technology. An important aspect of this autonomy is that technology radically modifies the objects to which it is applied while being scarcely modified in its own features (if not its forms and modalities). Let us take a simple example. We distinguish between open data and closed data. Open data relates to still unsettled questions, it has an indeterminate content, it implies the participation of the interested parties. Closed data concerns a well-defined object, it can be coded and diffused instantaneously, and, of course, it is closed to participation. Only closed data takes advantage of all the technological means, only it can be rapidly transmitted, etc. Hence, the instant that technology is applied more rigorously in coding and transmitting data, the faster it accelerates and the more the data tends to become closed, i.e., to exclude participation by everyone, despite the ideology and the moral desire one may have.

We will not take up here the problem of the relationship between technology and science and technology's relative autonomy from science, since we treated these matters in *The Technological Society*. We will merely add four things emerging from recent studies. The man who, once again, has investigated this most closely is Simondon. And after showing the interconnections, he concludes not so much—obviously—that there is an autonomy pure and simple of technology, but that there is a possibility for technology to keep developing for a long, long while, even without basic research:

> Even if the sciences did not advance for a certain time, the progress of the technological object toward specificity could continue. The principle of this progress is actually the way in which the object causes itself and conditions itself in its own functioning and in the responses of its functioning to utilization—the technological object, issuing from an abstract work of an organization of subensembles, is the arena for a certain number of relationships of reciprocal causality.

This text gives the precise point of the autonomy of the technological object and thereby specifies technology itself. In the same way, but going to extremes, Koyré (*Études d'histoire de la pensée scientifique*) opines that technology is independent of science and has no influence on it—which strikes me as impossible to support. J. C. Beaune, following Hall (*The Scientific Revolution*), likewise feels that science and technology have separate existences and autonomous developments, whose convergence was historically contingent; he also feels that the passage to scientific technology consisted in unifying the empirical and dispersed technologies, which I have called the passage from the technological operation to the technological phenomenon. These ideas merely take up what I wrote in 1950. Lastly, we can find numerous examples of both the correlation and the independence of technology in Closets. But they are not very significant!

The second remark: John Boli-Bennet (*Technization*), in another connection, offers a stunning analysis of the relationship between science and technology. His is the most recent analysis that I know of, after Ernest Nagel (*The Structure of Science*, 1961), Karl Popper (*The Logic of Scientific Discovery*, 1959), and Carl Hempel (*Aspects of Scientific Explanation*, 1965). There are, says Boli-Bennet, two essential characteristics of scientific knowledge. The first is the "empirical proof of error": a statement cannot be accepted as scientific knowledge if it is theoretically impossible to find empirical data in respect to which the statement is invalid. The second is intersubjectivity, a concept that has replaced scientific objectivity: a statement is scientific only if it is liable to verification or "falsification" which is not subjective and individual, but intersubjective, each scientist never being more than one subject; but each subject having a certain knowledge and a certain background can repeat the same experiment, hence arrive at the same result. In sum, a scientific statement is one that is potentially "falsifiable" on an intersubjective level.

On this basis, we can very clearly see the close relationship between science and technology, quite a different relationship from the one that observers have been hunting for years by setting up "causalities." We will come across this science/technology problem again when studying the finalities of technology. But the mutual relationship between science and technology cannot be divorced from the relationship between technology and politics. It is through, and because of, technology that science is put in the service of government and that politics is so enamored of science.

The third remark: The science/technology interpenetration has *inter alias* a radical effect that is admirably set forth by K. Pomian ("Le Malaise de la science" in *Les Terreurs de l'an 2000*, 1976): namely, the end of scientific innocence. There is no more neutral science, no more pure science. All science is implicated in the technological consequences. And the strength of Pomian's long and profound *factual* study lies in showing that there is no political implication here. As he demonstrates beyond dispute, the essential element is not the decision by politicians to use a scientific discovery in a certain way. But rather, the necessary implication of all scientific research in technology is the determining factor. It is the domination of the technological aspect over the epistemic aspect. And the factors operate in terms of one another. Militarization, nationalization, technicization are intercorrelated. In the same way, Pomian also points out that there is no good or bad use of science or technology. The two are indissoluble, so that science, he claims, is not neutral, but ambivalent. "To believe that a methodology is neither good nor bad is to tacitly assume that human happiness and suffering are quantities with opposite signs, canceling one another. Far from it. In moral arithmetic, if there *is* an arithmetic, the sum of two opposite quantities does not equal zero." And we are gradually led to reverse the customary proposition: any *scientific* decision entails *political* consequences. "The decision to build a giant accelerator has political implications that the physicists cannot allow themselves to ignore." Pomian cites numerous present-day cases of scientists realizing the consequences of what they are doing and demanding a halt to research (and not a better political application!). Take for examples, the group working around Berg (1974) and the Conference of Asilomar (1975). In contrast, Pomian reveals the politically oriented character of the manifesto of researchers at the Pasteur Institute (the group for biological information). The object of the manifesto is not really the science/technology problem but rather a political debate in the most banal sense of the word! It is politics which is more and more induced by technology and incapable now of steering technological growth in any direction.

Lastly, we have to bring up a new analysis (1975),[4] which fairly transforms the present study of the relationship between science and technology. First of all, we have to distinguish between mathematics (which develops deductively, starting with axioms, and operates upon abstract symbols) and the physical or natural sciences (which develop on an instrumental and material basis). These latter sciences can progress only from a technological ensemble, which is itself nothing but the materialization of theoretical schemata.

Technology is both ahead of and behind science, and it is also at the very heart of science; the latter projects itself into technology and is absorbed into it, and technology is formulated in scientific theory. All science, having become experimental, depends on technology, which alone permits reproducing phenomena technologically. Now, technology abstractly reproduces nature to permit scientific experimenting. Hence, the temptation to make nature conform to theoretical models, to reduce nature to techno-scientific artificiality. "Nature is what I produce in my laboratory," says a modern physicist.

In these conditions, science becomes violence (in regard to everything it bears upon), and the technology expressing the scientific violence becomes power exclusively. Thus, we have a new correlation, which I consider fundamental, between science and technology. The scientific method itself determines technology's calling to be a technology of power. And technology, by the means it makes available to science, induces science into the process of violence (against the ecology, for instance). "The power of technology (theoretically unlimited, but impossible to utilize effectively) materializes in a technology of power. "That is the ultimate point of this relationship." Which the text summed up here calls the "Technological Baroque."

\* \* \*

Quite obviously, an autonomy from the state and from politics does not imply that there is no interference with, or political decision-making about, technology. I will certainly not deny the existence of the famous "military-industrial complex." The state cannot help interfering. We have seen that it is tightly bound up with technology, that it is called upon by the technologies to widen its range of intervention. Hence, all the theorists, politicians, partisans, and philosophers agree on a simple view: The state decides, technology obeys. And even more, that is how it must be, it is the true recourse against technology.

In contrast, however, we have to ask who in the state intervenes, and how the state intervenes, i.e., how a decision is reached and by whom in reality, not in the idealist vision. We then learn that technicians are at the origin of political decisions. Next, we have to ask in what direction the state's decision goes. And we perceive very quickly that a remarkable conjunction occurs. The state is furnished with greater power devices by technology, and, being itself an organism of power, the state can only move in the direction of growth, it is strictly conditioned by the technologies not to make any decisions but those to increase power, its own and that of the body social.[5]

Finally, since the system is far from being fully realized, politicians sometimes intervene, taking measures about technological problems, for purely political and in no way technological reasons. The result is generally disastrous.

Those are the four points that we are going to examine rapidly.

Habermas, starting with the presupposition and the democratic ideology, vaguely poses the question: How can we reconcile technology and democracy? But since his view of the technological reality is inexact, since his discourse is purely ideological, the idea of correcting, of mending technology in the actual world of practice is purely illusory. Certainly, the first question to trouble us is: What is becoming of democracy?

Among the hundreds of articles on this topic, we can point out one by R. Lattès ("Énergie et démocratie," *Le Monde*, April 1975) as significant because, written by a scientist, it ingenuously expresses all the ideas assumed by the most unreal idealism. I will not repeat my criticism of identical positions, as set forth in my article "Propagande et démocratie" (*Revue de Science politique*, 1963). Instead, I will limit myself to underlining two particular features.

Monsieur Lattès rightly feels that for *the exercise of democracy*, all citizens must be well informed and judge with full knowledge of the facts. If parliamentary debate is to have any sense, all the deputies must be well educated and well informed. Then, regarding the problem of energy, Lattès asks seven "obvious" questions, whose answers one *must* know for any valid opinion in the energy debate. But he does not seem to realize for even an instant that this issue, paramount as its importance may be, is simply one of dozens: the risks of military policies, the multinational corporations, inflation, its causes and remedies, the ways and means of aid to the third world, etc. For each issue, the citizen would have to have a complete, serious, elaborate, and honest file. Who could fail to see the absurdity of the situation! People do not even have time to "keep up to date."

Furthermore, Lattès apparently believes that the correctly informed citizen could decide on the problem of nuclear energy beyond gut responses and panicky reactions. But (and I will develop this further on) what marks the situation is the inextricable conflict of opinions among the greatest scientists and technicians. The more informed the citizen, the *less* he can participate. Because the evaluations are perfectly contradictory. Lattès is deluding himself. But this is certainly more comforting! There is absolutely no way the citizen can decide for himself. Yet the politician is equally deprived (cf. "L'Illusion politique" in Finzi: *Il potere tecnocratico*).[6]

Thus, despite the advances made in understanding the state/technology problem, we must emphasize an opinion frequent among intellectuals: "To resolve the problems and difficulties caused by technology, we have to nationalize. We have to let the state run the whole thing." That is Closets's implicit thesis, straight through; he tries to prove that all the dangers and abuses of technology are due to its lack of direction. We have to work out a general policy of progress, set up planning agencies, reorganize, etc. But all this can be done only by the political authorities, although he does not come right out and say so. We know that this is also Galbraith's thesis.

Habermas does a superficial analysis of the relationship between technology and politics. He is content with arguments like: "the orientation of technological progress depends on public investments," hence on politics. He seems to be totally unaware of dozens of studies (including Galbraith's or mine) showing the subordination of political decisions to technological imperatives. He winds up with the elementary wish to "get hold of technology again" and "place it under the control of public opinion . . . reintegrate it within the consensus of the citizens." The matter is, alas, a wee bit more complicated; likewise, when he contrasts the technocratic schema with the decision-making schema. To grasp the interaction, he ought to study L. Sfez (*Critique de la décision*, 1974). And Habermas's discussion of the "pragmatic model" is along the lines of a pious hope, a wish: the process of scientification of politics, such as appears desirable to him, is a "must." But the reality of this technicization of politics actually occurs on a different model!

Habermas poses the philosophical problem honesty: The true problem is to know if, having reached a certain level of knowledge capable of bringing certain consequences, one is content to put that knowledge at the disposal of men involved in technological manipulations, or whether one wants men communicating among themselves to retake possession of that knowledge in their very language. But Habermas poses the problem outside of any reality. When reading this text, we need only ask: Who is that "one" who puts technology at the disposal of either group? Who exercises this (if you like) supreme "will"?

And Richta goes along with Galbraith! The state, they feel, returns to its true function of representing the general interest when it encourages science. "It is significant," writes Richta, "that the state intervenes most drastically in sectors in which science makes the most of itself as a productive force that, by nature, is hostile to private property and that endlessly exceeds its boundaries." The American federal government finances 65% of all basic research, the French government 64%, for the profit motive can no longer make technology advance. But we are forgetting that the state thereby becomes a technological agent itself, both integrated into the technological system, determined by its demands, and modified in its structures by its relationship to the imperative of technological growth.

And such is Dumont's way of thinking (*L'Utopie ou la mort*, 1975); but naturally, he never admits it! He merely talks of vast international organisms taking over the ensemble of technological progress, etc. Yet who can set them up if not a political authority?

That is also Sauvy's well-known position (e.g., in his book on the automobile: *Les Quatre Roues de la fortune*, 1968). Who can oppose the automobile monster? Only the state, which must also be responsible for housing. But, to be sure—and Sauvy is well aware of this—not the present state, not the state as we see it functioning now.

The same thing is taken for granted by Crozier (*The Stalled Society*): Technological innovation entails considerable difficulties in the body social, causing the upheaval of entire areas. . . . The economic organizations are unable to cope with this. The state must make the necessary collective investments to develop the ability of human groups and human organizations to overcome the effects of progress. "The state and the public authorities in general are the ones who must *naturally* take care of this. But extending their intervention and their necessary rationalization requires a new style of action totally different from the regulatory or distributory style of intervention in most modern states."

And we find—again implicit—that same secret appeal to political authority when the excellent project of "change or disappear" (*The Ecologist*, 1972) asks (and rightly so) for taxes on raw materials, the revision of the rates of social preference by force of law, the obligatory regulation of the quality of air, water, soil usage, etc. Who will do all these things, even if there is no question of it? Obviously, the state.

Besides, given that, in any event, technology produces a specialization (which is inevitable and the very condition of its success), but also given that the technological system functions as an overall system, no technician can thus grasp the technological phenomenon. Such a grasp would require the experience of the body social, a nontechnologically specialized collective organism—in other words, clearly the state. We find the same thing in the Mintz and Cohen book *America IMC* (1972). With enormous documentation, these authors show that the whole of American society is subject to two hundred ruling industrial firms—and for Mintz and Cohen, the sole issue is once again the supremacy of the government, which alone will permit the fight against technological abuses, against harmful effects (inequality, exploitation, etc.). It is, incidentally, once more the state that can assure technology its true place and its progress, because—they maintain—the giantism of economic ventures is one cause of blockage to technological advances (but Mintz and Cohen never raise the problem of government giantism).

Lastly (but, of course, the list is not closed), we have to recall Saint Mark's enthusiasm for having the state alone protect nature. Nationalizing and socializing nature is the way to save it—and such mastery would also make technology itself controlled, well oriented, useful, etc.

Before such a roster of authorities, one is surprised and amazed. But also confused. Just what are they talking about? That marvelous ideal organism, the incarnation of Truth and Justice, letting a sweet equality reign without suppression or repression, favoring the weak in order to equalize opportunities, representing the general interest without damaging private interests, promoting liberty for all by a happy harmony, insensitive to the pressures and struggles of interest, patient but not paternalistic, liberating while socialistic, administering without creating a bureaucracy, able to encourage new activities of regulation and concertedness without claiming to impose its law, in such a way as to allow the social actors to freely control the effects of technological progress. A state, finally, having Omnipotence, Omni-Science, without abusing them for anything in the world . . .

One can only pinch oneself before such a pastoral! Has anyone ever laid eyes on such a state? And if not, what guarantee, what chance do we have that it will come true? Who are the people who will staff it? Saints and martyrs? The huge, the enormous mistake of all those excellent authors is simply that they never breathe a word about this mythical state, which they entrust with so many functions.

Hitherto, the state, whatever its form, socialist or not, has been an organism of oppression, of repression, eliminating its opponents, and constituted by a political class that governs for its own benefit. Will someone explain to me in the name of whom and of what the state will be any different tomorrow—for the dictatorship of the proletariat is exactly the same thing. The marvelous state that will run technology and solve the problems is composed of men (Why should they no longer be dominated by the spirit of power?) and structures (which are more and more technological).[7] What those authors are proposing is that we hand over all power to the administrations, increase administrative power (an ineluctable growth, to be sure, but in no wise a remedy)—i.e., to transform an aleatory control into a technological organization.

In reality, not only is there no guarantee that the state will carry out its envisioned role. But, as can be demonstrated, this state, ruled by the technological imperative and no other, must unavoidably create a society that will be a hundred times more oppressive. It may be able to put order into the technological chaos, but not to control and direct it. It can only accentuate the features we are familiar with. Relying on the state (without considering the autonomy of technology and what the state will turn into under the pressure of technology) means obeying that so technological reflex of a specialist: Things are going badly in my sector, but my neighbor surely has the solution. Finally, it is interesting to note that the advocates of this position, while abominating technocracy, are summoning it with all their might. For a state qualified to dominate technology can only be made up of technicians! But we will come back to technocracy further on.

Observers are admitting more and more that the large-scale technological directions are a matter of high-level political decision.[8] (Thus, the construction of the 200 Ge V accelerator involves France's relations with Europe.) But this, from the lips of scientists and superior technicians, does not imply that politicians should decide for political reasons. On the contrary, it means that for these choices, politicians should heed the advice of specialists and that, say, in France, the famous commission of the Twelve Wise Men is notoriously inadequate. Constantly underscored is the fact that these political decisions cannot be left to the ultimate will of politicians.[9] Gradually, the USSR has at last come to realize that for planning, the "political decision" can be made only *after*, and *in terms of*, the technological determination of all the elements. "It is clear," writes one of the specialists in Soviet planning, "that scientific forecasting must precede the plan." Experts actually plan only what forecasting, qua science (or technology), establishes as possible and useful. The decision is therefore made by the scientists and technicians, not by the politicians.[10]

As always in these techological domains, Japan offers a quasipure model.[11] A remarkably swift technological growth has just been joined by state intervention (the M. I. T. I.: the Ministry of International Commerce and Industry, with its Agency for Science and Technology) for essentially political and nationalistic reasons in respect to the United States. First we note that here, politics is *following* technology, in time but also in the main aspects. And when the M. I. T. I. limits itself to aiding a technological branch toward financial independence from American firms, nothing much has changed—except for the nationalist sentiments! But, even in

Japan, no political intervention can leave well enough alone. Politics absolutely has to claim control. And thus we witness enormous decisions: the direction of aid (and hence of all technology) toward "large-scale programs" (of course!): data processing, nuclear energy, space . . .

Naturally, neither the soft technologies nor the individual distribution of the small technologies interest the state, which is more concerned with the peak sectors and the spectacular. Hence, because of this intervention, we may expect serious imbalances in the development. Furthermore, the errors caused by political intervention have once again been perceived. Thus, a Japanese group managed to build a purely Japanese rocketship and satellite outside the capitalist firms. The M. I. T. I. got interested and entrusted the space program to an agency (M. A. S. D. A.), involving the big firms and reintroducing the American influence through them. But above all, the M. I. T. I. finally decided that, for the moment, nothing could be done in these areas. Once again, state intervention is incoherent and obstructive.

It is always the mixture of and confusion between the two that produces the mistakes. Either the government selects or prohibits a certain technology (often because of the influence of a prestigious scientist or a pressure group). Or it turns one possible trend among several into an obligation by sheer political decision. Very frequently, a government adopts a technology and imposes it on a country. But is perverts the dynamics, precisely because that one technology is part of an ensemble, whereas the government, by its choice, gives it a preferential and, above all, obligatory character.

This simple passage from the pragmatic to the legal changes the tenor of technology, and all the great technological errors come from that political imperative: e.g., the choice of the atomic "line"; the choice of oil over coal as a source of heat; and also the choice of oil over dams for producing electricity.

In one precise point, L. Siegel's fine article ("Le Champ de bataille électronique au Vietnam" in *Science et Paix*, 1973) effectively shows the role of politics: Most of the electronic fighting processes were known for a long time; but it was the Nixon doctrine of ubiquitous recourse to automation that gave them a predominant role. Political choice takes place in an arsenal of technologies, which cannot all be employed at the same time.

But, in contrast, Illich perfectly attests the uselessness of politics in regard to the technological system. "As for the oppositions who want to gain control of existing institutions, they thus give them a new kind of legitimacy while exacerbating their conditions. Changing the ruling team is not a revolution. What does power to the workers mean, black power, women's power, or that of the young, if not that their power is to replace the power in office? Such power is, at best, that of better managing growth, which is thereby enabled to pursue its glorious course thanks to these providential takeovers of power! School, whether teaching Marxism or Fascism, reproduces a pyramid of classes of failures. The airplane, even if made accessible to the worker, reproduces a social hierarchy with a superior class." I heartily go along with these ideas!

To conclude, we will not go into detail about an issue already treated in *The Technological Society*: When the state makes purely political decisions, it is the politician alone who decides; and this always causes disasters on the technological level. I will limit myself to a few additional examples: (1) that of the affair of the French Commissariat for Atomic Energy, where it was discovered in 1969 that political imperatives were behind the bottleneck in technological development in the atomic domain; (2) and that of the posthumous work (1964–1969) of the great Soviet economist Varga, who formally accuses the political authorities (and not just the bureaucrats) of grossly interfering with technological (and not just economic) growth.

We will give further examples when we study the possibility of technological blockage due to the growth of political power.

To wind up, we will cite a fact that stunningly reveals the dependence of politics and the autonomy of technology. The technological demand is dependent on technological means and not on political ideologies. For instance, Peru has immense copper resources in Cuajone. Experts are unanimous in affirming the incredible wealth of these deposits. But they are very hard to get at and extract. In 1968, Peru turned to the USSR. Soviet experts carefully examined the problem, and their highly detailed report concluded that only the United States had the technology to properly mine the deposits. These experts advised Peru to confide the work to the Americans. In early 1970, the Peruvian government was in a quandary about handing over the "Cuajone contract" after expropriating the International Petroleum Company. But what strikes me as important here is that most of the nontechnicized countries must either leave their riches unexploited or else appeal to highly technicized countries—whatever their ideological outlook may be.

Ideological imperialism is nonsense. Only the technological weight gives true superiority.

\* \* \*

It might now be useful to focus on the idea of autonomy from economics, for misunderstandings abound. Quite clearly, one cannot *separate* technology and economy, as Simondon strikingly points out: "Thus there exists a convergence of economic constraints (decrease in raw materials, in work, in energy consumption, etc.) and of properly technological demands. . . . But it seems that the latter would predominate in the technological evolution." Simondon shows that the areas in which the technological conditions override the economic conditions are those in which technological progress has been most rapid. The reason, he says, is that the economic causes "are not pure," they interfere with a diffuse network of motivations and preferences, which rotate or overthrow them. And it is to some extent the "pure" character of the technological phenomenon that assures its autonomy.

Hence, sociologists imperceptibly slide from the primacy (and autonomy) of economics to the primacy (and autonomy) of technology. This is not generally formalized, clearly worded, or enunciated as an overall reality; but more often, it is a subliminal thought, latently taken for granted, as it were. "It goes without saying" for most observers that technology is what determines and causes events, progress, general evolution, like an engine that runs on its own energy. Technology in the intellectual panorama plays the same part as spirituality in the Middle Ages or the idea of the individual in the nineteenth century. Observers do not proceed to any clear and total analysis, but one cannot conceive of society or history in any other way. This trend is so powerful that it crops up even in those who deny it.[12]

I must, however, add some clarification. When I first analyzed technology's autonomy from economics, certain readers saw this as a declaration of *absolute* autonomy—and their criticism was aimed at this *absolute*. Yet I had emphasized that my term did not imply an equivalence between technology and divinity. It is no use saying, "Either there is autonomy, and hence it is absolute—or it is not absolute, and hence there is no autonomy."

This kind of theoretical argument does not go very far. Everyone knows that a sovereign state today cannot do anything it pleases with its sovereignty; belonging to the "concert of nations" is a practical limit on sovereignty. Yet being sovereign, being colonized, having a government imposed by an invader, are not one and the same. Thus, I never said that technology was not dependent on anything or anyone, that it was beyond reach, etc. Obviously, it is subject to the counterthrust of political decisions, economic crises. I indicated, for example, that a government decision at odds with the law of development in technology, with the logic of the system, could halt technological progress, wipe out positive consequences, etc., but that in the conflict between politics and technology, the former would inevitably lose out, and that such a political decision, going against a technological imperative, would ultimately be ruinous for politics itself.

It is quite obvious that technology develops on the basis of a certain number of possibilities offered by the economy. And when the economic resources are lacking, technology cannot operate at its full capacity, achieving what its possibilities allow it to achieve. The relationship between technology and economy is complex. Technology is a determining factor in economic growth, but the converse is equally true. Closets shows clearly that the impact of technology on economy is ambiguous and that economic advances are not proportionately highest where there is the most technological research. Still, technology develops most rapidly in the peak sectors, and it is there too that economy follows. The relationship between the two is striking. In the United States, exports rose an average of 4% in 1967, but 58% for computers, 35% for aeronautics, 30% for telecommunications hardware. Here, the direct relationship is reestablished, but with technology being decisive for economy.

The relationship varies with the periods. It does not appear certain, first of all, that a relationship exists between the great movements of technological *invention* and the economic or social structure. The technological inventions seem like unforeseeable givens of civilization and are by no means tied to the economic level. Nor is technological invention today tied to any one country. It breaks away from those who have encouraged it and benefits countries that did not take part in the effort of scientific or technological invention. But when we leave the domain of invention and proceed to application, technology presumes the involvement of greater and greater capitals.

Can one say that industrial development is what conditions the possibility of technological growth? (Considering that industry is itself a product of technology!) Most technological research in the twentieth century, so it seems, is conditioned and stimulated when the market causes an industrial boom. However, M. Daumas (*Revue d'histoire des sciences et de leur application*, 1969), on the contrary, forcefully asserts the autonomy of technology from industry. And he maintains (which has always been my position): "There is no denying that the evolution of technologies can be understood only if placed in its original historical context; but it is all right to think that the original task of the historian of technologies consists precisely in revealing the intrinsic logic of the evolution of technologies. This evolution actually takes place with an internal logic, which is a very distinct phenomenon from the logic in the evolution of socio-economic history. . . . Investigating this internal logic in the technological evolution is the only way for 'the technological history of the technologies' to slough off its character of data history."

With the spread and growing complexity of technological development, invention in its turn depends on already acquired technological bases (the outcome of earlier applications) and involves *more and more expensive* elements. Hence, technological invention comes to depend *also* on possibilities of economic investment. We thus perceive a mutual influence. On the one side, all modern economic growth depends on technological application, in all areas.[13] But, vice versa, the possibilities of advanced technological research and of the application of technologies depend both on the economic infrastructure and on possibilities of mobilizing economic resources. (Further on, we will examine the problem of economic restraint on technology.) Negatively, the economy can thus either block technological development for lack of power or prevent technological application. The technological program is conditioned by two series of economic imperatives: in a capitalist country by the profitability of investment; and everywhere by the possibility of obtaining the funds necessary for investment.

Nevertheless, at the moment, this is less and less so, for people are coming to realize how impossible it is to calculate the profitability of investments in basic research, and they are growing more and more "convinced" that this research is essential, cannot be neglected, etc. The relationship between technological research and profitability is no longer direct. Hence, the technological applications will be highly unequal according to the economic forms and levels. The latter cause an inequality both in the intensity of technological progress and in the rapidity of access to the profits of technologies.

All this is obvious. But the importance of the economic factor notwithstanding, I will maintain the concept of technology's self-sufficience in the sense that economy can be a means of development, a condition for technological progress, or, inversely, it can be an obstacle, but never does it determine, provoke, or dominate that progress. Like political authority, an economic system that challenges the technological imperative is doomed.

It is not economic law that imposes itself on the technological phenomenon; it is the law of technology which orders and ordains, orients and modifies the economy.[14] Economics is a necessary agent. It is neither the determining factor nor the principle of orientation. Technology obeys its own determination, it realizes itself. And by so doing, it naturally employs many other, nontechnological factors. It may be blocked by their absence, but its reason for functioning and growing comes from nowhere else. Modifying a political or an economic system is perfectly ineffective today and does not alter the true condition of man, because this condition is now defined by its milieu and its technological possibilities, and because the impact of political or economic revolutions on the technological system is practically nil. At most, these troubles can hold up technological progress for a certain time; but revolutionary power changes nothing in the intrinsic law of the system.

This autonomy will get its institutional face in self-organization. That is to say, normally, the technological world will itself organize technological research, the direction of application, the distribution of funds, etc. The autonomy of the technological system must be matched by the autonomy of the institutions that are part of it, that embody it. And this, incidentally, will be the only acceptable autonomy in our society, because it will be the only one providing an ultimate justification. The basic research oriented toward technology cannot develop unless it is sufficiently autonomous! There is an excellent study on this topic by Monsieur Zuckerkandl, research director of France's National Center of Scientific Research (*Le Monde*, November 1964).

One of the effects of autonomy is that technology is becoming the principle factor in reclassifying the domains of activity, of ideological directions. Thus, in 1950, I studied the way technology is making political regimes more similar and reducing the role of ideologies: e.g., the Soviet and the American systems. Likewise, technology is causing a reclassification of public and private activities: the distinction is fading between the economic activities of these two areas. All this was taken up and demonstrated at length by Galbraith in *The New Industrial State* and by M. L. Weidenbaum in "Effets à long terme de la grande Technologie," *Analyse et prévision*, 1969. But the essential point is to see that these effects derive from the autonomy of technology.

Evidently, it is hard for the Marxists to admit that technology has become an autonomous factor, dominating the economic structure and having the same nature and effects in both a capitalist and a communist regime. The most frequently developed argument is that, without any possible doubt, technology is simply in the service of capital, that the familiar effects are due to its integration in capitalism. The technician is merely a salaried employee like the others, the ideology of efficiency is not technological but rather the reflection of the profit need. The division of labor and specialization are not products of technology, but additional ways of exploiting the working class, etc. The most complete effort at systematically demonstrating this interpretation was made by Benjamin Coriat (*Science, technique et capital*, 1976).[15] That is why I will stick to his book rather than lesser works along the same lines.

The two themes to be demonstrated bear, first of all, on the fact that the power of decision belongs to capital. It is capital that decides whether or not to use technologies; the capitalist technologies are as much technologies of production as they are technologies of controlling the exploited class; and capital uses the technologies *only* when they can procure greater profits. If the author admits that technology is not neutral, then only in the sense that it serves capitalism exclusively. The capitalist mode of production has one single goal: the valorization of capital; and by examining the contributions made by the different types of inventions to capital in its process of self-valorization, one can expose the (social) causes determining the incorporation or rejection of the various technologies. Capital utilizes only those that increase the extraction of surplus value. Likewise, the law of value defines the very space in which the technological rationality can operate.

Naturally, the author accuses Richta of dodging the law of value and the production relations *in* and *under* which technology is put to work. But the entire basis of his demonstration rests on Marx's demonstration that capital resorts to mechanization only under two conditions: (1) when the use of dead labor (accumulated in the machine) permits obtaining more surplus labor (diminishing the part of the day that the worker devotes to his own production and increasing that part which goes back to capital); (2) when the technologies allow capital to better dominate the labor process.

Those are the chief arguments, and they are constantly reiterated throughout Coriat's book. The reader is somewhat surprised. For the upshot would be that with technological progress, the worker is more dominated today. Now is it accurate to state that the working class is more dominated today than a century ago? It would also mean that the rate of surplus value has considerably increased. Yet everyone, including the Marxists, agrees that the rate of surplus value is *de*creasing—just as, by the way, Karl Marx predicted. It would also mean that capitalism is discriminating between applied and nonapplied technologies according to the one criterion indicated; hence technological development ought to increase the power and security of capitalism. Yet it is rather clear that for the past half century, classical capitalism has been losing every contest and regularly weakening *because* of the technologies, which are developing towards socialism. Finally, there is the statement that technological progress can be appreciated only in reference to the concept of the productivity of human labor, the latter being the sole producer of value. But this statement obviously neglects the fact that the modern technologies tend to eliminate working-class labor and place man on the fringe of the production process.

What I find so startling about Coriat's work is his dogmatism and his inability to consider present-day phenomena. All his ideas rest on the implicit conviction that nothing has changed in 150 years, that technology is the same in 1975 as it was in 1848, that capitalism has not evolved. Technology has not modified the operating conditions of capital, such as Marx established; that is the basic decision. "The capitalist *must* and does reproduce the bases for the division of labor and for the ensemble of relations between production and labor that characterize the division of labor."

The "must" is typical. The reasoning is as follows: So long as we are not yet in the communist society, we are in the capitalist society. And the latter cannot change; it is always the same; "capitalism is capitalism ," and that's that. Hence, technology must remain subordinate and enter the framework of Marxian analysis. On the one side, there is capitalism, in which the productive forces develop in terms of the accumulation of capital. On the other side, there is socialism, with a collective capacity of mass production and mass initiative. Technology is nothing particular in this dichotomy. Hence, envisioning science and technology as a process bound up with the process of capital accumulation becomes a *necessity*.

Yes, to be sure, a necessity, so long as we take the prerequisites as demonstrated. But none of this is so. We are given presuppositions throughout. Presupposing that Marx was not mistaken, how can we admit modern technology into Marx's demonstration? That is the true problem that Coriat was confronted with. How ironic of him to quote Marx: "The word *process* expresses development viewed in the entirety of its *real* conditions." Whereas in Coriat, we have two unrealities: one of dogma, the other of living in the past. He will only concede: "Naturally, technology remains, but before technology there is politics, the class struggle, and the appropriation of technology by capital."

The two impossible lines in his reasoning are, therefore, hardline dogmatism and perfect unrealism. As to the former, his book can convince only those who regard Marx as infallible and as having said it all. For Coriat's method consists in taking Marxist notions or quotations and developing them abstractly, as though they were metaphysical truths, never once applying them concretely. The concrete situation cannot have changed so greatly as to render Marx's analysis inaccurate. That is the basis. But at no point do we find either an elucidation of real facts or a demonstration; all we get is a glossing of texts.

The second defect, unrealism, keeps manifesting itself throughout. When Coriat happens to offer examples (the reason why there was no chemical progress in France during the late nineteenth century, or the scientific specialization decided on by capitalism, or the domestication of science by capital after the construction of the atomic bomb), we enter the realm of sheer phantasmagoria. Likewise, he has to reply to the rather easy criticism that technology is the same in the USSR and in the Western world, with the same structure and the same effects. Coriat's answer is not new. He simply says that the USSR is not socialist. Luckily, we have China to fall back on. Precisely because China has not reached the stage of a technological society, one can say: "You see, technology there is not what it is here." But it never dawns on Coriat that this may be quite simply because her technological level (save for a few peak sectors, which, incidentally, are constructed altogether differently) is at a *pre*technological stage! Besides, how can anyone fail to see that it is a bit much to peacefully declare that the USSR is not socialist. We are not skirting the issue by asking if the impact of technology (and not one man's paranoid delirium) could just possibly have been what reversed the effects of the Revolution of 1917 and led to the present situation.

But the most characteristic thing about Coriat's unrealism is his living in the past. Coriat takes Taylorism and mechanization as examples, models, and the ne plus ultra of technology. We must be

# AUTONOMY

dreaming! Nothing fundamental has occurred; there has been no change in the technological structure since Taylor. Technology is summed up in and boils down to: the machine. We can obviously understand in these circumstances that Marx's analyses are accurate *for those facts* that are contemporary with, or very slightly subsequent to, Karl Marx. But the mistake is to claim that we are still back there. In Coriat, technology is nothing but the *industrial* application of science in terms of the production of *goods* (in the narrow sense). He blissfully declares that the technologies whose goal is not to produce goods are unemployed! And his critique of Taylorism (as if that were the present situation) corresponds to a labor situation of 1930. In other words, Coriat's "demonstration" is acceptable only for the reader who first grants total approval to the literal expression of Karl Marx's thought and who totally "pooh-poohs" the present facts about technology. Coriat remains enclosed in a problematics established on totally obliterated facts.

\* \* \*

We would like to dwell on a further aspect of that autonomy from values and ethics.[16] Man in his hubris—above all intellectual—still believes that his mind controls technology, that he can impose any value, any meaning upon it. And the philosophers are in the forefront of this vanity. It is quite remarkable to note that the finest philosophies on the importance of technology, even the materialist philosophies, fall back upon a preeminence of man.[17] But this grand pretension is purely ideological. What is the autonomy of technology all about in regard to values and morals? One can, I feel, analyze five aspects.

First of all, technology does not progress in terms of a moral ideal, it does not seek to realize values, it does not aim at a virtue or a Good. We will examine this in the chapter on causal progression.

Secondly, technology does not endure any moral judgment. The technician does not tolerate any insertion of morality in his work. His work has to be free. It seems obvious that the researcher must absolutely not pose the problem of good and bad for himself, of what is permitted or prohibited in his research. His research, quite simply, *is*. And the same is true for its application. Whatever has been found is applied, quite simply. The technician applies his technology with the same independence as the researcher. Now this is the great illogic of many intellectuals. They agree on the first term, which strikes them as obvious, but they want to reintroduce judgments on good and evil, human and inhuman, etc., when they come to the second term, that the technician ought to use his technology to do good. Yet this makes no sense at all after the first term, for application coincides exactly with research. Technological invention is already the outcome of a certain behavior. The problem of behavior (on which people claim to have a value judgment) does not arise only with application. (We will study the conflict between power and values in the last part.) It is the same behavior that dictates the attitude of research (claiming it to be free) and the attitude of application. The technician who puts something to work claims to be as free as the scientist who does the research. Thus it is childish of an intellectual to bring morality into the consequences if he has rejected it in the principle. The autonomy of technology is established here chiefly by a radical division of two areas: "each for itself." Morality judges moral problems. It has nothing to do with technological problems: only the technological means and criteria are acceptable.

An absolutely engrossing study was done by an American technologist on the following theme[18]: So long as the problems are purely technological, they can always find a clear and certain solution. But once the human factor has to enter, or once these problems become too large for any direct technological handling, they seem insoluble. Confronted with these difficulties, people have been developing "social engineering." This innovation appeals to the better feelings; a whole improvement of man rests on the finer instincts and it claims that the route will be the improvement of man, albeit obtained by technologies (psychological or psychosociological technologies). Now after a certain number of examples, the author feels that this route is unsuccessful and uncertain because there are too many nontechnological factors. The only way out is to transform all the problems into a series of specifically technological questions, each receiving its solution from the adequate technology. Here, we can be sure of getting results by avoiding a mixture of types. There is no finer example affirming technological autonomy! Morality, psychology, humanism—they all get in the way. Such is the obvious verdict.

And this is reinforced by the philosophical certainty that only man can be subjected to a moral appraisal. "We are no longer in that primitive epoch when things were good or bad per se: things are only as man makes them. Everything boils down to him. Technology is nothing in itself." But in formulating this oversimplification, the intellectual fails to realize that man is dependent on technology and that, since the latter has become free of all moral judgment, the above statement would imply precisely that technology could do anything. Man does what technology allows him to do. He has thus undertaken to do anything. Maintaining that morality should not judge invention or technological operation leads to saying, unwittingly, that any human action is now beyond ethics. The autonomy of technology thus renders us amoral. Henceforth, morality will no longer be part of our domain, it will be shunted off into the void. In the eyes of scientists and technicians, morality—along with all values and what can be called humanism—is a purely private matter, having nothing to do with concrete activity (which can only be technological) and with no great interest in the seriousness of life.

Here is a small example. In March 1961, the French Minister of National Education launched a survey among students at the scientific *Grandes Écoles* (the faculties specializing in professional training) and in the preparatory classes for these schools. The questionnaire dealt with the teaching of philosophy and literature. The outcome was significant. The students were almost unanimous in denying any sense or value in philosophy. As for the teaching of French, they made a distinction: Literature was totally uninteresting; but knowledge of the language, in contrast, was useful for writing reports and describing experiments.

That is a fine illustration. The technician does not see any bearing that the study of ethics or philosophy can have on his work. Naturally, he admits that the specialists on moral problems, the philosophers, et al., can pass opinions on this work, pronounce judgments. But that is no concern of his. It is pure speculation. There are more and more works of philosophy, sociology of technology (and the theology of technology is beginning to blossom); but their only audience is within the circle of philosophers and humanists. They have no outlet whatsoever into the world of technicians, who utterly ignore all this research. And this is not simply due to specialization. These technicians live in a technological world that has become autonomous.[19]

Since technology does not support any ethical judgment, we come to the third aspect of its autonomy. It does not tolerate being halted for a moral reason. Needless to say, it is simply absurd to voice judgments of good or evil against an operation that is deemed technologically necessary. The technician quite frankly shrugs off something that strikes him as utterly fantastic; besides, we know how relative morality is. The discovery of "situational morality" is quite convenient for putting up with anything. How can we cite a variable, fleeting, constantly redefinable good in order to forbid the technician anything or stop a technological advance? The latter is at least stable, certain, evident. Technology, judging itself, is now liberated from what was once the main check on human action: beliefs (sacred, spiritual, religious) and ethics. Technology, with a theory and a system, thereby assures the freedom that it has acquired in fact. It no longer has to fear any limitation whatsoever because technology exists beyond good and evil.

For a long time, observers claimed that technology was neutral, and consequently not subject to morality. That is the situation we have just described, and the theoretician who thus described technology was merely rubber-stamping the de facto independence of technology and the technician. But this stage is already passed. The power and autonomy of technology are so well assured that now technology itself is turning into a judge of morality. A moral proposition will not be deemed valid for our time if it cannot enter the technological system and be consistent with it.[20]

The fourth aspect of this autonomy concerns legitimacy. Modern man takes for granted that anything scientific is legitimate, and, in consequence, anything technological. Today, we can no longer merely say: "Technology is a fact, we have to accept it as such, we cannot go against it." This is a serious position which reserves the possibility of judgment. But such an attitude is looked upon as pessimistic, antitechnological, and retrograde. Indeed, we must enter the technological system by acknowledging that everything occurring within it is legitimate per se. There is no exterior reference. There is no asking the question about truth (for now, truth is included in science, and the truth of praxis is technology pure and simple), or the question about good, or the question about finalities. None of these things can be discussed. The instant something is technological, it is legitimate, and any challenge is suspect. Technology has even become a power of legitimation. It is technology that now validates scientific research, as we shall demonstrate further on.

This is very remarkable, for hitherto, man has always tried to refer his actions to a superior value, which both judged and underpinned his actions, his enterprises. But this situation is vanishing for the sake of technology. Man in our society both discerns this autonomy demanded by the system (which can progress only if autonomous) and grants this system autonomy by accepting it as legitimate in itself. This autonomy is obviously not the outcome of a struggle between two personified divinities, Morality and Technology! It is man who, becoming a true believer in, and loyal supporter of, technology, views it as a supreme object. For it must be supreme if it bears its legitimacy in itself and needs nothing to justify it!

This conviction is spawned by both experience and persuasion; for the technological system contains its own technological power of legitimation, advertising. It is shallow to believe that advertising is an external addition to the system, due to the domination of technology by profit seeking. Advertising is a technology, indispensable to technological growth and meant to supply the system with its legitimacy. This legitimacy actually comes not just from the excellence that man is ready to acknowledge in technology, but by the persuasion that in fact every element of the system is good. That is why advertising had to add public relations and human relations. By no means does "the mass consumer society vote for itself," but rather, it is the technological society that integrates the individual in the technological process by means of that justification.

There is, however, a further stride to be made, and quite a normal one at that. Independent of morals and judgments, legitimate in itself, technology is becoming the creative force of new values, of a new ethics. Man cannot do without morality! Technology has destroyed all previous scales of value; it impugns the judgments coming from outside. After all, it wrecks their foundations. But being thus self-justified, it quite normally becomes justifying. What was done in the name of science was just; and now the same holds true for what is done in the name of technology. It attributes justice to human action, and man is thus spontaneously led to construct an ethics on the basis of, and in terms of, technology.[21]

This does not occur in a theoretical or systematic manner. The elaboration only comes afterwards. The technological ethics is constructed bit by bit, concretely. Technology demands a certain number of virtues from man (precision, exactness, seriousness, a realistic attitude, and, over everything else, the virtue of work) and a certain outlook on life (modesty, devotion, cooperation). Technology permits very clear value judgments (what is serious and what is not, what is effective, efficient, useful, etc.). This ethics is built up on these concrete givens; for it is primarily an experienced ethics of the behavior required for the technological system to function well. It thereby has the vast superiority over the other moralities of being truly experienced. Furthermore, it involves obvious and ineluctable sanctions (for it is the functioning of the technological system that reveals them). And this morality therefore imposes them almost self-evidently before crystallizing as a clear doctrine located far beyond the simplistic utilitarianisms of the nineteenth century.[22]

\* \* \*

A very fine example of this autonomy of technology was supplied by a celebrated text: Jacques Monod's inaugural lecture at the Collège de France in 1967. He explained clearly and artlessly that the reason why our society is suffering from angst, and why modern man is living a life of anxiety, is the "distrust of our contemporaries towards science," their alienation from scientific culture. (This is a remarkable test of the psychology of the man of science, who interprets the slightest reserve toward science and technology as distrust and fails to perceive the blinding faith, the magical trust, the irrational resignation of all our contemporaries in regard to science!). We wish to go on living in an outmoded society with institutions, morals, a system of values rendered obsolescent by "science and technology," and already nearly annihilated. We wish to hold them as valid while "science and technology" demonstrate that they are nothing anymore, devoid of any meaning or basis. It is by sticking to old values and refusing to recognize new values, the ethics of science (and of technology), that man makes himself unhappy. All we have to do is adopt the ethics of knowledge (first adding that of action), and everything will be all right. The discord in man, the new society created by technology, the new universe known by science will be appeased.

"The only goal, the supreme value, the sovereign good, of the ethics of knowledge are not—let us own up to it—the happiness of mankind, and even less man's temporal power or comfort, or even the Socratic *know-thyself*: they are really the objective knowledge itself. I feel that we have to say so, we have to systematize this ethics, bring out the moral, social, and political consequences, we have to propagate it and teach it, for, as the creator of the modern world, this ethics alone is compatible with the modern world."

There is no better way of saying that science has liquidated everything constituting traditional society and that it has created a new morality. Unfortunately, our scientist has forgotten one detail. His science is not, is never pure; it is applied. And it is a serious error for him to continue as he does: "[This new morality is] a conquering and in certain ways even Nietzschean ethics, because it is a will to power: but a power uniquely in the noesphere. An ethics that will consequently teach a scorn of violence and of temporal domination."

What an illusion when it is a science that cannot fail to be applied and that not only furnishes the instruments of power but makes sure that these instruments have surpassed the spirit of power and have become in themselves the frenzy of Dionysius. What a voluntary blindness to believe in the social ethics of freedom through science, for it is a falsehood to say that the only end of science is knowledge. This is wrong even in the most abstract thoughts of the scientists. For science has only one true goal: application, the transition to practice, which is the true sense, the true criterion of research. Consequently, the decisive factor is technology, the new morality is technological. This follows directly from Monod's *unfinished* discourse.

\* \* \*

It is this autonomy of technology that makes it well-nigh useless to cite dangers and harmful effects. The issues that are specifically raised are then classified in separate domains. On the one hand, the analysis of the effects of radioactivity; but on the other hand, the technological research, e.g., the use of atomic energy in producing electrical power. Mixing the two will be deemed incongruous. When Monsieur Sauvy claims that nearly all pollution problems can be solved by developing atomic energy, he makes sure not to bring up the problem of atomic pollution (*Croissance zéro?*). Conversely, although well aware of these dangers, the technicians of atomic energy limit themselves to *advancing* their research in its own direction; the big problem is thus the use of plutonium. In reality, the imperative of technology suffices to legitimize further research while disregarding potential uses (the accusation leveled by scientists and technicians at the soldiers and politicians is naive) or actual dangers.

The big weapon in these terms is "division," which allows each individual to escape the responsibility for his acts; everyone obeys not a *judgment brought upon* technology, but the development imperative that is included *in* the technological system. And that is also what makes technology a justifying system. Here we have the same reversal that I studied in detail with respect to the sacred: The desacralizing factor becomes in its turn the sacred. Likewise, the fact of having become autonomous gives technology a supreme *situation:* There is nothing above it that can judge it. Hence, it transforms itself into a supreme *authority*: Everything has to be judged in technology's terms. And whatever is done for the sake of technological growth is justified for that very reason.

The celebrated formula "You can't stop [technological] progress" in no wise means "one can't," but rather "we have to participate in it." Remarkably, Sauvy, the grand killer of prevailing ideas, winds up his book on growth with, of all things, that platitude: In any event, you can't stop progress. He thus acknowledges that we are not the masters of technology, indeed that we cannot resist "progress." In other words, technology has become a moral value: whatever supports it is good, whatever hobbles it is bad. And ultimately, people accept as normal the monstrosities presented by Rorvik or Toffler for the future (e.g., putting a few electrodes in a newborn infant's brain to speed up his education, increase his capacities for assimilation, pleasure, etc.), or those monstrosities which have been already accepted (e.g., the therapeutic experiments on human beings as practiced in the United States since at least 1949 and permitted by the "charta on research bearing upon man" (World Medical Association, Helsinki, 1964).

French jurisprudence, which refuses to accept just any experiment whatsoever, even with the consent of the subject, is harshly judged by all technicians: The law is impeding progress . . . Physicians demand the power to decide when they should experiment, and, in quest of a technological morality, Fourastié seems to back them up: "The generation of discovery is also that of experiments. It is inconceivable today that a physician should not also be an experimenter" (*Colloque sur l'expérimentation,* March 1971). Of course, all that must be linked to a "garniture," i.e., everyone has set out to discover the foundations of a collective ethics. The right to manipulate the individual is for the good of society, the common interest, collective solidarity, etc. But we are here dealing with the ideological superstructure, which is meant to provide clear consciences. What is really at stake, however, is the autonomy of technology, which justifies what is done in terms of technological power. The moral discourse attached to that is a further justification for the man who knows that he is objectively justified in advance.

This reversal is altogether astonishing in Melvin Kranzberg's article "Technology and Human Values" (*The Virginia Quarterly Review,* 1964). As the author clearly shows, it is not the values that should authorize us to judge technology, simply because technology itself creates values. Kranzberg makes a point of demonstrating

## AUTONOMY

that freedom, justice, happiness are rationalizations of what technology has already effectuated. The values are secondary; it is technology which produces them, but which likewise renders them obsolete. It is because technology wiped out serfdom and slavery that man thought and spoke of "freedom." Hence, there is no contradiction between a properly understood humanism and technology. Since everything rests on the use that man makes of technology, "the question is not to know if man is going to master technology but if man can master himself: that is the technological imperative, that is the humanist imperative." This is a formula that we come upon often, namely, that technology reveals human capacity. The computer is "man laid bare," etc. In other words, in all these affirmations and all these fallaciously self-evident things, it is technology that is *ultimate*, that is a *value*, in terms of which everything has to be judged, appreciated, ordered, etc. Therefore, technology is quite autonomous, although no one has been audacious enough to articulate this outrageous truth.

* * *

To conclude these observations on technological autonomy, we have to add two remarks. One on the relationship between technology and its limit; the other on the neutrality of technology.

Of course, when we point out this trait of autonomy, we have to recall what we said about the determining factor. It is not a metaphysical and absolute autonomy, since technology is not subject to any determination, to any pressure whatsoever. Actually, there is always an interrelation. And Beaune is correct in saying that if technology is self-regulating, normalizing, etc., if technological progress is the chief cause of, say, the concentration of businesses, then the latter, conversely, are the privileged place of scientific and technological creation. All relationships are mutual, as between technology and the state. But before obeying the conditioning by an outside authority, technology pursues its development by virtue of its intrinsic imperatives. That is to say, external influence comes as an obstruction or as a direction, or as a deviation, or as assimilation and adaptation; but it is always secondary, coming after the intrinsic process unfolds. And because of its autonomy, technology upsets the traditional relationship between theory and practice. For technological society, there is a mistake in the Marxist analysis of the relationship between theory and practice; and this mistake is illuminated by B. Charbonneau: "How can we pass from theory to reality in a world in which, theory being the monopoly of science, practice becomes the monopoly of the state."

Technology in itself does away with limits. Nothing is impossible or prohibited for it. This is not an accessory or accidental feature, it is the very essence of technology. A limit is never anything but what cannot at present be realized technologically—simply because beyond that limit, there is a possibility to be actualized. There is never any reason to halt at any point. There is never any boundary delimiting an authorized domain. Technology operates in this qualitative universe exactly as rocket ships do in space. We can go this far because our means do not yet allow us to reach Mars or Venus. What else could keep us back but the absence of means? But is this true in the human, social, and other sectors? The limits here are qualitatively different than for technology, which therefore *cannot* recognize or accept them as limits.

Hence, there are two kinds of limits: those due to a lack of means and those that are qualitatively incommensurable (and therefore cannot be acknowledged as limits). Technology is thus not a transgressing phenomenon, but rather a phenomenon located in a potentially limitless universe because technology itself is potentially limitless. Technology presupposes a universe to its, technology's, own dimension, and therefore it cannot accept any previous limit. Everybody agrees that scientific research must be free and independent. The same holds for technology. So that our modern zealots, who advocate abolishing sexual morality, the family structure, social control, the hierarchy of values, etc., are nothing but spokesmen for technological autonomy in its absolute intolerance of any limits whatsoever. These zealots are perfectly conforming to the implicit technological orthodoxy. They believe they are fighting for their freedom; but this is really the freedom of technology, of which they are totally ignorant, and which they serve as blind slaves to the worst of all possible destinies.

Our final comment is about the neutrality of technology. When we call technology autonomous, we are not implying that it is neutral—quite the contrary—but that it contains its own law and its own meaning. Technology is not an instrument that man can use as he likes. It has its own weight, which goes in technology's direction. Richta very judiciously emphasizes that all the theories on the "neutrality" of technology came after industrialization. This, he says, is because "in no earlier period did the productive forces take this form, which is indifferent to the commerce of individuals qua individuals" (Marx, *The German Ideology*).

## AUTONOMY

It is therefore interesting to stress that when I pointed out the nonneutrality of technology in 1950, I was attacked on two levels. First of all, in terms of the ideology that Richta shows and that sees man as still in charge of using that tool for good or evil. Marx's sentence clearly reveals the birthplace of this argument. But on the other hand, I was reproached by the Marxists for turning man away from the political struggle and depoliticizing him by centering everything on technology. This too is obeying the ideology of the neutrality of technology by believing that technology is not innocent only because it is in the wrong hands (which must be changed by political means). But this too is anti-Marxism. B. Charbonneau (*Le chaos et le système*) implacably demonstrates that technology tends to become its own end under cover of neutrality. "It is not neutral; it seems neutral only when it imposes itself automatically upon us. What we mistake for the neutrality of technology is merely our neutrality *toward* technology."

Now, a reversal has taken place. Observers are admitting that technology is not neutral, but with a misreading when seen as the Marxists see it. For them, science and technology are not neutral because they express the relations of capitalist production. Science is an ideology (hence nonobjective), reflecting the ideas of the ruling class; technology is an instrument of domination by that class. I find all this fundamentally inaccurate. Science and technology remain identical in a socialist world (including China) with the same effects and structures, and only idealistic hocus-pocus convinces us that these signs have changed—comparable to the christian faith in paradise.

For me, the nonneutrality of technology signifies that technology is not an inert, weightless object that can be used in any manner, any direction by a sovereign mankind. Technology has *in itself* a certain number of consequences, it represents a certain structure, certain demands, and it brings certain modifications of man and society, which force themselves upon us whether we like it or not. Technology, of its own accord, goes in a certain direction. I am not saying that this is absolutely irremediable, but rather, that in order to change this structure or redirect this movement we have to make a tremendous effort to take over what was thought mobile and steerable, we have to become aware of this independence of the technological system, which is opposed by the reassuring conviction of technological neutrality.[23]

# 6
# UNITY[1]

THE technological system is, before anything else, a system, i.e., an ensemble whose parts are closely united with one another, interdependent, and obedient to a common regularity.

This trait of unicity is simply the concrete expression of the system. The technologies are tied to one another in such a way that they exist only in terms of one another and are dependent in every way. We will not come back to this issue, which was studied in the preceding section. We will only examine the conditions and consequences of this unicity.

This unicity, incidentally, is not a recent phenomenon; it has existed since the emergence of modern technology. Furia, in his excellent book, *Techniques et société-liaisons et évolutions* (1970), shows that all technologies have been tied to one another since the start of the Industrial Revolution. For instance, textile machines and steam engines, in order to run smoothly, durably, and without slack, required precision-made metallic parts—hence the importance of manufacturing and improving tool machines. But I am not so convinced that the machine-made product was any more precise than the craftsman's hand-made product, despite Daumas's certainty and the examples he offers in *Histoire des techniques*, III. According to Daumas, all the innovations transforming industry between 1760 and 1830 were linked to the development of industrial machinery. Thus, the invention of Wilkinson's boring machine was indispensable for obtaining a satisfactory tightness between the piston and the cylinder in Watt's condensing engine. No doubt, an artisan would have done just as good a job; but his work would itself have demanded the acquisition of a new technology!

"Technological progress constitutes a whole of which the different elements are interlinked by tensions making them dependent on one another" (Daumas, *Histoire des techniques,* III). As a consequence, each discovery can be applied in a huge number of areas; each engine or machine has become polyvalent. We know, for instance, that the computer can be applied to anything—administration, education, medicine, practical life, time allotment, etc. See the detailed study in Seligman, *The Programming of Minerva.* However, the same holds true for the Laser beam[2] and, in a totally different area, for the inflatable structures, which can be used not only as housing, but also in agriculture, transportation, telecommunications, etc.[3] This is becoming a deliberate objective. More and more polyvalent technologies are being sought (e.g., for the new NASA program). But the consequence is a fundamental unity of the entire technological field: the ramification of these applications tends to modify the ensemble of activities according to a single model.

\* \* \*

We very easily note the identity of traits in the technological phenomenon wherever it emerges. Whether technological growth occurs in England or Japan, in the United States or the Soviet Union, it has the same causes and the same effects, it gives man the same framework of living, imposes a form of labor upon him, brings the same modifications to the social and political organisms, demands the same conditions for its growth and development. And it does this regardless of the historical origins, the geographic locations or possibilities, the social or political regimes. Of course, there are nuances, distinctions, but they are very largely secondary. The demands of those immersed in the technological system may vary slightly, according to local customs; but all those demands are essentially identical. In reality, we are dealing everywhere with common traits of the technological phenomenon. And they are so sharp that we can very easily discern what is part of the technological phenomenon and what is not. The difficulties one may encounter when studying technology are due to one's method, vocabulary, the complexity of the facts, but in no wise to the phenomenon per se, which is eminently simple to take note of. We see more and more clearly that just as there are factors common to things as different as a rocket ship and a TV set, so too there are identical characteristics in the organization of an office and the methods for building an airplane. An extraordinary diversity of appearances exists in the proliferation of work, objects, machines, methods; but behind this diversity, we perceive a fairly similar texture everywhere and an immense system of uninterrupted correlations.

Many authors have spoken of "technological fallout": When working on an enormous, gigantic project, like the atomic bomb or the conquest of space, we are led by these accomplishments to create work methods, products, technological entities, some of which will then be employed in a very general and standard way in objects or forms concerning everyone. We all know that spaceship research brought an improvement in the technologies of metals, electronics, information, ballistics, and "miniaturization." The achievement of integrated circuits caused vast changes in so many industrial products, e.g., the huge improvement in radio and TV, leading to what is known as the "fourth epoch" of computers. Furthermore, this research has greatly advanced the technology of the "reliability" of materials, which implies remarkable changes in aviation, etc.

The notion of "fallout" was keenly challenged by Closets (chap. 5), and in part correctly. He claims that the fallout concept was spread by the military services and NASA to justify the enormous research budgets in those areas, and to explain that the technological discoveries in this context ultimately serve in many other areas, assuring an overall technological progress. Closets's affirmation is probably accurate. But that we are dealing with an "undemonstrated postulate"—i.e., building a rocket ship allows us to automatically discover some new technology—strikes me as less certain. Closets refuses to see the polyvalence in technological products and processes. Obviously, the finished products for the construction of a spaceship cannot be immediately placed on the market or put to general use. However, the foundations for manufacturing these products *can* indeed be put to general use, so long as a transfer is made.

In all likelihood, the most important examples of fallout are indirect, as Closets himself points out. "They bear upon the methods of organizations, the way to use new technologies," and he offers the well-known example of P. E. R. T. (Program Evaluation and Review Technique). Established for building Polaris missiles, this method was applied as an organizational model for complex operations in the most diverse areas. Now this certainly consists of (organizational) technologies and reveals better than anything else the unicity of the ensemble.

But for advances to be made in this way and for "fallout" to happen, we need a wide dissemination. In this area, we have to

# UNITY

recognize the openness of information in the United States. Americans are the only people who truly understand the "technological system" and its rules. Thus, they very quickly publish their technological inventions, knowing that others will do so more or less as quickly, and that this is the condition for the rapidity of technological growth. Conversely, e.g., in France, some of the reasons for technological blockage are the dispersion of the research teams, the lack of coordination between programs, and the mutual secrecy of the laboratories.

Technologies all have a reciprocal action upon one another, they interpenetrate, associate, condition one another. If it had not been for rapid transports, neither urbanization, nor industrial growth, nor mass consumption would have been possible.[4] Each of these sectors causes, demands the emergence of dozens of new technologies in all sectors—materials, organization, psychology—which have repercussions on the use and growth of transportations, which in turn brings new technological research in this domain.[5]

Technologies do not have a parallel development, they do not array themselves in a "dispersed order" in a different and alien environment. The truth of the matter is that the possibility of achieving each technology demands a certain number of other achieved technologies (sometimes very far away and, at first glimpse, unrelated). And, vice versa, the progress of each technology *causes* or requires, for its realization, a progress of diverse or multiple technologies. Nowadays, technicians are so well aware of this that they often try to link apparently unrelated technologies in order to see what the outcome might be. Bringing together mechanical, electromagnetic, biological, psychological technologies, etc., has become quite normal.[6]

For many of the best sociologists of technology, it is not the invention that is of primary importance, but rather the ability to join multiple technologies. The prototype of an invention is nearly always defective. America's lead is analyzed as due to her ability to produce series of models that are vastly improved when their structures incorporate elements from other technologies, and that are therefore capable of far greater performance and efficiency (Freeman). In other words, the big problem of technological advance is technological correlations and information.

These correlations, moreover, lead to imposing the technological weight where it has not seemed necessary. With society becoming technicized, education must also adjust. Universities have to be more technological in order to furnish men better qualified to use technologies in society. France's National School of Administration must abandon its trend toward humanist education. Its students must be trained to use all the new technologies, on all levels, inside and outside of administration. Such is the goal of the 1969 reforms at the National School of Administration. But conversely, the men thus trained are obviously going to speed up the application of technologies and reinforce the use of multiple means of this type. Everything functions by way of reciprocal effects. Thus, for examination and comprehension, it has become impossible to investigate a technology per se, its progress, methods, effects. For the true problem, and I will even say the true reality of our society, is the system of relations among the various technologies and the mutual repercussions among them, with ramifications so complex that observers wind up with generalized consequences. Hence, the proper object of study is the system of relations between the technologies.

Now this is a sociological object, because the synthesis between the countless diverse technologies has altered social bodies and human life. We are here reaching a certainty about the unicity of technology and the existence of a system. Everyone is talking about these changes. People know that the family, the factories, the offices, the associations, have been going through enormous changes for the past century: leisure, travel, the rhythm of work, the standard of living, etc. It is not worth listing the hundreds of examples that are demonstrated everywhere. And people even expect the changes. When they encounter a technological enterprise that does not seem to have great practical consequences for society or for the individual, they promptly ask: "What good is it?"

Hence, when someone wonders about the "conquest of space": "What use will it serve?" his is not a wretched spirit of utilitarianism. Rather, he is expressing the obvious fact that technology modifies all forms of life. It has created new kinds of behavior, beliefs, ideologies, political movements. It determines the factors of life, the levels and modes of existence. Anyone, no matter who, knows as much and says as much. Do people imagine that these effects are due to, on the one hand, airplanes and, on the other hand, TV sets, plus organizational methods, or, even further, psychological manipulations? If all aspects of human and social life have changed fundamentally, it is because the environment in which man now finds himself, his system of references, and all his modes of action, have changed fundamentally and thoroughly.[7]

But this is not caused by the appearance of a certain apparatus or a certain method. There must, on the contrary, be a new environment, a new reference system, a new overall complex of modes of action. And that is what the technological system is. Recognizing, discerning the generality of the effects of technology forces us to go back to the generality of the system. It is this system that now fashions the framework of unity in our society. Technology is no longer, as in the past, one factor among others in a society which produces a civilization and is the milieu in which a technology could be situated. It has, on the contrary, become not only the determining fact but also the "enveloping element," inside which our society develops.

We should really be aware of the relation that likewise exists between what seems to be technological to us and what seems to be something else. Even the most independent, the most nontechnological activities are located—whether we like it or not—in the technological system. Just as in the Middle Ages, for example, everything was located in the christian system (even when having no direct or visible relationship).[8] On the one side, everything is interpreted, understood, and received in terms of technology. On the other side, everything is ultimately modified by the sheer presence of the technologies: if we take the "crisis of the Churches," aggiornamento, the spiritual and liturgical changes, etc. This occurs not because of a direct influence by some technology or other, but because religious and ecclesiastical life is now situated within a technological world. The extreme point here is the systematic quest for the theological transformations and the effort to apply technologies directly: for instance, data processing, linguistics, group dynamics, etc. Needless to say, these temptations are explained not by the inventive genius of their originators, but by their being so deeply immersed in the technological system that they fail to see how any nontechnological activity could still be conceivable.

Finally, we have to remember that this unicity operates in time. Technological undertakings are long-term ventures. Technology does not evolve by leaps and variations: it perpetuates itself. Once a technological course is taken, it requires so much capital, human energy, so many organizations, other technologies, so much planning, that it is materially impossible to either stop, choose a different route, or go back. As we shall see, the effects are cumulative and the directions imperative. The equipments influencing our lives or the quality of our surroundings have long-term or *very* long-term effects. We feel the consequences of decisions that were made long ago and that we have no power to direct.

I tried to show this at length in *The Political Illusion;* Kolm demonstrates it in political economy. This unicity of the system makes it rigid and coherent—concretely (not ideologically, for one can always imagine any utopia of malleability of technologies). In now adopting a technological direction, we would have to foresee these "commitments," and calculate the welfare of generations to come. Yet none of this ever goes into our planning!

\* \* \*

The phenomenon of the unicity of technology appears both positively and negatively with computers in particular. Roughly, one may say that computers have an unimaginable power but are unemployed. They are blocked everywhere by the lack of progress in *other* technologies. Furia (*Techniques et société-liaisons et evolutions,* 1970) notes, for instance, that there is a third generation of computers but no third generation of applications. Because of these deficiencies, more than half of all computers are unprofitable. They are used with programs thought up by the previous generations. For lack of intellectual technologies, programmers transpose the applications studied for obsolete calculators. Software seems to lag increasingly behind hardware. Man thus is *obliged* to seek technological adaptions and invent apparatuses in which functions hitherto performed by programs (but no longer performable by man) will be integrated into the very logic, the very structure of the computer. A portion of software, too costly and hard to produce, must be replaced by an improvement in the computer.

If an instrument like the computer is to have its place, it must enter a highly advanced technological environment; for the computer connects all the parts of the system, while demanding from all technologies an "advance," which brings them to light in terms of this newcomer. Thus, the computer is often blocked by a breakdown in the communication instruments (Elgozy). There can be a perfect data-processing service, which other types of communication render inoperative. If the computer does not give all it can, this may be due to slowness in the telephone and telex. "Deprived of such instruments, data processing for its own sake is uninteresting." But this factor, presented as a demand, is far from immediate realization; it will require new technological changes.

UNITY 163

However, we have witnessed this phenomenon in regard to "peripherals." For years, the possibilities of the computer were blocked by the peripherals—devised essentially to handle the paper (punched cards, listing cards, then by the tape units. But all these things (even the magnetic disks organized into detachable groups, dispacks) are still very inferior to the computer itself. In 1972, it was held that we had been with the third generation of computers for years (integrated electronic circuits instead of the transistors and electronic tubes of foregoing generations) and were about to enter the fourth generation. But as far as peripherals were concerned, we had not even come to the second generation.

Data acquisition is as backward as data emission. The acquisition still takes place on paper; in France, the figure is 57%. But this is not just a matter of technological innovation. Like for TV several years ago, it is also a question of standardizing (a further imperative of technological unicity). There is still no standardizing of the "computer/peripheral" interfaces, for there has to be adjustment to the standards of each computer manufacturer. Now this lack clearly holds up any potential strides in peripherals, which can advance only if standardized. But then computers must be standardized first. This, in turn, entails, more or less rapidly, a new concentration—as explained by R. Lattès ("Les Sociétés informatiques de 1980," *Le Monde*, March 1971). The advances made by data processing require a "unity of control" for the creation of machines—as well as a tele-data-processing without limits: hence, new essential technological challenges to economic or political structures. The unicity of technologies tends to be so tight that no major innovation can be introduced at any point of the system without promptly causing hitches and demands for technological progress in all the other factors.

\* \* \*

The unicity of the technological system has a huge number of consequences. A first consequence, which we shall not dwell on is the necessity of a technological order once removed: namely, the multiplication of technological authorities to organize the unicity of the system, just as a scientific organization of scientific progress is necessary.

The above is well known. Let us also recall that the unicity of the system entails the necessary correlation among the technologies. This correlation seems so decisive that some people envisage creating certain "new organisms," even in a liberal economy. Their task would be to acquire sufficient competence in diverse technological areas. They would also have something like a diplomatic mission between businesses in order to aid efficiently in passing specialized knowledge all around. Strange to tell, we are thus ultimately renouncing competitiveness for the sake of necessary technological cooperation, which dominates everything.[9]

Of a different sort are the following consequences of this unicity: the impossibility of distinguishing between good and bad technologies; the relation between forms and contents of technologies; the identity of technology and its use; the polyvalence of each technology; the independence of the technological system from political or social regimes; the impossibility of confining a technology to limited use and preventing it from passing into public use, etc. These are the consequences that I studied in detail and with numerous examples in *The Technological Society*. We need not go into all this here. Let us merely recall that the unicity of the system, which permits both its rapid progression and its equilibrium, may be the cause of its fragility in certain cases: when one point is hit, everything risks being paralyzed. The technological system, in which all the technologies are related and coordinated, should be compared to the electric network on which ultimately everything depends. A broken line has far-reaching human and economic consequences because of the technological solidarity of the entire network: an interruption in the mass transit of workers, work stoppage in the factories involved, a delay in the arrival of raw materials, a loss of working time, with repercussions—e.g., in Paris, for the 260,000 suburban workers arriving at Gare du Nord, or the 300,000 at Gare Saint-Lazare. The collectivity has to pay dearly for the tiniest snag. The more unity in the system, the more fragile it becomes.

Let us now look at another set of consequences. To the extent that the phenomenon has this unicity, when one seeks a response to a damaging effect, a solution to difficulties caused by technology, a way of coping with some problem, one should not envisage a separate technological phenomenon isolated from its context. One must look at the whole system, because it is generally on the basis of an overall view that one can understand the why and wherefore of a factor which might otherwise seem absurd, and that one can measure the complexity of the questions raised. Usually, one focuses on one single element, which seemingly allows finding a satisfactory answer, yet one irritatedly wonders why that answer is not applied. One then seeks mythical reasons—influences by a political regime, an economic structure, an alogical ideology. However, the proposed solution is inapplicable quite simply because of the overall technological context in which it is meant to be integrated.

Let us cite a few examples. Technologically, it is now easy to supply the public with information that is correct, "objective," general, immediate. Even the knotty problem of honesty, noninterference by political or economic interests, can be resolved *technologically*. Hence, everything can run smoothly. But in reality, nothing can run smoothly, because we fail to deal with the actual situation in the technological milieu of the receiver and user of the information: the informed man. The life-style created for him by the technological surroundings *prevents* him from being correctly informed, he lacks the intellectual background, the time and the direction. And this lack is not due to any human flaw; the technological condition is at the bottom of it.

This problem of "good information," incidentally, is now worked out on the level of technological information, the only kind that can actually be processed. For we must distinguish between technological information (which concerns "data") and the general information of the average citizen. The former kind is as encroaching, as overwhelming, but it was believed (and uninformed people still believe) that it could be mastered with the computer, that all such information would only need to be stuffed into the computer, and data processing would do everything. Yet it is quite obvious that "general" information must be acquired and known by each citizen. Otherwise it cannot help him to form his opinion.

However, for technological information, too, we have come to realize that direct human knowledge is indispensable.[10] "Distributing and utilizing this information poses a problem that becomes all the more noticeable as the organizations grow and the lines of their structures get entangled. The decisions about the system of circulating technological information have a manifold effect under these conditions. Managers, executives, organizers, are equally involved by the disposition of this system."

But then we have an interesting example of the unicity of technologies. For passing on and correctly using information, we need a psycho-sociological type of intervention in order to qualify a group or individuals to receive and use the information. There must then be cooperation between the study-and-development sector, data processing, psychology, etc., in order to obtain the positive results from the ensemble of information technologies. We thus have blockages stemming from certain technologies, "contrary effects," as well as a greater and greater need for cooperativeness.

One can likewise find the best pedagogical technology, assuring a training for the individual plus a development of knowledge: technologically, that is already known. But this research ignores both the growth of the population, the increase of the "intermediary age" (young adults, whose intellectual training keeps getting longer, holding them away from practical life), and the professional equilibrium in a given social body. All these problems are also rooted in technology.

From an agricultural standpoint, it has been said over and over again that the optimum in France would be to reduce the farming population to fifteen percent of the total population. This evidence of economic technology is made possible by mechanizations and chemical products. But we run into very knotty issues of urban growth and further rural exodus, into psychological conflicts of adjusting to a new milieu, into economic difficulties of employment, etc. All these things depend on the influence of the technological environment on uprooted people or of technological possibilities in sectors adjacent to the rural sector.

We could multiply the examples. They all show that one cannot hope to solve an isolated problem in our society, for our society is an ensemble, whose structure is the technological system. The responses must be all-inclusive, like the society itself. Otherwise, we end up in either of the following two situations.

Everyone wants to give the response suitable to the specialization in his area. But if the solution is well adapted to the problem he is familiar with, then that solution is out of "synch" with the rest of the society, sometimes inapplicable, and in any event inadequate because each technological situation depends on the ensemble of the structure. The domain of each technician is in fact conditioned by the technologies of the neighboring domains. He can never claim to be doing an exclusively specialized work. All this, moreover, is perfectly known and acknowledged. We ubiquitously come upon the affirmation that there can be no more solitary work today, only teamwork. Every technician has to work with others having different specialties.

This is a platitude. But no one has even remotely gauged its true scope, because generally this platitude is applied in limited sectors. Thus we know that hundreds of different specialties are cooperating on rocket ships. But we have to apply the same notion to nonmaterial technologies. We realize that it took just about thirty specialties conjoined to prepare the astronauts physically and mentally. But on a lowlier level, do we not speak nowadays of a "medical team"? A patient can no longer be treated by *one* doctor, even if he has a definite disease. A team is required.

This notion must likewise be applied in the sociological or political technologies. Furthermore, we have to succeed in coordinating *different kinds* of technology. But here we encounter a major difficulty. The more familiar one becomes with a problem and the more one analyzes its givens, the more sharply one perceives the complexity of each phenomenon in particular. There are borderline zones; each phenomenon is surrounded by a sort of "aura," which is more or less distant from the center. Should one interfere technologically in this zone? The number of technologies to be used is growing, coordinations are getting more and more difficult, and ultimately, we no longer know for sure if a certain supplementary technology is useful or if it might even have the opposite of the desired effect. But if this is the true situation, well known to technicians, then it merely illustrates (and proves) the all-inclusiveness, the unicity of the technological system. Failure to realize this may lead to an impasse, and that is the second situation to be emphasized.

In his particular domain, a technician may not succeed in giving a satisfactory solution to a problem. He then decides to hand it to someone with another technological specialty. But this specialist may not take the problem seriously because it does not concern him directly, or he may not have any way of solving it. For example, the technician for the psycho-sociology of work, of biotechnology, of work organization may conclude that under the present circumstances, there is no remedy possible for factory workers suffering from nervous fatigue, depression, anxiety, "alienation," "reification" (to employ vague but convenient terms). But the technician can pass the buck by saying: "All these things can be solved by leisure. The technician of spare time ought to deal with them." But this "technician of spare-time activities," for his part, is getting to feel more and more that leisure has no virtue in itself and that everything depends on the personality of the individual using these spare-time activities. Leisure can be perfectly destructive if the person indulging in it is unable to manage his life. Leisure has no sense and no virtue if labor has none. There is no destructive work and constructive leisure. Work without value or meaning leads a man directly to leisure without value or meaning. This small (and very large!) example shows how far any technician is from getting rid of a problem by sending it over to a neighboring specialist. Only the coordination of research and application can bring about a result, *because* the various technologies do not function separately, they are integrated in a coherent ensemble.

But the converse, which is truly fundamental, is that one cannot challenge a technology without aiming at the entire system. It does no good changing a single aspect or procedure if one does not tend to destructure the whole! For instance, the book on working conditions by C. Durand et al. (*Les conditions de travail,* 1974) throws up an issue that has become very traditional in the critiques of Taylorism and industrial labor in general. This book sheds light perfectly on the absorbing and conformizing nature of modern technologies, and it shows how a challenge to the technologies as *means* is actually a challenge to the entire system, to the objectives in view.

In particular, Wisner demonstrates that the technological process keeps us from undertaking any *real* improvements in work if we do not challenge the objective of productivity. We cannot truly ameliorate working conditions unless we throttle our desire to increase productivity at any cost.

Likewise, Montmollin points out the absorbing power of the technological system with the example of Taylorism. Anti-Taylorism merely integrates the very principles of Taylorism in a higher rationality. There is no actual challenge. The principles are maintained (the same principles of technology, as I showed in my 1950 book), but raised to a higher level and inserted in a more elaborate, less "inhuman context."

Finally, in this orientation, Simondon has shown, with his usual depth, why there was (and could not help but be) unity among the material technologies bearing upon the "environment" and the human technologies, which appeared as separate technologies, at a second phase. This relationship comes not only from the relationship between man and his milieu, but from the character of the genesis of this ensemble. It is with the aid of his genetic theory that Simondon (see *Du Mode d'existence,* part 3, chapter 3) proves the existence of this unity, which is not fortuitous but stems from the very essence of the technological phenomenon. We are thus involved in a profoundly unsettling all or nothing.

# 7
## UNIVERSALITY[1]

UNIVERSALITY refers to the fact that we now encounter technology everywhere and that the technological system is spreading into all domains. This universality must be regarded from two points of view. First of all, there is universality concerning the environment and the areas of human activity.[2] Then there is geographical universality: the technological system extends to all countries on earth.

Thus, universalism means, first of all, that "the entire globe is tending to become a vast megalopolis, in which the parcels of nature still resisting this invincible thrust are merely a residual phenomenon: the logical and inexorable state is the artificial environment, fabricated by automated machines" (A. Molès). But the *sign* of this universalism is the change of attitude toward this world of objects. No longer is a humane, beneficial nature—corresponding to man and opposed to machines—conceived of as a necessary evil and just barely acceptable in view of production. Now we have a positive and joyous acceptance, not only through material benefits, but also through an esthetic consumption of the machine. The esthetic values of the factory, of new materials, of advertising, of electronics produce an accord between our means of production and our sensibilities. A universe of objects is then created, and this universe is not only spontaneous, but also voluntary and conscious. The former manual appropriation of the natural world is replaced by a mental appropriation, by the symbol and image of the technological world. Art is both testimony to this universalization and the means of our adaptation. Thanks to art, the "fleet" of objects keeps renewing incessantly toward finer and greater sensitivity and extends over the whole of the human environment. Because of art, technology is no longer content with its functional justification, and it, too, enters the world of apparently gratuitous esthetics. That is why "design" strikes us as far more significant of that universalism than the pace-setting and really gratuitous efforts of kinetic art, a reflection of technology for esthetes but by no means a creation of a new universe (*Journées d'Eurodesign de Nancy*, 1969).

However, it is not just the total environment; all human activities now tend to become objects of technologies. Each activity has been subjected to a reflection of technological orientation. Each activity has been equipped with intruments or "ways of doing" that come from technology. There is practically no area that is outside of technology. From the humblest to the most elevated tasks, everything is covered by the technological process. There is a technology of reading (speed reading), as well as a technology of chewing. Every single sport is becoming more and more technological. There is a technology for cultural animation and for chairing a meeting. And this list could be stretched out ad infinitum.

It is not just the—well-known—fact that for every activity, there is a multiplying of machines that entail a certain behavior; the activity itself is becoming technicized. There is a conjunction between the apparatus and the methods of using it and the technicization of gestures, activities independent of the apparatus. On the one hand, there is household "equipment," and, on the other hand, the best possible way of acting in such and such a circumstance, to obtain such and such a result. The interpenetration of the two processes makes technological universalism on the individual's level at the same time as the universalization of the use of technological products, not only a machine but also, for instance, remedies, whose general use leads to a specific behavior. This behavior is conditioned by the car, the TV set, etc., but also and simultaneously by the technology of relaxation or group dynamics.

Simondon shows perfectly how education, whose model, he feels, is the one assumed by the *Encyclopédie*, coincides with the technological boom, since education itself is technicized. It is therefore "doubly universal," because of the audience it addresses and because of the information it transmits. "This is knowledge meant for everybody. Knowledge given in the spirit of the highest possible universality according to a circular pattern, that never presupposes a self-contained technological operation in the secrecy of its specialty, but rather presupposes a technology bound up with others . . . and resting on a small number of principles. . . . For the first time [with the *Encyclopédie*], a technological universe was established. . . . This solid and objective universality, presupposing an internal resonance of this technological world, requires that the work be open to all and that it constitute a universality." He brilliantly concludes: "The *Encyclopédie* is a kind of Federation Festival of the technologies, which discover their solidarity for the first time."

And this universalism is clearly marked by an identification of needs. As people attain a certain technological level, the same needs appear—spontaneously, it seems—beyond any distinctions of nation or social category. Raymond Aron (*Progress and Disillusion*) very accurately notes "the tendency of any social group or any nation, upon reaching a certain income bracket, to desire the same goods that were bought by the groups who preceded it in this rise."

And likewise, I believe that A. Touraine is perfectly right when he shows that social class is no longer the explicative factor of cultural behavior. "The movie-goer or car-owner is no longer part of any social group, and he suffers from the incessant transitions he has to make from the mass working world to undifferentiated clothing, spectacles, and sports." Technologies do not fit into any one class; they decisively modify social behaviors and tend to bring about their identification, under the mask of divergent ideologies. Aside from such remarks, we must bear in mind that the technological phenomenon shapes the total way of life. It is a platitude to say so. But this entails the universalism of technology. Let me just mention domestic equipment. It is certainly a positive thing, but we also know that it brings a certain type of existence, which has been called one of "accumulation and solitude."[3] The housewife bends under the weight of objects, whether they are the ones she buys or the more tyrannical ones that she cannot afford to buy. Moreover, the housewife does all the old housework in solitude, whereas this same housework formerly involved a relation, a collective labor. We are dealing with an upheaval that is described as the liberation from household drudgery (indeed it is), but that also brings burdens and a new conception of life.

Jorge d'Oliveira E Sousa has written a fundamental article entitled "Les Métamorphoses de la guerre" (*Science et Paix*, 1973). Here, he admirably shows that every technological innovation acts both on the system of standards (removing prohibitions, burning ethical codes that are now antiquated, splitting positive standards) and on the (international) political system. But, in their turn, standards and systems appropriate technological innovations and regulate their use, assigning limits, and imposing modalities of existence upon them. We are dealing with three variables that react to one another. Technological progress has given preponderance to the technological variable, and the technological discourse contradicts the ethical and legal discourse. Technological military power, as the author does a fine job of pointing out, induces the creation of a sort of worldwide feudalism. But it is not atomic power that creates the absolute distance between the "big" and the "little" nations; it is the technological *refinement* (technology's trend toward miniaturization). For atomic weapons will never be used in local conflicts; whereas, in contrast, electronic armaments "push the asymmetry between the combatants and their means to the extreme." "Electronic warfare" explodes the ethical discourse on war (the promised outlook is no longer death, but suffering). New weapons are replacing the natural environment (destroyed by defoliants) with an electronic "natural" environment. "The traditional legal and moral conventions belong to a world of the past, the world of conventional warfare. The new forms of violence—technological—have not yet found an [adequate] discourse for their own law and their own morality." Altogether, this article reveals the extent to which technology has become autonomous and determinative.

We have to add the use of chemical factors, which modify, notably, activities or behaviors whenever we like. Recall the pill, which transforms the love relationship, or tranquilizers, which ensure the relay between the individual and his environment (relieving him of the burden of ensuring and mastering circumstances himself, of integrating experience—for it is precisely the lack of this ability that makes the tranquilizers necessary). Recall the many drugs for conjuring up mystical experiences or for directing a religious life. To be sure, man has always looked for stimulants (coca) and artificial paradises. But here as elsewhere, the difference is that these devices are transformed into technological procedures in the modern sense and that they are integrated into the overall technological system. The act of the Arab smoking hashish is not the same as that of the hippie. The former act is in a pretechnological stage, drawing its meaning and even practice from a certain number of physiological "lacks"; the hippie act is at the peak of technological development and becomes a way of complete integration into (through a *seeming* escape from) this technological system. Of course, we are told that the pill or drugs are liberating procedures for the human being, that the girl is now liberated,[4] and that the use of these devices is voluntary, that they are available instruments, etc.

Such reflections always posit that a human being is perfectly scatheless and autonomous. But we have shown that he is, first of all, integrated and modified within the technological system. He uses these products as signs and expressions of, as supplements and additions to, the total technologies that he never stops using. These products help to condition him in the same way. But, once again, let us not pass judgments about morality (it is good or bad) or liberty (man is thereby liberated or enslaved). That is not my object here. I am simply trying to show the extension of the technological system to all aspects of human life, which it absorbs and modifies.

Technology is called upon for the most diverse areas. There is no domain that it cannot penetrate. For a long time, it was felt that agricultural work might be open to some slight mechanization, but not more. At the moment, farm labor is submerged in technologies, both biological and chemical, for the pen-raising of pigs and calves, for the mechanical picking of fruit, for opening up fields and clearing pastures and forests. And now the computer can even be applied to the "fields." One would be hard put to find two worlds more remote from each other; and yet, of course, what the computer does is still an elementary task. Take for instance, the accounting for an ensemble of farming (such as exists in Charente-Maritime); and soon, an agricultural administration service will be added. The interesting point here is that we are dealing with small farmers (25,000 in Charente-Maritime, where the experiment began with properties averaging twenty-five hectares (1 hectare = 2.47 acres). These small farmers are obliged to unite in order to profit from such a system, and they have to gain some technological background, on the basis of which they can save an enormous amount of time.

Onimus (*L'Asphyxie et le cri*) does an excellent job of showing the invasion of technology into the most remote areas, love and religion. Love "boils down to pleasure and to technologies that produce pleasure. . . . We publish and teach how-to's on love-making with diagrams and instructions. . . . Sex is reduced to a laughable assortment of mechanical procedures." One of the great areas—like death—that once eluded technology has now been invaded by it. This is not astonishing, but it does elicit two essential comments.

The first, as usual, obviously bears upon the reductive and

separating character of technology. Love can become technological so long as it is *stripped* of all feeling, all commitment, of everything that involves giving, impulse, passion—all the merriment of love—and so long as it is brought down to an act. Reduced in this way and *separated* from the all-inclusiveness of being, it can truly be technicized. The sexual act detached from life (the life of the protagonists and of those who could be born from it) is a mechanism. But the very act of proposing and spreading technologies (from the pill to the Kama Sutra) obligatorily turns sex into a technology—and turning it into a technology necessarily causes this reduction and separation. They are ever and always the result of applying a technology.

The second comment is that the fervent advocates of this technicization are the left-wingers, the revolutionaries, the progressives, the freedom enthusiasts. These demagogues of liberty struggle valiantly against the moral obscurantism of the past in order to impose the freedom of love. But caught, as usual, in their own trap, they are simply making progress (and what progress) for the technological universe. They are the mythomaniacs of liberty and yet they serve technicization—thereby transforming love into its reverse and sterilizing both love-life and the merriment that should be part of it.

Onimus points out the invasion of technology into the religious area. The "religious revival" of these past few years, oriented toward Zen and Yoga, actually derives from the discovery of religious technologies and from the fact that certain religions lend themselves more readily than others to technicization. What these seekers are thus in quest of is neither a conception of the world, nor a reason to live, nor meaning or truth. They are looking for technologies (of contemplation, the void, the extension of inner space). "In the mental space of technological cultures, the highest philosophies deteriorate into recipes." It is always a matter of finding an *exterior* procedure, demanding *the least effort* (an eminently technological trait) to obtain the same apparent result (ecstasy via a drug, the expansion of spiritual space).

"Zen is perfectly efficient. It knows ways of exploding the structures of discourse, of liberating the consciousness through the dazzling and definitive assumption of the Absurd." The *procedure* becomes the essence. And this expresses the necessity for expanding the technologies into all areas. Little by little, the religious world is becoming dominated. Naturally, it has been dominated since long ago; and we may say that the magical procedures, the

# UNIVERSALITY

rites, liturgies, music and incense, were all technologies. But between them and what we see today, there is all the distance between the technological operation and the technological phenomenon. We have gained speed and efficiency, and have reduced effort. We have also gained purity, for in a new technological phenomenon, there is no longer exactly anything *but that*—and no longer anything of the "natural" religious texture. Why bother with the long asceticism of spiritual exercises, like Ignatius de Loyola, if a pill can give us the same result? Once again, here is the precise stamp of technology. Efficiency is prime—whereas an authentically religious person would say the opposite: Asceticism is prime.

And among the various modern religious movements, we are witnessing the same influence of technology. People are constantly comparing technologies and outcomes—which is precisely one of the traits of the technological process: The adepts recount their experiences and compare the results. "The container is in a fair way to replacing the content, the methods are driving out the meaning, a corpus of standardized recipes is supplanting religiousness."

We must never forget that nowadays, any action claiming to be efficient is always subjugated to technology. Hence, we cannot admire the guerilla as representing the human against technology on the level of the airplane or tank. Not only does the guerilla also employ the devices furnished by industrial society (weapons, communications items). But, if he wants to win, he must be, above all, a technician—of organization (parallel administration), propaganda, espionage, etc., which are technologies that are no *less* technological (on the contrary, often *more* so) than those of flying an airplane! The victory of the guerilla is always the victory of technology and the setting-out of his country upon the technological road.

And these inevitable universalized technologies bear on the actions of individuals, as well as of collectivities, ensembles, organizations. Offices are equipped with more and more numerous and complex machines, they are organized by more and more rigorous principles, and function according to more and more exact processes.[5] We should not imagine that this would bring any greater tension, growing overwork, less independence of the people involved. On the contrary, when equipment, organizational technology, and individual operational technology are conjoined, the employee is subjected to a less unsettling rhythm (even if it is really faster); he finds himself in a vaster situation, apparently enjoying a greater autonomy. On the highest level, we find the same phenomenon in organization and economic, administrative, and scientific research (because, for science to now keep on advancing, it needs a huge technological infrastructure, in machines, organization, and methodological training of researchers).

Intellectual and artistic activity is now directly dependent on technology—with the same double aspect. We have, on the one side, equipment—computers, calculators, tabulators, etc.—and, on the other side, the creation of musical and pictorial technologies more closely inspired by the technological milieu. Ultimately, we know the *nouveau roman*. And with the new methods of hermeneutics, we are tackling the most abstract and, for an intellectual, the most anguishing domain into which technology can advance. Of course, these efforts are still tentative, as they are in the political technologies. But given the rapid spread and progress of the phenomenon, we can expect these methods to develop and deepen in the next few years.

Hence, the entire field of activity, of human life, is the object of technologies. According to their application areas we can divide these technologies into: mechanical technologies (a very wide term, also covering things that are not, strictly speaking, mechanical, like computers); economic technologies (for research and intervention); organizational technologies (for all types of social organisms, including government, administration, etc.); and "human" technologies (for the individual or for noninstitutionalized groups, advertising, propaganda, group dynamics, psychoanalysis, etc.). It is now possible, I believe, to say that in the Western world, no activity of any sort whatsoever can claim to be nontechnological. The system is quite universal.[6]

But does no reaction exist? We know the generally accepted observation that modern man, by using machines or technological objects, is actually manipulating symbols, that the symbols are what draw him toward this consumption, and that the important thing in this universe is the symbol rather than the object itself. People thus try to reassure themselves by integrating the technological phenomenon into a traditional and familiar universe. But in reality, none of this is so! The symbol in the technological system has changed meaning and value for the plain reason that the symbolized object or the object provoking the reference to symbols is not what it used to be. It is no longer an object both alien to man and belonging to a "natural" universe in which everything *had* to be symbolized. The object of the technological world now has its own efficiency, its power, it can obtain results, it is a work of man and yet alien. Hence, the symbol no longer plays the same role as earlier in regard to the object.

We thus have to complete what we were saying previously. On the one hand, man's inherent power of symbolizing is excluded; on the other hand, all consumption is symbolic. The technological system is a real universe, which constitutes *itself* as a symbolic system. With respect to nature, the symbolic universe was an imaginary universe, a superordinated reflection, entirely instituted by man in relation to this natural world. It enabled him to *distanciate* himself and *differentiate* himself from that reality, and at the same time to master reality through the mediation of the symbolic, which attributed an otherwise undifferentiated meaning to the world.

In the technological system, there is no more possibility of symbolizing in that sense. First of all, this possibility is not present because the reality is produced by man, who does not feel mystery and strangeness. He still claims to be the direct master. Furthermore, it is not present because, if symbolizing is a process of distanciation, then the whole technological process is, on the contrary, a mechanism for integrating man; and finally, because now, it is no longer man who symbolizes nature, but technology which symbolizes itself. The mechanism of symbolization *is* technology, the means of this symbolization are the mass media of communication. The object to be consumed is an offered symbol. The symbolization is integrated into the technological system. There is no longer any distanciation, any possibility of mastering the system along this route, which was once the royal road for determining what made man man and set him apart as a species.

In particular, it is not the symbol that appears as a complement to the meaning or as an access to a new dimension. The meaning is already assured by the technological system, and all dimensions are covered. Likewise, the symbol is not the human means for imposing a significant order on what eludes man. Here, what causes the symbol is already a human means. Finally, the function of symbolization no longer attests to a specifically human power. It is now subordinated to a different order, a different function, which are both already created by man. And if that function is performed, it proves that technology is now the true environment of man (otherwise, he would not feel the need to operate with symbols in this connection). It also proves that the expansion of technology is total, since technology causes and actually assimilates the symbolization that man is still capable of. The hippie reaction is the desperate, unconscious, rearguard struggle to save that freedom.

Habermas strikingly confirms this analysis when he shows that we are witnessing a destructuring of the superego. "A greater development of adaptive behavior is merely the reverse or counterpart of an area of interaction mediated by language in the act of dissolving under the influence of the structures of rational, goal-oriented activity (here, the symbolic is eliminated by technology). This is matched on the subjective level by the disappearance from human consciousness of the difference between rational goal-oriented activity and interaction. The fact that this difference is masked shows precisely the ideological strength of the technocratic consciousness." (op. cit., p. 39).

\* \* \*

The second aspect of technological universalism is the geographic one. The technological system is developing throughout the entire world, despite differences of race, economy, or political regime.[7] This, although more readily admitted now than twenty years ago, is as yet not generally accepted. It is easy to note that a machine is still itself wherever it is shipped to, and that there is no Arabic or Chinese way, no capitalist or socialist way of using it. But, as we have pointed out, the machine is merely one element in the technological system, and this system has characteristics similar to those of the machine. It is not machines that are shipped to all the countries on earth; it is, in reality, the ensemble of the technological world—both a necessity, if machines are to be usable, and a consequence of the accumulation of machines. It is a style of life, a set of symbols, an ideology.

We know all about those machines that were given to African nations but remain in sheds, unused, wasting away. This is not primarily a question of competence; it is far more an absence of conformity in the life-style, the social organization, etc. And there is no escaping this dilemma: "Either the machine is used, and it then brings about a certain type of family relationships, economic organization, a certain psychology, an ideology of productiveness, efficiency, etc. Or else it will not be used." All the elements of the technological system condition one another mutually; the machine is one of them. We should not think of it as a puzzle that we could assemble as we like. Each piece has its place, and if we have not put it where it belongs, then the ensemble will not function.

This does not mean that the form cannot change in details. Of course it can! The political organization may be more or less dictatorial, more or less democratic; but within narrow limits, that is, the political regime must, in any event, be bureaucratic and rely on experts. It must allow optimal use of the ensemble of technological means. There will then be an elimination of unfit regimes and a selection favoring the fitter ones. As the divergences between the forms of government gradually lessen, those forms refusing to employ technology will be purely and simply excluded. The others (with, of course, their necessary differences in terms of psychology, history, etc.) will wind up as neighboring types, i.e., neighboring from a structural but not a formal or constitutional standpoint.

Japan offers a remarkable example of universalization after the Meiji revolution.[8] It is the ideal model, in a pure state, for the transfusion of Western technologies. At present, Japan keeps following the technological lead of the United States. She adopts and then adapts every American technological development, and we know the upshot: on the one hand, a tremendous economic leap forward; on the other hand, a heavy price to pay. Japanese firms (with rare exceptions) are dependent on American firms, and that entails a political dependence. Still, once technology reaches a certain degree of development, it cannot keep growing by sheer imitation. And, aside from the nationalist motive, that is what we are now witnessing: the trend toward creating a process of autonomous growth, which, however, while challenging American supremacy both economically and politically, nevertheless consecrates technological universality.

The same holds for life and economic organization. Contrasting socialism and capitalism is quite antiquated by now, that is simply a matter of ideology and propaganda. There are the economic forms that can best absorb and utilize the technological ensemble, and there are the other economic forms. The latter are doomed, they will have to align themselves or disappear.[9] With his icy irony, B. Charbonneau sums up the unification between the capitalist and the socialist countries by the grace of technology: "After the thesis, capitalism, and the antithesis, socialism, here is the product of the synthesis: the society of plastic."

Mitscherlich (*Die Unwirtlichkeit unserer Städte*, 1965) like so many other authors, shows that the technological phenomenon produces the same results, no matter what the political and economic forms of government may be. For instance, in regard to urbanism and the urbanist technocracy: "In the Communist countries, the limitations imposed on private property have not favored the emergence of an original style, and above all, they have not brought an end to isolation. . . . These countries have gone on building lugubrious cities."

Furia (*Techniques et sociétés*) shows the convergences between various socialisms, e.g., Russian and Chinese, because of technicization. The Chinese have adopted the measures recommended by Khrushchev for technical training. Technicization, first achieved by the Russians, is leading the Chinese along a road very similar to that of their adversaries. They both agree, Furia underlines, that the technologies play a paramount role in the social revolution; they both reproach capitalism for curbing technicization; they both feel that technology is the basis of socialization; hence they both give top priority to technical education, letting the cadres spread the technological spirit among the young and the workers.

These resemblances strike me as far more essential than the spectacular contrasts, apparent and actualized, between the two regimes. The Chinese imitate the Russians in the desire for productivity in the socialist organization of work, in forming technological teams. The Chinese have struck out on the same road of technicization as other nations—exactly the same. I wrote about it in 1952. And everything confirms it. There is no originality. Mao's idea that the technological revolution must be accompanied by a cultural revolution is nothing new. That was the Russian position in 1927 with the *Piatiletka*, the Five Year Plan. And if Mao declares that the dominant factor is man, we should not forget that Stalin once wrote a book entitled *Man, the Most Precious Capital*.

As for the so-called original features of Chinese Communism, the evidence offered that the Chinese have taken a different route because they associate intellectual, rural, and industrial work, because they appeal to the do-it-yourself mentality and to ingenuity, etc.—all these admiring witnesses simply fail to see that this is not a new route, but an antecedent stage and that's all. The do-it-yourself period has preceded the stage of evolved technologies *everywhere;* the factories installed in the countryside were part of the industrial stage in England and France during the eighteenth century. The appeal to the initiative of workers is the stage of the beginnings of the bourgeoisie. In all the books and stories on China, I have found nothing strictly new in regard to technicization. The Chinese are merely at the dawn of this phenomenon, which allows them to still have illusions about its future and to imagine a different outcome. But the conditionings are the same; and the Chinese, thinking themselves original, are striving tooth and nail to reproduce the very same conditions for technological growth and, if not the present-day forms, then at least the placement of the ensemble of the mechanism, which will impose its laws upon the cultural ideologies.

For there is no other choice. Either the Chinese will prefer sticking to this apparent line and go on building the village blast furnaces and the do-it-yourself factories. In which case, they will reach their maximum very quickly. Or else this "original Chinese route" will turn out to be merely a stage, a phase for accustoming the people to technicization and preparing a certain number of necessary foundations for the later strides. And in this case, China will become a technological society exactly like the others. For—let us keep reiterating it—the technological system brings along an ensemble of conditions and consequences that are always identical. But if we present those two alternatives, we should not delude ourselves: The choice is already made—in favor of the second possibility.

Indeed, numerous declarations by Chou En-lai (reported in *New China* or in the *Peking Review*) attest that the major concern at the moment is technicization—at *any* price, including American aid, the return of "material incentives," the rehabilitation of technicians and experts who were dumped during the Cultural Revolution. Everything is dominated by China's technological lag behind the Western world. When a country starts out on this road, i.e., technological competition, then it obligatorily adopts the entire system.

The problem of this lag was first raised (1971-1972) in regard to the "blockade" and imperialist aggression. China had to advance technologically in order to confront imperialist politics. But let us not forget that this was the same argument that Stalin used for mass industrialization and technicization. When you set off on this road, the consequences are ineluctable. Even more so in that technicization covers all sectors. In particular, China has to make a special effort toward electronics, automation, computer processing. But this stage is already passed. Mao himself proclaimed the necessity of an intensive technicization (June 1973) "in order to make communism more agreeable." (It would seem that Lin Piao was removed partly because of his *ascetic* sectarianism.) This agreeableness is tied to consumption, the application of technology to ends that are very specifically the consumption of technological objects. Given these things, any discourse on the uniqueness of the Chinese route and Chinese socialism is truly discourse. The Chinese debate on economism and moral incentive was quite characteristic. But the return of Teng Hsiao-ping is the sign (and also the quarantee) now of the triumph of technology over man, the "politics of steel," modernization at any price, nuclear power, yield and profit. The Chinese Revolution is aligning itself to technology at any price, once and for all.

The tragedy of the third world is precisely its (present, of course, but not essential) incapacity for using technologies. It is perfectly moral but intellectually ludicrous to be scandalized because the rich countries are getting richer and the poor ones poorer. Posing the problem in this way is very idealistic and virtuous, but it dooms us from the very outset to understanding nothing. The matter is in no wise "capitalist"; it is technological. The "technological gap" is widening because the third world is not yet fully integrated into the technological system. So long as this is the case, the third world can only keep growing poorer while being more and more outclassed by the technological powers. It has no chance of improving its situation either by political disorders and dictatorships, or by revolutions in the technicized countries. If such revolutions succeeded, they might at best destroy the technological power of the West. And that would not improve the position of third-world countries one iota. On the contrary, they would fall even lower, having neither aid from "Western" countries, nor a chance to export their merchandise.

The only possible route for the third world is technicization (I am not saying, industrialization!), the establishment of political and economic structures able to make optimal use of technology—a psychology of work and yield, a social organization that is "individualistic and massified," etc. In other words, the development conditions of the technological system in its entirety, as a system. But so long as people talk about "socialism," "nationalism," "democracy," these ideological outpourings will block any chance of technicization, as, on another score, the top-priority pursuit of unionization, or the mass spread of machines, the attempt at rapid industrialization, etc. Furthermore, when I state that the only possible route is technicization, I am merely saying that it is the route *imposed* by the technological system, by universalism. I am not saying that this route is morally, ideologically, or humanely

# UNIVERSALITY

*desirable,* or that it is *good.*[10] It is simply inevitable if these nations wish to survive. Otherwise, they will be doomed to greater misery, agitated by incoherent movements, revolts, internal ravagements (we can already, alas, see wars multiplying everywhere in the third world, caused not so much by the Chinese, the Russians, or the CIA, but rather by tragic responses to the growing poverty due to lack of technicization). And these countries will get more and more dependent on the technicized powers, even if the latter are full of good will.

Goldsmith vividly points out that little by little we are forcing the third-world nations (seemingly for their own good) to abandon their very sound farming methods, which respected the natural cycles. Instead, they are turning to an intensive agriculture with machines, chemical fertilizers, and pesticides. This development has the twofold effect of making these nations more and more subordinate to the technological countries and plunging them into the vicious spiral of unlimited technicization. However, the immediate result is an improved situation for the consumption of agricultural products. Technicization always takes place in the name of an immediate obvious necessity.[11]

The excellent account of the West African Conference on Science, Technology and the Future of Man and Society (*Oecumenical Review*, March, 1972), at the University of Ghana, offers a complete panorama of the demand for technicization and its effects. The obvious goal of technicization is "the end of neocolonialist exploitation, the dignity of the African, social justice, economic development." The debate commenced between partisans of "intermediary technology" (light, especially rural), adapted technology, and native technology. The first of the three was rejected as not permitting the establishment of a strong power over and control of their future by the people involved. Appropriate technology, which wants an adaptation to local circumstances, was also rejected, because it was not known *who* would do the adapting, and it was feared that, once again, it would be White technicians. Enthusiasm favored native technology. But, curiously, this referred to African perfecting of technological products, which would put these in line with what is being done in the West. The first great achievement of purely native technology was the manufacture of a new rocket by Black technicians in Nigeria—over which they so greatly preened themselves.

To be sure, this rocket is indispensable for waging war against South Africa. But it merely shows how identical the technologies and the development processes of technologies are. Obviously, this development of technologies (identical to Western ones) must be stimulated by the state, which has to deploy all its resources in order to create technicians, etc. Yet, the "experts" at this conference fully acknowledged that technicization spelled a religious downfall, the elimination of rites, the metamorphosis of mythical thinking into rational thinking, which produces a psychological and social vacuum. In particular, there is a tendency toward absolute domination by the technological minority over the rest of the people.

P. Sarpung's paper is extremely pessimistic. Dealing with the social disintegration caused by technicization, he notes that in the face of social and religious collapse, there has been a return to the most primitive magic practices as a defense. We already know that magic and technology are fine bedfellows. Africans are going through the cycles more swiftly than we! But whatever the dangers, the technological imperative is forced upon them.

A. Aluko's report analyzes, without problems, the social changes necessary to make technological development possible in Africa; especially, the creation of a new ideology, one of self-reliance, that is nationalist, rationalist, and socialist. But never for an instant does he suspect that this self-reliant ideology is actually the pure and simple adoption of the Western ideology! He presents the exact "values" of the technological ideology of the West. To assert the independence and autonomy of Africa, the Africanization of technology, they must adopt not only the technological objects and processes, but also the values and the ideological context.

And the final recommendation of the conference bears out this point: The entire social, ideological, etc., context *must* be overthrown to allow the rise of African technology. None of this is very new, except for the confusion of values produced by technicization, the acceptance by the Africans of the heaviest price to pay, the illusion that technology will help Africa to come of age and achieve independence.

As for the technicizing passion and the ideology of progress among third-world nations, Z. Brzezinski cites numerous and moving examples: third-world students heading more toward the United States than anywhere else for technological studies; a ubiquitous shift towards a technicized agriculture dependent on Western technological inventions (the green revolution); the spread of literacy to allow more rapid adoption of technologies (a subjective and cultural revolution *destined* for technicization!); with an

## UNIVERSALITY

overlapping growth of communications, professional training, technological instruction, and the corresponding apparatuses (radio, TV, etc.). Brzezinski gives eloquent figures for all third-world countries. He is correct in underscoring the inadequacy of literary or legal education and the trend among these students to adopt Western cultural models along with the technologies. What is formed by that instruction, transmitted by technicization, is a totality because, in effect, technology has become a totality.

And Brzezinski points out features common to just about all these nations, particularly, indirect technicization (by the transistor) of the most traditional peasant masses. In reality, everything rests on a veritable passion for technology, an obsession in all these nations. Especially, all the rulers, all the elites can imagine only one single road of civilization, one single road of development, one single road to "enter history": the road of technology. Any attempt to make them realize that they are setting off on a dangerous road, that technicization might be an impasse, and that they ought to find their own specific road of development, will reap accusations of colonialism and antiprogressive thinking.[12]

Technological passion is leading the third-world countries to impugn anything that may now be said about pollution, the dangers of technology, the ecological imbalances, and so forth. All that seems like words to prevent a technological upswing. They are utterly unaware of the universality of the problems and have in mind solely their own desire to profit from the technological boom.

Thus, Brazil, proud of its space, its forests, its mineral resources, has no qualms about inviting all industries to set up shop there. As C. Vanhecke put it (*Le Monde*, August 1973), Brazil is announcing, "Come and pollute us!" This is very characteristic.

"Here, technology still does not have a monopoly on the works of civilization, but they are summoning technology in a fetischistic manner to come and receive all the realities. Here, everything is measured by the mile of tar and by the weight of concrete. And the intellectuals are participating in this frenzy." These lines, written to me by a colleague in Togo, can be generalized.

On the Ivory Coast, Simonnot ("L'exemple et les vestiges de la Côte-d'Ivoire," *Le Monde*, July 1973) notes the unification brought by technology. Corrugated iron has replaced straw. The new villages are infinitely dreary and ugly, but they "fulfill the wishes of the villagers themselves: the corrugated iron is more solid and does not require upkeep." They have not yet experienced the harmful effects (for estheticism is certainly not the issue here). Obstruction—production—work—and soon the creation of a proletariat, not by exploitation, but by disintegration of the traditional social tissue.

And education everywhere is oriented to technicization. I. Illich's verdict is virtually accepted by several Western intellectuals but completely unknown in the third world, which obeys the logic of the system: "It goes without saying" that reading and writing are good things and that education *must* be developed on the Western model! But it is perfectly wrong and stupid to claim that there was no education in Islamic countries. The difference, which is all that justified this new education, is the necessity of gaining access to technology. Hence, the trends of rejecting native culture. Hence, questions like the one reported by J. Dejeux in *Le Monde* (January 1971): "If we Arabize, can we aspire to scientific and technological progress?" Rejection of the world of storytellers and poets, destruction of a culture remote from efficiency—such are the themes of the new Arabizing! The issue is not a synthesis or the creation of a new culture. At best, there may be a juxtaposition, as in Japan, between folklore in private life and technology, the latter allowing people to attain universalism by sacrificing symbolic peculiarities. The passion for technology among all third-world nations lies beyond the ideologies of the ruling political forms and even the rejection of the West. This technicization can be found in the very struggle against the West. It is a state of mind, a way of organizing oneself, of situating problems, etc.

\* \* \*

There is much talk about the interdependence of all the countries in the world today, for better and for worse. But we must not forget that this "mechanical and obligatory solidarity" comes from technology, and that the universalization of technology and the coherence of the technological system are what produce the interdependence, which causes each event to have repercussions everywhere. This altogether changes, say, the problem of "crises." In the past, "the world system" was so uncohesive that local solutions were possible. But this is no longer the case. And since evolution was slower, people had time to look for remedies. Today, technologies are combined so rapidly that the conditions of a crisis change before anyone even manages to find a response. We saw this in the "oil crisis" and its disastrous effects on the third world, whose industrial and food output went down some twenty percent in 1974, by and large *because of* higher oil prices.

If I trace this globality back to the all-inclusiveness of the technological system, then I am going against Pestel and Mejarovic, who see technology as *one* of the factors in the ensemble but not as the determining factor, and who do not view technology as constituting in itself a system. To my mind, this warps their forecast and the orientation of their strategy for the future, in terms of what they call "counter-intuitive" behavior. The word itself is accurate, but the reason for this behavior lies in the reality, until now, of its constituting factor: technology. In all domains, the sole issue is an overall approach to problems, a quest for stable technological and economic development for all regions, a worldwide economic diversification with complementarities, an effective demographic policy. And all these factors would have to be combined. This implies a voluntarily total system, a world-governing organization, operating with a technology that is far more developed than at the moment.

Nonetheless, the existence of this universality of the technological system, its identity wherever it is introduced, the reproduction of its conditions for existing, do not necessarily mean that the world is being unified. Previously, we saw that the technological system is not transforming society into a megamachine. And here we have the same problem. First of all, it depends on the level of analysis. If technology is alike everywhere, producing comparable effects and creating identifiable structures, this does not imply any unification on the political level (just as nationalism is an ideology that is comparable everywhere but arouses the mutual hostility of the nationalist nations). There is obviously no universality of modern *society*.

Raymon Aron (*Progress and Disillusion*) has shown that the ideological universality of technology is expressed in two postulates: the truth of science and individual equality. But this does not do away with any conflicts, social or national. I also feel that Aron is asking the wrong question when he writes: "Is it legitimate to pass from the universal truth of science, the universal efficiency of technology, to the universal vocation of industrial civilization? . . . The notions of equality, personality, liberty, are vague. . . . Are they borne in upon non-Western minds? Are they adequate for defining a joint project of all the industrial societies, Soviet or Western? . . . Does not every society need its own principle of cohesion?"

In reality, there is no contradiction. The universalization of technology involves an ideological and sociological remodeling that is quite the same everywhere. But it does not wipe out the local peculiarities, or the risk that these diverse technological societies may enter into conflict with one another. Universalization does not spell fusion or submission to a world government or, of course, the existence of principles of specific cohesion on all sociological levels (just as there is a cohesion principle for the national, which is inadequate for ensuring family cohesion).

But there is a far more complex problem. Within this process of universalization, technology, which "marks the advent of the global comunity," also causes ruptures and aggravates divisions. It fragments humankind, separating people from their traditional customs, on the basis of which a universal modus vivendi was established. Technology widens the range of human conditions and deepens the gap between human material conditions. Technology is set up everywhere as a foundation, possibility, demand by societies; but it creates the means of destruction that trigger fear and mutual distrust. It creates the means of production that separate the poor and the rich more harshly than ever; it appears to increase tensions and conflicts. "While the means of transportation and communication are bringing together the diverse factions of the human species, the means of destruction are driving them apart. . . . The inequalities in development have never been as great as in our epoch, or more precisely, the very notion of inequality in development is meaningless outside of industrial civilization" (Aron).

Thus, without a doubt, *some* technologies help to bring men together, and *some* technologies drive them apart, cause ruptures. But this accurate picture once again results from considering the technologies *separately*. The technological system is indeed universal and, as a system, it has established itself everywhere, more or less completely. It does not, however, guarantee peace or good feeling among countries. It actually produces the breaches that we know about but that are powerless against this universalization. In fact, if these divisions come about, they are due to the universalization of the technological system.

So long as technology was the property, the prerogative of a tiny number of countries, who were the only ones to wield technological power, the world could be unified under their rule. But it is in the "nature" of technology to universalize itself. Technology cannot be kept private, it is objectifiable and must go to the utter limit of whatever is possible. Hence, it must extend to all nations. They cannot remain subordinate. Once they achieve technology (and this is bound to happen), they demand political autonomy. Moreover, technology obliges them to compete with other nations on their own terrain. The formerly colonized peoples take over the notion of society or of history that stems from technology and that was first articulated by the West (because the West was technicized first). That is how the ideology of growth (the opposite of any traditional creed) is foisted throughout the globe. The third world rejects all its ancient philosophy in favor of this single value—which is purely technological and Western. But this is obviously what launches competition and conflicts (recall the ideology of nationalism, which has the same character).

The truth is that the universality of the technological system *causes the rupture* of the human world for a long time, and not its unification. This is one of the basic features of the system. It produces competition, if only because of different rates of development in the technological sectors. As a result, new fragmentations replace the old. Technology renders obsolete the divisions in society and the human world according to the ancient patterns or for the ancient motivations—such as have been studied everywhere by sociologists. And in their stead, it creates new differentiations, or else, maintaining the old ones, it provides them with new justifications and foundations, for instance, the elites. Technology is developing equality and democratizing; but it is also producing the phenomenon of technological elites. Hence, it is no accident that, at this moment, technology is striking breaches in the "unified" world. We cannot believe in any "globalization," any rapprochement of nations, any world solidarity; this is an idealism founded on a very superficial view of things.

In a like manner, people thought that the meaning of the discovery of the New World was to save the poor heathens by converting them to Christianity. This is the same kind of illusion that causes some moderns to believe that, thanks to the means of communication, we are advancing toward a united world. The universalization of the technological system does produce an *identity* of foundations and structures in diverse societies, bringing human groups together materially; but it puts them, without fail, in a position of power conflict. For we must never forget that technology is never anything but a means of power.

We are inevitably led by the extension of the technological system to a gradual identification of cultures as well as of economic and political forms. We must bear in mind that the problem of development, when seen from the aspect of the catching-up of underdeveloped countries, is rooted in the existence of the technological system with its traits of unicity and universality. If there were any chance for pluralities of civilization, we would still be in the traditional historical situation. Each society had its technologies and its civilization, it was *different* from the others and therefore noncomparable. There was no real *inequality* during the first century B.C. between the peoples in the Chinese Empire and those in the Roman Empire. This was not, as a shallow view might have it, because they did not know one another. The reason was that they were too different to compare themselves with one another.

Once there is universality of a type, technology, in which everybody aligns himself on this structure and adopts its ideology, comparison becomes inevitable, and inequality sticks out like a sore thumb. Raymond Aron is perfectly correct when he says that "the very notion of inequality in development is meaningless outside of industrial civilization." The "problem" of development has become a "problem" because of the ideal of well-being and the general spread of technicization. But for this very reason, universalization produces a conflict between nations at different levels of growth: "Inequality in development radically excludes humanity's worldwide political unification; the most striking upshot of statistical investigations is not the persistence of these discrepancies, but rather the tendency of any social group or any nation, upon reaching a certain income bracket, to desire the same goods that were bought by the groups who preceded it in this rise." This phenomenon is not due to wealth, for wealth could be applied to multiple and diverse needs. No, such identical consumption is caused by technicization. Men are polarized by their universal technological faith toward a purely technicized consumption.

However, the identification of cultures is neither absolute nor rigid, it perfectly supports the diversity of spectacle and tourism. There will still be (more and more) local crafts, folk songs and folk costumes; festivals and marriage rites will be marvelously aboriginal, and religions will flourish . . .

Needless to say, when we speak of universality in the technological society, we are not saying that there is *identity* in all countries and on all social strata. Plainly, technology acquires specific traits and unifies ways of acting and even being. But hot countries necessitate a different way of life from cold countries, and nationalisms persist despite the basic unity of technological society. The technological world does not entail the great rectilinear avenues of the identity of ideologies! The greatest apparent diversity can reign, provided it does not interfere with the basic fact! For, under the seeming pluralism of cultural forms, a universal and common system is crystallizing, identical in all parts of the world.

\* \* \*

We are witnessing a new development of reflection about technology with a trend toward intermediary technologies (i.e., à la China) and appropriate technologies.[13] These appropriate technologies are the ones adapted to countries in a process of growth. Supposedly, the technologies are no longer marked by efficiency or profitability. But actually, the debate is distorted. Notwithstanding claims that efficiency is disregarded, for some (Austin Robinson), the technology in question must nevertheless maintain (for the specific country and in relation to its standard) an economic efficiency (otherwise, why bother using technology); for others, (e.g., Mercier) even if one need not worry about the maximum quantity produced, it nevertheless goes without saying that a technology must be utterly economical (though for a long time now, economic efficiency has not been the gauge of technological efficiency). Hence, people admit that technology must be evaluated from four points of view: objectives, available resources, population makeup, and later results. But note that the issue is always an ensemble of technologies meant to promote *economic growth*, and that the evaluation criteria are perfectly consistent with what is expected of technologies.

In other words, the notion of "appropriate technology" signifies a technological adjustment to circumstances, which is quite "normal" in the technological phenomenon. And the limitation to *economic* effects and services considerably limits the interest of such research. The point each time is simply to determine how the technological system can be set up in developing countries. All that can be done is to figure out what is more profitable (e.g., the Taiwanese way or the Filipino way), what brings the least amount of trouble and upheaval.

The central issue is obviously to know the nature and range of options available to the third world in technology. For some people, there are choices resulting from the option of a certain type of "development," a certain economic orientation, hence, a political choice. But one is forced to note two things. People, rather vaguely to be sure, admit the notion of the "technological package"—i.e., the extremely simple idea that *one* technology cannot be implanted alone, it requires a technological ensemble. But this notion lacks rigor, due to a misconception of what the technological system is; yet the same notion points out that there is not much choice. The other obvious point is that the technological choice is narrowly determined *in third-world countries* by the natural resources. This dependency has been done away with only in the highly technicized nations. The others are still tied to their resources, which will be exploited by single technological procedures, for which there is no choice. Technology (as Rad-Serecht so excellently puts it) is no longer a variable to be determined, but a given fact to which we must adapt the different economic and social variables with as little damage as possible. However, the weakness of this lecture, as of all present-day research on "appropriate technologies" is that it still views the economic criterion as determinant, and separates the technologies for production of resources from the ensemble of the technological system. Hence, any analysis is askew.

All these things, and so many other diversification factors, are necessary for the expansion of the technological system, in order to fight anything dreary, desperate, and insignificant about it. Hence, there will be no identity of all the aspects of cultures, but rather a modeling of each culture in terms of what has already become and can only become its fundamental structure. This technological universalism is not manifest at all times and in all places. But the ideological turn has been taken everywhere. It is not just the ubiquitous emergence of machines; above all, it is the fact that now, whatever a country's degree of evolution, the only point of interest, the only focus of ideological fixation and hope, the only vision of the future is technology. All countries are teaching that the degree of civilization is to be judged by the degree of technology.

We have previously analyzed the desire of African intellectuals to demonstrate the technological and scientific validity of their past civilization. And we already know their distrust toward the folkloristic idea of negritude: It would be very wrong to "fixate" Africa on an ineffective past; it seems unacceptable to glorify Black arts, dancing, costume; that can only keep the African nations inferior to Westerners. Instead of negritude, Blacks need political action, socialism, and, above all, a grasp of technologies. This, in reality, spells the adoption of the technological system and the necessary adaptation.

More and more, in all countries on the globe, the proposed ideal is technicization. When someone says "civilization is becoming global" or "the African and Asian nations are entering history," he actually means that the technological system is universal—and that people start belonging to history only upon reaching a certain level of technological development. For all African or Asian leaders, the prime objective is always, ultimately, to develop technological resources in their countries. Of course, they do not see clearly what this entails—and how could they, since the issue is so controversial in the West! They do not know "how" to go about it, nor where to start in with the technological system; but the objective is always quite the same, the problem is to advance along the road of technicization and to develop by means of technology!

Naturally, this is perfectly legitimate from a human and psychological standpoint, given the poverty of the third world. What has made for the material happiness of the West is its technological power. Hence, to escape poverty, each third-world nation must develop a similar technological power. What could be more obvious!

Nevertheless, after the great efforts made from 1945 to 1960 in this direction, people have come to realize that technicization cannot take place from the outside, by the infusion of technological means; for this involves a thorough metamorphosis of the society in question. That is why the application of technological means has not brought the intended results. Vast discouragement has seized hold of the nations and their leaders. Instead of asking why this failure has occurred on the level of technologies, the leaders, inspired by Western ideologues and propagandists, have preferred to create a political fabrication, which can only aggravate the situation. This fantastic analysis will obviously delay growth, but the error cannot hold out for long. At bottom, the veering towards technicization has already begun, and all nations (except India) are basically convinced of the unique value of this route. Hence, the principle cause now of technological universalism is that conviction, which has won out, from the Western countries to the entire world.[14] Therefore universalism rests on two complementary givens.

*An objective characteristic of the technological system* is that technology is necessarily progressive. It cannot, "by nature," remain stationary. It cannot stop advancing.[15] We always think in terms of linear expansion: a "step forward," an improved technology *succeeding* another. But this progressivity is also spatial expansion; technology cannot find sufficient breadth unless it is applied everywhere. It cannot leave any domain intact, because it always has to keep mobilizing more and more energy, resources, raw materials, etc. We cannot conceivably fetter the application of technologies to a limited geographic site. This is true especially because the two aspects of this technological progressivity condition each other: every improved technology is also universalizing, in all senses of the term, both because it demands identical competences everywhere and because it tends by its very power ("improved," for technology, means more efficient and more powerful!) to widen its domain of application. Needless to say, aviation in 1915 did not make communications worldwide, whereas the sheer technological development of the airplane, which flies faster and further, necessarily entails global networks, with offices, airports, etc. Geographic universalization comes with the progress of each technology. It cannot be helped.[16] This is not due to capitalism or profit seeking or politics, or socialist propaganda, or whatever.

The other basis of universalism is the *psychological and ideological change*, the human factor, man having renounced his religious hopes, his myths, the quest for virtue, his rootedness in the past, in order to play out his life in the future, pin his hopes on technological progress, and thereby seek a solution to all his problems.

These two conditions have now been met. We can thus speak of a technological universalism even if there is no very visible or satisfying technological growth in a large part of the world. But the phenomenon is virtually established, irreversible, and the technological system can only develop. For, addressing the individual, technology produces behaviors in him, sets up habits, which can be neither integrated in a different ensemble of values nor repressed, because they are carried by an obvious material support, and they also respond to models that are both hated and desired. On the other hand, addressing the social body, the technological factor develops in such a way as to thoroughly modify the body social. However slightly technology has penetrated a society, one may say that an irreversible process has been launched and that it will not end before the whole society is technicized.

Thus, technological universalism makes us aware of *a triple reversal of relations*.

Traditionally, technology was engulfed in a civilization which it was a part of. Now, it is technology on which everything depends, it rules all the other factors, and it is technology which is the engulfing element, inside of which everything is situated.[17]

Technology was once a means of obeying exterior finalities; now it has become its own finality, developing according to its own rationality; universalism ensures its "ipseity."

Technology, in the West, developed thanks to the fortunate and surprising conjunction of a whole set of factors, social, intellectual, economic, historical; but now, in order to develop according to its own necessity, it artificially and systematically reproduces everywhere the factors necessary for it. They are the condition of its expansion; previously fortuitous and natural, these factors are now voluntary and artificial. We will have to elaborate on these two aspects later on.

Thus, technology now defines, according to the very will of the nations, their sole future. Technology, i.e.—for there is no other kind—the West. Technology brings along ways of being, thinking, living for everyone. It is an all-comprehensive culture, it is a synthesis.

In these past two decades, the major discovery of historians, sociologists, anthropologists (Western) was the specificity and dignity of all cultures. After the hubris and power of the nineteenth-century West declaring "I" and only "I," we are now bowing in admiration before the wonders of many civilizations. There is no universal history, there are many histories, each original. There are no primitive peoples and evolved peoples, there are different structures, all of them well equipped, all of them well adapted. "We must describe them in their own terms, with their own systems of references, of specifications," nonjudgmentally. "It is simply possible, historically, in certain circumstances, to pass from one system to another by a mutation of the code of societies. To believe in universal history, interpreting savages in terms of a future that is merely our own present, is tantamount, for Lévi-Strauss, to projecting upon other societies the system of thought that characterizes ourselves and to interpreting by our own myths" (M. A. Burnier).

No doubt, no doubt . . . But we have discovered this exactly at the point when technology is invading these nations more surely than colonial armies and assimilating these cultures. Right now, at the very moment that their value is being discovered, technology is destroying them. And technology is today confirming the earlier discourse of the superiority, the truth of Western culture. *Western culture* is the future of those societies, just as it is our present, and there is no myth involved; except precisely the myth that these cultures have a different future ahead of them. Practically all we have left of them is a poignant memory.

\* \* \*

Nevertheless, we should not picture this universalization as occurring in a brutal fashion. It has been ascertained that the human factor is indispensable for technological growth, and also that technology causes disorder. We must therefore have a new technology that contributes to technological expansion and to the development of technology as a system. This would be what is known as "the transfer of technology."[18] Until now, the influx of technologies was random and haphazard, according to capitalist interests or local circumstances. But now we have come to see that this procedure is no longer possible and that we must undertake a methodical transfer. We cannot let just anybody employ just any technology; we cannot abruptly pass men from a nontechnological milieu to a different one. We realize that technology is not transmitted as easily as a material good by sheer contract or as a contagious disease by sheer contact. We need a method for the transmission of technologies. We need a complex ensemble, for it is not enough to "learn" how to use a device. A whole conception of life is being transferred. But all this has been reduced to precise technologies [French, *techniques*]: the "transfer" of technology [French, *technologie*].

Two preliminary remarks are necessary here.

First of all, we are delighted to see that these specialists know what they are talking about. The transfer of technology [French, *Technologie*] does not mean the transfer of technolog*ies* [French, *Techniques*]. They are not confusing the two, as is so often the case! This is truly technology [French, *Technologie*], a discourse on the technical [French, *Technique*], i.e., on the entire intellectual, cultural, and psychological apparatus that permits the use of technologies [French, *Techniques*] and adapts man to that use.

Secondly, the objective clearly remains the diffusion and universalization of technology. What is certain beyond any doubt in this new progress is the need for expanding technology. The sole problem is to prevent this expansion from creating disorders; the sole question then is, "How do we go about it?" This means new technologies, period. And, as usual, technology will turn out to be scrupulously simple and attentive. Hence, we will firmly impugn what has too often been done: "the transfer by a certified true copy," by "grafting"—which will be replaced by a transfer that one might call organic. For example, we will realize that it is useless to reproduce an American industrial model and ship it off as such to Africa. Technology can exist only if there is a human group properly qualified to receive it. The transfer of technology is thus not a method of transferring technologies from one human group to another. Rather, this transfer is a technology that, given a certain technological objective, consists in molding a human group in such a way as to make it capable of utilizing as well as possible the new machines, the new structure, a factory or an organization; and, of course, this also implies, conversely, remolding certain technologies to adapt *them* to this group.

"There is a transfer of technology, we can say, when a group of men, in general part of an organism, become effectively capable of assuming, in conditions judged satisfactory, one or more functions linked to a definite technology." We must take into account the sociological context, the psychological aspects; we will try to integrate the technology in such a way as to adapt it to a certain cultural context; but in any event, we have to make the group, these people, capable of using the new device and of adapting to it with a minimum of suffering and a maximum of efficiency. And of course, as usual in technology, we will stress that there is no absolute transfer per se, every transfer is relative, according to the abilities of each group. A certain group was unable to run a certain factory, and it becomes able to; i.e., by running the factory, it obtains a certain output, while reducing the damage done to materials, the number of rejects, etc.

The transfer technologies apply to diverse situations: the transfer to an individual starting out in a factory, the transfer when a new technology appears in a factory. (The standard case is obviously the appearance of the computer in an administration: we must thoroughly transform the structure of the group as well as the knowledge and psychology of each individual. Transfer posits the disruption of routines.) Another kind of transfer takes place when a country passes a technology from one organism to another (e.g., the NASA technologies to hundreds of American factories). Finally, and this is the kind that we always think of, there is the transfer of technologies from a "developed" country to underdeveloped ones.

But bear in mind that the estimate of development is technological. Take for instance, the initial transfer of *European* nuclear science to *American* industry (which was underdeveloped), or the transfer of German space science and technology to the USSR and the United States. The point is thus to lead the group to technological mastery. But, let us be quite clear. This means the ability to use a technology as efficiently as possible—that's all! And we perceive that this mastery always relies on a high level of organization, hence, structural modifications.

But it also presupposes a cultural change; the transfer of a technology entails the modification of social behaviors and of the way people understand and assimilate events. This transfer is possible only if there is a joint effort between the receiver and the emitter. The receiver is even more important. But the emitter must be fully aware of the cultural, psychological, and other obstacles in order to avoid, say, putting up a factory that the native population does not need or whose technologies it cannot assimilate.

We then go on to elaborate a meticulous technology of technological transfer, which supplements both the study and development of projects (transfer of technological material and the ergonomics (adaptation of work to man). The transfer of technology is bound to commence with a study of the receiver's situation, the available population sources, the local systems of education, the existing industrial structures. The transfer is, above all, a matter of communication. And if the cultural differences between the emitting system and the receiving system are too large a gap, the emitter will have to install "interpreters" capable of knowing the technology that is to be applied as well as the concrete situation of those who have to apply it, and capable of making themselves understood by these people. We thus see that the automaticity of the application is expressed through human groups that perform the chosen work among various technologies according to their maximum proximity to the group. But this choice is quite "automatic," for the only criterion it obeys is the technological one.

"The macro-conception bears upon the choice of the process, the pattern of production, the characteristics of the huge machines." Technology is never so constraining that it cannot adopt diverse structures. Normally, diverse solutions are conceivable, but the automaticity consists in the fact that the solution imposed is the most "technological," i.e., the most effective in regard to an environment, a climate, a group. "The choice of a structure adapted to the present culture and probable evolution of the group is a factor in simplifying the transfer." The action will thus include pedagogy, psychology, information, planning; and, in each of these areas, it will be rigorously calculated with exact methods that are the very object of the science and technology of transfer. Which does not, of course, prevent us from gloriously recalling that technological transfer is the *"intrinsic feature of man,"* for "the gradual, then universal ascent of man toward his industrial development was possible only because of the vertical fertilization and the cross-fertilization permitted by the transfer of technology. Vertical: in one place, from generation to generation; cross: from place to place, from ethnic group to ethnic group."

# 8
# TOTALIZATION

THE technological phenomenon thus appears, like science itself, both specializing and totalizing. It is an all-inclusive ensemble, in which what counts is not so much each of the parts as the system of relations and connections between them. (The parts can, no doubt, be studied as specified technologies, but they never give us a view of technology as a whole.) This means that from a scientific standpoint, one can study a technological phenomenon only *overall*. A particular study of certain aspects or effects will get us nowhere. Not only does it fail to take the technological phenomenon into account, but the study of this particular point is already inexact per se because *this* issue is engulfed in the technological ensemble and receives its true formulation *from it*. For each problem, we assume that there is an integral and absolute man, a man issuing from the Platonic dialogues; but, in reality, man has been profoundly transformed and manipulated by a technological *ensemble*.

A problem we will find later on is that technological specialization *entails* totalization. The reduction of each active ensemble to a series of simple operations, the indefinite growth of the applications of technologies, with no reason ever to stop, would bring a dispersal, a wild incoherence if, at the same time, the process of development did not involve a sort of concatenation of all the fragmentary technologies. This concatenation produces a totalization of the technological operations; but this totalization, concerning technologies that bear upon *all* aspects of life and action, produces an ensemble that tends toward completeness. This is reinforced by the tendency to add up technological operations, which are always preserved, accumulating without ever getting lost. When a technology disappears (since the upswing of technology, of course!), it is replaced by another of the same kind, only superior. Nothing is lost in technology. Hence, totalization is simply the "flip side" of specialization.

The most striking image of this state of affairs is furnished by the constantly repeated assertion that in ten years, twenty years, the technological system will be "complete" (cf. Rorvik, op. cit.), and that everything will function without human interference. Even Brzezinski sometimes yields to this magic. He tells us, for instance, that the satellites will soon have enough power to transmit images directly to receivers without the intermediary of broadcasting-and-receiving stations. This would be an important step towards totalization.

Such "forecasts" reveal the extent to which the image of totalization is foisting itself upon mankind. We must understand that this totalization responds to a deep technological desire of man. Little by little, technology has solved a large number of problems that humankind was faced with. When men walked on the moon for the first time, there was a delirious explosion of joy (in newspapers and on TV) that "man's age-old dream has come true." Naturally, all the slow scientific and technological advances in developing rockets, then satellites, then space suits, and so on, had nothing to do with the poetic dream of flying to the moon. But people receive a technological feat as the fulfillment of a wish.

Yet man has a far more basic desire than walking on the moon, and that is the wish for unity: to reduce everything to One, destroy exceptions and aberrations, assemble everything in a harmonious system—a great concern of the philosophers. And once again, what man intellectually sketched out, technology accomplished. Unity is no longer a metaphysical construction, it is now assured and given in the technological system. Unity resides in *that* totalization. But man has not yet grown aware of this relation between his striving for unity and the constitution of technology as a unitary system. He does not yet know, does not yet see, that this system exists as a system. In other words, man is not *intentionally* bringing technology to this point. He has no plan along these lines. The elaboration of the system, i.e., "specialization-totalization," is an intrinsic process per se. This phenomenon is established by an ensemble of mechanical actions. We can observe it only after it has taken place.

But we must then cope with a twofold problem. On the one hand, the transition to a per se, and then to a reflexive per se. When I describe the system as it is constituted and exists, I am obviously

## TOTALIZATION

trying to make known a reality that hitherto has eluded our gaze. I am trying to explain what occurs and hence to point out both an objective phenomenon and our participation in this phenomenon—but I leave the reader on the level of his simple knowledge, that is, I do not intervene in the creation of the totalization. Man, made aware of what is happening, can react in a certain way and perhaps seek to master the fact that he now knows.

On the other hand, one can try something entirely different, starting with the ideal and obsession of unity, which we spoke about earlier. Not only is the totalizing system constituted in itself, not only can one study it as such, but one can consider that we have now fulfilled the deepest striving of man. This kind of undertaking was tried, on a rather summary level, by Teilhard de Chardin. It was then recommenced with the powerful synthesis done by E. Morin ("Le paradigme perdu," in *La Nature humaine*, 1973).

Morin's book strikes me as one of the most dangerous that have ever been written—for it offers a voluntary grasp of all the results of the human sciences in order to lead them to a synthetic ensemble, to unity. In other words, he forges the theory of the de facto technological totalization. Not that his theory *concerns* this totalization; but rather, just as totalization has been accomplished on the level of facts by technology, so too Morin accomplishes it on the level of theory. And his totalization is the exact pendant and complement of the preceding totalization because it has the same origin: science. He does not account for what exists, quite simply, but he elaborates the theoretical complement of this (involuntary) praxis, so that we find the closure of the system here: So long as theory was either faltering (not following the ensemble) or contrary (*refusing* to play along with totalization), the totalization, pursuing itself in itself, could not be completed and closed. There was always a chink on the theoretical level, an escape hatch for man. Morin's work shows what road to follow toward closing the system and trapping and dispossessing man.

I realize that this is not Morin's personal intention—any more than the atomic bomb was Einstein's intention. But Morin is moved by a passion for explanation and unity that inevitably makes him play this role (which he repudiates), because he himself has not seen what the totalizing technological system really is. He cannot know what the consequence of his theory is, simply because he is not cognizant of the reality of the system *in which* that theory is going to be integrated. He brings it the "solemn complement" which is going to speed up totalization. His theory—although Morin explicitly rejects totalization and closure—is closure and totalization because it does not remain limited to employing all data of the human sciences and tying them together for a profound explanation. His theory takes its place in a technological totality that supplants the natural totality and abandons man to its necessity of development. Morin wants to furnish a total explanation, to the extent that science permits this explanation today, and it is right here that the deadly complement to the technological system resides.

Thus, not only is global society tending to become a primary society (according to MacLuhan and on condition that we push his theory to the limit); not only do we need more of a social order the more technological order wins out (and the tiniest disorder is intolerable); but far more important, the science of man that Morin lays claim to (and that is *inevitable* in the perspective of the technological totalization) assembles the still separated factors, concentrating all technological possibilities on man himself. For the explanation precedes the action. The instant we *know* for sure, technological innovation is bound to come.

This theoretical advent could easily be translated into what would be most contrary to Morin's intention. In point of fact, his science of man cannot remain on a conceptual level, precisely because it is totalizing. Not only does his science help the system to close, but, even worse, it takes its place *in a technological society*, and nowhere else. Hence, it can produce only the very opposite of what Morin writes in his "Introduction to a politics of man." His total science of man, had it come in Periclean Athens, would have been an admirable step forward in developing a just politics. But it comes in the technological society, in the process of totalizing the system, of assimilating the society to its function as a producer/consumer society of technologies.

In other words, within the society, Morin's science translates into a totalitarian socio-political organization. Morin risks exactly the same mishap as Marx. The latter's theory, meant to liberate man and allow him to take his history into his own hands, came during the early development of the technological system (with the structuration of the state and industrialization). And for that reason, it was turned upside down. It produced a dictatorial system that is in no wise a mistake or heresy, but simply the inevitable combination of the technological system and the total theory—the latter ineluctably in the service of technological totalization, or else doomed to wander in the limbo of idealism. A total system has a corresponding total theory—that is what has come about. But it is translated into a total dictatorship. Such is the case when the created entity proposes a theory that is not only total but also *closed*, i.e., claiming to account for everything that is intellectually grasped and explained, but also graspable and explicable—when this theory is not only the reflection of the reality but the solution of the reality. The theory can then produce only the socio-political systematization[1] that will express itself somehow or other in a technological dictatorship. By this I do not mean a technocracy or a political dictatorship like Hitler's or Stalin's: each age has its specific forms.

In the now beginning era of the computer and of the synthesis of the human sciences, there can be no more question of Fascism. It seems marvelously old-fashioned in the Greece of 1970 or the Brazil of 1975. However, the abstract and beneficent technological dictatorship will be far more totalitarian than the preceding ones. All that is needed to develop it is the team of men able to conjoin theory and practice, to conjoin the totalization per se of the system and the construction of the equally totalizing science of man.

When Morin's book came out, many people proclaimed that we had now reached the year one of the science of man; yet this wonderful invention could easily mark the triumph of the technological totality. It is not by an antiscientific, retrograde prejudice, nor by an unreasonable reaction, but as the result of the sociological analysis of the technological system and also the historical experience of the twentieth century that I can declare: The total science of man is the end of man.

Actually, we must not forget that this totalization of technology covers all the elements making up the social body and that gradually all expressions of human life are becoming technological. This means that technology has a double effect on society and human existence. On the one hand, it disintegrates and tends to eliminate bit by bit anything that is not technicizable (this has been brutally felt on the level of merriment, love, suffering, joy, etc.). And it tends to reconstitute a whole of society and human existence *on the basis of* technological totalization. What is being established is no longer the subordination of man to technology, etc., but, far more deeply, a new totality. It is the process that causes such vast malaise in man and such a keen sense of frustration. All the elements of life are bound up with technology (to the extent that technology has become a milieu); and the totalization of technology produces a veritable integration—and a new type at that—of all the human, social, economic, political, and other factors. Hence, this society, this human being, while not becoming technological objects, robots, and so forth, now receive their unity from the totalizing technology. But the latter cannot provide any meaning; that is its great lacuna. The reconstituted totality is devoid of significance.

PART THREE

# The Characteristics of Technological Progress

OBVIOUSLY, we cannot retain the definition of technological[1] progress in terms of its economic application alone. "By technological progress, we mean all the innovations resulting from the application of science and technology to the economic process. . . . The object of these innovations is either to create new products and/or services, and/or to improve those already existing, or to augment the efficiency of economic operations, normally in order to lower their costs." This definition is apparently accepted by Beaune (modern technology expresses itself in the economic domain according to its announced attributes: self-regulation, etc.; what pure science regards as its inferior parts, the economic repercussions, now become the essential factor). But it is so fragmentary a definition and pays so little heed to the immense range of technological applications that one cannot really go along with it.

It is clearly easier to *calculate* a technological stride in the economic sector than elsewhere; but this is the same old problem. To achieve "scientific" precision, one radically denatures the object of study. Economic calculation can take certain advances, certain technologies into account, but only by arbitrarily snipping out whatever is calculable from the technological universality! A very bad scientific method. When I speak of technological progress, I am referring to the totality of the phenomenon, and hence I am not restricting myself to the issue of productiveness.

Hetman devoted a first-class study to technological progress in economic production (see "Le Progrès technique, une illusion comptable?" in *Analyse et prévision*, 1970). He shows, first of all, that technological progress in this area derives in a straight line from analyses of productiveness; that, furthermore, its definition is very uncertain; and that, finally, the evaluations of its importance in the production process are highly variable. He offers an excellent survey of all attempts by economists to explain the notion, influence, and reality of technological progress. Utmost uncertainty prevails. Technological progress is discerned by some observers as a residue (after they define all other factors of productivity), by some in the component of positive data (progress of knowledge, diffusion of knowledge, rationalization, etc.). For some, technological progress is the determining factor in ninety percent of the cases for the growth of output per man work unit (and this, therefore, reduces the importance of capital). For others, technological progress has a negligible influence (something like three percent). Hetman concludes that it is therefore difficult to know what observers are talking about, and that it is well-nigh impossible to do a statistical analysis in this area. He sums up the causes of this situation by saying that in regard to technological progress, we have a basic insufficiency of statistical data; a methodological disarray, due to the absence of any definition of technology; and an adherence to concepts from a theory born in an era whose problematics are not adapted to those of the society of innovation. In other words, when studying technological progress, we are dealing with an intellectual problem of the same kind as the one posed by the social classes: It is impossible to grasp them by the strict application of a statistical method or of any sociological method known to man.

And yet the fact exists: *Eppur si muove!*

# 9

# SELF-AUGMENTATION

BY self-augmentation, I mean the fact that everything occurs *as if* the technological system were growing by an internal, intrinsic force, without *decisive* human intervention. Naturally, this is not to say that man does not intervene or play a part; but rather, that he is caught in a milieu and in a process, which causes all his activities, even those apparently having no voluntary direction, to contribute to technological growth, whether or not he thinks about it, whether or not he wishes it. Self-augmentation signifies that technology represents a center of polarization for all twentieth-century mankind, and that technology feeds on everything that people can want, try, or dream. It transforms human acts into a technological factor; this is not self-creation, but the integration of the most diverse and seemingly most alien factors into the system, for its own benefit.

Self-augmentation thus encompasses two phenomena. On the one hand, technology has reached a point of evolution at which it keeps changing and progressing, with no *decisive* human intervention, by a kind of inner force, which compels it to grow and necessarily entails nonstop development. On the other hand, all people in our time are so passionate about technology, so utterly shaped by it, so assured of its superiority, so engulfed in the technological environment, that they are all, without exception, oriented toward technological progress, all working toward it, no matter what their trade, each individual seeking the best way to use his instrument or perfect a method, a device, etc. Thus, technology progresses thanks to the efforts of all people (except for the nonintegrated nations of the third world and the very tiny number of antitechnological individuals in technological society).

The two phenomena are actually identical. First, man was

assimilated into the technological system, which, of course, develops only by human acts. These acts, however, are so precisely caused, determined, defined, summoned, elicited, that no one escapes and each individual's activity is ultimately integrated. The All and the Individual are identified. Since everybody is working in this direction, it is not the individual's small deed that counts, but rather the anonymous product, which is nothing but technological augmentation. This is self-augmentation because technology induces each person to act in this direction, and the result comes from an addition that no one deliberately, distinctly wanted. Man appears between the two as the necessary—albeit narrowly necessary—factor.

Twenty years ago, when I first pointed out that technology develops by a process I could describe as "self-augmentation," my idea was put down as "mythical exaggeration" and "unfounded artifice." But since then it has been more and more frequently taken up, accepted, and demonstrated. I will cite a few examples:

"Technological progress is virtually self-generating. We must no longer await future scientific discoveries from technology; it is technology itself which causes expansion in new discoveries and new dimensions" (Diebold).

Karl Mannheim shows that technology causes by itself the planning, which extends to vaster and vaster areas of our life and which engenders and exacts technological progress. "We will no longer be capable of progress without planning, even in the cultural domain. . . . There is no asking the question of whether or not we prefer a planned society: we cannot escape it" (*Man and Society in an Age of Reconstruction,* 1967).

"It is thus essentially the discovery of functional synergies that characterizes progress in the development of the technological object. One must then ask if this discovery occurs at one swoop or continuously. As a reorganization of structures intervening in the functioning, it occurs suddenly, but it can pass through multiple successive phases" (Simondon). Once again, Simondon's profound analysis makes what he writes about the technological *object* applicable to *technology* in general.

Likewise, B. de Jouvenel, without mentioning self-augmentation, does point it out: "There is a difference in nature [between our civilization and all others] especially in that efficiency continually progresses: our civilization has a permanent revolution of procedures" (*Arcadie,* 1968).

"It is its own acquired speed that makes technology progress.

And there are two reasons for this. The first is that the traditional industries must be kept up . . . the second is nothing other than the fundamental law of technological civilization: 'Anything that can be done will be done.' This is how progress applies new technologies and creates new industries without seeking to find out whether or not they are desirable" (see Dennis Gabor, *Survivre au futur*).

R. Richta too, incidentally, recognizes the principle of self-augmentation in technology; labeling it "self-development," he links it to the principle of automation. Where the production process remains broken down into independent cycles, automation of systems will only be partial. Where a process of uninterrupted mass production occurs, we have complete automation: Hence, self-augmentation accelerates with the possibilities of automation. However, this self-augmentation, as Richta abundantly demonstrates, rests primarily on a capacity for research, a standby of scientific knowledge, permitting the constant application of more efficient technological solutions. Thus, the development of science and research is far more important in creating and reproducing social productive forces than the extension of direct production. This is Richta's decisive contribution to analyzing the system.

In clarifying this trait of self-augmentation, I do not deny the existence of the celebrated "process of decision." De Jouvenel always insists on decision-making, which he sees at the origin of each technological development ("Situation des sciences sociales aux États-Units" in *Analyse et prévision*, 1968). A decision as such, he holds, is a social act. This statement is true. But it lacks two elements of analysis. First of all, the decision-maker is technicized man, preconditioned by technology. Then, the options are fixed exclusively by the technological field; the decision never bears on anything but the applicational validity of some innovation, which will or will not impose itself according to its technological value, efficiency, and, perhaps, profitability. The decision-making process is, in reality, integrated in the phenomenon of self-augmentation.

Donald A. Schon (*Technology and Change*, 1967) offers a useful analysis of the different stages in the process of technological growth: invention, innovation, diffusion. He underlines a paramount aspect of self-augmentation, namely, that innovation and invention must be taken as facets of a single continuous process rather than as a series of actions coming before or after one another in time. He correctly rejects and refutes the "rational view of invention" (intentional, an intellectual, a goal-oriented process) in favor of a "process" that develops and ramifies incessantly "thoughout the life of any new technology, with no precise beginning or end," and in which "need and technology mutually determine each other." This analysis strikes me as remarkably exact and very different from the simplistic diagrams of the rational and finalist character of technological invention. Very generally, however, writers distinguish between "discovery" (which is more and more abandoned), "invention," and innovation." For some, there is scientific invention and technological innovation. There is no "invention of the radio": there is only innovation by applying a scientific invention and combining previously existing technological elements.

Each technological advance is an innovation resulting from series of convergent inventions.[1] But observers try to distinguish several types of innovations and even (see Russo) the *levels* at which innovation takes place: elementary technologies, technological units, industrial units (from the most simple to the most complex). And they distinguish the *stages* of innovation: essential conception, new processes, the combining of old processes, the components of improvement that was affirmed by the intervention of diffusion. We can then establish the following pattern (Daumas):

(a) essential conception (origin of conception, conditions of its realization, integration into the technological unity);

(b) tests and final adjustments;

(c) innovation (nature and relative importance of the problem to be solved—circumstances of the diffusion of the process, motivations, technological or economic difficulties of application);

(d) developments (improvements, adaptations, economic consequences).

This is the kind of analysis that can bring home what is covered by the general term of innovation.

We must, in sum, realize that technological innovation does not exist per se. It responds to a certain number of *needs* (even though observers are more and more contesting their preexistence: needs depend on the technological object rather than vice versa). It occurs within the dynamics of a certain number of tensions (all kinds, but always relative to time), *in relation to a certain socioeconomic milieu* (favorable or unfavorable to this innovation) *and finally in an overall technological context* which can be receptive or prohibitive. It is the relationship of all the factors that allows concrete understanding of the technological development.

Thus, when considering a technological product, one can always ascertain that it is only a combination of previous elements: there is no invention of television, or radio, or the automobile. The detached parts first appeared on the market and existed; and only on their basis was the final product possible. Some observers even go so far as to discard the very word *innovation* and speak only of "technological change." But this seems rather hazy.

On the other hand, we certainly ought to go along with B. Gille ("Note sur le progrès technique," quoted by Daumas) in distinguishing several types of innovation: compensational, marginal, structural, overall.[2]

We are still left with the question of when, where, and why innovation takes place. The habitual Marxist answer is that innovation occurs in response to a rise in salaries. The employer is interested in replacing expensive manpower with machines. The introduction of new technologies results from higher pay, the effect of which is lower profits. Management must then try to bring down the aggregate of wages by introducing methods that save direct labor (automation of production). But as Beaune points out (*La Technologie*, 1972), "focusing exclusively on higher salaries, such as a certain British and American trade-unionism does, without appreciating the technological element in its own right, is playing capitalism's game." Profit can be replenished only by innovation. Yet we are forced to recognize that this simple explanation does not clear up everything. For, after all, a specific domain does not necessarily have to have "labor-saving innovations" available: The opposite can be proved all too easily![3] In reality, even when concretely examining the phenomena of innovation, we perceive that there is no necessary and generalizable correlation, but only an accidental one.

M. Crozier (*The Stalled Society*) maintains that large-scale organization is an environment favorable to innovation. The latter, he says, is not an individual phenomenon determined by a strict economic rationality, it is a collective system whose success depends on human factors, and in this area, large-scale organization can be superior to the crowd of small producers. And Crozier dwells at length on this collective aspect (both before and after innovation), which corresponds exactly to the idea of self-augmentation. In particular, if innovation depends on a certain individual liberty, it is probably more assured in large-scale organization than in a tiny business. Likewise, a large-scale organization can draw on greater resources to aid innovation. And above all, it can anticipate the possible consequences: "The capacity for innovation grows with the ability to control the unfavorable effects that one might await from innovation."

Thus the growth in size of social and economic units seems to furnish a favorable milieu for innovation. Organizing more and more coworkers is the condition for innovation. Hence, what I wrote in 1950 is now confirmed: Self-augmentation *is* the participation of everyone in the technological work. "The activity and efficiency of the technicians do not stop growing with their number [It is in the numeral growth of the protagonists] that the cause of spectacular achievements may be found. . . . Each technician taken separately is no more gifted . . . than those who preceded him. A hundred men studying the same problem in the same time span obtain greater results than one man devoted to the same work a hundred times longer. Furthermore, the progress of technologies has been its own stimulus. . . . It has continually created more improved means favorable to its own acceleration."[4]

Therefore, only the big firms can meet the conditions of this growth, by coordinating the research of technician teams—so that, as Furia excellently points out, "research is even more concentrated than production." These firms try to appeal more and more to the young, even the untrained, in order to get them to enter the process. Hence, there is really a tendency to integrate *everyone* into research, at least potentially. A teeming of very tiny businesses is not favorable to self-augmentation. The latter requires a certain overlapping of each technological subsystem; technology takes its rate of growth as of a dimension that allows investments, unsuccessful experiments, unprofitable capitals during a certain period. Therefore, it is wrong to think that the concentration of businesses is due to technology but could be challenged, and that technology could be used for deconcentration. The truth is that concentration is not a consequence of, but a *condition* for the development of technology, for the phenomenon of self-augmentation. Thus, French chemistry stagnated so long as it was scattered. When Rhône-Poulenc absorbed Progil and took control of Péchiney-Saint-Gobain, this *brought about* not only economic equilibrium, but the possibility of technological development. The issue is not capitalist competition but the size of a subsystem that must be integrated in order to offer multiple possibilities of action.

Finally, the framework of big business (whether capitalist or socialist) will allow what strikes me as a fundamental aspect of innovation, what I will call *essayisme*—trial and error. Technological innovation seldom results from mathematical reckoning; it continues to function on a level of trial and error. And this seems to quite specifically mark the technological mentality: Technicians test. Anything and everything. And we see what comes of it. It is not curiosity but rather an absence of certainty and deep-rootedness. "Why not this . . . ?" Here we have a general feature of our society. For the sake of innovation, religious, moral, and collective certainties must be done away with. Every individual is left with his experiences—why not do that? And amid thousands of errors, a lasting innovation comes about. But with technological innovation, we see the positive face of trial and error. Further on, we shall see what this means for man engulfed in the technological society.

In contrast, innovation seems limited by a strange phenomenon ascertained by Jouvenel: "The crafts that have progressed the least were those that could have improved the material lot of the majority." So, Teissier du Cos: "The more an industry responds to a basic need, the less it innovates." In other words, technological growth (i.e., innovation) occurs first in the areas of the superfluous, the useless, the gratuitous, the secondary. And this seems to be generalizable. In the period of spontaneity, innovation was applied to things that did not respond to essential needs.

Thus, no innovation is in man's true interest. The obvious things we note today (more innovation for walking on the moon than for feeding people) have *always* been a trait of technological progress. And this confirms the trait of self-augmentation. It actually means that technological growth has taken place in terms of itself and by its own process, and that there has never been a clear human intentionality able to direct it. Man has never chosen to make innovations where they are really needful. They occurred in places where the technological system had in itself its reason for progressing. To be sure, with planning, men now claim to direct innovation; but actually, we realize that all planning is polarized in advance by the growth imperatives of the technological system, which completely ignores real needs (everyone everywhere is always bent on more turnpikes rather than *quality* food). And innovation, on the contrary, thanks to the minute analyses of these past few years, has been integrated into the process of self-augmentation. It is not the marvelous, dazzling sort of innovation that causes growth in this new domain, but rather the ipseity of this growth that defines innovation. The latter is comprised in the mechanism and takes place according to its needs.

An excellent (and involuntary!) example is given in Kaufmann's book on invention (Kaufmann, Fusten, Drevet: *L'Inventique*, 1970). It refers to "creative methods" whose development responds to the needs of the society. Businesses have to keep inventing constantly—every executive, every engineer has to be a discoverer. The mechanisms of discovery can be analyzed, understood, hence reproduced and utilized. This study shows ways to grasp and elicit "intuition," including a climate of play and relaxation, recourse to "nonexperts" (indispensable catalysts!), the process of bisociation (bringing together two ideas or two technologies than can combine), "breaking down," playing with words, superimposing ideas and analogies, etc. The most complex combinatory methods are analyzed: Molès's matrices of discovery, Zwicky's morphological research, etc.

All this perfectly demonstrates the integration of inventiveness in the technological system—invention is no longer the affair of a man who, left to the devices of his genius, discovers within his particular orientation the innovation that excites him. Invention now results from a set of procedures and manipulations, and it comes about by a sort of collective mobilization (experts and nonexperts), inevitably on a very low level—i.e., it is always a product inherent in the logic of previous growth. It cannot escape it. Hence, innovation is utterly domesticated. There is no conflict at all between innovation as a triumphant act of the individual and the blind self-augmentation of a system; the system has perfectly assimilated, gained control of, and integrated the innovation. There is no growth unless there are innovations, but these result more and more from applying technologies to technological areas that correspond exactly to the necessity of self-augmentation—without our being able to discern the least independent, intractable, or forensic factor.

Of course, this self-augmentation does not signify a lack of very deliberate and voluntary reflection of research on this growth. The remarkable "Post Apollo Program—directions for the future" is quite specific in this regard. This is the programming of research for continuing the NASA work after the political "slam on the brakes" (February 1970). The report selects the basic choices for doing research and pursuing operations. It is thus a very explicit effort, such as is furnished, incidentally, in many sectors of the technological world. And yet, even here, one can speak of self-augmentation because this project is situated within the technological system, which involves that growth. Everything in this report is open to question, everything is reconsidered, except the obviousness of continuation and progression. The authors of the report were moved by the need to pursue this development, hence they took part in a self-augmentation that made this development both obvious and necessary. The only thing that had to be achieved was research along the most judicious road, the choice of polyvalent vehicles, etc. All these things are issues raised only in terms of a self-augmentation of the system.

Massenet perfectly expresses this self-conditioned technological augmentation: "Do we want these technological changes for themselves? Obviously not, unless we fall back upon a collective unconscious. We want their effects, we measure the efficiency of social devices by quantitative progress and perhaps tomorrow a qualitative progress of our living standard. Hence, technological progress, which only a minority of researchers take upon themselves, . . . is only implicitly desired by the collective as the means obliged by actual progress. Technicity is no longer an adventure but a necessity" ("Du changement technique" in *Analyse et prévision*, 1971, XI, p. 345).

And yet, one of the conditions of self-augmentation, albeit not absolutely indispensable, is government intervention. The latter is obvious in socialist economy, but less certain in capitalist economy. Still, a certain stimulus and coordination are nonnegligible factors; although there is no reason in the world to believe that they reintroduce an element of intention and decision into technological growth. Of course, "research and development" (R and D) is a voluntary position and a political decision; hence, people thought that the state (as a substitute for man) was directing. But in fact, the state is first conditioned by technology, and the decisions concerning research and development are purely and simply sparked by the technological necessity. Technological growth leads to a point at which the body social can no longer refrain from establishing a research-and-development organism. Thus, government intervention strikes me as being situated *inside* the phenomenon of self-augmentation (like technical education) and not as forming a precondition. Intervention then *becomes* a condition during further self-augmentation.

And this poses the fundamental problem of research and development. R and D is the whole set of activities from basic research to the final touches on new methods, procedures, and prototypes in all domains. Classical R and D is now being joined by the formula T and E: the "testing and engineering" of the product by "engineers" in the broad sense. R and D is included in the ensemble of the scientific policy, which requires setting up objectives, allocating and distributing subsidies, administering programs and researchers, interacting with other economic and social areas, and, finally, evaluating the results. As was emphasized in a report by the Organization for Economic Cooperation and Development, it also envisages the way in which science affects politics and technological discoveries influence scientific decisions. For R and D is closely related to politics, it is called upon to pursue objectives that are first posed by the state; but actually, the political organizations have very little power or control over it. R and D was forcefully developed by the United States because of wars, and three sectors were differentiated: the military program, university research (financed by the government but free in its directions), and industrial research (financed largely by corporations). R and D profited from an extraordinary growth in funding between 1948 and 1967 (2.4% of the federal budget in 1948, 5.8% in 1957, 10% in 1962, 12.6% in 1965). And then came the crisis toward 1966: first, stagnation; then, a decline of resources (even in absolute figures), and then a challenge to the objectives of the scientific policy and the "military-industrial-technological complex."

R and D was the big thing in the United States after World War II and in Europe ten years later. It was actually a concentration of forces, funds, and minds on scientific—really technological—research, the ultimate goal being development (economic and, in these circumstances, capitalist). In 1946, the R and D outlay in the United States was 300 million dollars; by 1971, a peak year, it reached 25 billion. This was 3.5% of the gross national product (as against 1.68% in France). The United States also had a tendency toward curbing once it realized that indisputable technological growth did not necessarily spell economic growth. The figures are quite clear: Great Britain earmarks 2.5% of its GNP on research and development, while the per capita income went up only 2.2% annually from 1960 to 1970. And Japan, at the head of world growth, devotes 1.5% of its GNP to research and development.

In the United States, the yield in economic productivity for the enormous sums spent on research is tiny now that a certain stagnation is occurring; but research is heading more toward the "qualitative" and toward solving problems like pollution, etc. Hence, if there are misgivings about the economic result, there can be none about the technological results. But this does not interest countries like France, where R and D is still completely tied to industrial policies (e.g., the Ortoli Declaration, December 1969).

## SELF-AUGMENTATION

Science and knowledge are thought of more and more as instrumental goods, as means to an end.[5] Of course, basic research is still carried on, but it is not the center of interest, although theoretically and intellectually it should be. In reality, applied—i.e., industrial—research, on the one hand, and development, on the other hand, are the chief focus now. And they have led to an amalgam of all *three* in research and development—which also explains the present crisis of this ensemble. People are questioning not only the economic yield but also the significance—the researcher asking himself: What am I doing? What use will it serve?

People therefore assume that man is still in control of the situation, that he decides to launch into research, that he grants funds, and that when he asks himself the above questions, everything stops. Hence, there is no self-augmentation of technology! This is anything but the truth. I indicated earlier that American technology is directed toward ways of cleaning up and reconstituting the environment, yet pollution does not stop. The difficulty here is the *social* change that such a technological reorientation involves. Yet after two or three years of qualms, the technological growth is not challenged. I would even say vice versa. It is the imperative of technological progress due to self-augmentation that has brought a reorientation of R and D and that demands socioeconomic adaptation. Far from being determined, technological growth is the determining imperative—blindly ineluctable. This is confirmed by interesting declarations made by J. P. Beraud, the director of France's National Agency for Valorization and Research (*Le Monde*, February 1972). His declarations were taken up again by the Minister of Industrial and Scientific Development (July 1973). Research is not the privilege of a few specialized individuals, "it is a permanent necessity, to which everyone must be open. . . . It is an activity opened upon the outer world, our daily individual or collective needs. . . . We even must integrate the researchers pyschologically and socially into our society." (Hence, make them adjust in such a way that they will not ask any paralyzing questions! That is the service imperative coming from self-augmentation.)

In reality, the ensemble of funds, institutions, and organizations of R and D is not the autonomous factor determining technological progress, it is the instrument the technological system employs for obeying its own law of self-augmentation. The latter is *mediated* by R and D. The people involved are the agents of this self-augmentation. We must repeat that there is no anthropomorphism in such formulations. I am not saying that there is some kind of omnipotent divinity with the clear and deliberate intention of fabricating R and D in terms of his imperatives. Nothing of the sort. But we can take the comparison of the market in liberal economy. Nobody wants to create the market. It results from the combination of multiple supplies and demands, apparently incoherent, of particularized policies of independent businesses, and of spontaneous needs, etc. Yet this disparate ensemble constitutes a reality that obeys its own laws. And, once the market exists, it is given a certain number of mediating and regulating organisms. That is exactly the level on which we find R and D. It actually is subject to the stimuli or restraints due to the (irregular) phenomenon of the self-augmentation of technology. Like Leprince-Ringuet ("Concluding Lecture at the Collège de France," May 1972), we might have been anxiety-stricken by the budget cuts for space and nuclear research. "What, then," he asks, "will be the major objectives of applied research tomorrow? How are we to utilize the enormous present-day technological potential that has been liberated?" Have no fear. When technological growth is halted in one domain, the process of self-augmentation causes a change in the field of application. There is, inevitably, a delay, which may be regarded as a stabilization or a crisis; but in reality, self-augmentation resumes in an area where it is possible.

Thus, everything derives from the situation of the technological phenomenon in the overall society. A very fine study on self-augmentation was penned by Marie Moscovici ("La Recherche scientifique dans l'industrie," *Analyse et prévision*, 1966). The author particularly goes into the phenomenon of nationalizing research, which becomes a sort of joint program, an overall ideology, legitimized a priori by the body social as a whole. Here we have the overlapping between autonomy/legitimation and self-augmentation. We actually have to realize that each characteristic of the system must be considered in correlation with the others. From this perspective, research becomes a kind of spontaneous activity of the entire body social. The research laboratory, which does exist, of course, is a particular organization whose goal is to produce inventions. But it can exist as such only on the basis of self-augmentation as a previous approval. Inventing is now administered, the scientist and the research technician have, first of all, a social role (which, the better they are integrated, the better they perform), and they are now passing from aleatory creativity to induced creativity.

## SELF-AUGMENTATION

Self-augmentation rests on the a priori legitimation of technology in consciousness. A problem we shall come back to later on. Habermas rightfully stresses that this is matched by the ideologies "which replace the traditional legitimations of rule while presenting themselves by citing modern science as their authority and justifying themselves as a critique of ideology." But the fact that technology has thus invaded the precinct of ideology does not mean that it can be boiled down to that!

Naturally, in this aspect of the technological domain, one must also pay heed to the obsessional and polarizing force of vocabulary. Words are emotionally charged by the general context of the society. Thus, from the fifth to the thirteenth century, it was the theological words that sparked actions and reflections. In our society, it is the political lexicon; but serious action is prompted by the beacon words of the technological world. Terms like *planning, productivity, forecasting, computer processing, management* pop up, and the intellectual forces promptly change bearings according to these crystallization points. There is no need to *incite* individuals to do any forecasting, to prepare for careers in computer processing, or to organize along principles of management. Research and application take place of their own accord. And to the precise extent that many people are attracted to progress, it goes on without our wanting, seeking, or knowing it. These words are put in the limelight because they link economic interest to the technological preoccupation. It is not a matter of fashion, but of polarizing attention, to the very extent that anyone drawn by such a word basks in the general atmosphere of the technological society and is sensitized to anything that may develop.

\* \* \*

We have just seen that self-augmentation, resulting from intrinsic features of technology, implies the existence of certain conditions of possibility. We have to think of this exactly as, at the start of technological development, there had to be a set of ideological, economic, scientific, and social conditions that were favorable and united. J. Boli-Bennet shows, for instance, that the desacralization of means is a necessary precondition for technology to develop, to the extent that this is possible only if one can ask the question about the efficiency of the means and not about its conformity to the sacred. Likewise, it is obvious that the success of a certain number of technologies, concerning certain aspects of a culture, increases the propensity of this social group to apply technology to other aspects of the culture. There is a necessary previous acceptance of new technologies.[6]

This, incidentally, is what makes the application of a technology possible experimentally so that there may be a kind of "testing bench." As a rule, a technology undergoes long laboratory testing before it is handed over to the public (marketed, if in a capitalist regime). But this condition is hard to meet for an all-inclusive technology, a technological ensemble, because it involves a huge number of people or a society. Yet, we realize that self-augmentation occurs only if there can be experimenting. That is why wars are so useful within this framework: at such times, all experiments are possible. But it is wrong to think that the Spanish Civil War or the war in Vietnam were mere "testing benches for future wars." Of course, there are the directly military technologies, but they are relatively secondary. All the others are the important ones; they are momentarily applied in war to relieve us of worrying about the disastrous or exorbitant results of a particular technology. War is the field of experimenting necessary for self-augmentation, because it authorizes any audacity, any technology, any *in vivo* work, which is irreplaceable.[7]

We must point out other indispensable factors in this autonomous progression. One is the existence of technical education. Obviously, if technology has an intrinsic tendency to grow in that manner, it requires a "matter-of-course" participation by people. We shall see further down how each person is integrated into technology; but technicians are needed to assure this progress. Professions are getting more and more technological. If you want to learn a trade, you have to know a technology; but this necessity felt by man causes a reciprocal effect: the more people are trained for technology, the more deeply they become participants in its rise. Technical training is not only career training, but, involuntarily, a training to take part in technological growth: not by transmitting knowledge, but by delimiting a field of interests and inducing an unconditional adherence. In these circumstances, the phenomenon of self-augmentation occurs through the participation of all people. Each technological invention *causes* other inventions in other areas. There is no halt. In a civilization, technological progress is never questioned. It is irreversible. It cannot be annulled, it keeps going accumulatively, never doubling back. I will not return to this.[8]

Progression is like counting. There is no reason to stop at any number, any technological level. One can always add a number. One can endlessly add some improvement resulting from the application of technology itself. Of course, I mean this in regard to the whole of the technological system and not just one particular technology, which, obviously *can* be stopped for a certain period. Technologies summon one another.

But this can happen under different aspects, both positive and negative. On the one hand, each technology brings its practice, its efficiency to the great ensemble, contributing to all technologies through the unicity of the system. This is the most obvious aspect. On the other hand, one technology appeals to other technologies because it can advance only if certain known problems are solved, if new materials and new instruments are created. Technicians ask around. Technology thus raises a positive problem and technology responds to it. Naturally, when I say technology "appeals," or "responds," this is an anthropologism that may appear naive, but is not. For if technicians pose the problems and other technicians respond, they are so exclusively determined by their role and by their competence that they are actually just simple mouthpieces.

In this self-augmentation triggered by the needs that technology creates for itself, we must place, say, the extraordinary research in new materials. A technology can now develop only by using materials that do not exist in a natural state. The material having a specific quality, determined by the use that a technology wishes to make of it, *has* to be invented. The idea, the qualities of the material are given in advance. And at the present, the lack of adequate materials is what slows down a very large number of technologies; therefore, we may say that now the research in new materials has the highest priority, is the chief concern, and is also most rapidly extending.[9] There is self-augmentation because technology defines its own needs for itself and satisfies them itself. But the problems raised by technology are not always just "positive," there are also the questions of necessity. A new invention comes not for the sake of progress, but in response to an unexpected and difficult situation brought on by technology itself; although, at this point, we cannot yet speak of the necessary compensations.

Self-augmentation can be engendered, when, say, technology economizes on manpower: automation, for instance, presupposes a transfer of workers from one occupation to another. But the great discovery was that the level of employment can be maintained wherever we like by adjusting the demand: "If there is not enough work in automobile manufacturing, we can take care of that by going to the moon" (Keyfitz). This is remarkable. Any release of manpower, if unemployment is to be avoided, is an urgent appeal for technological growth in another domain, which, for a while, will absorb this manpower, until, pushed to an extreme, this progress in turn will render that same manpower useless.

But beyond that, and this is the last term, self-augmentation occurs to the extent that technology has harmful effects which only technology itself can cope with. We have already sought out the difference between the problems that technology can resolve and those for which it is impotent.

The great mechanism of production is self-augmentation; this is actually the emergence of problems, dangers, and difficulties. One can present them in a very simple way. Any technological intervention (simply by putting us on the level of operation) gives rise to problems and difficulties—and we very quickly realize that only a technological response is useful or effective. Hence, technology nourishes itself with its own failures. "Our progress is a complex of solving problems and creating problems" (de Jouvenel). Thus formulated, it is a banality. But the new factor is that by being integrated into the technological system, each failure might challenge everything. The problems are not posed *by* man, they are posed *to* him by technology itself, and he is not free to put off their solution till tomorrow. It is a matter "of life and death" each time.

The absence of a choice in regard to problems is, strictly speaking, self-augmentation. When a technology functions, it causes disturbances; they must be dealt with. The "must" determines self-augmentation. The raison d'être of a greater and greater number of technologies is simply to respond to difficulties: "Discarded wrappings force us to build factories for burning garbage. The congestion at the center of Paris has led to building Sarcelles and highways. The general pollution has forced the Japanese to buy oxygen and drink mineral water."[10] Nobody wants it, but that's the way it is! It is not only through dangers or pollution that technology engenders itself; it sometimes directly asks itself questions. A fine example is offered in G. Bertrand's *Enigma* (1973): the creation of a machine for encoding (military) texts and the gradual perfection of the decoding technologies through the comprehension of the machine itself.

At bottom, it is the old argument between "the breastplate and the projectile." And in this indefinite competition, we see the process of self-augmentation, for every obstacle presented by the breastplate is an obvious and indispensable provocation to find a more powerful projectile, and vice versa. There is no human "participation" here; deliberation is wiped out by the crushing presence of technology. We would have to reach a peak of *collective spiritual* independence to challenge this process, and this gets all the more improbable and difficult as technology *creates* inevitable situations in which there is no other solution than to keep advancing. Once pesticides are used, we cannot go back, because the insects, having adapted, will be worse than ever. Once we have chemical fertilizers, we can select "miracle" species of rice or wheat (as permitted by the Green Revolution), but growing them *demands* the use of chemical fertilizers, and so on.

Thus, Closets says, "Only city planning will save the cities, only the fuel cell will clean up the atmosphere, only contraception will end population growth, only chemistry will help us to conquer hunger, only computer processing will solve the problems of permanent training. . . ." Of course. In other words, technology raises problems, brings difficulties, and we need more technology, always more and more, to solve them. Nothing but self-generation.

This is quite characteristic of the garbage problem. We must absolutely multiply the technologies for disposing of waste and making up for any damage. It is not enough to build automobiles, we also have to destroy them, compress them, reduce them to recyclable "pulfer." We build factories for that (the one in Athis-Mons, France, can handle 75,000 tons of cars every year). But none of this is enough. We have to coordinate the activities of eliminating old cars. This task can no longer be left to an inadequate individual initiative. We have to forge a concerted policy, create an administration, a second technological level for organizing and systematizing the removal of technological waste. However, the automobile is one case in a hundred. If we do not want to perish under the refuse,[11] we have to devote a growing part of technological activity to this problem: a suction system through the sewer network (as used in Sweden), incineration, etc. There is a self-augmentation of technology, for we cannot keep using the old methods of gathering and dumping. And technology raises the issue in the first place, for the greater increase of garbage is due to the packaging that has been perfected. However, beyond this impulse that technology gives itself by demands that have to be met and by difficulties that have to be overcome, many other factors operate in the same direction.

Certain factors operate for the very reason that human groups take part. And here is a very simple and frequent concrete example. A task seems necessary from an economic, a social, and other viewpoints. Technologies are developed in response—and, of course, a body of professionals is established to apply them. Eventually, the objective is reached. *But*, the body of professionals still exists; there can be no question of discharging them. The stock of new equipment is installed; there can be no question of not using it. We then keep functioning by applying technologies and activities to useless domains, to superfluous extensions. For instance, building useful roads demands administrations, workers, better and better materials; and when the network is adequate, we still keep building roads because we cannot stop the technological machine that has been put into place.

However, at the other end of the scale, very general elements enter public opinion, political life, and they link up to produce the same effect. Good examples of self-augmentation based on the obvious necessity of technological progress are supplied by Closets: "Once an avenue of research opens, dozens of teams are engulfed in it." He shows how competition, whether between nations or between firms, inevitably brings on a technological growth that nobody wants as such. This growth is the only way of evincing the superiority of individuals or groups.

To conclude this point, I could cite the remarkable study done by Bela Gold ("L'Entreprise et la génèse de l'innovation," in *Analyse et prévision*, 1973). This study entirely confirms my views on self-augmentation. Gold does a thorough analysis of all factors leading toward technological growth, and he always winds up with a skeptical attitude, showing that we misunderstand the system of technological progression so long as we attribute it to clear decisions. Furthermore, he says: "The great strides forward are nothing but the accumulated results of small,gradual improvements"—and anonymous ones, I must add!

\* \* \*

And that brings us to the consequences of self-augmentation. There is, however, a reciprocity of the phenomenon. Self-augmentation occurs because everything functions by combinations of thousands of small discoveries, perfecting the ensemble; and that is also its consequence. Progression too results from this reality of the system. The repercussions are vast. The eminently technological character of all work allows just about anyone to advance the work;

for technology progresses far less by huge, brilliant, and spectacular inventions, than by thousands of small improvements that anyone can contribute, provided he knows "his" technological sector well. One need not be intelligent or educated to make technology progress. Any average student or diligent professional always lends progress a hand—at best, progress takes place through research by thousands of people on each issue; but the quality of these researchers is ultimately insignificant. The important thing is that they keep experimenting on a problem indefinitely until all possible hypotheses and combinations are exhausted. They are bound to obtain a result, provided they have the necessary material, are within a total structure, and obey a rigorous and complete system of research. In these conditions, anybody can do it. And the thousands of small discoveries occurring throughout the world ultimately add up to a technological step forward that will be deemed extraordinary at a given moment. But this also explains the perfectly interchangeable character of these technicians. They can proceed anywhere so long as the resources are available to them.

To the extent that technological progress depends on its own structure, an individual's qualification is less urgent. He has to be both far more competent in his specialty and far less capable of reflection. "The more factors there are, the easier it is to combine them, and the clearer the urgency of any advance—the more obvious the advance itself, and the less human autonomy can be expressed. Actually, a human being must always be involved. But anyone can wind up doing it so long as he is trained right for this game. It is now man in his most common, most inferior reality who can act, and not with anything superior or particular about him, since the qualities demanded by technology for its evolution are acquired qualities of a technological nature, and not a particular intelligence."

In this decisive evolution—of technology toward its constitution as a system and toward the gradual formation of the trait of self-augmentation—man does not intervene. He does not seek to make a technological system, he does not move toward an autonomy of technology. It is here that a new spontaneity occurs; it is here that we must look for the specific, independent motion of technology, and not in an "uprising of the robots" or a "creative autonomy of the machine." In this sense one may speak of a *reality* of technology, with its body—its particular entity, its life, fairly independent of our decision-making. For our decisions are either political, hence with no purchase on the technological fact, or microtechnological, hence entering the general motion of growth. The technician's specialization is thus an essential factor of self-augmentation. But, as always here, it is both a factor and a consequence.

Everyone acts in his particular domain, each individual advances a gesture, a small tool, a fragment of a machine . . . All the questions dealt with, no matter how delicate, are always specific.

Everyone doggedly tries to find solutions to very precise, very concrete problems, or to develop efficiency in a determined area. No one has a view of the whole, no one can really direct the technological system; and both scientific and technological progression occur as an indirect consequence. There is, moreover, far less of a *will* to invent, to innovate, than the pursuit of a general movement in which everyone is caught; there is a general orientation of this civilization; there is the exercise of the professional function; there are the possibilities offered by the new equipment (material or mental), which we cannot help using. Then, obviously and inevitably, a technological advance occurs, indefinitely joining the others. And the phenomenon will be alike everywhere. Technicians work with the same equipment everywhere, coping with the same problems, obeying the same impulses; technological progress tends to occur everywhere at more or less the same time. Of course, I am referring only to the countries that have both sufficient technological equipment, a certain economic level, and the technological passion. Given those things, the "discoveries," the "innovations" can emerge at several different points, and only months apart.

That is why we should not place too much credence in espionage affairs, with agencies ferreting out scientific "secrets" (normally *technological* secrets) that nations steal from one another. There is not much substance to that. Any "advanced" country is capable of doing by itself what any other has done. The nineteenth century already knew that the "great inventions" (technological) could be claimed by lots of countries. Each nation has an official truth on the invention of movies, the telephone, the radio, the automobile. Today, the identity of the technological route leads to identical inventions everywhere because they are made with the same resources and respond to the same needs. No government can make a decisive advance in any field, all states will quickly be at the same point. This is evident in astronautical research: the United States and the Soviet Union alternately take the lead or soon catch up.

However, it may be more difficult to carry things out: realizations depend on resources. For after a discovery or invention, its realiza-

SELF-AUGMENTATION										229

tion demands huge investments, which are not always possible. Nonetheless, we are now faced with the problem of the perhaps decisive technological advance of the United States thanks to the computer system, with other countries having "missed the boat."

This advance can spell political supremacy. Yet, on the technological level, the United States is forced to put other nations in a situation of progress, without which its own development would ultimately be useless. For self-augmentation brings solidarity between centers of technological advancement.

Finally, we may note this last consequence: the thrust of technological growth toward the concentration of businesses. We have already seen that only businesses of a certain size are able to do research.

Now research is held to be both fundamental and truly necessary for companies: "The great corporation [*must*] be able to attain the *critical mass* on the basis of which its research budgets are efficient."[12]

Technology's type of growth demands our furnishing it with possibilities of its own realization. In this regard, the research paper of the Philips Society (at Eindhoven, October 1969) is quite characteristic. It reveals that self-augmentation functions mainly in the vast, but unspectacular sectors; and also that self-augmentation occurs chiefly through accelerated communication between parcellary research areas. Philips comprises numerous companies in numerous countries, research centers scattered throughout Europe. There is steady communication among them through the center at Eindhoven, but also with research centers that are not part of the Philips network. Intercommunication accelerates self-augmentation. And we find a new example of reciprocity here—which is an effect of this feature of technology and at the same time a condition of its reality.

However, the mechanism of spontaneous progression that we are describing cannot operate fast enough. The present trend is to cut down the delay between invention and technological application. It is toward this end that new organisms are created, pieces that will become essential to the technological system. The relation between researchers (of fundamental research), on one side, and engineers and technicians on the other, is quite certain and direct in the United States. The economic and psychological climate likewise assures contacts, and the diffusion of innovation runs into few obstacles.

This is not true everywhere. In France, an institutional or

psychological gap sometimes exists between engineers and researchers. This circumstance has led to forming the European Economic Development (a private organism created in 1964) and the National Agency for the Valorization of Research (a state agency created in 1968). The goal of these bodies is essentially to discover the holders of new ideas and help them toward industrial applications. Canvassing is done in any university, any laboratory where a new idea, an invention appears. In some cases, the idea must already be "developed"; in others, it is caught at birth in view of its interest and its technological or industrial future. Next, the discoveries are plucked out and the means of application are given.

These organisms, which are multiplying, do not contradict what we call "self-augmentation"; they are an aspect of it. They are meant to speed up the process of growth; and also, they bear witness that the technological system, engaged in the irreversible necessity of this growth, produces the necessary institutions to assure the growth. This is a new element of what is actually self-augmentation. And it is obviously in this area that government intervention may be required. Robert W. Prehoda (*The Future and Technological Forecasting*, 1966) shows that the liberal regime and the nationalized regime both have their advantages. At bottom, he is saying that in a liberal regime, the spirit of intervention is more active, but innovation and diffusion (hence, the passage to application) are "chancier," while the opposite situation prevails in the Soviet Union, for instance. But the goal is to understand the process of research and diffusion. At that moment, a true technological programming is possible, conceived as a voluntary combination of technology and economy. When this programming is done, we will be able to say that the phase of self-augmentation is concluded. And yet, I do not believe it. For what we will have will be the ensemble of resources and the process of stages.

However, both the polarization of all forces and the motor energy of the system will remain quite outside this programming. Nevertheless (as Prehoda clearly points out), the programming, which is itself a technology, will be able to serve a capitalist as well as a communist society, a democratic as well as a totalitarian state.

\* \* \*

"Thus technology is gradually organizing itself as a closed world" (*The Technological Society*). It utilizes what the mass of people does not know. It even rests on human ignorance. Man no longer has to keep abreast of civilization in order to use technological instruments (and participate in their functioning). No technician dominates the ensemble anymore. What connects the parcellary notions of men and their incoherence, what coordinates and rationalizes, is no longer man, but the internal laws of technology. No longer does the hand grasp the cluster of means, or the brain synthesize the causes. Only the intrinsic unicity of technology ensures coherence between resources and human actions. Technology reigns, a blind force that is more clear-sighted than the highest human intelligence.

Self-augmentation gives technology a strange barrenness. Technology always resembles itself and never resembles anything else. Whatever domain it applies to, whether man or God, it is technology and it undergoes no altering of its motion, which is itself technology's being and essence. For technology is the only place where form and being are identical. It is only form, but everything is molded by it. And here it assumes intrinsic features that make it a being apart. A very sharp border runs around it. There is that which is technology, and there is everything else which is not technology. Anything entering this form is compelled to adopt its features. Technology alters anything that touches it, and is itself insensible to contamination. There is nothing else in nature or in social or human life that may be compared to technology. Hybrid but not sterile, even capable of generating itself, technology draws its own limits and shapes its own image.

Whatever adaptations nature or circumstances demand of it, technology remains exactly identical, in both its traits and its course. On the contrary, any difficulty seems to oblige it to become nothing else, but rather more of itself. Everything it assimilates reinforces its characteristics. There is no hope of seeing it transformed into a subtle and graceful creature, for it is neither Caliban nor Ariel; instead, it has managed to take both Ariel and Caliban into the unconditional circles of its universal method.

# 10

# AUTOMATISM

ACCORDING to a pertinent analysis by Simondon, the automatism of machines is not their perfection point but, on the contrary, a fairly low degree of technicity; the true perfection of machines is that their functioning contains a margin of indetermination. We therefore have to have a precise concept of automatism in technological progress. The latter, as we have seen, does not operate in a repetitive fashion, but rather by absorbing new areas, which become technicized. Hence, there is no comparison *on* this point between the machine and the technological system. The system's automatism is not that of automation (and that is why, as we have seen, the technological system is not a mere addition of machines or a megamachine). The system's automatism is the application of technologies according to choices that are induced by previous technologies and that can be shunted and diverted only with great difficulty. Hence, this automatism has a large measure of indetermination. In each new situation, for each new area, the technologies combine in such a way that *as a result*, and independent of human decision, a certain technology (new or old) is applied, a certain solution is contributed. At the start, however, nothing seems definite in advance. There is no progression according to a computer program. There is a situation that seems fluid at the outset; but actually, it eludes man, and it is structured according to the workings of technologies in a manner that, to be satisfactory, must become automatic.

But that is why, too, there are always several technological possibilities at the start. There is even a choice to be made. Automatism does not alienate the choice *at the start;* it sifts out those effectuated choices that meet the technological imperative and those that do not. We know, for instance, the mistakes made in using atomic energy. When it came to opting for enriched uranium, heavy water, etc., America chose enriched uranium. France and Great Britain chose natural uranium (as dictated by the desire to build a plutonium bomb), with each of these "channels" presenting numerous variants, among which the choice was not obvious. And according to what we indicated earlier, they tried everything . . . Finally, after a lot of testing and spending, when they at last managed to produce electricity with atomic energy, they had to acknowledge that the only usable formula was that of enriched uranium. The same holds for the famous story of the long-range variable-geometry supersonic aircraft in the United States. After spending millions of dollars on the project, they abandoned it.

In other words, when a new technology appears, there is no single and obvious decision; the choice is not "to do or not to do," as Closets accurately points out. The choice is among several possibilities, and, generally, the person who obeys exclusively technological reasons (without bringing in politics, "national" motives, as was often the case in France) will ultimately make the best choice. But this choice is actually imposed by the technological result. Little by little in the experimenting, with no one having to make a real choice, technology crystallizes, becoming obvious at a certain moment in the process.

Everything takes place as if the technological phenomenon contained some force of progression that makes it move independently of any outside interference, of any human decision (a point treated differently in *The Technological Society*). The technological phenomenon chooses itself by its own route. It obeys a certain number of automatisms. But we have said, "Everything takes place as if . . ." It is not our aim to formulate a theory of a sort of dynamism, a mystique of the progression of a new being. We do not intend to relapse into the original conception of the Laws of Nature or the Laws of Society. Nevertheless, a precise examination of the facts of technological progress leads us to conclude that human decision, choices, hopes, and fears have almost no influence on this development.

However, in the previous chapter, we saw that if man produces the self-augmentation of technology (which could not generate itself, of course), he does so by assuming only an occasional and not a creative role. He cannot help but produce this augmentation; he is conditioned, determined, destined, adjusted, and preformed for it. Technological automatism does not cover the totality of the phenomena, but in the sense that we may say that an automobile is automatic, i.e., that certain operations occur that do not stem from human intervention. This automatism bears upon the technological *direction*, the *choice* among technologies, *the adaptation of the milieu* to technology, and the *elimination of nontechnological activities* in favor of others. All this happens without man's thinking about it or wanting it; and if he did want it, he could not change the obviousness of the choices. For ultimately (and we must remember this for each sector), it is man, who formally and apparently chooses (e.g., one technology over another). But the choice, as we shall demonstrate, is vitiated at the base, for he could not make any other choice.

\* \* \*

The technological direction is decided by itself. The problem is complex. On the one hand, the disparate growths of the technologies must be taken into account (to be studied later on). On the other hand, two different elements must be combined: the growth of technologies in all possible directions and the establishment of a line of growth. Normally, technology develops in all directions. In any domain, each objective, each difficulty, problem, effort, obstacle will trigger research, so that technology proliferates at a growing speed. And this proliferation seems to occur with no choice, with no preference for an aspect. Anything that can possibly be done is done by man. This growth takes place in terms of possibilities not options: it is now possible to perform a certain operation, ergo, we perform it. And this possibility is not only that of what has already been acquired but of an evaluation of what will soon be possible: i.e., we not only use what is now usable but we also evaluate, according to what we have in hand, what is immediately realizable as a new technological stride to create a new instrument. Given this, we can assert that, without exception, "every technological apparatus, when discovered or about to be discovered, is (or will be) necessarily useful. At no time does man forgo using a technological apparatus."

Anything that can be done must be done: this is once again the fundamental law of automatism. Rorvik marvelously presents this image of the limited "technician" who sees only the technological feat and who, ignoring all the effects on man and society, doggedly sticks to that principle. Historically, it is very rare to find man deliberately renouncing the use of a technological possibility. We know the United States gave up the supersonic passenger plane. That was certainly the case. But technology must adapt each time to the most advanced, most rapid, most efficient model. In 1950, I pointed out the influence of container ships. At the time, there were only isolated cases, and maritime shipping was obviously not affected; but with the advantages of speed, ease, etc., it could not help being affected. Meanwhile, all the maritime and harbor technologies have had to adapt by a veritable automatism to this new shipping technology. It is hard to picture what this represents when we say it like that: e.g., the terminal container of Port Elizabeth in 1968 was designed to load and unload two containers at once, vertical and horizontal handling; this requires a complex of machines and buildings covering twenty-one hectares, a parking lot for 3,500 cars, and an eight-hectare area for storing the big containers!

Conversely, we feel the need for this automatic adapting to peak technology when an obstacle crops up. It was very odd to note the scandal blocking the first color TV channel in France during 1970 because of too many "old" receiving sets. There was no technological difficulty for this "stride" being foisted upon us. It was simply that consumers still had their old sets (819 lines, whereas color TV has 625 lines: another fine example of automatism. France was the only country to adopt 819 lines in 1947; she now had to abandon this choice in order to conform to the common standard and advance to color!). The customer *must* go along with technological progress; he was not free to keep his old set. Soon, color would be forced upon him—there would be no more telecasting in 819 lines—he would be choosing in full liberty. All obstacles must yield to the technological possiblity. Such is the principle of automatism.

This goes back to the autonomy of technology. In the name of what will man do without?[1] Naturally, we can say that it is man who decides. But technological growth has manufactured an ideology for him, a morality, and a mystique, which rigorously and exclusively impel his choices toward this growth. Anything is better than not utilizing what is technologically possible. We know the definite risk that humanity is made to run by the growth of bacteriological, chemical, and nuclear weapons, as well as by the general pollution of air and water, the domestic and agricultural use of countless chemical products (and no doubt the research in the chemically caused changes in the living being). But none of this matters; we must, above all, use what technology puts in our hands. The determining factor is the technological passion; everything else is merely a rationale and ideology for hiding the reality: especially, the "national necessity," the "armaments race," the "necessity to have revolution," etc. These are superimposed ideologies. It is wrong to think that national defense pushes researchers to operate in this direction. It is wrong to think that technological progress is diverted from what it is by such elements. The very oposite is true. Man first obeys technology and then gives himself ideological justifications that allow him to have, in everyone's eyes, a reason accessible to the passions and, above all, to assume the appearance of freedom (if I jump into technological progress it's because I want to, I'm working in this direction because I believe in my country, or in the proletariat, and so on). It is wrong to think that any grossly pecuniary interest, the drive for profit, leads the nasty capitalists to use technology. We have to recall once again that the use of technology is the same and the threats to mankind just as great in socialist countries.

Galbraith has a wonderful analysis showing that now it is not the quest for profit that is determining but the motion of the techno-structure: a technological system that functions best in terms of discovery and the application of all possible technologies. Thus, the technologies develop in all directions. Of course, progress continues at different speeds. In some branches, it may stop altogether at a certain point, when no more new combinations are possible in a given sector. People will then mark time for a while, and difficulties will seem insurmountable. But the course is always the same. The difficulties cannot be solved by any direct approach. The progress of other technologies, sometimes adjacent, sometimes apparently unrelated by any stretch of the imagination, will in some way "overlap" with the question, the previously inaccessible domain. And we will finally get across the "wall" by the roundabout way of new products, new procedures, new machines. In this generalized growth, however, lines of force can be discerned. This seemingly anarchic and proliferating development gradually orders itself in terms of a major technology; or else we make out a deeper and secret structure in this progress. But these structures add up, this primacy of a technology is decided without debate, discussion, assembly, or vote. This order emerges of its own accord, in terms of relations between diverse technological sectors, priorities, disparities, growth, multiplicity of applications, etc.

Nevertheless, when major technologies are perceived and the technological universe is being shaped, man cannot remain passive. We then see another dimension of the system emerging: it is the conclusion—inevitable and automatic in a society where technology functions—of a forecast. This fact is essential: adjustment is both automatic and reflected. The forecast bears not only on what will come if we let things happen but also on what has to come if there is to be the best conjunction between the social and the technological. Forecasting is not an instrument to steer technology in a specific direction, it is the indispensable apparatus for preventing insoluble conflicts between society and technology. Adjustment to the technological phenomenon, in the technological environment, can only be conscious, but it is inevitable. Forecasting enables us to situate ourselves on those two levels. This is what challenges Soviet planning, which was too voluntaristic with respect to the technological imperative.[2]

So far, we have been saying that wherever technology develops, we witness inevitable and involuntary adapting, e.g., of large organizations: innovation actually must first be ensured in organizations.[3] But this raises a series of institutional problems; for the climate favorable to innovation depends on a thorough transformation of the power dynamics in the ensemble concerned. There will be either a trend toward centralizing, a blockage between opposite pressure groups, or acceptance of the competition between groups by acceptance of both a certain structure and a certain level of conflicts. Technological action allows us to replace constraint with forecasting. Orientations in one direction or another are due to very diverse reasons, but there is a tendency to accept what is most favorable to technological progress.

Crozier, in *The Stalled Society*, demonstrates what a society ought to be like in order to adjust well to technology, and how—if it is not adjusted—technological progress brings on a social blockage of its own accord. The change is not ineluctable, to be sure; but when it fails to come about, the society can no longer function. It is thus a kind of challenge thrown out by technology. Now nobody knows exactly how the body social *should* be organized; but it tends to organize toward continuing to exist in the new context; hence, forecasting. At the same time, however, Simondon demonstrates that technological progress takes place through individualization of technological beings, which individualization is made possible "by the recurrence of causality in an environment that the technological being creates around himself and that conditions him as he is conditioned by it. This environment, both technological and natural, can be called an associated milieu. It is that by which the technological being conditions himself in his functioning. This milieu is not manufactured—at least not totally manufactured: it is a certain organization of natural elements surrounding the technological being and linked to a certain organization of elements constituting the technological being." Hence, the adjustment by the milieu is both inevitable and indispensable in terms of the configuration of the technologies.

Of course, this configuration, which has been forecast, is not eternal or very durable. If we observe the technological systems of the past half century, the configuration seems to change roughly every ten years; i.e., every ten years or so, a major technology emerges and all the others arrange themselves with respect to the new one. But this orientation is not a function of utility or human benefit or needs or reason or the "good." It is a purely internal matter of the technological system, and the reasons are purely technological.

However, Simondon, although discussing the technological object, emphasizes that evolution, even if necessary, is not automatic. It is not enough to show that the technological object passes from an analytical order to a synthetic order (like technology in its ensemble); this transition has causes, both economic and properly technological, residing in the imperfection of the technological object. In this sense, I agree: The imperfection triggers the evolution; but sociologically, in this case, there is a true automatism. Technology approaching, by necessity, its most efficient and most perfect functioning—that is what Simondon himself points out when he explains that the technological object, for which the user asks for alterations according to his individual taste, loses its character as a technological object to acquire a whole set of inessential features. Technological automatism is precisely the tendency to reject these inessential features.

\* \* \*

Automatism works on a different level, likewise, for the choice between two possible technologies for the same operation. This choice occurs exclusively for the efficiency or dimension of the results achieved; and we can say that the "judgment" is purely automatic. The new technology allows us to go faster and further, to produce more, and so on.

There is no real choice, strictly speaking, about size; between three and four, four is bigger than three. This is not contingent on anybody, no one can change it or say the opposite or personally escape it. Any decision about technology is now of the same order. There is no choice between two technological methods: one foists itself inevitably because its results are counted, are measured, are obvious and indisputable.

The surgical operation that could not be done and now *can* be done is not debatable, it is not the object of choice: it exists. Here we have a decisive aspect of technological automatism: it is now technology that makes the choice ipso facto, with no remission, no possible discussion, among the means to be used. Man is absolutely not the agent of the choice. He is an apparatus registering the effects, the results obtained by various technologies, and the choice is not based on complex or in any way human motives; man decides only in favor of whatever gives the maximum efficiency. This is no longer a choice. Any machine could perform the same operation.

And if man still seems to be making a choice by giving up a method that is excellent from one standpoint, he does so only because he analyzes the results more profoundly and ascertains that this method is less efficient on other scores: e.g., the deconcentration efforts of large factories after planning maximum concentration, or the abandonment of record production systems in favor of a productivity that is less per capita but more constant. It is never anything but a matter of perfecting the method in its own direction. We are confronted here with matter-of-course insights and an automatism of application. Hence, we can say that when it comes to choosing between trees (which, we know, are more and more indispensable for good health) and the highway speed of cars, then there is no deliberation: speed wins. Thus, *Le Bulletin des domaines* (December 1969, p. 1) regularly apprises us that huge quantities of trees are being chopped down to clear the approaches to highways. We may rest assured that no true choice is involved: the option was taken in advance.[4]

These "choices" do not cause any impoverishment of the technologies—i.e., we cannot imagine any resulting loss, exclusion, diminution of a certain number of procedures for the benefit of the ultimate winner. Of course, the winner will cause some reduction in the long run. But this system of elimination operates within the proliferation of technologies. Hence, we cannot generally say that *one* better technology replaces *one* less efficient one; normally, *several* procedures correlatively replace an older means. The automatic choice comes from successive refinements, i.e., the reduction of technologies. In particular, we take into account more and more circumstances in which the technologies must be applied; we manufacture different instruments for adapting to a specific climate, soil, and even to a psychology or set of habits if they are consistent with technological application. We must take them into account; this facilitates technological growth, for it is sometimes easier to alter a type of machine or a method than customs or character traits.

One aspect of this "eliminating" automatism must be particularly examined: the operations of the computer. Creating data banks and thoroughly using the enormous ensemble of knowledge that can accumulate in reference computers involves something like an overall revision of human knowledge. What the computer has to register is precise, uniform, and general data. We are thus establishing a "thesaurus" of data processing, including the list of terms conventionally standardized for each discipline and forming the documentary lingo of the science in question. Each term represents a semantic field, with its precise contents and limits; and it must show three common traits: generality, specificity, associativity. For the so-called exact sciences, this is not very difficult. Jurisprudence likewise has a rather precise vocabulary and univocal terms. But what a problem for the human sciences! Who can tell us the exact meaning of words like *system, ideology, myth, state, class, role,* etc.? We would have to accept *one* definition offered by a specific school and ignore all the rest. There are solid reasons why each doctrine gives a different sense to *social order* or *information*. In other words, the semantic choice is a doctrinal choice. And once a certain vocabulary is fixed and all the information in the computer is established, in terms of that lexicon, no more heterodox thinking will be possible in a doctrine or theory. For the sole choice will be to accept the vocabulary with the established meanings or else not to utilize the possible data offered by the computer and, hence, to remain on a very low level of documentation and not do any "scientific" or "scholarly" work. This automatism can have considerable repercussions.

\* \* \*

The third aspect of automatism is a very different one. When a technology develops in a sector, it demands a certain adjustment by the individual, the social structures, the economic factors, and the ideologies. In the spontaneous thought of modern man, this adapting must be automatic, and he is scandalized if it does not come about. Technological development is both necessary and good;

hence, everything and everyone must adjust in order to promote it, and any possible resistance must be wiped out.[5] It is actually held that the social and human material must be completely plastic so as to be molded according to the needs of the new technologies and constantly follow progress.[6]

E. G. Mesthene (*Technological Change, Its Impact on Man and Society*, 1970) very accurately analyzes the processes whereby technological innovation inevitably (I would say, automatically) causes changes in the society: "Organized groups of people" have to find forms of particular organization to profit from opportunities offered by, say, new equipment. Technological progress imposes the need for social and political innovation so that the advantages offered by progress may be realized and its negative effects minimized. The acknowledgement of science as an instrument of social action, the existence of science and technologization entails a constant augmentation of the scope and influence of the public domain: the decisions made by the public authorities keep getting more numerous as technology grows. The public structures change at the same time that the jurisdictions augment. Society is complexifying. These statements, although not very original, are interesting because of the hidden conflict in this book. The author *involuntarily* shows that these adjustments come inevitably, automatically, whereas his clear thought leads him to the conviction that technological progress has the goal of reducing imposed behaviors and increasing freedom.

The simplest example of this adjustment is obviously that of urban space, the layout of housing, etc., which have to conform to the transportation technologies.[7]

In these problems of adapting, we are sometimes faced with a conflict between two equivalent technological orientations. For instance, it was correctly said that the engulfment of the computer in large businesses and administrations made antiquated structures efficient, and this administrative efficiency permitted the neglect of more basic structural reforms, that would have come had it not been for data processing. The structures did not adjust to the computer, it was the latter that accommodated the existing structures, producing new dysfunctions. See the very remarkable article by C. Balle, "L'Ordinateur, un frein aux réformes de structure des entreprises" (*Le Monde*, September 1975).

In this automatic adapting, we obviously have to note the trend toward a certain economic concentration.[8] The more technological the products, the more we observe the following phenomenon:

"Because of the complexity of the systems and the number of different components entering into manufacture, it is almost impossible to make a product without having the right to use a large number of patents. . . . For these reasons, the patent pools, the granting of licenses and know-how among the principle firms, are one of the characteristics of modern industry. The more patents a firm has, the greater its chances of obtaining the know-how and licenses of other firms."[9]

Hence, industrial concentration, which is the adaptation mode for business, takes place more for technological necessity than for financial imperatives. But in reality, there is only the fact itself: everyone expects the milieu to be shaped by the technologies; we hope for, we await automatic reactions of adoption and service in the body social. This adapting occurs through the technicians, the users, and the consumers, who are all agreed on the necessity. Likewise, we have cited the studies that aim at attacking and destroying the behaviors, ideologies, beliefs, and values unadapted to technology.

As Massenet emphasizes ("Du changement technique à l'éclatement social," in *Analyse et prévision,* 1971, no. 4), technological change is expressed for individuals in changes of information; and it is this alteration not only of the channels and quantity of information but also of the quality of the object that brings on the social change. Information trends in our society are affected by a double mobility: that of exchange and that of incessant renewal, which enters the technologies. "Our society is an information society par excellence because the intensity, the variety of the information streams are inseparable from the rhythms of an industrial society. . . . But what truly characterizes our society is a certain mode of distributing and renewing information. Now this mode is in turn characterized by change: . . . modification *of* information and modification *by* information." Massenet draws the correct conclusion that our society is therefore *obliged* to take on a certain style, particularly a style of opposition between the most rigorous technological constraint and the lack of profound coherence. The type of society is *dictated* by technology, even if the orientation and structuration takes place through human beings and by way of information.

Undoubtedly, these adaptations do not come about in an a-human fashion; they are desired, hoped for, and believed.[10] This is why in this aspect of automatism, we are describing not so much what happens in reality as what the average Western man desires;

the pressure he exerts on the body social leads to this (always imperfect) refashioning, whereas he himself remains fairly unadapted. Obviously, the political and social structures are not completely flexible and mobile: they are heavy, sluggish. And the problem of the necessity of adaptation by the social is recognized only when that resistance crops up, i.e., when automatism does not operate.

What is actually desired (albeit not clearly expressed) is a perfectly malleable social organization, because in order to progress, technology demands a great social mobility; it requires huge population shifts, changes in the practice of professions, allotments of resources, and alterations in group structures and in the relations among these groups or among individuals within the groups. It seems altogether simple and obvious that nowadays, in the course of his career, a man must foresee the possibility of changing his profession (i.e., his technology) three times in thirty years. He must therefore be polyspecialized, rather than specialized in one branch; he has to be retrained en route and mobilized in mid-career.[11] But since a man of forty is less flexible, less open, with a poorer memory and a lower aptitude for learning than a man of thirty, it is taken for granted that he should be paid less because he is less adapted to the new technology. This notion is already widely followed. We know that for an executive (the prototype of technicized man), the maximum salary comes at around thirty-five and then gradually decreases. In the United States, the executive of fifty-five already earns less than one of twenty-five. This seems quite normal: an automatic adjustment to the technological necessity. Each technological advance threatens better and better qualified specialists with loss of jobs. In the past, the manual laborer was threatened by economic recession, but he kept his labor power; he was always able to work. Nowadays, with disqualification by advanced technological inventions, the most highly trained employees are suddenly and totally unfit. In 1948, the invention of semiconductors disqualified hundreds of thousands of radioelectricians. Hence, the need for permanent retraining of the most qualified: it goes without saying.[12]

However, people are trying to reduce the human suffering caused by this automatism. The whole system of "engineering" (now admitted into French as *ingénierie*) and the sciences of "engineering," i.e., organization, are technologies for adapting individuals and businesses to technological growth.[13] Organization (planning) analyzes, determines, and defines the problems. Engineering puts to work the new resources, the data furnished by psychology, psycho-sociology, physiology, computer processing, ergonomy, etc., to solve those problems.[14] And this quite obviously produces a humanization. We manage to break through man's isolation in the midst of machines, find a better distribution of labor power in time through production administration, P. E. R. T. (program evaluation and review technique), etc. But we see that everything actually functions "in an integrated circuit." Given the technological system, new technologies make the best integration possible, with a happy balance that is painless for both the collective and the individual. This is the point at which the automatism of adjustment joins self-augmentation.[15]

Here is a further example from among a hundred. It seems natural for the Black African nations to try and alter their social structures so that technological development may take place, unless, conversely, we decide—interestingly enough—on a discriminatory aid. To be effective, assistance has to concentrate on the countries and regions with the greatest development potential. This potential is reckoned less by the old norms (e.g., the abundance of raw materials or energy reserves) than by the presumed adaptability of the inhabitants and the malleability of the social structures. Thus, in 1964, India received an aid of two dollars per capita and Chile twelve dollars. Chile was the pet child of technological help because it seemed best qualified to adapt totally, i.e., not squander what it was given. This position is rationally defensible. People want to stop dispersing an absolutely useless "development aid" if a country does not have the facilities for attempting an autonomous development. Here, the verdict is prior, but it corresponds to the same vision: the need for human transformation in order to make technological progress applicable. Now we have to speak of automatism even when adaptation does not come by itself, because on no account should anyone discuss the excellence of technological progress in regard to a given socio-economic form.

Adaptation has to be the same for economic and political structures. One can draw up a chart of relations between a certain energy source and a certain type of economic structure. This would seem far more accurate than Marx's celebrated formula. Let us say, for instance, off the top of our heads, that the steam engine produced economic liberalism; electricity, planning, and atomic energy, a return to liberalism. But, indisputably, the structures of each economic system are altered by the new contributions of technology—and that is practically the sole mover. Notwithstanding the resistance of individual interests, this adaptation is more obvious, inevitable, and spontaneous than that of social structures. There is no need to belabor this point.

But, as we must stress, it goes without saying (in appearance) that one of the major elements in our society, the university, has to adapt immediately and without further ado to the technological structure. The debates on this topic are endless. The university has to become a technical school so that each student may instantly fill a position in this technological society. And people are horrified that the university does not accommodate faster and better. These imbeciles are totally ignorant of what the university's role should be, they sneer at the value still attached to the "humanities," at the uselessness of Latin, of history and philosophy. They want the university to be a technological cog in a technological society. Of course, these are the same imbeciles who give pompous speeches on tomorrow's civilization and technological humanism. In contrast to these simplistic views, it is interesting to emphasize the opinion of a man coping with the problem of the university. Seligman (*A Most Notorious Victory*), observing the evolution of American universities, holds that, on the contrary, "the universities are responding so well and so rapidly to the demands of technology that they risk a self-disaggregation due to their overly easy adaptation to the world of tomorrow." In effect, it is quite likely that this adjustment to the technological world will condemn any possible university to death.

As for the adaptation of political forms, the big problem is the application of technologies of governing (e.g., psychological action upon the masses) as well as the growing influence of technicians in political quarters.

Elgozy shows clearly that the growth of the technological factor in budgetary choices (Planning, Programming, and Budgeting System, Rationalization of Budgetary Choices) in planning, in "decision aid," automatically reduces the political choices and possible applications of decisions and the democratic or parliamentary controls; especially, as he points out, when political rationality does not coincide with technological rationality. However, the former must accommodate itself to the latter. It is clear that the political structure *has to adapt by itself* to technology, i.e., *by its own means*. That is the gist of the problem. Needless to say, the administration must restructure itself in terms of the computer. But from that point on, there is *no* mastery over what the computer might possibly do. Since the structure is *adapted* to it, no one can control the computer. Ralph Nader denounces the "tyranny of uncontrolled computers," but there is no other choice. Controlling them means *renouncing* their power and operating with an antiquated political-administrative structure. Seeking the best possible application for the power of the computer in order to perfect administration means giving administration a power that can no longer be arbitrated from the outside.

We realize that all previously devised constitutional forms do not square with these demands.[16] Still, there is no way of not appealing to technicians (since most political issues are now technological issues), of not using advanced administrative or (for instance) police technologies. However, the political personnel is no better adapted than the institutions. In our forms of government, we note that adaptation is poor. There is an energetic resistance by what we call the political class, the group of professional politicians who do not care to be plowed under by the technicians.[17]

There is an ideological resistance in the name of old values, democracy, popular sovereignty, freedom translated into elections, and so on. The majority of people are deeply attached to this ideology, which seems to guarantee political truth and protection against dictatorship. But these same people wax indignant if the government is not efficient enough, if there is disorder, if the technologies do not help to solve some problem. The population favors both technological progress and classical democracy, and, of course, it absolutely fails to perceive the utter conflict between the two. This contradiction recurs in intellectual circles, which fiercely cleave to democracy, national self-determination, the rights of man, and so forth.

Intellectuals, moreover, have a particular vice. On the one side, they are very consciously and ardently well disposed toward technological progress; they are more wonder-struck than anyone else by its developments. But on the other side, they are very hostile to it in the political arena, which must remain a field of palaver (their chief occupation), choices, chance elements, personalities; and they are excited, above all, by what politics represents as the total expression of man, the decision on his future, the utterance of his freedom.[18] By verbalizing both these aspects, the intellectuals strike me as more naive and unthinking than the average man in the street.

It is these hindrances to automatic adjustment by political institutions that create the troubles, uncertainties, difficulties besetting the political world. Sfez (*L'Administration prospective*) admirably shows the dynamics of this automatism in administration: "The true reforms come only through objective and blind mechanisms that grind down routine and sclerosis. . . . The machines and the technologies of conceptualization that are linked to them spark an irreversible process of innovation. . . . Machines *allow* us to take heed of the most complex data . . . rationalization technologies *postulate* the integration, into reasoning, of variables that were previously left to the politician. The administered individual is integrated not because it is good to integrate him in the name of a liberal, personalist, and socialist philosophy; he is integrated because he has to be, so that the calculations may work out."

The citadels and feudal systems of administration do not come tumbling down under the blaring trumpets of reformist Joshuas; instead, they tend to crack under the impact of the necessary coherence of decisions as revealed by modern administration methods.

No doubt, one may object that it is human beings who do the reforming, human beings who introduce new machines and methods, and that, hence, the appeals were not in vain. But this interpretation would be erroneous. The directors of public or private administration who have introduced innovation were forced to do so by technological advances. A private business is threatened by competition. The government has to use new technologies in order to cope with its own needs; what with resources dwindling and needs growing, the public managers have to rationalize the use of resources to a maximum. The prime goals of public or private managers are efficiency and rationality, the sole chances of survival. It turns out that participation was posulated by these chances.

There is no better way of describing the automatic character of this choice, of these adaptations and transformations: the administration adopting modern technologies *must be* what these technologies allow *to be done*.

Thus, technology challenges the social structure; there is nothing original about this, but it automatically triggers the necessary adjustment. Massenet describes this process perfectly ("Du changement technique à l'éclatement social," *Analyse et prévision*, 1971–1974), when he characterizes the society of technological progress as showing constraint and a lack of deep coherence. The cohesion of a society was once of a moral nature; it now becomes purely organizational and external. And Massenet adds this essential remark: "We cannot overlook the possibility that the high degree of material cohesion exacted by the functioning of our societies may be the very source of their disharmony." In other words, the automatism of adjustment is perforce *external* and leads to an apparent rationality, the only one that technology can necessarily produce. However, technology, in order to progress, will itself challenge all the values and all the symbolics and prevent any *autonomous* internal cohesion of the social system. The social system (aside from the after-effects of the past, which are far from being liquidated, aside from its sluggishness, which we shall study later on) tends, therefore, to be thoroughly malleable and plastic. The adjustment, tending to be automatic, is at the price of internal cohesion and organic solidity.

That is why, as Massenet again so well points out, social change must now take place through contestation; the latter is not revolutionary in any way; it expresses the need for adapting to the technological. It expresses itself wherever this adaptation does not occur. Unanimity prevails in accepting technological progress and its consequences. But, Massenet emphasizes, "it is an abstract unanimity, which stops existing as soon as we have to determine the rate of progress or the distribution of its fruits" (and, I would add, its modalities). On this level, we find those conflicts that are conflicts of *form*. Technological progress forbids clear conflicts by large masses: the old oppositions between large ideologies, compact social groups (classes, parties, trade unions) are utterly depassé and decrepit. Any coalition is challenged by the "whirlwind rapidity of evolution." It is within this framework that contestation occurs; it has no revolutionary meaning, but it does express the blind and unconscious automatism of society's adjustment to the demand of technology: as prompted by the obvious contradiction between the marvelous possibility of technology and the concrete unacceptability of society as we experience it. Contestation against the consumer society is actually a protest against a "bad use of technology," i.e., the demand that a bad society adapt itself to good technology.

Of course, when structures and institutions do not adjust spontaneously, there is still a choice to be made. We have already said that in certain cases, it is easier to shape a technology according to the existing reality than to modify the latter. The choice will then favor the greater facility and efficiency of either of two operations. Naturally, this choice will never be worded as explicitly as I am wording it now. It takes place on the level of work by technicians and also on the level of relations among the groups and sectors

## AUTOMATISM

involved. On the one side, there is a tendency to apply technologies, with the resulting pressure on some group or tradition; on the other side, there is adoption or resistance. And depending on the firmness of this resistance, the technician will correct the method or the tool to achieve the best possible return under the given circumstances. But there may be deeply emotional resistance, an addiction to the past, blockages, individual or societal sclerosis, institutional rigidity, all hindering any alteration, any innovation. Then again, technicians may refuse to allow parcelling, because they often view their perfected technology as irreplaceable and tend directly or indirectly to modify the milieu, which will happen if the technology in question is actually applied. We have to remember that it is applied not so much because of human needs or sociological imperatives as because of the technological context in which the new procedure will be integrated.

In such cases, the conflict between milieu and technology will bring disorder and often social, economic, and political disturbances, until one of the two factors has negotiated the adjustment. This conflictual relationship explains most difficulties in Western society between 1900 and 1940 and in third-world societies at the moment. It would be easy to do a detailed study of this. The ideal is thus (only *unconsciously* desired) the automatic adjustment to the milieu. But this adjustment implies the corollary of control. One can say that the extreme point of this automatism is reached when it is no longer man who really controls the machines but when he himself is included as a piece in the overall system and controlled by machines to coordinate his action with that of others and of devices at the same time as materials, installations, etc. This is the application of Program Evaluation and Review Technique.

In the dynamics of human, political, and societal adjustment to technology, as we have said, the technological system produces its own facilitations and compensations. Spare-time activity is one of them. Automatism would be a very harsh law if there were no compensating equilibriums. We will not bother reviewing all the studies done on leisure, but it is essential to emphasize its function. Without ever openly articulating it, each study implies that spare-time activity chiefly makes up for automatic progression; robbed of decision-making power in this area, man needs *total* recovery as a setoff. Empty time is greatly unnerving; we wonder how to use it; primarily, however it is empty of automatism. Of course, man does not know how to use it. He is utterly unaware that technological automatism is so painful that he has to escape it. For not only the mechanization of work is involved but also, far more deeply, the integration of man in a system that functions outside of him. And yet that is exactly what he tries to palliate.[19] This is obvious whether man is bewildered by the vacant time itself or by the sudden absence of constraints.

But this is not the true problem, anymore than the relation to work. Likewise, the statistical studies about the way we cultivate spare-time activities (e.g., Credoc, *Consommation*, 1970) provide information that makes no sense. We have to transcend these classic questions in order to see leisure as making up for compulsory submission to the automatism of technological progress. This is its true state and also reveals its impossibility as profound experience. Leisure is the institution of an emptiness that would authorize choices. The normal mistake is to confuse spare time with the games, fun, palaver, the *dolce far niente*, the relaxations of traditional societies. We are then forced to state that it does not have the same value as any of them and that it is impossible to "garnish" empty time with such activities. They were tied to traditional nontechnological activities; they cannot be reproduced in our new environment. In contrast, technological automatism, killing the true possibility of choice, makes life unbearable and stifling for man, who cannot accept the fact that he is no longer in charge. Leisure is the respiratory function of the system. It is the aperture that lets us breathe, the escape hatch that gives the illusion of freedom; hence, the spontaneous, unreflected rage for spare time (vacations, weekend trips, TV, etc.) as well as the twofold reflected and systematic maturation of the engineers and vendors of leisure activities and the intellectuals striving to make leisure the justification of the system.

\* \* \*

Technological automatism has one last trait. When a technological procedure enters a new domain, it encounters older ways of doing things, from a pretechnological period. They tend to be eliminated, for nothing can compete with anything technological. The choice is made a priori. Neither man nor group can decide to follow any road that is not technological. Man is placed before this very simple dilemma: On the one hand, he can decide to safeguard his freedom of choice, he can go on using the traditional or personal, the moral or empirical means, and he then has to compete with a power against which he has no effective defense. His resources are useless, they will be plowed under or eliminated, and he will be vanquished. On the other hand, he can decide to accept the technological necessity; he will then be the winner, but he will submit irremediably to technological enslavement. Hence, there is absolutely no free choice. We are now in an evolutionary stage of *eliminating* everything that is not technological.

Today, the challenge to a country, to a man, to a system is only a technological challenge. A technological power can be opposed only by another technological power. Everything else is swept away. Chakotin constantly reminds us of this. What can we say in response to the psychological assaults of propaganda? It is no use appealing to culture or religion; it is no use educating the masses. Only propaganda can reply to propaganda and psychological rape to psychologial rape. Hitler formulated it before Chakotin: "This tactic, based on a precise evaluation of human weaknesses, must almost mathematically lead to success if the opposing party does not learn to fight poison gases with poison gases" (*Mein Kampf*).

The exclusive nature of technology provides one of the reasons for its staggering progress. Today, a man can have space to live in only if he is a technician. A collectivity can resist the pressures of the surrounding milieu only if it uses technologies. Having technological ways of coping is now a matter of life and death for all of us. Because there is no equivalent power anywhere in the world.

The same is true for the individual. He is obliged to choose the most advanced technology. Plainly, an engineer who continues applying century-old technologies is not going to find a job. And just as plainly, artisanry is eliminated because it competes with technological procedures. The important thing in judging this automatism is that it very often affects the practice of a trade. Now, whatever the country, this trade will inevitably be a livelihood. Hence, the individual must apply the most advanced technology because it is the only one allowing him to survive. There is still no choice here. The choice is made in advance and always in the same direction. Of course, it may be stressed that in highly technicized nations, various crafts are developing or recurring anyway: the Americans are excited about Navajo products and the Soviets are encouraging Bashkir and Tungese craftsmen. By all means. But, once again, these things are luxuries, extras, an adventitious reprieve from the society of rigor and efficiency.

The path is always the same. To produce fabrics, technology competes with traditional craftsmanship, taking over the market by first using the same raw materials: wool, cotton, linen, for instance.

The textile industry reigns supreme. Then, chemistry creates fabrics from raw materials that have nothing to do with the classic ones: nylon, orlon, dralon, etc. From a utilitarian viewpoint, this development offers all the advantages. But then comes a return, for luxury, fantasy, attractiveness, and what not, to the old raw materials and to craft procedures. This is no competition. Just a supplement to needs that are otherwise completely satisfied.

We can show the same pattern for music. In a first stage, the radio set kills off the village guitarist, the small orchestras at local movie houses, and so on; all village music-making disappears. But when we come to a new technological phase, with transistors, LPs, and industry flooding the market with canned music, there is a kind of general permeation, and the individual, living in a climate of permanent music, starts playing himself. It is not the same thing as the artistic hobbies of the nineteenth-century bourgeoisie, but something like a regurgitation of too much musical absorption. This music by an individual or a small group in no way competes with technicized music, it merely adds a bit of pleasure, a luxury, that of human warmth, of the musician's physical presence, the charm of a possible false note, an error (which we never get from mechanized music), the piquancy of unimportant "chanciness."

Thus, technology, triumphing automatically over all nontechnological procedures, allows them a new life, which does not menace it—the benevolent dictator who authorizes some flimsy caprice and smiles at the initiatives of his subjects, while order reigns implacable elsewhere.[20]

But then comes the following (still hypothetical) problem. What would happen if the modern technologies, trampling the older forms underfoot, were to reintroduce choice, flexibility, and indeterminateness? This thesis is maintained by Richert and Sfez. In his book, which is very much to the fore (*Critique de la décision*, 1974), Sfez shows with extreme clarity how institutions adapt to different technological stages: When faced with rigid technologies in industrial society, technologies causing centralization and hierarchy, people had "instrumental institutions . . . centered on resources," which were linear and semi-mechanical. And this category must include all authors who hold that society can become a simple social mechanism (e.g., Naville, *Vers l'automatisme social*). However, at a more developed stage of technology, especially with the emergence of the human technologies, we conceive of a different form of institutions. These are called "pragmatic institutions"; they are linked to definite objectives, representing empirical facilities to ensure the efficiency of tasks in technological planning and in implementation. But we are still in a linear organization.

In contrast, with the most recent technological advances in automation and data processing, we could arrive at a different institutional model, the self-adaptable institutions, which combine decentralized initiative and centralized synthesis. These institutions, furnished with a regulation for adjustment, entail decentralization; characterized by operational, strategic, and structural flexibility, they are supposedly "ideal" and are made possible by the most recent technological progress. But here we are dealing with a fundamental issue: they are only possible. They do not seem directly conditioned and necessarily produced. They imply choices and decisions. But how can these come about in a system that has so far eliminated choices and decisions? And if they do not come about, there will be a contradiction between the new technologies and the political and bureaucratic structure that has adapted to the preceding stage. The problem is a seminal one. Self-administration is the wrong answer.

\* \* \*

There is a final aspect connecting automatism and self-augmentation. To perceive it, one must start with a very important remark by L. Schneider and S. Dornbusch (*Popular Religion: Inspirational Books in America*, 1958). It was quoted by G. Vahanian (*The Death of God*)[21]: "It is surprising that when faith fails, what it ordinarily allows us to do without any particular thought or effort on our part becomes the object of a technologically oriented behavior. This observation is interesting both inside and outside the domain of religion. It has been suggested that the technology of physical love will most likely develop if love becomes problematical and gives way to doubt. In the same way, the technologies of pregnancy appear when 'natural' love for children is no longer manifested precociously and spontaneously."

This is a fundamental observation, which can be generalized. It is commonly said that when man discovers a technology to do what he used to do pragmatically, he abandons his former practice and prefers the new and more efficient practice. We have repeated this over and over again here. Furthermore, it can bring the loss of a certain feeling, ability, aptitude, vitality, etc. Hence, the technologies of eroticism are certainly doing away with the deep and true relationship of love, its authenticity.

But, with Vahanian, we also have to view the converse development. When modern man, because of his life in this society, loses a profound force, a wellspring of vitality, a motivation, and no longer knows how to act by virtue of that basic reason, a reason for action and meaning, when he is so lackluster that he has no more purchase on the outside world, then, automatically, a technology is born to allow indispensable action despite everything. This action, becoming more efficient, is therefore easier and requires no such great motivations, no such total judgment, no such full effort. Thanks to technology, man can not only do harder things more easily, he can also act meaninglessly and remain perfectly outside his action. We know this from the difference between killing an enemy face to face with a knife and bombing an area from four miles up. We can posit as a consistent and permanent feature that when man loses a deep reason for acting, a technology appears that allows him to act in the same area, but without any reason. The means has entirely replaced the meaning. There is a technological aping of man's most profound expression. This is apparent in all the psychological technologies when people can no longer engage in a human relationship, when friendship no longer inhabits the human heart, when there is no longer authenticity in a group. These things are supplanted by the technologies of human relations and group dynamics, perfectly mimicking from the outside the things that should only be spontaneously invented in the inmost heart of man.

We have said that this is an area of technological progress linking automatism with self-augmentation. When a vacuum replaces these essential realities in man, when only social roles and behaviors are left, then, like an indraught of air, a kind of technological automatism leads research into this domain. We cannot stay in this situation for long. Indispensably, previous experiences must persist; hence, technology, obscurely but definitely, enters this void, gradually adjusting its mechanisms, though no one either sought or wanted it. This is self-augmentation, because the technological system inevitably grows in the vacuum left by the retreat of a deep existential activity. No one thinks per se of doing this substitution work; it foists itself. We cannot let human relations deteriorate and deaden indefinitely: the deficiency must be made up for. This simply stands to reason. Everything that man loses in presence, spontaneity, reason, will, decision, choice, commitment, freedom, everything he forsakes because it is too difficult, because his life is too complicated, because he is too tired or inhibited—all these things cause both a "spontaneous" augmentation of the technological system and the automatism in the orientation of that growth. On the basis of this general orientation, it is quite easy to apply this analysis to many experimental areas.

We can, no doubt, say that these social and human relations are always sociabilized, hence they become the object of technologies, more or less assimilated (which also obtains for our feelings). Granted, education, courtesy, and the like are also "techniques": but we have to repeat the distinction—already studied—between original and pragmatic technologies and the technological phenomenon. The new thing here is the calculation, the systematization, and the consciousness: the technologies that supplant "spontaneous" action due to profound impulses are deliberate and are applied as technologies (e.g., group dynamics). And that is what disrupts the old structure of relations.

# 11
# CAUSAL PROGRESSION AND ABSENCE OF FINALITY

WE generally have the spontaneous notion that technology develops because human beings—scientists or technicians—want to reach a certain goal, because other men express needs that technology must make good, because man has ends to attain and technology is the ideal agent. This conviction surfaces constantly, dictating the basic idea that no judgment about technology is possible because the latter is only a means (hence, as a means, unimportant—everyone knows that for our philosophical elevation only the ends count), and everything depends on the ends we pursue. This notion, I believe, is one of the most serious and most decisive errors concerning technological progress and the technological phenomenon.

Technology develops not in terms of goals to be pursued but in terms of already existing possibilities of growth. Daumas shows that, in its evolution, technology obeys "an internal logic which is very distinct from the evolutionary logic of socio-economic history—this can be demonstrated for nearly all periods and nearly all episodes of technological creation. The close connection between mining, the steam engine, and smelting are a classical example. The study of horizontal or vertical filiations confirms this." And this intrinsic logic is essentially causal.[1]

## FINALITIES

However, we must first ask whether technology obeys a finality, whether it pursues an objective. And we must obviously distinguish between ultimate *finalities*, half-time *objectives*, and immediate *goals*.

## CAUSAL PROGRESSION AND ABSENCE OF FINALITY

Are there true finalities for technological growth? No doubt, finalities emerge in the progression of the technological system. But the point is that these finalities appear during the very course of the process; in other words, they in no way direct it, they are adventitious. Ex post facto, we discover that what has been done (according to a purely causal mechanism) could easily be applied to a certain problem and can answer (in general, partially, and fairly abstractly) a question that was being asked. Unless we are to believe that this matter was working away in the depth of the human unconscious, guiding man (what a marvelous arrangement between this unknown desire and the causal mechanism that brings a discovery or transformation!). But that is something I refuse to acknowledge, for as soon as I have tried to make this unconscious dream precise, it dissipated. We have to get back to the idea that these finalities, *produced* by the system, never determine it. They are merely justifications that are tacked on because man is unwilling to lose face, unwilling to appear subjugated to causalist mechanisms, and always wants to affirm himself as master of the situation!

Let us leave aside the delirious talk about the "trip to the moon" supposedly "making the dreams of mankind come true." It is downright absurd to believe that the technicians who worked on airplanes did it *because* they wanted to realize the myth of Icarus! True, there has, occasionally, been a vague sentiment (crossing the oceans, flying, going to the moon); but can we claim that some dream was at the origin of radio, printing, gun powder? This rationale is a poetic addendum, taken on by technicians with a literary background. But one cannot seriously view it as the driving finality of technological growth!

If we question scientists and technicians about their ideas, we always get the same answers and the same vagueness. Why technological progress? The first end they cite is "the happiness of mankind."[2] But as soon as we ask them which happiness, the greatest uncertainty reigns. We sense that pure leisure or consumption are not altogether sufficient. *Happiness,* a word that is satisfactory because it is perfectly vague and insubstantial—satisfactory because it responds to the most widespread of the current ideologies. People believe in happiness.[3] Technology assures happiness—a formula that is all the more effective for its lack of content.

We get the same hazy and floundering result when we are assured that technological progress works toward the realization of man. Which man? Normally, there is not the least anthropological thinking behind such a proclamation. And we find something here that has already been pointed out, namely, the total divorce between, on the one hand, scientists and technicians and, on the other, humanists, philosophers, theologians. The latter group pursue their analyses of man without knowing the technological phenomenon, and they wind up with perfectly aberrant conclusions. They are, however, getting more and more honest in refusing to supply an ideal model of the human being to be achieved. They do not offer a useful anthropology or the desirable model as a transcending finality of technology. In contrast, the scientists and technicians, for their part, are utterly incapable of this reflection. When they advance along this road, their visions are rather silly and full of lovely sentiments and antiquated humanism (like Einstein's). Or else they are unsettling[4] because what they project as the type of human being to be achieved is that which technology allows them to achieve. Here (and only here) we are approaching the robot ideal—how very frightening the possibility of altering man by chemical techniques without ultimately knowing what we are after.

We should not fool ourselves. If an ideal human type were proposed, it would not be easy to agree on it. Who can say, for instance, if we ought to wish for a human being who is far more free (although how can we do that by an intervention decided from outside his personality?) or more social and cooperative and conforming to the group? A more intelligent, more efficient, more powerful man—or one who is good, humble, inefficient, and joyous . . . ?

Let us not expect the technological miracle to reconcile all these irreconcilables; since technology is involved, there is no miracle to await.

Thus, we still have the two questions that I once asked (Ellul, *Lucidité de l'Au 2000*, 1967) and that were taken up and developed at length by L. Mumford (*The Myth of the Machine*, vol. II). First of all, what type of man do we wish to make? And secondly, are the manipulators truly the fittest to establish this desirable type of man; what qualifications other than purely scientific and technological do they have for going about these manipulations? I have no reason to believe that Monod or engineers like Bell, Cannon, Kingsley Davis, et al., are in any way capable of telling us *who* man *must* be. We are thus in an area that, more clearly than any other, shows the absence of finality. We are on the point of being able to manipulate man

## CAUSAL PROGRESSION AND ABSENCE OF FINALITY 259

exactly as we want him to be, genetically, chemically, electrically; but we do not really know what we want. This problem will be taken up again a bit later.

One of the texts quoted by Mumford is this remarkable passage by the biologist and Nobel Prize laureate Hermann Müller: "Man as a whole must elevate himself in order to be worthy of his utmost realization [and what would that utmost realization be?]. Unless the ordinary man can *understand* the world that the scientists have discovered, unless he can learn to understand the technologies that he uses today . . . unless he can join in the exaltation of conscious participation in the great human enterprise and find his satisfaction by playing a constructive role in it, he will become like a less and less important cog, the mass line of a vast machine." That is the only model! To understand science and use technology! A bit flimsy! Unless we have absolute faith like Monod.

We can do anything. But we do not know why. However, the why will be furnished gratuitously and spontaneously by the system itself. That is the key. We should not, alas, imagine a glorious demiurge that ultimately holds the secret of life and *therefore* accomplishes something wiser than what existed before![5]

The common attitude is to believe that man became "wiser" upon attaining such power! This is absurd. We have, incidentally, demonstrated that the growth of power always and necessarily destroys human values and capacity for judgment. In any event, the "wise" will not be individuals in their globality, who will be left with the artificial paradise, but rather those controlling the means of manipulation, who are going to establish the human model to be manufactured. Yet this can only be a model consistent with and perfectly adapted to the technological system. When these scientists, these Nobel Prize winners speak (and how vaguely) about "happiness" for man, their words quite obviously chime with a situation in which man is no longer in disharmony with his milieu, in which there are no more breaking points, confrontations, conflicts, for happiness today is quite commonly regarded as that happy concordance. But the environment is solely the technological environment. Man is to be made happy by having an easier time of living in this system. Something that is obviously challenged by no one—not the counterculture, not the hippies, not the brilliant youth of contestation and anticonsumerism! Because, in order to challenge it, one must first conceive of it as a system. It is not the replacement of capitalist whiskey with LSD, the rejection of Hollywood spectacle by underground cinema, that is going to change anything! It is not the sensualist, irrationalist explosion that is going to shake the system per se, even the slightest bit.

But now these modes of intervention are leaving the laboratory to meet up with the thinking of other technicians! Here is an example: the architect and city planner Yona Friedmann.[6] For the moment, his thinking is still altogether utopian, and relatively unknown; but what strikes me as unsettling is the warm welcome he has received among many intellectuals. His thesis is infinitely simple: Compared with the mechanism of "electronic brains," the human brain functions very poorly. "Our brain *is* a deforming mechanism." If we wish to think correctly, we have to model ourselves on the "thinking" of computers; that would be the true operational mechanism of human "thought." The deforming factor, which does not exist in the computer, includes all the things Friedmann groups under the heading "animism": feelings, conceptions, irrational impulses, etc., a whole set of "abstractions" and "extrasensory observations." All these things must be eliminated if we want to achieve a satisfying social system—satisfying because it would be consistent with unlimited technological growth. "Animism" is bad because it introduces elements that are "uncontrollable in our rational system."

If Friedmann's first model is technological, then his second one, on a vital level, is the animal. There is no animism in animals. They live on the level of their biological reality and are therefore in rational truth. They are a superior social model. "One can hope that in a few thousand millenniums, man will reach the superior social level of donkeys. . . . We have to establish animal well-being for the urban society." Animals do not work, they do not own anything, etc. These arguments are old hat. But interestingly, the author shows that to set up a rigorously rational society, we have to alter the human brain. And this is now possible with chemical means. The author incessantly maintains that the city planner must not impose his views on building the human habitat; he must leave the inhabitants free to choose the form of their city and hence establish "mobile architecture." But to make sure that everything works out, we first have to condition the human being so that he will have no unpredictable or irrational reactions.

We are thus confronted with the ultimate and extremist reflection: the use of all possible technologies to fashion the human being *according to the type foreseen* by Yona Friedmann. Most remarkable of all, in his theory of communications, he is very protective of humanism, democracy, and the predominance of small groups. But in his studies on architecture, his attitude is resolutely technological: we must formulate what is good for others and figure out how to impose it on them.

Now what disturbs me is that such ideas can be given credence. Friedmann teaches at Harvard, at the Carnegie Institute; he is subsidized by France's National Center of Scientific Research. All we need is a fraction of public opinion and a sufficiently important group of intellectual or political leaders to sway in his direction— and the experiment could be made. From that moment on, Huxley's brave new world will be in view. We have numerous ways of bringing it about; all we lack is the ideological impulse. And the latter can come by agreement on a simplistic materialistic ideology like the kind we have just discussed. Such agreement can result from unforeseeable irrational factors, but the results would be irreversible. To the extent that we are thus pursuing "technological progress," who knows what, from a human standpoint, will prevent this agreement!

We are then faced with the possibility of a reversal in the situation we have so far described. If an ideology like the one we have just gone into were given approval (clear approval by intellectuals, diffused approval by the masses), it might become the finality proposed for the technological system. It would have the same nature as the technological system; it would show all its characteristics and be perfectly coherent with it. This finality would be totally included in the system of means. But it would appear ideologically as a finality. Such is the true and probably sole danger of technological growth. So long as technological growth is a system of means, there will be, as we shall see in the end, a relative human autonomy and a possibility of keeping aloof, if not gaining control. In contrast, if a goal foists itself, appearing certain and obvious to everyone, then, at this point, the system will close altogether, having become complete.

The hope of discovering a finality for technology is, thus, invalid, because the proposed ends have no common standard with the technological factor, or else that hope is the decisively alienating and dangerous factor. Yona Friedmann's prototype, uninteresting in itself because of his weak thinking, is important in signifying that possibility of evolution. And that is also why I utterly distrust any utopian movement, for it will not sidestep the trap of reconstructing the rational and perfect city, i.e., where technology will be everything and in everyone.

\* \* \*

But given these forecasts and possibilities, these obvious rationalities, there are two things I wonder about: the how of the intermediary period and the human ideal that is suggested.

Here is my first question. How can we socially, politically, morally, and humanly reach that goal? How will we solve the enormous unemployment and economic problems caused, say, by automation if we really wish to apply it? How can we make all humankind agree not to have any more children in the natural way? How can we get people to undergo constant and rigorous health controls? How will man accept radically transforming his customary food? How will we evacuate the one and one half billion people who live off agriculture and who will become totally useless, and what will we do with them? (This conversion will have to be ultrarapid because we have been promised this new world in some fifty years.) How will we redistribute this population *equally* over the face of the earth, since that must be the first condition if the world is to have four times more inhabitants? How will we set up a stable modus vivendi among the nations to share the planets, control the airways, the satellites, etc.; or else how will we manage to do away with national structures (one of these two hypotheses is indispensable)? There are plenty of other how's. But no one talks about them. When we stop to think that coal and oil have caused several economic and social problems (very feeble ones), and that, after a century and a half, we still have not managed to solve them, is there any chance of our learning in the coming fifty years how to deal with these new how's, which are ten thousand times more complicated?

There is, indeed, a route, but only one: the most totalitarian worldwide dictatorship that could ever exist. This is the sole way of allowing technology its full surge and overcoming the prodigious difficulties that it keeps piling up. But we have no trouble understanding that the scientists and "technolasters" would rather not think about it; leaping blithely across this gloomy and uninteresting intermediary period, they hope to land squarely on their feet in the golden age. One could modestly wonder if we would ever get out of the intermediary period, and if the amount of suffering and bloodshed that it announces is not an exorbitant price to pay for that golden age.

My second question overlaps with the question asked by one of the most eminent psycho-sociologists today, D. Krech ("Controlling the Mind Controllers," *Think*, 1966): "Who will control those who control the human mind? [I would add: And those who intervene genetically?] The scientists are neither philosophers nor moralists." Indeed, if we look at the texts quoted by *L'Express* in a 1967 survey, we are struck by the incredible naiveté of these distinguished scientists and their inability to formulate a desirable human model. Without glimpsing even the shadow of a contradiction, these scientists declare *at the same time:* (a) *On the one hand*, we will be able to manipulate and remanipulate human feelings, desires, and thoughts at will, arrive scientifically at efficacious (preestablished) collective decisions, develop collective desires, set up homogeneous units on the basis of aggregates of individuals, forbid people to bring up their own children or even have any; (b) *on the other hand*, we have to assure the victory of freedom and avoid dictatorship at any price. All these are textual quotations. And Müller placidly talks about genetic engineering and artificial pregnancy, while at the same time assuring the victory of freedom.

And once these scientists hazard comments about the objective to be pursued, they cite perfectly hollow formulas: "To make human nature more noble, more harmonious, more beautiful" (Müller). But what does this mean? What reality do these adjectives refer to? We are left with fuzziness. "To ensure the victory of peace, freedom, and reason." Admirable sentiments, but it would be nice to know what they mean and *in what way* psychological manipulation assures freedom, and what this peace will be like if it is not part of an overrepressive society. And *who* is going to determine *what* structure? What sort of human being must be produced?

The thing that seems alarming right off is the immense lag between the powers of technological action developed by science and wielded by scientists and technicians, and their incapacity to criticize this power, to really control it. To do so, they would have to have: an ability to remain detached from their science (i.e., an absence of faith in science); a sense of the relativity of its works; an exceptional clearsightedness (which neither Einstein nor Oppenheimer revealed) of the normal consequences of their inventions; a very powerful transcendent thinking; an absolute self-control (in these works). And they would have to indulge in a very profound reflection on man. But everything I have read by these scientists (including Einstein) shows neither this attitude nor this ability. When they start talking about ends or objectives, they have good will, excellent sentiments, but an infantile attitude.

We keep stumbling across the formula of "happiness" with,

incidentally, its self-destruction. Just look at what was written by Dr. J. Weir in this symposium: "We will be able to modify the emotions, the desires, the thoughts of man as we do rudimentarily with tranquilizers." In other words, we will actually be able to give man the feeling of happiness, the conviction, impression, emotion of happiness, with no external cause, no material substratum. Man can then be happy even in utter penury. Well? Why promise comfort, health, food, culture, if a simple manipulation of his nerve cells could render man perhaps really happy without comfort or health?

Thus, the flimsy motive one might attribute to the technological adventure risks being swept away by technology itself. But ultimately, the most serious point is the inability of those scientists to provide us with a model of man. When they talk about "preserving the semen of men who deserve well of humanity," who is to judge? By what criteria? After all, Pasteur may have been a genius, but he was odious in his private life and not particularly likable in his dealings with colleagues. Are we going to choose the modest, humble, kind, good, helpful, generous man? I fear that this sort will not draw much attention. For some, it will be Napoleon's or Hitler's semen that ought to be preserved; for others, Mao's or Guevara's. Or that of the members of the French Academy. Or the Nobel Prize laureates. And behind these scientists' utterances, we glimpse a conviction that they are the ones who should furnish the offspring of mankind. But when we consider the mental mediocrity of these scientists, then the instant they bring out their speciality, we can only shudder at the thought of what they may regard as "favorable" for man. And we are seized with the anguish of the contradiction between the enormousness of the means and the inability to plan a desirable human model.

Nor do I feel that the philosophers and moralists are any more capable. If we asked all possible groups, according to races, according to religious, philosophical, and political options, we would have a hundred, a thousand ideal human types. There is not even the slightest edge of agreement on this matter. So we will produce hundreds of different types, all contradictory, according to group and national interests. And they will promptly conflict. And then all of them will manufacture the most efficient man in order to win out over all the others. Or else, the choice will be made a bit randomly, and they will manufacture an unreflected, unmeditated human model—because of circumstances. Just as today, with the most wonderful means of diffusion possible, we spread a culture that might at best be called an absence of culture, randomly produced. The problem still remains the irretrievable gap between the most admirable means and the total lack of reflection on what could possibly be done. Irretrievable because one does not board a supersonic airplane in mid-flight.

People are just as vague, hazy, and indefinite when claiming that the progress of technology will bring about socialism. Which socialism? No one is able to tell us. The confusion grows when we perceive that socialism is consistently altered in definition and content at each technological stride. Socialism is not a finality of technology. A certain social structure that one can dub socialism, if one cares to, will no doubt be the still unelucidated consequence of technological growth.[7]

Very often, incidentally, the goal of technology is identified as its growth and development; technology progresses in order to achieve the best development. Later on, we will delve into the relationship between growth and development. For now, let us make two observations.

First, all modern studies tend to dissociate growth and development, as Lefebvre points out. On the one hand, there is a simple increase of power, means, production, etc. On the other hand, there is a development of both the balanced social organization and man's intellectual, moral, etc. being. We could say, to schematize, that one is quantitative, the other qualitative, and the further we advance, the less we see a direct kinship between the two. Growth can even cause underdevelopment. To be sure, technology brings growth, but it does not guarantee development. It appears certain that the finality presupposed by technology is in no wise development. For countless technologies are applied nonstop, clearly producing the contrary of the hoped-for result. If technology and development overlap, then they do so only by chance, and seldom because anyone has that goal in mind. However, if technology produces growth, we cannot speak of any goal here. Growth is not the finality of technology; it is the result. No one sets up the ideal of growth; the latter appeared as a phenomenon only to the extent that technological progress dangled growth in front of everyone's eyes. Anybody who speaks of growth as a finality is simply confusing the end and the means.[8]

We sometimes come across another suggested finality: science. When people discuss the validity of technology, someone promptly brings up science. Now we have to distinguish the practice and use of technology and research. In the former, it seems quite obvious that the technician who employs his technology has no such objective, he has no scientific aim. It may happen, accidentally, that a technological practice will put us on the trail of a scientific discovery, and, moreover, very frequently, that the technician who employs his technology will take part in scientific research.

Naturally, we realize more and more that science can develop only through a vast technological infrastructure. But the latter serves science only accidentally; technology develops totally outside this scheme. And here, we are already entering technological research. The specialists of the various sciences keep repeating that most research is of no scientific interest. We need only recall (among so many texts) E. Perrin's statement that "the experimental explosion of an atomic bomb has no scientific interest." We also know that the work done at the various atomic research stations in France has been consistently judged in the same way. Incidentally, on another level, this situation is fully confirmed by J. Monod's declaration, which we have already reported: There is no other objective to science than science itself.[9] This declaration is debatable, but it certainly holds true for technology. Technological creation is justified in technology itself. It is acknowledged, for instance, that the space technologies have a far more technological than economic or political interest; and the use of communications satellites does not ultimately justify the huge sums spent and the prodigious research and development in those areas.

Nevertheless, it seems obvious that science raises problems, which require an enormous technological apparatus if we are to solve them. Looking closer, we realize that the scientific problems now emerging are actually the fruit of previous technological progress.[10] In other words, a certain development of certain technologies raises new scientific questions for the scientists, and these problems can be tackled only with a new technological means. Thus, we revolve in a reciprocal condition, and the scientific objective is in no way primary. Quite the opposite, it seems that in the last half century, the relation to science has reversed. Technology is no longer subordinate; rather, it legitimizes scientific research. All the protests of these past few years against the low funding of scientific research in France center around the notion that "true research is always profitable" (Chombart de Lauwe). If we must engage in scientific research, it is because the technological future rests upon it. The sole issue is the evaluation of when research becomes profitable: at a short term, says the businessman or politician; at a medium term, says the scientist. This difference

CAUSAL PROGRESSION AND ABSENCE OF FINALITY 267

in evaluation is a "complete revision of the notion of profitability," but we clearly see that the basic attitude is the same: technology justifies science.

And lastly, could one say that technology must be oriented by national grandeur or national sovereignty? Here, we come back to the problem of subordinating technology to a political objective. We have already indicated how the political factor has itself been modified. One illustration is the affair of the French Atomic Energy Commission (1969-70). The year 1952 brought the first Five Year Plan for nuclear power. For political motives and for the sake of independence from the United States, the French decided to choose a specifically French "line": "natural uranium/graphite/carbonic gas." But after a certain time, this led to an impasse; they could not continue with their research and implementation. In 1969, the government was forced to own up to its mistake. This spelled the crisis of the Atomic Energy Commission. It now decided to construct nuclear plants using only enriched uranium, à l'américaine. For fifteen years, enormous sums had been spent on a politically motivated antitechnological policy: the primacy of the political over the technological, which normally leads to failure.

There is no finality possible for technology. At the end of this review of generally admitted finalities,[11] we have to conclude that unless we want to content ourselves with ready-made words and formulas, it is impossible to discern any real finality in technological progress or in the men working away at it. One quickly realizes that any finalities cited are in no wise real or essential to technological progress. They are brought up for the nonce when justifications are asked for. And that, essentially, is what they are: justifications for some technological project, justifications added a posteriori, which the technological phenomenon, by itself, does not need. It is what it is—nothing more. Technology develops because it develops.[12]

Finally, we go along with Lefebvre (*Positions: contre les technocrates*) in his very remarkable analysis of "terrorist" (really, technological) society. Here he shows "the apparent ends—culture, happiness, well-being—are means, while the apparent means—consumption, production for profit, organization—are the true ends."

Simondon shows clearly that the influence of technology ultimately transforms the very problem of finalities. "Integrating a representation of technological realities into the culture by raising and widening the technological domain must put the problems of finality into their place, *as technologies*. These problems have been wrongly viewed as ethical and sometimes as religious." But this purely technological consideration of the finalities actually leads to obeying a causal process and to translating simply into terms of finality what is the intrinsic movement and the certain outcome of that process. To speak of technological finalities (i.e., ones that are integrated into the system) is tantamount to saying that technology evolves according to a causal pattern. Simondon explains our reluctance to admit this process exists: We see only the superior ends as important, we confuse life with the finality; but all this is just pure justification: "That of which there is technology cannot be an ultimate justification." The process of technological organization excludes the other finalities by making them seem inoperative, and this "technological production of teleological mechanisms allows us to bring out from the magical domain the most inferior aspect of finality. . . . The new technological forms cannot be justified by any finality, because they produce their own ends as the final term of evolution." Hence, the imbalance between causality and finality disappears. Naturally, "the machine is *externally* meant to achieve a certain result, but the more the technological object becomes individualized, the more this external finality wanes for the sake of the internal coherence of the functioning. The functioning has a finality with respect to itself, before having one with respect to the exterior world. In self-regulated functioning, any causality has a meaning as finality. Any finality has a meaning as causality."

OBJECTIVES

What would now be the medium-term objectives, which at a future point, would bring on, call forth, and determine technological progress? Let us first make out who sets these objectives. If nontechnicians (politicians, administrators, capitalists) establish them, then these assigned objectives are disastrous for research. We have spoken about this in our analysis of technology's autonomy when, for political or sociological reasons, the scientist and technician are told: "You must look for *this, here* is the problem to solve, *that* is what we expect of you." The result is feeble, as witnessed a hundred times. For technological progress to take place, it requires an indetermination at the start, the trial and error of attempting anything and never quite knowing where it will go. But obviously, these experiments are based on existing data that the technician has available to him.

Nonetheless, there are indeed objectives.[13] They are not, however, legitimate; they are not correctly established and formulated; they have no chance of realization unless they are set up by the scientists and technicians themselves. An objective is never chosen for its interest, for human needs,[14] lofty ideas, etc. It is fixed by each specialist in his specialty.[15] And how does the specialist determine that? The exact point is the limit between the possible and the impossible. The medium-term objective that every technician has to set up is to cross the limit of the impossible. "We can now *do this* in this area of activity. But we stop at this point; we cannot yet do that. The objective is to succeed in doing what is still impossible today. The route is open until *this* point. It is mapped out but not open until *that* point. Beyond that, we know nothing." Each technician follows his route, adding a new section, stage by stage. That is the valid objective. In other words, nothing interferes within the closed system of technology, which progresses in terms of itself.

Incidentally, it is very difficult to distinguish between objectives and finalities. B. Cazes has written a fine article (in *Critique*, April 1969) on the problem of ends and means in these areas. He tries to define the acceptable ends of *economic* growth. Cazes rightly emphasizes the difference between objectives and finalities, pointing out that "there is no automatic equivalence between the operational goal that is aimed at and the resulting impact on the finalities! . . . The finalities can be the permanent goals of a society which result from the value system that the society adheres to." There can thus be a huge number of finalities and "dynamics" of finalities. But Cazes shows clearly that making the finalities intervene in, say, an economic plan, means relativizing the objectives and gradually redefining them.

I agree fully with these points and with Cazes's conditions for determining what the finalities are. But then he reviews the themes frequent in the literature (solidarity with the third world, national independence, national development, social progress, economic growth) or the potential choice established by P. Massé (among an economy of power, an economy of leisure, an economy of consumption, an economy of creation, an economy of solidarity) or the three finalities offered by a group of experts (better distribution of professional power, improvement of the framework of life, the fight against poverty). And at last, he proposes the finalities that strike him as responding to all the necessary scientific criteria (national position in the world, development of human potential, economic growth).

In regard to these things, the following remarks are in order. First of all, these finalities make sense for the orientation of economic growth, no doubt (which is all Cazes was aiming at); but they do not make sense for technological growth. Moreover, there is obvious confusion between purely ethical finalities (solidarity with the third world, economy of solidarity, economy of creation, improvement of the framework of life) and concrete finalities resulting, in turn, from technological activity: power, leisure. There seems to be confusion between desires and realities. Of course, when people claim to be guiding economic activity in some direction according to a plan, they can pay heed to wishes, values, lofty moral strivings. But technological activity is of a different order from economic activity. Technological activity is not mixed up with moral or social values; whereas such values are impossible to eliminate, despite all rigorous attempts at making economy the "science of economic activity" (work, essentially, cannot help being a moral value too). In other words, economy can and must take moral values into account when defining the objectives, because economy cannot be "purged" of its relationship to ethics. This does not hold for technology, which contains nothing moral, spiritual, or human.

And if I try to relate these various motions of finalities to technology, I realize that practically no relationship is possible. To be sure, technology enters into all these sectors, reinforces national power, contributes to a certain human development, serves economic growth, and so on. But these are not "finalities"; none of these things is the finality of technological progress. And one cannot shunt it off into a direction exclusive of the others. How could one augment technology without augmenting power? So long as the world is divided into competing nations, how could technology help but be the instrument par excellence of national (hence military!) independence? How could it help but be the source of the consumer society? These are not objectives, but inevitable results. As for objectives that are not linked to technology—e.g., solidarity with the third world, social progress—either they remain pious wishes about technology or else they are radically transformed (and often inverted) the instant that, being converted into reduced objectives, they are subjected to the law of technology, which is determining by its mode of application.

## GOALS

Can one, finally, speak of short-term "goals"? One may, for instance, be tempted to say that the goal pursued is money. But ultimately, I do not believe it. Again, several aspects must be differentiated here. In regard to the technician who limits himself to practicing his technology, we are dealing with a profession. He is attached to his technology by the necessity of making his living; he serves the growth of this apparatus because he is attached to it, because he receives satisfaction, prestige, money. But he is not pursuing any real goal by using some means or other.

Then there is the inventor, the man who expressly tries to solve technological problems. In his case, the concern for money does not seem to dominate, he is obviously prompted by his personal temperament. But I would be willing to believe that the researcher applies himself out of love for technology itself, by his integration in the technological system.

One can, in contrast, hold that the capitalist promotes technological progress for reasons of money.[16] Everyone knows about the financing of research by the large petroleum and pharmaceutical companies. It is pointed out that in the United States the capitalist firms devote a lot more cash to research than the government, and increasingly larger percentages of investments. These facts are quite familiar. Plainly, these "capitalists" are doing all this in the hope of making money. But this is where the profit motive is alien, by nature, to technology. The profit motive compels an unsuitable finality upon technology from the outside. Hence, money contradicts technology as much as it summons it. Thus, for a long time now, people have been worried because in privately financed laboratories, "basic research" (without which no other research is possible) has been neglected in favor of applied, i.e., industrial research. No doubt, Americans are now trying to correct this trend and to accept a research with no profitable objective. But often, the financier imposes a simple improvement of known medicaments, a perfecting of manufacturing methods, rather than research for original products.[17] Very often, all they do is change the formula of an old product by incorporating a new substance that is useless, harmless, but expensive! And finally, the profit motive can totally block technological progress when a conflict breaks out between the interest of capital and overly innovative technologies: those demanding too rapid a renewal of material, those devaluating the means previously used, and so forth. At that point, we know, capitalists are tempted to halt the technological development that the capitalist system cannot absorb. In other words, goals like earning money are in no way the reasons for technological progress.

Here too, the only valid immediate goals[18] are the ones the technician sets himself in his experiments, his use of the technology, etc. But this action is solely in terms of the means available to the technician and within the previously acquired technological orientation. We can therefore say that technology never advances toward anything but *because* it is pushed from behind. The technician does not know why he is working, and generally he does not much care.[19] He works *because* he has instruments allowing him to perform a certain task, to succeed in a new operation. The consideration prior to establishing a goal or an objective is always the evaluation of the already existing means.

J. Boli-Bennet (*Technization*), picking up on an analysis by Boguslaw, whom he quotes, shows that in regard to "goals," the technological system has a very remarkable process of substituting inferior goals for the objective (the principle of "subgoal reduction"): "Making progress by replacing the achievement of an objective with the achievement of a whole lot of smaller and easier goals." Here, we are dealing with a specific phenomenon of the technological system. Man sets himself an objective that is very rich in meanings, connotations, and values; but when the technological stage is reached, a huge gap yawns between the ideal objective and what technology is doing. This is where the curtailing of the ideal begins; the ideal is shrunk each time to whatever technology is realizing—by demonstrating that the accumulation of hundreds of small technological strides will constitute the equivalent of the ideal goal.

Thus, as we see, happiness, the ideal objective of the eighteenth century, was transformed by the nineteenth century into a series of technological improvements ultimately constituting well-being: happiness was finally reduced and assimilated to well-being. And generally, as Boli-Bennet emphasizes, it was affirmed that the realization of material objectives *entails* moral, political, and spiritual satisfactions for humanity by demonstrating that what mankind was seeking on this level by a spiritual and moral route was impossible. This is not materialism, which would imply a philosophical choice. It is simply the motion necessary to technology obeying its causality and thereby substituting the goals it makes accessible for the goals that were ideally proposed.

\* \* \*

In other words, the real technological work is done in areas in which it is *possible*, with methods that are *possible*. Now what makes an operation possible? Previously existing material, method, organization, resources, competences, know-how—this combination allows not only performing the exact task for which all that was done, but also trying a new step along the technological route. It is precisely the use of acquired instruments that not only permits but even provokes technological development. The technician gets the idea of applying a certain procedure that was hitherto confined to some domain or other—of employing a certain chemical product in an original composition with another—of treating the organization of an army the way people have been treating an industrial ensemble, etc. In other words, technology progresses only in terms of and because of prior technological results.[20] There is a sort of pressure astern, forcing advancement. It is the pressure exerted by the mass of ideas, tools, machines, organizations, ideologies, manual or intellectual training, all of which is technology. There is no call toward a goal; there is constraint by an engine placed in the back and not tolerating any halt for the machine.

In this self-generation of technology, we must obviously recall that technology is ambivalent, causing new problems the instant it solves old ones, and that it grows by itself through the problems it raises. We can thus say with Boli-Bennet that "the problems appear because the solutions create them." And these problems are recognized and accepted as problems because the technological solutions are admitted as such in an "intersubjective" manner (which replaces the celebrated "objective"). However, the problems issuing from technology are also conceived intersubjectively. Problems emerge in a technological society in response either to the demands of efficient planning or to the capacities of the technological system itself, which demands being applied. The complexity of the system entails such numerous interactions that we cannot really see where a finality might have a place. Actually, each solution is technological, defining by itself the problem. The difficulty of understanding the technological system lies precisely in this reversal.

We are in the logical and scholastic habit of assuming that one begins by posing a problem and then arrives at the solution. In this case, a finality can be integrated (on the level of why I am posing this problem). But in the technological reality, the order must be reversed: the interdependence of technological elements makes possible a very large number of "solutions" for which there are no problems. Research and development keep bringing forth new procedures whose use is discovered *afterwards*. When we have the instrument, we can tell that it may be applied to such and such a situation; and naturally, the huge expense of research and development *forces* us to find useful applications for discoveries. Hence, the "problems" thus identified are automatically resolved, since the solutions come before the problems. In these circumstances, there is no place to integrate any finality.

Each technological situation is the outcome of what has been decided a moment ago, as is put excellently in a book by Dérian and Staropoli. We should not "forget that the electricity demand which the decision-maker asks the analyst to project into the future is what it is today because he himself, like his predecessor ten years ago, has made investment decisions to furnish this same energy to its consumers."

We may then set up two principles. The first is that *there is no technological research unless previous elements make it possible.* It is not only the application of technologies that presupposes a certain infrastructure (both human and economic), it is also the possibility of technological growth. In other words, it is absolutely useless and shallow of third-world nations to hope for complete autonomy from Western countries so long as they have not accumulated the technological factors allowing a specific progression. It is not enough to reach a point of using a certain number of technologies; one has to reach the point at which combining brings progression. Until it has reached that point, the third world will depend on technologies infused from the outside. We already know that development aid to Chile has borne exceptional fruits because, first of all, she went through an initial industrial stage with nitrates in the late nineteenth century. Even after the collapse of this mining, there was a crude technological substructure as well as a certain technological development in the rural and mining sectors.[21] On this basis, United Nations development-aid becomes beneficial. It consists mainly of coordinating and combining all the technological possibilities.

By contrast, the Chinese model is completely distorted. In technological growth, there is no possible way of substituting manpower, energy, ideology for the combination of technological factors. The extreme use of overabundant manpower can achieve (nontechnological) results equivalent to those obtained by technological means; but it can never launch technological growth, which cannot take place on the basis of a human factor. This lesson is taught by China's successive failures in this area during the last twenty years.

The second principle is that *any acquired element will be used in later research.* For the application of technologies, we have asserted that whatever exists is sure to be applied; nothing that is possible will be neglected. And the same holds true for research. Some procedures may be neglected, some technological factors may seem to have no future for a while; but they reemerge in some new application and are suddenly thrust back into circulation. Nothing is lost in the technological world. One progressing technology affects all the others and sometimes revives them.

Simondon excellently demonstrates this process of *causal evolution* on multiple levels. First of all, as the technological object evolves, it suppresses secondary effects which may prove to be obstacles and specializes each structure as a "positive synthetic functional unit": "The concrete technological object is one that is no longer struggling with itself, one in which no secondary effect damages the functioning of the whole." Thus, technology itself evolves by eliminating, in its own movement, anything that hinders it from being perfectly realized; this is a progression with no external objective.

But Simondon himself generalizes: "The evolution of technological objects can become progress only to the extent that the technological objects are free in their evolution and not necessities in the sense of a fateful hypertely. For this to be possible, the evolution of technological objects must be constructive, i.e., it must construct the third techno-geographic environment, each change of which is self-conditioned. This is not progress conceived of as a march in a pregiven direction or a humanization of nature."

Thus, the connection is established between technology as an environment and the nonfinalist, but causal process of development. Causality operates inside the milieu and moves from technology to technology. Simondon analyzes the very process of this causality, which moves from overall and previous (technological) ensembles to subsequent elements. These elements appear in a technological unit, modifying its characteristics, which causes a change in a given technological ensemble. There is the causality from the small element to the ensemble. But then, the mechanism produces a second causality, which moves from the ensemble toward each of the factors. This is characteristic of a system that contains its own causality. It occurs not only when new machines are invented but also when new products appear. As the technological process develops, new chemical products come forth (e.g., in atomic energy production), and something has to be done with them. They are not just refuse. Similarly, the combination of lines of chemical research causally brings new products—for instance, makrolon. No one was looking for a product that would be transparent, unbreakable, warp-resistant, and heatproof. But once the new substance is here, it obviously becomes indispensable.

Finally, research done by physicists on the basis of theoretical calculations (e.g., on transuranian elements) also gives birth to chemical elements "that do not yet exist" but are bound to exist in the future. Research—completely theoretical here and hence different from the two preceding cases—is thus causal. Physicists are oriented *toward* the discovery of heavy elements; they calculate that elements 112, 114, 126 are apt to exist. But this is because the researchers were pushed in that direction by a previous hypothesis, which determines the sequel.

To fully perceive the way technology progresses, we would have to apply Thomas S. Kuhn's research on science to these domains (*The Structure of Scientific Revolutions*, 1970).

We must not forget that technological growth results from *the procedures of the technicians;* and these procedures, briefly, are characterized as procedures by practitioners, based on a rich harvest of experiments and observations. Every technology progresses experimentally, by trial and error, with adjustments, and confrontations of experiments. Each technology must be successful and form the basis for a subsequent practice. It is a *progressive* procedure, always moving toward diversification and growing complexification, corresponding, of course, to an expectation, but with no real break or brutal innovation. And naturally, every technician must be informed about the progress of comparable methods, solutions to neighboring problems, and new findings and practices in connected areas. We are brought back more and more often to the experimental method, comprising—let us recall—six principle terms: observation of phenomena, selection of meaningful amounts, construction of a representative model (in all technological investigations, the construction of a model is growing more and more important), extrapolation from the behavior of the model, experimentation, definition of the scope of validity. Here, we see clearly to what extent everything functions causally.

Kuhn insists on the causal nature of scientific development: "The process of development described in this study is a process of evolution *from* a primal origin. . . . But nothing of what has been said or what will be said can make it a process of evolution *toward* anything. . . . We are all accustomed to viewing science as an enterprise that keeps getting closer to a certain goal set in advance by nature. But is this goal necessary? Can we not take account of the existence of science, as well as its success in terms of evolution, on the basis of the state of knowledge of the scientific group at any given moment?" Which is what Kuhn demonstrates excellently.

The general idea of Kuhn's presentation is that science does not proceed by linear accumulation—contrary to what is currently believed. It is usually thought that one discovery or invention is added to the other, but Kuhn demonstrates that this is wrong. Science progresses by leaps and bounds, by changes in direction. In reality, every linear evolution is based on "paradigms," and when we are forced to change a paradigm, any evolution is accordingly modified. Paradigms, for Kuhn, are "the scientific discoveries, universally recognized *for a time*, that furnish researchers with the problem types to be solved and the solutions." But simultaneously, these paradigms, being ready-made ideas, delimit the field of work and research for scientists during a shorter or longer period. Scientists purely and simply do not see reality, which is obliterated by the paradigms. They see only the reality delimited by these concepts. The paradigm gives scientific research both its basis (the context of discovery) and its legitimation (research has to take place on a certain basis and in a certain direction to be legitimate: this is a context of justification). The researcher, without even realizing it, works on the basis of these given theoretical ideas or this "tacit knowledge."

The paradigm is not simply a matter of method or research rule; it is actually the *Weltanschauung* within which the scientist has to work. Thus, the ensemble of paradigms can determine the progression of science without the intervention of perceptible rules. In general, only an alteration of paradigms makes us perceive the ones on whose basis we have worked. When we pass from Ptolemy's astronomy to Galileo's, from Newton's conception of space and time to Einstein's, etc., the paradigms then spawn a whole activity destined to draw all the inferences, illuminate all the facts thanks to the "theory" founded on the paradigms. These pardigms must be structured and specified in increasingly stricter conditions, and scientists go as far as possible into these domains.

Generally, for a certain time, people refuse to see the contrary facts or pay heed to failures. The paradigm is considered true. It is both the vehicle of a scientific theory and an instrument of work and interpretation. It has a cognitive and also a normative function. What is constituted as a body of "laws," experiments, theories, solutions within the framework fixed by the paradigm is regarded as "normal" science, which is constituted by the determination of significant facts, the concordance between facts and theory, the growing precision of the theory. All scientific literature during a period is focused on those three objectives. The paradigms, finally, are always reinforced by the fact that scientists make up a social body; they exchange ideas; they need solidarity; they check one another mutually. There is a sort of group orthodoxy that gets stronger as they get closer to the origin of the paradigm and heavier as the group increases. Scientists have had a similar professional training and initiation, which both differentiate them from other specialists and enclose them in the paradigms that have served to establish this specialty.

But little by little, the failures multiply, inexplicable phenomena start forcing themselves upon the researchers, new problems crop up, insoluble in the framework of old paradigms. Most often, it is the young or new researchers in the specialty that are alive to these lacunae and setbacks. They go to the origin and challenge the paradigm. The role of youth in basic scientific research and in discovering a new paradigm is essential. A conflict then occurs between "normal science" and the results of a new paradigm. This is not a possible addition but a qualitative leap. "Even though the world does not change after a change of paradigm, the man of science henceforth works in a different world." For hitherto, "the man of science, by virtue of the accepted paradigm, knew in advance what the givens of the problem were, what instruments could be used to solve it, and what concepts could guide its interpretation. But this interpretation can only *specify* a paradigm, not change it." Hence comes a tearing down of everything that was thought to be science, which is replaced by a new science, with new paradigms. Next, there is a kind of sifting of what was discovered previously, and then a reinterpreting of old phenomena and old laws. Thus, science proceeds by breaks and changes of direction. And technology suffers the consequences of these paradigm alterations, but also contains in its intrinsic development a process likewise made of ruptures and replacements. Technology, contrary to what people believe, is not only an indefinite addition of procedures; it is also ensembles of means superseding other ensembles of means.

And that explains the vast difference between the technician and the scientist. The latter, as Kuhn shows, is inevitably forced at a given moment to question the theory behind his work. Such is the effect of the paradigms, as Kuhn demonstrates. And it is an intellectual matter. The scientist is, in fact, limited only by the paradigms he works with, is accustomed to, and was trained by. If his mind is free enough, he can challenge them and construct a new interpretative system. The technician, on the other hand, is locked up in the network of functioning practical applications. Investments have already been made; when we notice an error, we cannot correct it because that would mean wiping out with a single stroke of the pen the billions already involved (and this is true even in a socialist state!). Furthermore, there are the groups taking part in the work. To be sure, the scientist also has his "professional corps," but he does not destroy it by leaving it; at most, he himself is excluded. We cannot overthrow a technology, because thousands of people earn their living through its application. And ultimately, the technology forms the framework of life for people; it cannot be dumped; we cannot scrap a set of processes, products, apparatuses, for *they* are a livelihood. We have to have the agreement of these people, we have to "reverse" public opinion, to make this transformation possible. The technician cannot overthrow or reorient technology, because the latter is defined in its very progress by the professional "apparatus" (both mental and material). This is a further decisive aspect of causality.

In point of fact, technology advances within a sector to the utmost possible point,[22] until it comes up against an impossibility (stemming, usually, from the outside—a limit on money, raw material, etc.). And so long as technicians are going in one direction (within a paradigm, Kuhn would say), they see no other, they do not look for anything in another area. When a blockage occurs, e.g., a missing energy source, then, to achieve the same result, they supplant the old technology with a new one. Research thus proceeds from impossibility. For instance, solar or geo-thermal energy was considered uninteresting so long as we had no oil problem. New technological progress is conditioned by the impossibility of going on with petroleum-based energy.

Let us consider "space research and astronautics." It has become standard, even in the USSR, to claim they serve no purpose, and to contrast them with expenditures regarded as useful: housing, agricultural research, etc. Faced with such opposition, scientists mention a certain number of uses for the development of communications, instantaneous diffusion of information (Tel Star), which will allow a remarkable advance of worldwide education in certain useful domains (e.g., learning the most highly developed farming technologies, contraceptive practices, etc.—the use for a possible war is modestly veiled). And, at a longer term, serious scientists are talking about ore mining[23] and even agriculture. They have already forecast that soon after the year 2000, it will be possible to grow algae on the top atmospheric layer of Venus; this will absorb the excess carbon monoxide, giving off oxygen and perhaps serving as additional food.

But when we examine the numberless "uses," we notice that we will simply be employing what exists or will exist. We are not pursuing this research *in order* to grow algae on Venus. But, given that we can fly to the moon, what can we do *on it* and *with it?* If we have the instrument—we have to use it, and it ultimately has to be useful. It is not a specific objective, a specific use that has guided and determined the research. When technicians came to a certain degree of technicity in radio, fuels, metals, electronics, cybernetics, etc., all these things combined and made it obvious that we could fly into the cosmos, etc. It was done because it could be done. That is all.

The technician deals with certain products, certain methods, certain instruments; he has to use them as best he can. This use, of course, combines all the existing factors. Innovation *is* the combination of these factors.[24] We should stop worrying about the difference between the simple user (on the lowest level, the driver of the car) and the inventor of new technologies. The two draw closer together as the technologies get more refined and more numerous. Thus, we know that the astronauts (users) are intimately associated with space research. Technicians work in terms of past technological strides; for these, it is obvious that the users are the best judges. A technician acts with what previous technological progress has put in his hand: earlier technology is the real cause of later technology.

It triggers certain effects that are themselves either a new technological advance or a component of this advance.[25] Technological progression does take place, but without any goal. It is no use wanting to suggest ends for technological progress or to discuss such ends. We can keep talking on and on, it will not matter at all. The concrete manifestation, as we have pointed out, is that the philosophical and humanistic discourses on what ends should be proposed for the technologies have no effect or influence on these technologies. One might think that this is accidental. Quite the opposite, for if we understand the true conditions of technological progress, we can see that this lack of communication stems from the very nature of the phenomenon. This progress occurs with no end in view. Nor can any end be proposed—much less changed. That may satisfy the intellectual or politician who is conscious of having done his duty and everything in his power; but it has no value at all.

For several years now, we have realized that when the ends are challenged, everything keeps jogging along as if nothing had happened. A huge amount of political change has occurred; but nothing anywhere has been altered in regard to technological growth and its effects. The finalities of medicine have been upset by what is known as social medicine, but nothing has changed for creating a mentality of a collective patient, and so forth. The finalities of automobile construction have been seriously challenged, but these challenges have not altered the existence of the car. On the other hand, when some resource grows short, then the finalities disappear! The oil crunch is a splendid example of our unbelievable sensitivity to means. We thought we were doomed because the "petroleum resource" was about to run out. It is not the technological system that is fragile, it is we who have become fragile. We suddenly felt it was unthinkable, inconceivable to have a bit less heat and light, to limit the use of cars. It was an absolute "crisis"! We also noticed this fragility when the TV pylon was destroyed in Britanny! Panic! An impossible situation! To deprive a whole region of TV for a whole week. Even *Le Monde* carried on about it. A loss of means appears out of the question: the very purpose and value of our lives is affected!

Having no end, technology has no meaning either. By seeking to discover an inner meaning, we prevent ourselves in advance from making any correct analysis of the phenomenon. As for trying to attribute meaning, this is really a mythological operation. Confronted with this enormous object, man wants to humanize it, find a common measure with himself, and he therefore embellishes it with a meaning. But that is exactly the operation that some people have pictured as occurring at the origin of religions. I hear thunder; it is not possible that something which frightens me and acts upon me can have no meaning, since it does have an effect. It is not possible that this can be a perfectly alien phenomenon. I can therefore attribute it to a more considerable personage than myself, but one similar to me, a God who has feelings as I do. And thunder becomes the comprehensible, sense-endowed manifestation of that God. (Of course, I know that this kind of explanation for religion is no longer accepted today!) The philosophers who want to give an end or a meaning to technology are unconsciously taking that road. They "anthropologize" and "mythologize" the technological phenomenon. However, we have to place ourselves squarely in front of this phenomenon, and we will then see that technology per se is not justified by anything forming man's previous universe. It does not belong to any constellation already known. It suffices unto itself, it conditions itself, it is situated only in regard to itself. If one claims that one can therefore act upon it, one cannot do it either on the level of finalities or on the level of meaning (i.e., of discourse).

One can intervene concretely on only two levels.

*Either:* One can try to act upon the components making up the next technological advance. But in that case, one has to be a technician oneself and, at the same time, a critic of technology, a lucid critic resolved to change the system. But this strikes me as a hitherto inconceivable human combination. When a technician claims to disengage himself from his technology and to act, he is launching into politics, which is the absurd attitude par excellence.

*Or else:* One must try to invent nontechnological yet applicable means for living and surviving in this technological environment—means exacting great inventiveness and energy, allowing one to be situated differently in relation to the technological universe—the attempts made by hippies, for instance. But little can be expected of them on this level, for they lead to setting up a marginal society, with no influence on technology, and with a way of life that is highly dependent on outer technologies, for this marginal society develops only through the enormous possibilities of the technological infrastructure.[26]

# 12

## THE PROBLEM OF ACCELERATION

HERE, for the first time, we encounter the problem of forecasting[1] or predictability in the technological system. And it is better to confront this problem directly, albeit on a particular point. To ask about the acceleration of technological progress is to ask about the possibilities of predicting the evolution of the entire system. On the one hand, there are obvious things; but on the other hand, there are incredible complexities in establishing facts and applicable methods.

Everyone knows about the Meadows Report (Club of Rome, M.I.T., etc.). Even though its scientific method can be contested, even though its conclusions are not as obvious as one might think, everyone knows that it asked the tough question about the limits of technological growth: Do any physical limits exist for the population expansion and the industrial expansion at the rate that has been noted for the last twenty years? We know the answer. The arable surface of the earth is limited, the expansion of food output is tied to nonrenewable resources, and it is calculated that the reserves are not considerable. Even if natural resources are not exhausted, they will reach prohibitive prices within fifty years; technological growth is accompanied by a pollution growth that will make development impossible. And Gruson, in his remarkable study "Affamé d'énergie," (*Le Monde*, 1972), confirms these conclusions in one essential point: Mankind risks having a lack of energy very soon. The oil deposits are not inexhaustible. Within thirty years, we will have to choose between a general return to coal or a massive recourse to nuclear energy despite the dangers.

For all these reasons, and many others that we know, Meadows proposes zero growth, the passage from a state of growth to a state of equilibrium, in which the problem will be not to develop production, but to correctly distribute the output. Thus, the problem raised in this chapter is:[2] Are we going to witness a voluntary curb presided over by man himself (the Meadows hypothesis); an involuntary and catastrophic blockage due to a collapse (the Vacca hypothesis); or a gradual halt because of a slowdown in technological progress? The last would be the most satisfactory answer, but I am forced to note that it is envisaged by almost nobody. Given the system of causal progression of technology, no one can see how such a gradual braking can come about. I myself do not accept any of these three hypotheses. I believe that the imbalances and dysfunctions will keep augmenting within the system, and, for lack of feedback, cause not a restraint but a disorder, which can, in turn, make the whole system slow down.

A simple look reveals that for a century and a half, technology has been evolving more and more rapidly.[3] It may be banal to say that there is a greater difference in all domains between the society of 1800 and that of 1950 than between the society of 5000 B.C. and that of 1800. But it is no less banal to point out that technological progress was quite slow between 1780 and 1850, much faster between 1850 and 1914, accelerating even more between 1914 and 1945, and reaching an incredible speed between 1945 and 1970. A good example of this rapidity is the computer. Not just for its expanded use, or even its many improvements, its speed, its size; but for the transformation of its basic givens. That is what is meant when people speak of "three generations" of computers since the first assembly-line calculator (Remington's Univac 1951). There was the phase of electronic tubes (with a double triode), lasting twelve years; the phase of transistors, from 1958 to 1964; and the phase of miniaturized circuits, toward 1975. But now a fourth generation is envisaged, a phase of integrated circuits. These advances have been toward an augmented pulse speed, greater reliability, and greater compactness.

As far as speed goes, adding two ten-figure numbers took 4/1,000 of a second in 1951, several tenths of a millionth of a second in 1955, 1/5,000,000 of a second in 1960, several hundred billionths of a second in 1964. The compactness of the new type of "memories" is considerable: stripped of tapes and punched cards, the means of grasping data allow over a billion words to enter a bank.

At the present, observers are starting to glimpse the speed "limit" which can be attained but not surpassed: the speed of light. But if *this limit* imposes itself, it will in no way stop the improvement of computers—the creation of a "buffer storage," the attempt at anticipating the result of a computation in order to make it enter a following computation before it is even finished, the separation of subsets that can be replaced by more improved ones, the flexible adaptability of the computer system, etc. Advances are so swift and the results so vast that one might possibly speak of a fourth "industrial revolution" only thirty years after the third.

As a further example of technological growth, one may take the series of cyclotrons with nine different types from 1930 to 1960 and with acceleration from one to 100,000 mega-electron-volts. But here too, a limit can be reached quite rapidly.

These are simple examples, and one cannot deduce a general movement from specific examples. But we must, in any event, point out the essential fact that it is always, in all branches, the most modern, the most advanced technology that determines the trend. Here, too, we find the automatism of choice working without fail. Still, it is useless trying to heed this acceleration in a practical fashion. It is impossible to precisely enumerate all technological improvements in all areas during one or more years. Even if this list could be drawn up, it would be impossible to compare it with a similar one for the years 1920, 1930, 1940. Not because of the same difficulty, but because one cannot be satisfied with comparing the number of technological inventions. One would also have to compare the respective importance of these inventions and the scope of their application. This is so since, naturally, in order to analyze the technological phenomenon throughout history, one cannot take the same attitude as toward science. For science, it is important to find, say, the date of the scientific discovery itself, its intellectual context, etc. But for technology, what counts is neither the invention itself nor its application in the laboratory, but rather its diffusion, its application through large-scale consumption. A marvelous technological invention remaining closed and confined to small circles would be uninteresting for the sociological analysis of the technological phenomenon. It is impossible to know exactly as of what date the diffusion of some procedure became sufficient to be taken into account for the growth of technological progress. Hence, it would seem that a precise factual study of the speed of this progress is absolutely out of the question. Those who hold that there is a continuous acceleration and those who feel that a slowdown is due after the period of growth are divided on impressions, feelings, and facts that are chosen as exemplary, but are highly approximate.

Thus, we are told in regard to scientific development: The number of creative scientists living today is the same as the total of all who have existed since the start of mankind; and the number is twice now what it was in 1930 (Report by P. Auger, Scientific Research Section, UNESCO, 1963).

It sounds very impressive and very unconvincing. What is a creative scientist? At what point does one become a scientist? What is the criterion? And how has anyone managed to count up the scientists who lived in China, India, or even the European Middle Ages?

We are also told that the quantity of human knowledge has doubled in the past ten years. But here too, what type of "knowledge" is meant? Is, say, legal knowledge included? And by what standard can we measure knowledge in history? Obviously, with research augmenting, we are submerged in knowledge. Thus, for an International Scientific Congress on Atomic Research (1964), a very complete documentation had been gathered on discoveries and new applications since 1950. And this documentation was so enormous that it would take one scientist twenty years to read it through.[4] Since all these discoveries are scientific, but turned toward application, it goes without saying that technology can only grow faster and faster.

One is obliged to note that the minds of respectable men are dominated by this obvious state of technological progress. A single example—Sauvy writes: "A conquering despot, technological progress will suffer no halting. A slowdown is equivalent to a setback. Mankind is doomed to perpetual progress." Progress in what? Technology, of course. A setback in what? And suppose technological progress is a setback in regard to something else? Charbonneau, in contrast, writes lucidly: "To believe in fated progress is tantamount to emphasizing material and collective organization: to stressing one of the conditions of freedom and not its subject, individual man. If we accentuate material, power logic [technology], we can only choose the impersonal."

A huge number of authors take the acceleration of technological progress for granted. G. Berger, writing in 1957 about educational reform, said that we had to rediscover "the deep meaning of education and invent the methods suitable for *an accelerating universe.*" That goes without saying.

Moving to the other extreme of the scale of seriousness, Toffler claims to demonstrate the "general process of acceleration," but without adding anything new aside from gratuitous affirmations and spectacularly insignificant facts (actually, he just parrots verbatim my demonstration of the geometric progression of technological progress).

Vacca, always far more precise, shows how the technologies adjust to one another in a growth that may be considered indefinite. (He regards the end as catastrophically accelerated, but he contributes few decisive elements.)

Closets, for his part, points out that there is acceleration, inter alias, by maintaining, like Toffler, that "the process from basic research to the finished product unrolls more and more rapidly: it took forty years for the electric motor, thirty-five years for radio, sixteen years for X-rays, ten years for nuclear reactions, eight years for the atomic bomb, five years for radar, three years for the transistor, etc. This is simply a statistical fact. Innovation can come up against a technological obstacle for decades. But industrialization takes place very rapidly once these difficulties are overcome. . . . The film of history unwinds at an accelerated speed."[5]

Actually, I am not at all convinced by these figures. As usual, we are offered a few examples in lieu of a synthesis. It would have to be proved that during these periods *all* technological strides in all branches followed the same acceleration. We must also ask what acceleration bears upon. At the start of the paragraph, Closets speaks about the passage from basic research to the finished product, and at the end of the paragraph, he speaks about industrialization. These are not the same thing! Moreover, when he indicates time periods, is the starting point the innovation itself or the components of the innovation? Or even the industrialization process? Is the finishing point the manufacture of a prototype or the mass marketing? There, too, the time periods are highly variable! Likewise, when we know about the plurality of technological factors involved in any innovation, we have to ask ourselves *which* is the true point of departure. Finally, Closets seems to reckon in terms of a direct line from scientific research to technological application, a process that we have shown to be inaccurate. Thus, we can get nothing from such examples; and above all, we cannot extrapolate as Closets does when declaring that "each time one draws a curve, it translates the same acceleration." Here, he mixes up consumption, the gross national product, and technological progress. It is obvious that there is acceleration in consumption (for technicized countries); and it is even more certain that there is greater acceleration in energy consumption.[6] But we cannot strictly infer any acceleration of technological progress.

Likewise, it is certain that the technological gap is widening, that the chasm between nations with, say, mass use of the computer and those without it is deepening. But here again, one cannot draw any conclusion about the acceleration of technological progress. Actually, the technological gap might result just as well from qualitative as from quantitative effects, or even from the stunted growth of certain countries that collide with an impossible situation: e.g., for the computer, as Elgozy so clearly points out, the low salaries in the third world.

Rorvik, in his abstract idealism, claims to show this acceleration concretely, on the basis of lists of probable technological achievements. Among other things, he emphasizes Helmer's famous "Delphi model" for the Rand Corporation. According to Rorvik, the moment one can predict the technological actualization of teaching machines for 1975 and the use of robots for all material tasks and certain administrations for 1988, then these things *will be*—regardless of any psycho-politico-economic possibilities of acceptance. In other words, when demonstrating acceleration, he once again regards technology *in vitro*, without realizing for an instant that technology is an environment integrating into an environment. Thus, one cannot infer anything about its acceleration.

In contrast, we must set great store by Vacca's demonstration. Vacca (*Demain le moyen âge*, 1973, chap. II) analyzes and criticizes the most common reasons for assuming that technological expansion will halt. He shows that although the drawbacks and harmful effects, the irrationalities, the congestions, the psychological insecurity, etc., do exist, they are incapable in themselves of seriously restraining technological development. Technology will keep growing despite the noise, despite the moral collapse, despite the costs, until the breaking limit. In other words, all the very real disadvantages cannot curb its growth; preferring technology to anything else, man is ready to endure incredible scourges and to adapt himself, until the breakdown. However, this will not be "zero growth" or gradual deceleration. When the accumulated effects start acting, it will be too late—i.e., it will be a catastrophe, with an enormous decline in technology and population.

R. Richta (*Civilization at the Crossroads*) too leans toward the idea of acceleration. He holds that the acceleration of technological inventions keeps growing, that the lag between a scientific discovery and its application keeps shrinking (he gives thirty-seven years for 1900 and fourteen or nine years for 1960—but I do not know

## THE PROBLEM OF ACCELERATION

where he gets his figures), and that "the amount of scientific knowledge now doubles in less than ten years." This last comment strikes me as a very flimsy statement for such a restrained man! And all the more so because on page 335 he contradicts what he says on page 223: In this other passage, he maintains that the cycle of an innovation now lasts twenty years, a figure corresponding "to the period of technological reconstruction of the basis of production and to the training time for researchers."

Can one really generalize? It would be cogent only if here again we drew up an inventory. Now the closest thing to this, the Rand Corporation Report of 1965, comes to the opposite conclusion on this score. The gap between discovery and application has remained practically the same from 1900 to the present. Moreover, it is felt nowadays that, on the contrary, a longer and longer delay is necessary between the start of technological research and its termination. The more complex the technology, the slower it moves on that level! We will have to get back to this point, for most of the people involved in futurology base their forecasts about technology on that presupposition.

Nonetheless, on the basis of the "ascertainments" that we have just surveyed and on similar ones, a few observers speak of an exponential growth of technology. The most frequent attitude will then be to consider technologies or scientific methods already known and to directly prolong their effects, to draw the possible and predictable inferences of scientific discoveries, and to show that this development will get more and more rapid. In the same way, observers demonstrate that the rural flight caused by applying new technologies has to accelerate or that the big cities are becoming vaster and vaster because of new technologies of transport, concentration, and so on.

In this view of the linear, indefinite, and increasingly accelerated growth of technology, we must pay heed to G. K. Chesterton's warning in *The Napoleon of Notting Hill* (1950): "All these clever men were prophesying with every variety of ingenuity what would happen soon, and they all did it in the same way, by taking something they saw 'going strong' as the saying is, and carrying it as far as ever their imagination could stretch. This, they said, was the true and simple way of anticipating the future. 'Just as,' said Dr. Pellkins, in a fine passage— 'just as when we see a pig in a litter larger than the other pigs, we know that by an unalterable law of the inscrutable it will some day be larger than an elephant'. . . . so we know and reverently acknowledge, that when any power in human politics has shown for any period of time any considerable activity, it will go on until it reaches to the sky."

R. U. Ayres (*Technological Forecasting and Long Range Planning*, 1969) rightly shows that technological forecasting is now indispensable because of both the planning and the orientations of neo-capitalism, but that it cannot be scientific because science illuminates the three laws that rule the functioning of the system under study. Hence, he says, technological forecasting is useless, and we are left with highly variable certainties and elementary information. He is altogether correct so far as this critique goes. But he fails to see that technology is actually a system, and that if we do not sufficiently understand it in its *totality* and *all-inclusiveness*, if we remain on the level of material technologies, especially production, and if we are obsessed with predicting "innovations," we condemn ourselves to grasping nothing and being able to predict nothing. Obviously, so long as we try to paint pictures of "inventions" in 1985 or 2000, we will be dabbing about at random and get nothing serious done. But Ayres himself confuses technology (*technologie*) and its object, the technical (*technique*) (and hence, the *technologians* would have to replace the technicians!). And Ayres himself envisages nothing but the economic technologies. Therefore, he prevents any possibility of his conceiving technology as a system.

The first question one should ask is whether the necessary forecasting is possible, and this has two aspects. The first aspect is the predictability of technological growth; the other aspect is the predictability of human and social development.

People often seem to admit that technological growth is somewhat predictable: the Rand Corporation specializes in very serious extrapolations. Likewise, in looking at the Kahn and Wiener book *The Year 2000*, we easily see that if the attempts at political and economic forecasting are very risky and furnish many possible models, the only part that seems surer and clearer is the part concerning technological progress. Here, in theory, one can set up something like a probable pattern; one sees what the more likely inventions and technological applications are, the ones already imaginable if not in progress. But, if it seems perfectly logical to undertake such an evaluation, what strikes me in this kind of forecasting is the lack of two issues that ought to be regarded as decisive. The first is the relationship between technological expansion and economic growth. If we are situated *inside* technology, we

## THE PROBLEM OF ACCELERATION

can indeed sketch a relatively clear pattern of the progress to be expected. But, as we have frequently said, *invention* in technology has only a very relative importance; what counts is application and diffusion. These two latter aspects depend on possibilities of economic mobilization. And here, we are in terra incognita. Not that a certain economic forecasting is impossible; but what does seem impossible is *the relation* between the economic potential and the technological potentialities—this is the correlation of growths.

The second difficulty is that of the very method of forecasting. One must first receive Ayres's "lesson in humility." This technological forecasting has nothing to do with the earlier extrapolations; but it still does not contain any scientific certainty. We are dealing here with an accumulation of multiple elementary data (like those that Closets gives in his book), highly variable in their weight and relatively uncertain. And they are juxtaposed in order to draw a picture that is possible because it is coherent. One can then try something like a more or less systematic inventory of possible futures, and one chooses the least unlikely construction. But we are not doing a general study here on the possibility of forecasting. We are not looking for what progress will be like in twenty, thirty, or fifty years. These charts have been drawn up by countless institutes, with dazzling disagreements. All we are interested in here is the problem of acceleration.

In regard to acceleration, we also have to consider the phenomenon of causal growth that is analyzed in the preceding chapter. We thus see that a technological development takes place by combining earlier technological elements. Logically, when their number increases, the combination possibility grows in a geometric progression. Schematically, if we have four factors to combine, they can produce twenty-four combinations. If we add a fifth factor as important as the others, then, assuming equivalent combination possibilities, that gives us 120 possible combinations. We have already said that each scientific and technological stride has repercussions on all other knowledge and applications. Progression now takes place no longer in a single domain, but through a combination of processes and sciences belonging to sectors that were previously viewed as distinct. One can actually maintain that while not all possible combinations are realized, it is not one new factor that is annually proposed for combining with the previously known factors, but tens or hundreds. And when these combinations bring forth a technology or a technological application, the latter also enter into contract with a hundred others as potential factors of combination.

Thus, the more technologies we have at our disposal, the faster technological progress accelerates. Each technological discovery has repercussions on and causes progress in several other technological branches, not just one. Hence, also unintentionally, the sheer combining of new givens produces ceaseless innovations and applications. Moreover, entire fields, hitherto unknown, open up to technology because several trends come together. Observers are trying more and more to define the "crossroads" (see L. Armand's report in *Réalités*, 1965), where diverse technologies and disciplines interpenetrate: crystals, bionics, low temperatures, so-called "space" technologies, etc.[7] Such knowledge and practices are not melded arbitrarily. The knowledge acquired in a certain number of disciplines converges—one might almost say—"spontaneously" toward an area of study; and the teachings thus gathered make other branches of science bear fruit ipso facto.

How can low temperatures help the study of plasma, that fourth state of matter, which forms at temperatures of thousands of degrees? Low temperatures have also led to superconductivity, which has in turn led to building superconducting magnets, used in a growing number of devices and also for scientific research. Thus, we are witnessing an unlimited growth of technology and a constantly increasing speed. But given the theoretical slant adopted here, it is better to speak of a potentiality. If the technological phenomenon evolved in a vacuum, one could say that it was developing by the principle of geometric progression. There is no visible reason for it to stop evolving in this manner.

This led us in 1950 to formulate the law of geometric growth for technological progress. We have to add an interesting idea by R. Lattes (introduction to Mesarovic, *Stratégie pour demain*) that the nonseparation of variables leads to the phenomenon of coupling. "Linear behavior, in which the effect is directly proportional to the cause, is replaced by a coupling, nonlinear by definition, between phenomena that, interlocking with one another, keep amplifying their effects in turn, sometimes to the point of divergence." This offers a perfect view of the reality of reciprocal effects of technologies within the system. With, precisely, the ambiguity of this accelerated growth; for the coupled variables produce phenomena of amplification, but also, inevitably, phenomena of mutual neutralization. This is what we ascertain. Vacca gives an excellent formulation, saying that all these technological activities and creations have "a character of continuous and exponential growth, and their variation is ruled by a well-known mathematical law: the law of the phenomena of growth in the presence of limiting factors."

But one cannot even picture technology developing in a "pure" environment. By its very nature, it is in touch with the concrete, it is meant to be applied. Hence, one can evaluate the real progress of technology only with respect to its application environment. This intrinsic potentiality of indefinite and accelerated growth must be shifted to the concrete. When reintegrated into its milieu, technology runs into obstacles that are external to it (and here we realize that the adaptability of institutions or economy is not indefinite). Or else, technology reveals a different aspect of itself: a kind of self-curbing, self-regulating.

First of all, let us push aside facile opinions that are no more valid than those quoted at the start in favor of acceleration. Periodically, some intellectuals proclaim that "it can't go on like this for long." A few, like E. Wolf, declare: "The law of the limit of technico-economic development involves the fact that past progress closes the way to future progress, i.e., future progress is left with a margin that is only a fraction, nay, a small fraction of previous progress." These words were uttered in 1945! Before the enormous technological development of recent decades. This "law" ignores the deepening and widening of the field of scientific knowledge. It was strikingly refuted by L. H. Dupriez ("L'Intensité du progrès technique," in *Mouvements économiques généraux*, I, 1950). We are dealing with a simple philosophical opinion. But someone always regularly announces the end of the possibility of technological improvement. Victor Hugo proclaimed it for the railroads. And L. Mumford (*Technics and Civilization*), generally better inspired, also declared that some of our inventions cannot be perfected any further and that the domain of mechanical activity cannot be extended: mechanical progress being limited by the nature of the physical world. True, no doubt. But we are very far from knowing the limits of the physical world. And ever since Mumford wrote this in 1937, the explosion of new inventions and technologies in all domains has singularly contradicted his forecast. It is quite true that one cannot imagine indefinite progress. But the question is whether this is due to lack of imagination or to actual limitation. We cannot, in any event, rely on such general reasons to predict the halt of technological progress.

Statements that further technological progress is impossible have always been given the lie. Even in 1970, an expert could say that, in the present state of things, we could scarcely envisage any improved performance in computers and that it made no sense gaining a few millionths of a second, that this area was reaching its ceiling. But since then, two considerable advances have been made: in terminals and in storage; in what IBM calls "virtual memory," which seems to be a decisive step forward (1972). Thus, on no score can we foresee any arrest in technological growth.

Finally, let us recall Colin Clark's opinion (after Mumford) that the progress of organization tends to cut down the use of certain machines. It is, of course, true that *certain* machines are going to disappear or have already disappeared; but not by a curb on technological progress. Quite the contrary, the cause is an acceleration of progress. Moreover, one cannot announce the end of technological growth by stressing the passage to a new "era," that of organization. This would, annoyingly, reduce the technological dimension to that of machines. We have seen that organization has become a technology. All one can say is that if the growth of organization leads to a certain regression in the use of machines, it is because we are entering a new era of technology and one kind of technology takes over for another. This is no setback, no sign of "deceleration" in technological progress. But, vice versa, when Richta shows clearly that the acceleration of technological progress is tied to a direct relation of the developments of the "science/technology industry," one can only remain undecided. According to the Keldych principle, "science *must* develop more rapidly than technology, technology must develop more rapidly than industry," in order that growth may occur.

Now it does not seem as if any such hierarchy is actually crystallizing. We are in the domain of wishful hypothesis. But if acceleration is due only to such a hierarchy, we cannot be assured that acceleration will take place.

\* \* \*

We may therefore say that, taken in and of itself, the technological system tends to accelerate its growth and progression incessantly and, in theory, indefinitely. But, at the same time, we must realize that when this acceleration takes place, negative consequences result.

This growth makes it harder and harder for the environment in which technology is integrated to adapt.[8] As we have seen, ob-

## THE PROBLEM OF ACCELERATION 295

servers note adjustments by the economic, political, etc., environment to technological demands. But malleable and uncrystallized as the environment may be, there are limits (and they are very quickly reached) on the speed of its change. It is materially impossible for social, legal, political structures to change several times in a few decades in order to supply the favorable context for new technological demands.

This is inconceivable. And it is, no doubt, an important aspect of the generation gap. Young people are directly adapted to the latest impulses of technology, whereas adults do not manage to follow. Which recalls one of the major curbs: the difficulty of finding men who are both adapted and competent. Here, we are dealing with not only the unmalleability of the human environment, the difficulty of parents in even imagining a totally new kind of work for their children, but also with the length of the necessary training. The faster technology moves, the more it produces the following situation. Young people begin training for one type of computer; but when their studies are over, three years later, progress confronts them with new types—and they have to readjust at once. We must pay heed to the enormousness of the demand. One sole example is data processing. This new instruction is being launched almost everywhere. But in 1970, it required 50,000 additional programs (140% over 1966) and 25,000 additional analysts (170% over 1966). Not even half were produced. Yet elsewhere, we have unemployment!

Perfecting the machine causes a lag between its capacity and man's capacity, and this lag seems insurmountable. The human cost keeps rising as the computer is improved. The cost of programming represented 10% of the whole electronic system in 1950, 50% in 1960, 70% in 1970, roughly 80% in 1973! The fragility of the computers, their demands on their attendants keep growing. The parts jam at the most imperceptible variation in voltage or intensity (this seems to have barely improved); the adaptation of the entire system to the computer appears to be more and more difficult; the preparation for using it requires enormous work. Elgozy cites a few interesting cases. Merely for recognizing the authenticity of signatures on checks, the employees of Crédit Lyonnais worked a million hours a year to prepare the technologies for electronic use. Likewise, it took Charbonnages de France two years to calculate the models serving general programming for five years. The need for highly qualified personnel keeps growing faster than the possibility of training. "Thus, the technological utopia comes up against the economic and social [and human] realities of our society." In other words, at a certain degree of technological growth, man is the decisive curb on development. We can skip Elgozy's many examples of computer errors, for they strike me as perfectable and reparable.

Z. Brzezinski also stresses the restraint on technological progress by a lack of ability and intellectual training. This is essential: a society would have a difficult time getting technicized if at least ten percent of its population between twenty and fifty years of age did not have a superior education and, moreover, if at least thirty percent did not have a secondary education. Furthermore, the education must correspond to a certain intellectual aptitude. Can we be sure of having it in these proportions?

It is thus possible that man, unsuccessful in controlling, orienting, or utilizing technology reasonably, may in his turn become a restraint and cause a recession. And this can happen in two ways.

On the one hand, we have to remember C. Wright Mills's statement (*The Sociological Imagination*) that a high level of technology and rationalization is not necessarily accompanied by an equivalent level in individual intelligence or social intelligence. Technological rationality does not necessarily increase tenfold the individual's will or faculty of reasoning. On the contrary! Man, becoming more and more self-rationalized and more and more unsettled, is gradually losing freedom and reason and growing less and less capable of truly reorganizing society or revamping scientific research. Thus, the type of man created by technology is incapable of maintaining the process of growth. He directs technology into repetitiveness—the same process we have seen in regard to the state.

On the other hand, we must take into account the extraordinary arousal of public opinion, the disappointment, fear, and questionings (which I would certainly not call awareness). And the press has been echoing this excitement since 1970. It is the generalized revolt of workers against efficiency, against subordinating work to profit.[9] It is the violent reaction to the technological imperative,[10] echoing the survey made by *Forbes* magazine on whether American technology is going bankrupt. The political preponderance is directly accused of causing sure recession, as are the emerging antitechnicization opinions. The term "contested research" is used by N. Vichney (*Le Monde*, July 1971).

From faith to disenchantment—the more hope was pinned on technology, the more traumatizing the discovery of drawbacks or setbacks. Equally significant is the May 1971 report of the Organization for Economic Cooperation and Development. On the social level, contestation is triggered either by the subordination of technology to capitalism or by technology's inability to solve social problems. But more than anything, the technological risks are what now influence public opinion. Such topics were taken up in the Science and Society colloquium of the Fondation Maeght (June 1972), with a strong trend toward contestation by American scientists. Contestation has encroached upon a domain untouchable twenty years ago: that of technological progress and its applications to work.[11] It is no longer the consumer society that is being attacked, but the technological society. In trade unions as well, the idea of an indefinite progress of technology is far from being accepted as yet. Some observers are even no longer depicting the future of the working class as a liberation by technology. Everywhere, the interpretative theories (economic, social) are being challenged *by* this contestation of technology.[12]

There is thus a kind of psychological recession that might deprive the technological system of its human foundation, which is indispensable even from a concrete viewpoint. What will happen if the young turn their backs on the system and refuse to furnish the "human capital"? French data processing is already in a dither about whether it can recruit the 220,000 computer experts now needed in France. This is a detail. But all these bottlenecks and refusals are on an emotional, passionate, irrational level. They are manifestations of fear, escape, the "freedom reflex" so dear to Pavlov. Nothing here strikes me as lucid, conscious, or basic. Hence, this crisis may be quite transient once the emotions have passed. And already numerous signs appear to indicate that we are in the process of veering once again. If, in contrast, people could reach a level of awareness and theory, they could envisage a regular curbing of technological growth. Otherwise, we must witness a stoppage made incoherent and dangerous by the inevitable disorder it will cause.

Restraint also occurs in a different form. The environment is so shocked by the impact of ceaselessly renewed technologies that it reacts to change and inserts curbs, usually spontaneous and noncalculated.[13] The issue in the preceding case was the impossibility of adaptation. Here, it is the reaction of a too deeply shaken environment, greatly brutalized; it is a simple defense reaction, but one that is perfectly understandable. A human group tries to "persevere in its existence," it adopts innovations only gradually and tends to absorb them. We have seen that the relationship has reversed. Now, it is technology that engulfs and determines the cultural forms, the "civilization." But this is neither accepted nor achieved.

In other words, the behavior of human groups in regard to technology is according to traditional forms and relations. Man claims he still controls and uses technology. But in this way, he restrains what strikes him as threatening, frenzied, etc. We must therefore pay heed to these refusals, which grow more extreme as the movement grows more rapid. The curb that might ultimately be the most effective is man's anxiety and even panic at what technological innovation demands of him. And it does no good whatsoever to say that "one must adjust." For the essence of the books or reports on this topic is the maladjustment of their authors. Upon rereading such texts after an interval of several years, one perceives their perfectly retrograde character. The authors suggested adapting to a technological stage that is completely over.

There is another possibility of curbing technological growth—by the growth of the state. Apparently, a contradiction exists between the development of government and technology. Despite research and development, I believe that people are admitting more and more that the imperative of political organization blocks scientific progress. Without going along with Eccles (*Facing Reality*, 1970), who views political freedom as the condition for discovery and innovation; I would assume that the very structure and imperatives of the modern state are altogether contrary to scientific research. The latter does not endure rigid planning. The state as such, being a total and absolute ruling organism, blocks scientific research and halts its applications. It actually organizes a technological society, but it forces that society to engage in a process of repetitive technicization. Thus, the state becomes vaster and more technological the more it tends to curb technological innovation by the excess of inevitable organization often called bureaucracy and by the imposition of goals external to technology.

It is quite illusory and idealistic to believe that if government concentrates its strength and means on technological research and development, if it subsidizes, then it does so in a liberal, neutral, and disinterested way. In reality, the state imposes organizations and objectives. But in so doing, it disarranges the system, making it grow incoherently. It would be wrong to infer that the state can *orient* research in any direction (e.g., military). This *orientation* (which is real) actually corresponds to a disorganization, a desystematization. If the technological-military complex that is so much talked about is obvious, if technologies keep developing more and more rapidly for wars and for the army, then this is because the defense need appears to be the most "obvious" (just as danger multiplies an individual's strength) and arouses all the more.

However, the reality is altogether different. We realize that the technological strides accomplished in these conditions are factors of irrationality in the ensemble (as we shall see later on). And if there is any acceleration in certain areas, the imbalances caused on all levels (social, economic, etc.) are actually crisis factors in technological progress and, secondarily, factors of possible deceleration in this progress. Now if this, *finally*, is the influence of government, we must, vice versa, note that technology causes the expansion of the state. It is technology that has made the modern state what it has become; it is technology that not only gives the state its means and domains, but also exacts this centralized power of coordination. This is so true that in the past thirty years we have seen the content of the word "socialism" changing. What is called a socialist revolution today is the awareness of the technological phenomenon, the desire for a lucid consciousness about it, and the wish to adapt everything to technology, to submit the social and political conditions to the need for technological application without discrimination. Socialism is now the form of government that is aware of technology's possibilities and the equal application of all these possibilities. There is no longer any doctrinal criterion of socialism, and the social structure is no longer characteristic (i.e., the end of private property). There is now a choice between a government aware of all the implications and necessities of technological development and a government that permits the social irrationalities, the inequalities, the consequences of the past, the survival of private interests from a pretechnological epoch.

One cannot say that technicization is pushing us toward socialism. But certainly, *socialism has become the absolutization of technology by politics*. This definition is the sole common denominator in all the regimes that style themselves socialist, although being of such diverse types (USSR, Cuba, China, Algeria, Yugoslavia!). Thus, technology helps the growth of the state, and this growth, arriving at its apogee, pulls technology into a blocking bureaucracy.[14] Something that is a NECESSARY consequence of technology risks becoming its *curb*.

We find another interesting example of the political obstruction of technology in the story of satellite liaisons between airplanes and control centers. Technologically, such telecommunications satellites are easy to actualize. But any project is halted by the political competition between the United States and France. The controversy began in 1965 and is still going strong. We have seen it in practice. Each time "free" political decision intervened, it interfered with the possibilities of technology.[15]

Of course, let me repeat, I am not inferring from this that politics is useless or ineffective. Like anyone else, I can cite a hundred examples of technological research made possible by the political authorities. Earlier, I showed in detail that the conjunction between the two has become ineluctable. But political decision is positive in those areas only if its motives are technological and not political, and if the decision is made by an organism that became technological *before* its momentum became political.

\* \* \*

Among the obstacles exterior to technological growth, the most striking is the economic obstacle. Technological progress, as we have already said, is tied to a certain number of economic possibilities. This would mean that technological growth must be accompanied by the same kind of economic growth. However, the further we advance, the more we perceive that the costs of economic growth are rapidly going up. This study of the costs of growth is probably the most important issue in present-day economic research.

We know that these are not just positive costs but also negative ones. Investments are required and, it is realized, continued economic growth entails greater and greater investments of funds, people, and knowledge. Perhaps the growth of these demands is even faster than the growth of technology itself. And that obviously puts a curb on this growth, because these possibilities are not indefinite. Now perhaps the more the system tends to accelerate, the more vigorous the curb will be, because there are no new corresponding resources, and the resources created by the new technology are always insufficient for the needs of new progress.[16] We must pay attention to the following. We are now probably going through a reversal of the well-known trend of technological progress, i.e., the production of surpluses that allow investments toward further technological progress. At the present, the surpluses are never enough, because technological progress is too rapid and its demands are getting harder and harder to meet. Investments are increasing in disproportion to the result obtained. There seems to be a generalization of the law of diminishing returns. But this is merely a tendency.[17]

In contrast, we must add the negative costs that were long ignored, such as destruction. There are direct costs, like human labor or investments, corresponding to a desire for growth; and there are indirect (or external) costs, which are due to the overall economic trend. We thus find damages and pollutions, noise, and all the "harm caused to others without those responsible accepting the responsibility" (B. de Jouvenel). For instance, the progress in the means of communication increases the damage and great cost of urban remodeling. If one wishes to evaluate the real cost of automobile growth, one must take into account accidents, medical expenses, disability pensions, higher insurance rates, road works, losses due to lower work efficiency in a noisy environment, health problems caused by air pollution, etc.[18]

"Coal mining, oil drilling, exploiting forests, producing proteins—a demiurge is enough for that. Manufacturing sky, water, space, and time—that would take a God." Using hundreds of examples, Charbonneau demonstrates the illusion of growth through the increased costs, errors of technicians (e.g., regarding atomic plants), the manufacture of "social gadgets" (seemingly useful but actually *useless*), gigantic works that are profitable only in prestige, and the destruction of the primary elements of nature.

Then there are the costs of various kinds of congestion: problems of moving, living space, travel expenses (for weekend outings or going to work—each being as necessary as the other). And there is also a congestion of knowledge and information, a congestion of minds.[19] Congestions overwhelm the individual and upset the society's life. But as in all technological domains, they are not a final stage; defense reactions set in. The organization of education and invention, such as Massé describes, is certainly a way of decongestion. Nonetheless, it must be observed that congestion is with us, increasing day by day, whereas the reaction is hypothetical, in the realm of possibility.

Then there are the costs of change. The things we have discussed—administrative, judicial, ideological, and other adjustments—do not come gratis. We were speaking of the need for greater human investment, but this assumes a very expensive technological, intellectual, and ideological training. We can see the problems caused by university overcrowding, which is itself a cost of change. We must transform education, curriculums, and pedagogy for the new professions that the young will have to take up—and such professions are new because of technology! This transformation will be both difficult and expensive—so much so that society does not seem able to afford it. We must also add the incalculable expenses of retraining, of permanent refresher courses. All this can be effective only if we are truly on the level of real technological progress. But in that case, such a difficult undertaking will immobilize an ever-growing portion of educators, who, cut off from research and from teaching the young, will tend to cause technological stagnation. So far, educational recycling has been very superficial, not preparing anyone to take his place in technological development.

Finally, we have to consider the price of complexity. The more the social, administrative, and economic system increases, accelerates, involves larger and larger numbers, the more complex it becomes, and, hence, the more it augments the services of coordination, of second- or third-degree administration, such as we have talked about. But they too are extremely costly. It is no good saying that such services can be performed by machines and data processing. These facilities are extraordinarily high-priced and more and more specialized, they presuppose a larger apparatus, and technological progress quickly renders them obsolete.[20] Hence, they will in no way lessen the burden of complexity on economic life. On the whole, we see that economic growth is assured, even conditioned by technological progress. But at the same time, the costs of this growth are increasing so greatly that its results may become less and less satisfying, and, *all things considered,* the *ultimate* balance may not be positive. But then, adequate resources cannot be made available to technological growth, which will then be slowed down if not blocked.

In sum, the further the *possibility* of technological innovations increases (according to the geometric progression I have described), the further the number of innovations in all areas augments, and the more we realize that it is materially impossible *on all levels* to accept, apply, and endure those innovations. Psychologically, ideologically, man cannot put up with *everything.* That is the correct (though banal) argument of Toffler's book. Economics cannot follow, any more than administration, management, organization, no matter how hard they too try to become technological. The malleability, the plasticity of the social organism are not indefinite. Hence, choices must inevitably be made among technologies, among innovations. We cannot, today or tomorrow, do

## THE PROBLEM OF ACCELERATION 303

everything that technology overabundantly proposes. The gap between the technological potential and its realization tends to increase overall. But we are still left with the technological imperative (anything that can possibly be done technologically must be done) and the accumulation of the technological potential (any dormant innovation can, at any time, be aroused and applied). Nevertheless, the examples of blockage are multiplying. The speed of computer innovations now demands a "pause" (the growth rate in the computer industry has gone down since 1970). Industry can no longer "show off."

And, let us note, incidentally, that under these circumstances, a great attack is being mounted against the computer. I might suggest that the project against nuclear energy, then space technologies, then data processing, has come exactly when each respective area has reached the ceiling of its application possibilities. In other words, when the gap widens between the technological potentiality and the actual general application, then people virtually justify not carrying out everything that technology allows us to do. And this justification (involuntary, of course) is precisely an accusation against *this* unachieved technological potential. Man, as usual, claims to be still in charge of the situation, and since he *cannot* use this resource, he declares it bad, harmful, dangerous. In his great wisdom, man does not want it. Naturally, we will forget our misgivings once application is possible.

When a new technology appears, its application is more and more difficult if it proposes to dethrone older technologies. We know the melodrama of the fluidic, which allows us to perform logical operations solely with the help of flows and without the intermediary of electronics. But after the huge investments necessary for developing electronics, how could anyone, as of 1970, question electronics! It has not yet been fully developed, after all, and the personnel is only just being initiated! This is not a matter of capitalist structure, of lack of financing. Under any regime whatsoever, it is impossible to suddenly replace one technological ensemble with another. The further we advance, the more the technologies require a material infrastructure, an immobilization of capital, and a vast human training. Hence, the less capable they become of being rapidly superseded. A technology can keep improving in its own being; but we are having a harder and harder time leaping from one technological ensemble to another, a new one. Such is the case with fluidics.

This obligation to choose among the technological possibilities makes the universe of a Toffler or Rorvik highly improbable. Both authors stick to the simplistic vision of the universe of kiberts, robots, electroprotheses, the generalized artificialization of the human body, and so forth.

Even on a more modest level, if we take, say, the use of the oceans, we perceive the gigantic abyss between the knowledge acquired in laboratories and the true possibilities.[21] Aquaculture is an instance. We may create two small stations for basses and salmonidae. But then we are promptly forced to admit that these two experiments raise *enormous* problems for the *overall* handling of the coastline! Far worse is the question of tapping the mineral wealth at the bottom of the sea. This is technologically possible—but . . . who has the right to do it? Whom does the ocean floor belong to? This is not merely a legalistic quibble. We may very well end up with the same problem as colonization in the sixteenth century. The country with the technological power has the right to exploit. And it will thereby enlarge its power. But if we refuse to go along with this, if we divide the ocean equitably among the nations, this would mean that nine-tenths of its "riches" would not be tapped, for only two or three great powers are capable of exploiting them. Such are a few of the many problems showing that reality cannot follow the rhythm of technological innovations.[22]

\* \* \*

Yet there are also, it seems, internal blockages, a kind of self-regulation in the technological system. Here is one example, based on Closets's fine analysis of the medical technology. In point of fact, there has been vast improvement in all domains—and it occurs so rapidly as to devaluate the peak technologies every three or four years. At the same time, new technologies appear in unexplored areas. But these two kinds of growth are of interest only if these technologies are applied to a sizable number of patients. Otherwise, they are purely laboratory affairs and of little interest. Here, we once again find the gap between discovery and application, the latter alone being a constituent element of technology. But application to a large number of patients requires a specifically trained medical personnel (which will be harder and harder to obtain) and a hospital equipment that is very expensive and will take a long while to set up. By the time it is installed, by the time "the most modern" technologies are made available to thousands of patients, these technologies become largely obsolete. In the course of this process, technology virtually suffocates itself. The installed apparatus forbids the application of what might be possible. It is not enough to set up a computer possessing the whole of medical science. We have to be able to put to work everything that it indicates! Technology thus ultimately curbs itself by being unable to keep endlessly readapting application, because *one* application of medical technology implies an infrastructure of dozens of other technologies. And the more swiftly the first technology evolves, the less capable the others are of adjusting, because they have been adapted to a technology that is *already* highly evolved.

It has been observed that in any growth of a technological sector, there is a change of rhythm and possibilities. At first, numerous choices and options are possible. Gradually, one of the variants is imposed, excluding the others for many reasons (which fits in with what we have examined as the technological automatism). At first, likewise, the sector has a large number of innovations. But little by little, these innovations, necessary to its development, become less and less numerous. An important fraction of research in this sector moves toward marginally improving the initial product or making it different from competing products. In other words, within each sector, in turn, success coagulates the technological process into repetitive forms and modes. The essential thing would be to find out whether this situation has an impact on the whole of the system, or whether the static area is normally replaced by other sectors.

This acceleration of technological progress, if it is to be fully achieved, would require a harmonious and concordant growth of the subsystems. In point of fact, the more acceleration, the more the distortions, dysfunctions, incoordinations are rudely felt. When certain technological sectors "do not follow," the repercussions are felt everywhere.[23] Overly great possibilities in a peak area set tardier areas moving. We know there is uneven growth; but so long as the movement is not too rapid, there are compensations, replacements, polyvalences (J. R. Platt, "The Evolution of Man," *Science*, 1966). However, in the contrary case of accelerated growth, the system cannot balance itself on its own. We may then await slowdowns due to these imbalances, until the overall equilibrium of technology is restored. "The object meets hindrances within its own functioning: it is in the incompatabilities spawned by the gradual saturation of the system of subensembles that one finds the limits, the crossing of which constitutes an advance" (which I already noted in *The Technological Society*). This advance is basically a change in the internal distribution of functions, a rearrangement of their system.

The same holds true for the technological system. When the subsystems block one another, the ensemble, obviously, cannot keep growing. This is Vacca's analysis of the present-day situation when he demonstrates that the large subsystems are becoming unable to function. We now seem to have reached this saturation point. Every new technology has a hard time finding its place in the system. It causes a hitch in the ensemble, which, for its part, seems more and more fragile.

Simondon asks about crossing this limit. Given the size we have reached, is such a crossing possible? No one knows. This is why we can be certain that acceleration is not indefinite and that it will be curbed more and more often. But it is almost impossible to say at what precise level the slowdowns will appear, whether the trend will be reversed, whether we will pass from acceleration to deceleration, or whether we are moving toward stabilization or merely normalization of growth.

Very detailed studies of these specific, but generalizable, points (Simondon) lead one to think that the technological changes cannot go on at this rate and are now reaching a limit in most domains. An astonishing acceleration is taking place in the social and human milieu, a kind of "bang" causing considerable disorders just about everywhere. But this climb over the wall of technological possibilities must inevitably be followed by a time of stabilizing and putting things in order. We are thus in the midst of a transition crisis, and we can await a perceptible slowdown in the entire system during the next thirty years. This opinion is shared by Sheldon (former member of the NASA general staff). For him, after an era of wasting and squandering technological resources, we are about to enter an era of conservation and orderliness. The problems now caused by the technologies, he says, are so enormous that we will be going through a "recess" and mankind will be forced to devote all its strength to overcoming the damages and disorders. The present technologies will no longer be developed in their own direction; they will, instead, be applied to "heroic measures," bringing a certain halt in technological progress.[24]

Similarly, Closets writes: "Just as we must admit that there will never be more researchers than individuals, and that the science budgets will never exceed the GNP, so too we must admit that the actual curves of progress are sure to round off: progress follows S-curves."

One can observe the same stagnation trend in the medical domain. The advances of the medical sciences since 1960 have been more apparent than real, more theoretical than practical. It is all as if, in overdeveloped countries, the vast growth of medical consumption were not being translated into an improvement of public health. "Increasing or decreasing the health budget by one half would probably change nothing in the average longevity of Americans," says Professor Béraud, from whom we take this analysis. The true amelioration of health now comes more through mass education than through spectacular therapies. We must rethink the training and informing of the public. But we would then collide with the extreme slowness of this training and the difficulty of reversing the "hypno-technological" current, which leads the public to conceive of medicine only in terms of a glorious surgical operation or reanimation. Here, it is slowness that seems to characterize the next stage.

Likewise, in one particular point—though we could multiply the instances—Vincent has very scientifically demonstrated that hourly work output has been climbing for years in the West at the rate of five percent, yet there is no possible way that automation can allow this growth (European Colloquium on Automation, Grenoble, 1967).

Of course, we must not count on any general reversal of the trend, which would cause something like a regression of the system. Charles Reich's reveries strike me as highly dangerous: to wit, the machine is starting to self-destruct, the state is achieving its own ruin (without a communist revolution—oh, Lenin!). The state, he explains, can no longer be governed, the causes for malcontent among the workers/consumers are on the rise; the more spare time a man has, the less he likes doing his work; the more satisfied the consumer, the less the worker wants to work; technological products can be totally consumed only in wars, and, he firmly declares, the war in Vietnam is the decisive crisis for bringing the enterprise state and the technological system to a standstill.

One can only be stupefied at such infantile rubbish! Reich shows that he has no synthetic view of the technological system and no deep knowledge of history. He keeps his nose to small present-day facts, which he takes for huge general trends. He might recall that no war has ever halted technological progress—quite the opposite. Five years from now, young Americans will have totally forgotten the Vietnam War, and the only traces will be quantities of technological improvements. Indeed, there is no reason to believe that the system will self-destruct, no reason to count on any blockage for the reasons listed by Reich—especially because of any change in consciousness. By now, three years after the publication of his book, we may note that in the United States, the grand appearance of Consciousness III is a façade that is just toppling. The hippie movement, drugs, the counterculture, communes, the rejection of the consumer society are all waning, and students are "back to normal." We are returning, lock, stock, and barrel, to Consciousness II, which, in my opinion, we never left in the first place!

In other words, there can be no forecasting about true acceleration or stagnation in technological progress. If it seems more cogent to believe in a slowdown, one cannot foresee the exact moment at which, or the precise sectors in which, it will occur. What is certain, in contrast, is that we do not have the right to make predictions simply by prolonging what already exists. Or to claim that the rural areas will be more and more depopulated, that the overall population will continue to rise, that transportation will accelerate, that there will be ever-growing problems of commuting, and so on. These hypotheses are absolutely gratuitous when extended beyond a dozen years. The same concerns the overall spread of automation or the four-hour day.

In any case, the probable slowdown tendency affects only one technological sector (immense, to be sure!): the application of the physical and chemical sciences.

Which raises the question: What will the expected stasis be used for? To restore order in a disarrayed society, to allow efficient organization, to assimilate the vast progress already made, to allow man to integrate and adjust? In other words, we will keep making strides, but most likely in the hitherto disadvantaged technologies, the organization and adjustment technologies, the psychological and manipulational technologies, the preservation and compensation technologies.

Reparation activities are going to absorb more and more strength and power. According to Baudrillard, this will cause "a kind of self-deviation of the system. . . . a threshold of slippage, which all the excess productivity will pass to maintaining the conditions for the survival of the system." This may be perfectly accurate. But we must note that it would in no way correspond to any lowering of acceleration. In fact, for such deceleration we would have to consider that the only technologies taken into account are the technologies of producing for consumption. These are diminishing, however. And while the psychological, sociological, ecological, administrative, and similar technologies may develop very rapidly, the rhythm of the system will not slow down. Technological

## THE PROBLEM OF ACCELERATION

activity will merely *shift* its zone. Nor can these technologies, which are meant to cope with dysfunctions, be contrasted with technologies that are supposed to increase the "positive satisfactions." For it would be a perfectly positive satisfaction to eat healthy food, suffer less noise, live in a balanced environment, do away with traffic jams, and so on. Hence, technological acceleration can persist under these conditions—only *elsewhere*. The dysfunctions do not necessarily challenge the acceleration.

It cannot be said that the technological system as a whole tends to stablize. Let us merely say that a few sectors will probably slow down their development, while others, more underprivileged today, will develop necessarily and unfailingly. There is no trend toward general blockage. On the contrary, the system will return to the mode of growth that we indicated in self-augmentation.

*Conclusion*

# MAN IN THE TECHNOLOGICAL SYSTEM

FOR more than thirty years now, people have been wondering what man's place is going to be in regard to technology. We can discern two currents in these reflections.

For some, the essence is the relationship between man and the machine. This group is subdivided in two: those who feel that man and machine will combine and those who feel that man will simply be excluded by the machine. And again, each of these two interpretations is further subdivided in two. Some people speak of the "man/machine" coupling, which is the more reasonable conception (both man and machine perfectly adjusted to one another and functioning in terms of one another). And then some people, in science fiction, speak of a mutation in man, who will turn purely into a brain and nervous system, while the machine will become man's body, the integration being thus whole, like a graft.

In the exclusion current, we find two views: an optimistic opinion (man excluded from all hard work and able to devote himself to spiritual elevations and the joys of creation); and a pessimistic opinion (man excluded from all activity, becoming parasitical and superfluous, or ultimately wiped out by the revolt of the robots).

All this is very shallow, because it sticks totally to the fragmentary and parcellary vision of machines, thousands of machines, regarded singly, with man also perceived as an individual. There is no grasp here of the technological system or even the technological phenomenon. We can leave all this aside.

The other great current (if we skip mystics like Teilhard de Chardin) attempts a more inclusive view and more or less accepts the idea of a technological society. But these people remain far too vague and utterly hazy. They talk about consumption, leisure, etc.

The point is no longer machines or mechanization but that we are living in a technological system. And this makes it obvious that the problem of the relationship between man and technology can no longer be posed in a traditional way. This conclusion will not try to sketch any solutions (to be saved for a later work). Nor will it deal with disadvantages and dysfunctions of the system (to be studied in the book following this one), which can be envisaged as the starting point for feedback toward completing the system. Simply, we have to ask ourselves what will actually become of man in this system and whether we can preserve the hope, so often formulated by idealists, that man will "take in hand," direct, organize, choose, and orient technology.

Seligman, in a striking formula, has emphasized the technological mutation in this area: Homo faber no longer exists; he has become a working animal. And the man who used to be at the center of work, for whom (as Marx kept pointing out) work had a decisive meaning—that man is now gradually being evacuated from work. He finds himself, as Seligman puts it "at the periphery of work." We must then ask the question: Who is the man to whom one attributes the power of choice, decision, initiative, orientation? No longer a Greek in the time of Pericles, or a Hebrew prophet, or a twelfth-century monk. He is a man who is entirely immersed in technology. He is not autonomous in regard to these objects. He is not sovereign, nor does he have an irreformable personality.

Man's situation in the system can be analyzed in five propositions.

First of all, man, achieving consciousness, finds technology already here. For him, technology constitutes a milieu which he enters and in which he integrates.[1] It is quite futile to say that technology is not a true environment. Anything man lays eyes on or makes use of is a technological object. He does not have to choose between alternatives. He is instantly within this universe of machines and products. And the most innocent items, the electric button or the water faucet, bear the most immediate witness to this technicity. Now without our realizing it, this environment shapes us in the necessary forms of behavior, the ideological outlooks. Who would contest this "already here"? It is taken for granted and acquired. It is taken for granted that rapid transportation and medicine are used. They are not questioned. Why shouldn't they be used? Very quickly, man thinks in conformity with this environment. He is formed for comfort and efficiency. If a person awakes to consciousness, he would no more dream of challenging or contesting the technological milieu in its perceptible aspects than a twelfth-century man would dream of objecting to trees, rain, a waterfall. These are self-evident things that very swiftly adapt this man to the engulfing reality of the phenomenon. Of course, he does not clearly see what it is all about, he does not discern the "technological system," the "laws" of technology. But neither did the twelfth-century man know the physical, chemical, biological "laws" and the processes uniting into a whole the phenomena that he perceived as separate. Being situated in this technological universe and yet not detecting the system is the best condition for being integrated into it, being part of it as a matter of course, without even realizing it.

This situation is complemented by the fact that all intellectual training prepares one for entering the technological world in a positive and efficacious way. This world has so thoroughly become a milieu as to be the milieu to which the culture, methods, and knowledge of all young people are adapted. Humanism is antiquated and has given way to scientific and technological training because the environment in which the student will be immersed is, first of all, no longer a human, but a technological environment. He is being trained to perform his function[2] here, i.e., he is being prepared to exercise a profession; but the latter requires knowing certain technologies and using technological apparatuses.

Education and instruction no longer have anything "gratuitous" about them; they must serve efficiently. And criticism of education always boils down to this: "Students learn masses of useless stuff. The important thing is to prepare them for a profession (i.e., the technologies of some branch)." All present-day schooling tends to become technological, and it is justified in the eyes of the public only if it is rooted in that concrete situation. How, then, could a young person trained in this way make any choices, any decisions about technology? Not only is he born in the midst of technology, not only are his toys technological devices, not only does he use cars, cranes, electric motors from childhood on; but schools prepare him for technological functions; and, more and more, this is the only kind of knowledge he receives.

The celebrated "crisis" of the French university has no other deep source than the maladjustment of this system to technological training. That is what we call "preparing students to enter society."

We must not forget that education is getting more and more

specialized, with unbelievable rigor. The training of, say, a computer programmer involves six very distinct specializations (system programming, administrative programming, real time programming, etc.). How can we expect a man thus trained to have even the slightest possibility of criticizing or taking over the technological system. Furthermore, when he enters a profession, all he encounters is the exercise of technologies. Whatever his job it is chiefly a participation in the technological system, either by what is produced or by what is diffused. There again, how could he challenge what is ultimately the warp and woof of his life?

In short, technological man is divided into two modes of being.[3] On the one hand, he is at close quarters with his technology, his specialty. He is very competent in his domain, he knows and sees clearly what he has to do with increasingly greater efficiency. But this remains within a narrowly limited sector. On the other hand, he is on the same level as anyone else: he knows the world and the political and economic problems only through partial and partisan information, he has half an understanding of the issues, a quarter knowledge of the facts, and his competence in his own domain is useless for helping him to grasp or know the general phenomena on which, ultimately, everything depends.

This influence is a lot greater than that of school or work. The technological system contains its own agents of adjustment. Advertising, mass media entertainment, political propaganda, human and public relations—all these things, with superficial divergences, have one single function: to adapt man to technology; to furnish him with psychological satisfactions, motivations that will allow him to live and work efficiently in this universe. The entire mental panorama in which man is situated is produced by technicians and shapes man to a technological universe, the only one reflected toward him by anything represented to him. Not only does he live spontaneously in the technological environment, but advertising and entertainment offer the image, the reflection, the hypostasis of that environment.

This mode of conditioning has already created a new psychological type (see the detailed account in L. Mumford's *The Myth of the Machine*): a type bearing, almost since birth, the imprint of the metatechnology in all its forms; a type incapable of reacting directly to visual or aural objects, to the forms of concrete things, incapable of functioning without anxiety in any domain, and even incapable of feeling alive unless authorized or commanded by a machine and with the aid of the extra-organic apparatus furnished by the machine deity. In so many cases this conditioning has already reached a point of total dependence. This state of conformity was hailed, by the most sinister prophets of the regime, as the supreme "liberation" of mankind. Liberation from what? Liberation from the conditions in which men prospered: namely, an active relationship, a relationship of mutually gratifying exchange with a human and natural environment that was "nonprogrammed," varied, responsive, an environment full of difficulties, temptations, hard choices, challenges, surprises, unexpected rewards.[4]

Here, once again, the first steps toward control seemed innocent enough. Consider B. F. Skinner's teaching machine. It is apparently and immediately legitimate! And yet, it is a simple means of technological adaptation. Admen and PR men do not, of course, have any deep, perverse intention.[5] But the true and ultimate result of their work is to defuse the spontaneous reactions against the technological system, more completely integrate every spectator or consumer into it, and induce him to work toward technological growth. Certain advertising technicians even have those express aims. All who are preoccupied with the society of tomorrow assume that the only thing to do is deliberately prepare people for life in the technology of tomorrow. Thus, since TV will progress in any event, since we roughly know what the strides will be like during the next twenty years, all we need do is prepare mankind in *advance*. "We have to get organized today for tomorrow's TV" (Closets).

However, the future they envisage is one of culture and freedom. It is therefore quite remarkable to note that when appearances lead us to think that the created image is nontechnological, we quickly perceive that it is actually even more integrating. The media do not always reflect the technological universe directly and straightforwardly; they do not always present it as it is, cultivating its virtues. Often, they give us seemingly reverse images of reality. For instance, the idea of spare-time activity is propagated more and more. Naturally, it is correct that our society has more means of distraction available and that we profit perhaps from more spare-time activities (a very moot point). But this must instantly be corrected. This image we receive is, first of all, the reverse of the true situation, for this world is one in which man works more than he has ever worked before. This wishful image of spare time is meant to help us endure the excess and boredom of work. The more burdensome our jobs, the more glorious and triumphant the propagated image of free time. Work is not brought up, it is the grayness of everyday life. Leisure is the "meaning" of life, it is the grace "given" to us—but there is no contradiction here; in reality, the image of leisure helps people adjust to the technological necessity.

This theme of spare time granted by technology must be viewed parallel with the praise of technology for increasing and improving culture. I do not want to get into a discussion of whether this notion is accurate, if there is not, in fact, a deculturation caused by technology, if the very concept of culture is not ambiguous (B. Charbonneau, *Le Paradoxe de la culture*). I will simply take the fact of the encomium to and profound conviction of modern man's intellectual and artistic growth thanks to technology. This widespread outlook only expresses man's gratitude to technology. It expresses the profound conviction of validity, of authenticity, that all of us have. We are spontaneously grateful to TV, the stereo, or the marvelous pictorial reproductions. And we are utterly frustrated when deprived of such boons, which are part and parcel of our very lives. This gratitude puts a nimbus around technology and reveals our thorough assimilation.

It is essential to realize that the man always spoken of is now a technicized man.[6] And there can be no other orientation. When we investigate a "culture" or a humanism for technological society, we always do so on the assumption that the human being in question is, above all, meant for technology, and that the sole great problem is adjustment. And this state of affairs is even more striking when the people who do see the gravity of the issue and take fright at "technocracy" fail to perceive any other solution than permanent "continuous education," in the charge of those using it—but an education that is basically and ultimately technological.[7]

Are we to believe that the society of leisure or culture is not technological? Far from it. Obviously, we are shown an access to leisure or culture only in league with the development of technologies replacing human activity and making human labor superfluous. And leisure? All it ever consists of is using technological things, transportation, games, etc. And very swiftly, as leisure becomes a "mass" thing (what else could it become), spare-time activities have to be organized. Imagine allowing anyone to be completely independent and do whatever flashes into his mind! The organization of spare-time activities is mainly a technological task, requiring a high degree of technicity to achieve satisfactory results, i.e., results giving a full impression of leisure and seemingly effacing the technological imperative. For the apex of technological development is the disappearance of the apparatus, the ugly, cumbersome device that is too reminiscent of materiality.

Modern apartments no longer have any heating gadgets. The electric wires have vanished. All mechanical things disappear backstage, letting you live in a marvelously nonarduous universe, where every gesture brings satisfaction without revealing the technological intermediary, which remains imperceptible. Thus, the technological system engulfs the individual, and he never even realizes it. He only receives immense satisfactions from it. But one of the specific features of this universe is its diffusion of images that are the reverse of reality: the maximum technological complexity produces the image of maximum simplicity. The intense mobilization of man for work convinces him that he dwells in a society of leisure. The decrease of means conjures up an appearance of immediacy. The universality of the technological environment produces the image of a Nature.

And this leads us to a new proposition. Everyone knows and takes for granted that technology responds to human needs, to permanent desires. No use belaboring this point. Man has always run after anything that would still his hunger; he has always sought more efficient means; he has always tried to spare himself drudgery; he has always wanted to ensure his safety. He has tried to know and understand. He has dreamt of walking on the moon and traveling through space. He has dreamt of mastering the fire in the sky . . . Technology makes his oldest needs and his youngest strivings come true. It gives body to his dreams. It responds to his desires.

I cannot understand the people who exalt desire as the form of man's independence and liberation from the technological universe—as if desire could have any nontechnological object, any nontechnological means of realization today! It is utterly childish to speak of unleashing desire as the final human expression against the environment of rigor organized by a technological society. Desire is responded to in technologies. And if people exalt the total liberation of sexual desire, they ought to ask what makes liberation possible. The answer? The pill—a technological product. Technology is not only enshackling and rigorous in the simplistic way that is now pointed out: it is "liberating" by making us enter more deeply into the technological system.

Yet some observers try to oppose desire and technology, making desire the escape, the response, the opening of possibility; and they base their outlook on Freud's analyses. This outlook is doubly fallacious, invisibly leading to a metaphysical position. It is quite true that desire is fundamental, that it far exceeds any realizations, that it pushes man forward without respite, and that anything satisfying desire today is promptly obsolete. But what eludes this beatific vision is that man in our society knows and is able to picture only one way to realize and satisfy his desires: the technological way. Technology works so many unexpected wonders that when a desire crops up spontaneously, man automatically seeks the answer in some technological product or other. Nor do the student revolts, the critics of the consumer society avoid this error. Anything but! Hence, the exaltation of desire plunges us all the more rapidly into technological growth.

And this brings up the other error. Since technology is rational, it seems to contradict the fundamental impulse of being. But this is a misassumption about technology, which is far more deeply an utterance of hubris. At this point, I can only call attention to J. Brun's remarkable study *Le Retour de Dionysos* (1969). Brun shows quite cogently that technology is not a cold, blind machine, but an exalting dance of Dionysus. Hence, technology and desire are perfectly matched. In our society, the exaltation of desire can only advance via technology. To reveal this deep kinship between human needs and their technological satisfaction, we do not have to add long discussions on the subject of what some people call the "new or artificial needs" created by technology and advertising, while others hold that there is nothing new and that we cannot distinguish between natural and artificial needs. Let us merely say that basic needs (food, protection against bad weather and danger) are met, on the one hand, and turned into an infinity of secondary needs, on the other hand, thanks to modern products and processes. These secondary needs are tacked on to older and essential desires, dreams, tendencies, but they swiftly become "natural" and necessary.[8] Now they all have a technological origin, since the means available to satisfy them are what makes them urgent.[9]

Man "dreamt" of flying to the moon. Technology makes it possible. More and more people are going to develop a need to stroll about on the moon. Such needs have a technological origin, and only technology allows them to be fulfilled.

The Wiener/Kahn characterization is the most striking: "These technological developments produce needs beyond the demands of the environment *in order to* satisfy technological capacities. . . . Every new technology triggers a marginal effect, and each of these changes will generally be considered desirable and beneficent." Technological growth is based on an a priori consent by man, who views the gift of each technology as a response to a need, which, however, really exists only to utilize the technological capacity. Under these circumstances, how can we believe that man would care to contest, impugn, challenge what strikes him (not clearly but through obvious experience) as the only source of his satisfactions, gratifications, and what, moreover, assures him of a livable future, i.e., the future in which his needs and desires will be fully met.

And here is the final proposition. Man in our society has no intellectual, moral, or spiritual reference point for judging and criticizing technology.[10]

Illich very accurately observes that the technological instruments tend to create "radical monopolies, a monopoly of consumption by advertising, of circulation by the existence of transports, of health by the existence of official medicine, of knowledge by schools, etc. This domination by the tool causes an obligatory consumption and hence restrains the autonomy of the individual. . . . Once the role is accepted, the simplest needs can no longer be satisfied except by facilities that are, by professional definition, subject to scarcity."

Likewise, interestingly, as E. A. Willener acknowledges,[11] it is by technology that man gets to know himself better, to realize better who he should become, and finds a way of identifying. In other words, technological experience teaches man who he is (in place of the old critical rhetorical experience!); and we end up with a kind of technomorphism and technocentrism of man—rather amazing since Willener's book is supposed to demonstrate that TV brings choice, freedom, autonomy! These two observations, which could be followed by so many similar ones, merely attest that man is entirely "on this side" (*diesseits*) of the system and has no more "beyondness" to "see" and criticize the system.

The sociology of the death of ideologies (D. Bell) and the theology of the death of God bear witness, accidentally, to the disappearance of this reference point.

The process of technological growth causes, by itself, either the destruction or the assimilation of the alien universe. The nontechnological sacred, the nontechnological religious are eliminated. Thus, man has no place from which to evaluate this process. He has no possible "point of view." If he thinks dialectically, technology is not one of the terms of this dialectics: it is the universe in which the dialectics operates. If he thinks religiously, he seeks primarily to make the new form of religion chime with this universe. (This seems clear to me in structuralism and the efforts of modern hermeneutics.)

\* \* \*

Such is the human being who is made to live, think, and act in our society. That is why we turn in a vicious circle when the lauders of technology explain that technology compels man to assume responsibilities, make up his own mind, and exercise choice. Closets develops this at length in regard to the politics of health, the moral problems posed by technology, the choice of allowing some people to live and others to die, of directing the technologies of health. By all means. I have never said that man would be mechanized or rendered servile by technology. But the man exercising this choice and this responsibility can only be the man who is first technicized, who will reach his decisions in terms of technology and toward the greatest technology. The central problem here is that of "technology and freedom," and it expresses itself in choices.

The partisans of technology try to rationalize by explaining that technology frees man from age-old constraints (which is true), that it allows man to do so many things that he could not do before (walk on the moon, fly, speak long-distance, etc.), and permits him to make countless choices.[12] When Toffler declares that technological society opens the way to greater liberty, he is talking exclusively about possibilities of change, possibilities of choosing among "different styles" (?), of shedding our habits and consuming a wide diversity of products.

Everyone sees that, thanks to technology, man can choose and, moreover, that his modes of behavior are liberated; he can go anywhere, grasp any culture. Thanks to technological resources, the pill or abortion, man (woman) is set free. Free to have children or not. But is this not a vast illusion? In writing about the film *Histoire d'A*, the *Le Monde* reviewer said: "By presenting the images of an interrupted pregnancy as a normal phenomenon, normal because it is clearly explained, approached without fear, in full liberty of individual choice and under medical supervision, this film removes the drama, the guilt from abortion."

It is no use dwelling on this issue. Plainly, modern man can move around, choose consumptions, etc. (I am disregarding political restrictions). But does this imply a growth of freedom? We have to ask a number of questions: Who is this man who is to choose? Is the choice autonomous? What does it bear upon? What is the influence of the technicians?

Mumford writes: "Even though every new technical invention can widen the field of human activity, it can do so only if the human beneficiaries are free to accept it, modify it or reject it, utilize it when and how it suits their own intentions, in quantities consistent with these intentions." But this is never so in the technological universe.

And Toffler announces: "For there comes a time when choice, rather than freeing the individual, becomes so complex, difficult and costly, that it turns into its opposite. There comes a time, in short, when choice turns into overchoice and freedom into unfreedom."

Let us start with the easiest problems. First of all, freedom is not necessarily having lots of consumer goods to choose from.

A person can be utterly free and yet never have anything to eat but rice. And he can be utterly alienated in a restaurant where he has his pick of a thousand different dishes. In reality, all that exists is *kinds* of choices, which are not of the same nature (choosing the man or woman to build one's life with is different from choosing an electric coffee grinder), and *zones* of choices.

In regard to the latter, the zone of my choices is completely delimited by the technological system. All my choices are made within the system, and nothing goes beyond it. Hence, the ingenuous protest for free love and against long-term coupling. These poor young people, who think they are thereby affirming their liberty, fail to realize that they are only expressing their integration in the system. They reduce the partner to an object giving satisfaction, like any technological product, and the fickleness of choice is merely part of the kaleidoscope of consumption. They make no *other* choice than what the technological system proposes.

In the area of consumption, Baudrillard has made what I feel is a startling demonstration. But one that must be developed. Everyone is caught between two poles. "The individual is free as a consumer, but he is free only as such." First point. "The ultimate end of the consumer society is the functionalization of the consumer himself, the monopolization of his needs, a unanimity of consumption that corresponds to the concentration and absolute planning of production." Hence, "censorship is exercised *through free behavior* (buying, choosing, consuming); through spontaneous investment, it is somewhat internalized in *jouissance* itself." Second point, and the matter is clinched.

But here, once again, we cannot help citing Closets's book, which bristles with contradictions. In one stroke of the pen he can admit that technological progress brings growing regimentation, prohibitions, stricter surveillances, incessant numberings, collectivization of private behavior, and sweeps out the "old liberal ideal." But at the same time, full of hope, Closets announces that "the individual aspirations impose themselves, that the collective demands recede, that the authoritarian regimes, the dogmatic morals, the imposed behaviors decline as the technologies advance," and there is "an increase in freedom brought by technological progress." This obvious, this flagrant contradiction is far more frequent than we think, and it is easily explained. In the first case, Closets is speaking as a technician, on the level of facts, of concrete statements. In the second case, he formulates (without noticing the change in register) his wishes, hopes, beliefs: It just can't be, it would be too sad if man were no longer free. . . . But he thinks it has already come; and what he wishes qua humanist moralist is of the same order as what he notes qua technician. Alas![13]

We have to do away with the myth that technology increases the possibilities of choice. Naturally, modern man can choose from a hundred automobile makes and a thousand kinds of cloth—i.e., he can choose *products*. On the level of consuming, the range of choice is vaster. But on the level of the role in the body social, on the level of functions and behaviors, there is a considerable reduction. The choice among technological objects is not of the same nature as the choice of a human conduct. There is no theoretical category of "choice" that would express freedom. The word "choice" has no ethical content per se, and freedom is not expressed in choices of objects. What we are offered is the choice between two objects, whereby we can take one and leave the other. But never do we have the more fundamental choice between, say, what is to be produced and what is to be eliminated by the growth process of the system, between one possibility and the suppression of the other. The "either/or" refers to "either the car or the TV." Never, for instance to either more electricity or fewer atomic risks. The proposed choice is always false, because the normal technological discourse consists precisely in affirming that it is not necessary to make a choice, but that it is possible to accumulate everything, i.e., become wealthier and more spiritual, more powerful and more solidary, and so forth.

On a different level, we may say that the choices in the technological society are exercised *next to* the reality of the chooser. The consumer can pick among vast numbers of diverse objects to consume. But he never makes a choice in regard to investments;

and yet investments are what dictate and decide consumption. Thus, the countless choices proposed (among voyages and cruises, among spectacles and machines, and what not) are always on the level of the ultimate consequences of the system, never at the origin. They are always in the margin of indifference (being for or against the pill is a matter of indifference); we even apply bright colors, which is basically a matter of indifference, to make our choices look more valuable. You can choose from huge numbers of professions, but extremely rigorous mechanisms decide this choice, which is never open anywhere. For the technological system reduces all choices to one: "the choice of faster or slower growth. The social changes intervene only as useful factors and necessary consequences of this growth" (Jouvenel). Our present-day method as Jouvenel so well puts it, is to "take without grasping [i.e., understanding], which is what a barbarian does. To grasp merely in order to take is the rationalization of barbarism, and that is the spirit of our civilization. We have a mind for snatching, but not for fellow feeling."

Is there any possibility left to make any other choice and, as he asks, to pit the social components that are factors of growth, with only instrumental value, against those that we find desirable and that have a value as finalities? The integration of the technological system tends to negate that alternative.

The possible choices are delimited by the system, and proposed to a human being who is haunted by technological values. These choices cannot be offered in all their dimensions; hence, they are induced and provoked by technicians. Let us take up these various points. Freedom of choice operates in a situation, a situation in which "one" places man. It is not the movement of conquering liberty. Moreover, one set of constraints is replaced by another. And the system particularly suppresses the possibility of being "disengaged."

"The man in the productivist city cannot in any way be disengaged: he is engaged in the numerous, changing, and pressing social relations" (Jouvenel), which others call alienation. The rapid changing of these social relations gives an illusion of freedom. But it is not man who causes these changes. It is they, stemming from the progression of the system, that determine man, and it is their "pressing" character that restrains his liberty. He is constantly more and more defined by his situation in the system. He has less and less chance of defining it—which would be his freedom vis-à-vis the system. It is impossible for just "any" man to correctly pose the problems and the very terms of choice: because he is incapable of doing so (which is maintained too frequently); above all, because the mentality of magic still persists; and even more, because we are unable to see the negative aspects of the means that we risk employing. We are obsessed with power and happiness, and we are incapable of posing the problem of choice correctly, because that would presume the clearsightedness of realizing that "accepting X automatically entails Y." That is where the problem lies, and not in the choice between having product X or product Y at my immediate disposal.

Reckoning the consequences is infinitely complex. Our choices are therefore never real, they bear solely on what the technological society makes available to us. The optimization of choices, the rationalization of budgetary choices, reveals even more pointedly that the choices are not up to the citizen! For every combination of variables or decisions, there is a corresponding possible solution to the problem, and we have to examine the technological and economic makeup of every decision with its consequences. But that is out of the question. Even at the highest technological summit, making decisions is aleatory, and so is making choices. One may say that on all levels, the greater the means of power, the more irrational the decisions and choices. And this seems even more serious when the demand is made for a certain quality of life, which eludes present-day technology. (For Jouvenel the problem is that the choice is not between building or not building housing, for instance, but either to build as fast as possible and cheaply, or much more slowly, more expensively, and more *attractively*. With the present choices, the French standard of living will double by 1985, but half of France will be living in *new* housing that is actually a *slum*). Ultimately, the choices we are offered are foisted upon us by the technological means and the technological mentality.

And what about the problem of an existential choice, like having a child or an abortion? How can we fail to see that we are dealing with means that theoretically, metaphysically allow man an existential choice but that, being within the technological system, are *in themselves* a negation of any possibility of that choice. The woman who chooses abortion is rigorously moved to that choice by the entire system. How could there be any individual choice if all this is dictated by a set of beliefs in naturalness, in the objectivity of science and technology? How could there be freedom with scientists and technicians whose entire thrust is in a determined direction? Does clear explanation suffice? We are going back to the scientistic illusions of 1900. Removing guilt when we terminate a potential life? In this not the prodigious growth of irresponsibility that characterizes the technological system? Far from being an act of freedom, abortion is a chance to wipe out the consequences of one's doings, and, therefore, it increases irresponsibility. (I treated this problem very thoroughly in volume 2 of *L'Éthique de la liberté*. I will merely recall that here.)

And this brings us to the complementary problem of the choice of death. Technological control allows us to prolong life artificially, to bring people back to life; but also to keep alive people who would "normally" be dead. Does that increase freedom? And, as a corollary, what about the technological means of letting someone die totally unconscious, whereas, at the cost of sure suffering, he could have "naturally" remained conscious, thereby taking death upon himself? Does that increase freedom? Is this not, as has been said, robbing a man of the most important moment in his life, his death! Is it, as in the foregoing case, diminishing responsibility and the capacity of choice before life and death? The problem is simply: Do the technologies increase freedom here?

I do not deny that the technologies allow us to ease suffering and lengthen our life spans. But that is not the issue *here*. The real point of this discussion was admirably articulated at the Colloquium on the New Powers and New Duties of Science (September 20–24, 1974, at the Sorbonne). And what was seen chiefly was the mastery of technology over the issue. Despite good intentions, a decision is always left to "conscious, competent persons" who "evaluate" the necessity of experiences, the chances of survival, the quality of the life being prolonged, and so on. In other words, it is practically never the patient himself who is asked to decide. Only the technician.

What it comes to is that technology increases the technician's freedom, i.e., *his power, his control*. And the so-called freedom due to technology always boils down to that growth of power. It always leads to further growth of the technician's role. The technician, legitimized by his competence, feels that *in his domain*, he has all rights, including, under the circumstances, the right of life and death. And we must realize that this is strictly consistent with the character of technology as a milieu and a system. So far as technology allows us to modify, interfere with, and turn back the natural process (which, for instance, might lead to death), it is obvious that human decisions replace "nature's decisions." But human decisions are not made by men affected by the phenomenon; they are made by men as operators of technology—the power of man over man. The full-scale illusion of those who wish to "let the user or the bottom man speak"!

That is why the "humanist" problems are false problems. How could this human being, who is the real one and not the one imagined by Sartre or Heidegger—how could he sovereignly perform what is expected of him: i.e., make choices, judgments, rejections in regard to technology as a whole or individual technologies? How and in terms of what could he give a different direction to technology than the one that technology gives itself in its self-augmentation? What initiative could he take that would not be primarily technological?

Once again, we should by no means conclude that man is mechanized and conditioned, that he is a robot. I have never said that. Man is still perfectly capable of choosing, deciding, altering, directing . . . But always within the technological framework and toward the progression of technology.

Man can choose. But his choices will always bear upon secondary elements and never on the overall phenomenon. His judgments will always be ultimately *defined* by the technological criteria (even those that seem humanist: the debate on self-administration is typical in this respect). Man can choose, but in a system of options established by the technological process. He can direct, but in terms of the technological given. He can never get out of it at any time, and the intellectual systems he constructs are ultimately expressions or justifications of technology—for instance, structuralism or Foucault's epistemological research.

Of course, as we have seen, man is not perfectly integrated in or adjusted to the system. But it suffices to note that it is not the human presence that hinders technology from being established as a system. The human being who acts and thinks today is not situated as an independent subject with respect to a technological object. He is inside the technological system, he is himself modified by the technological factor. The human being who uses technology today is by that very fact the human being who serves it. And conversely, only the human being who serves technology is truly able to use it.[14]

# POSTSCRIPT

THIS book is to be followed by a special study on the dysfunctions of the technological system. Divided into three parts, it will investigate the following issues: (1) The absence of feedback in the system, and particularly the ambivalence of technological progress, the irrationality of the system, the damaging effects and pollutions, etc. (2) The inadequacy of the remedies proposed (particularly, the uselessness of Marx's thinking in this area). (3) Finally, the system's tendency to institute feedback (the relationship between man and the computer) and its chances of passing from a process of growth to a process of development.

# NOTES

INTRODUCTION

1. Needless to say, of the countless studies that have attempted to "define" our society during the past few years, I have picked out only a few of the best examples, deliberately ignoring the pseudo-realistic studies, the shortsighted and unperceptive discussions, and the disarmingly innocent pamphlets like Maurice Clavel's *Qui est aliéné?*

2. David S. Landes; *The Unbound Prometheus* (1969). This book is the most remarkable history of Europe's industrial development during the eighteenth and nineteenth centuries. But the chapter on the post-1945 period, commonly seen as a period of transition to technological society, is quite disappointing. Landes more or less sticks to identifying technology and industry and to highlighting the relationship between industry and economy. When he delves into the speed of technological change, for example, he studies only the technologies of industrial production. Hence, he contributes little to the investigation of the technological system. He merely confirms a certain number of principles that we have been able to derive by observing the industrial process (the relationship between science and technology, the trend toward concentration, the universal participation in technological development, the anonymity caused by that universalizing, etc.).

3. D. Bell, "The Measurement of Knowledge and Technology," in *Indicators of Social Change* (1968).

4. Nothing in A. Touraine's *La Société post-industrielle* (1969) justifies this qualification. When he categorizes it as technocractic in its programmed organization, its motives dominated by economic growth, we do not see why the decisive element is "the antiquated industrial" element.

5. The best analysis of the consumer society was certainly made by Baudrillard in the system of objects. For him, consumption is neither a material practice nor a phenomenology of abundance. It is not defined by food and the like. It is the virtual totality of all the objects and messages now organized in a more or less coherent discourse. Consumption is an activity of systematic manipulation of signs. But vast as Baudrillard's conception may be, he is unable to show that consumption was the same in

any other era but ours. That is to say, consumption is as he analyzes it because it is based on technological objects, because it is practiced in an abundance, and because, finally, it is integrated in a more total system. It is only in this context that the systematic manipulation of signs finds both its reference and its possibility.

6. Jonas quite obviously understands nothing about this fact when he uses the term *ideology* for an attitude that consists in trying to determine the contents and nature of the technological phenomenon per se instead of being content with approximations or detailed investigations of *several* technologies. See Jonas, "Technik als Ideologie" in the collection *Technik im technischen Zeitalter* (1965). This criticism, taken up by Jürgen Habermas in *Technik und Wissenschaft als Ideologie* (1968) strikes me as being due to an a priori political choice. Considering the sociological analysis of technology as an ideology (whether a justifying or mystifying one) is really a way of preserving the explanatory schema drawn from Marx. But this is not the first time since 1904 that pseudo-Marxism has been used to conceal reality under a dogmatic explanation!

7. We have disregarded so many other formulas about our society; because they are too superficial (leisure), too general (masses), too old (urbanization). Yet for each of these, one could make the same comment. If there is leisure, it is a function of the time that man gains by developing technological means. And these spare-time activities must, in turn, be organized along technological processes. Mass society is quite properly analyzed by Friedmann as being: mass production, mass consumption, mass culture. But these three phenomena, in turn, are directly dependent on the technological factor, which both permits and generates each one. Finally, urbanization is likewise sanctioned and produced by technology: industrialization, mechanization of farmwork (which causes rural unemployment), means of transportation, increase in the distractions from urban pressures, etc. These elements are not exclusive characteristics of our society, and they are contingent on the same factor.

8. The point at which I disagree with Friedmann is when he speaks of a technological *civilization*. I am less certain than he that we are dealing with a civilization. He derives his outlook from M. Mauss's conception of the "complex aggregate of the factors of civilization." Today, these factors of civilization are the organization of work, mass production, mass media, mass consumption, mass tourism, etc., which add up to a technological civilization. See Georges Friedmann, *Sept Études sur l'homme et la société* (1966).

9. H. Lefebvre, *La Vie quotidienne dans le monde moderne* (1968). Moreover, Lefebvre's entire essay *Position: contre les technocrates* is blemished by his totally confusing several different things: (1) the *myth* of the technocracy (the fact that people imagine that technology rules); (2) *technocracy* (the attempt by a group of technicians to exercise power, the actual influence of technicians on a political, economic, or administrative level); (3) the *conformization of society* by the technological phenomenon; (4) the *determining factor*. In none of his arguments, in none of his discussions, does Lefebvre succeed in keeping the four elements apart. He continually switches around in them, which crucially weakens his debate.

On the other hand, it goes without saying that I fully agree with his

# NOTES

criticism of technocracy when it quite deliberately presents itself as being able to solve all the problems of society with the appropriate technologies—something that is the prerogative of both the political right and the left.

On this point, there was no great difference between De Gaulle, Marchais, and Tixier Vignancour. Furthermore, this unity of political thought is a mark of the decisive importance of technology. Lefebvre fails to see that the technocratic myth he condemns is merely the reflection of the primacy of technology—a primacy that is involuntarily recognized.

10. The concept of a technological society is indirectly challenged by Baudrillard. He calls it a functional mythology spawned by technology itself. His essay (which is excellent and, in all points, inadvertently confirms the notion of a technological system) repeats the standard Marxist argument that technology or the system of objects is what it is only because it is subject to a certain system of production, a profit motive. However, Baudrillard's conclusion does not come from analyzing the technological system as a whole. His is merely a structuralist analysis of objects in the environment, furniture, gadgets, etc. It is obviously quite easy for him to claim to be demonstrating that *this* system of *these* objects appears as an imaginary solution to all kinds of conflicts; that the profit motive is turning technology away from its true ends; that the minor perfecting of objects shores up a false idea of progress, masking the urgency of essential transformations (of society!). None of this is wrong. But a general conclusion is based on a partial analysis of an object chosen especially for the demonstration. The lacuna is crucial. Baudrillard would have to fit this system of objects back into the technological whole, allowing for its logic. He would have to go way beyond the social conflicts (whose givens are modified by the technological whole) and the means of production (which have been subordinated by the technological whole). Baudrillard's study is profound and his method is precise, but his conclusions are very superficial and valid only for the so-called affluent society.

11. See my books on revolution (*Autopsie de la révolution* and *De la révolution aux révoltes*) and *The New Demons*.

## Part One

### CHAPTER 1

1. Thorstein Veblen may be the first to introduce systemization into the phenomenon of mechanics when he describes it as being characterized by a "rational procedure" and a "systematic knowledge." But the center of his reflection remains the application of the machine to industry, i.e., the production of economic goods. In contrast, Max Weber (*The Theory of Social and Economic Organization*, 1947) gives "technology" such a wide meaning that it is almost useless for sociological study: "The term *technology*, when applied to an action, refers to the totality of the means employed as opposed to the meaning or the objective of the action. Rational technology is a choice of means that is consciously and systematically oriented according to the agent's experience and reflection and that consists of scientific knoweldge on the highest level of rationality." See the discussion

of these definitions in John Boli-Bennett's remarkable study *Technization*, 1973.

2. See A. Sauvy's excellent critique of the model mania, *Croissance zéro?* (1973).

3. See Hamon, *Acteurs et données de l'Histoire*, vols. 1 and 2.

4. Report by the Church and Society Department of the World Council of Churches, prepatory for a study of the future of man and society in a technological world, October 1969.

5. In any event, to understand the concept of technology and the technological system, we cannot *start* with technology's effects on man or society. Sociological or psychological considerations will not lead us back to the concept of technology. We have to focus on the technological object itself and its interrelations, as has been admirably done by Simondon, *Du Mode d'existence des objets techniques* (1956). The countless studies on alienation, the impact of television, work organization, the effects of mass media on voting, urbanization, etc. can be useful *afterwards*. They can then help us understand certain aspects of the technological system. But we cannot take off from them to work out the concept of technology. We have to *begin* on the highest level of abstraction and then *proceed* to the reality constituted by technology's relationship to man or society.

CHAPTER 2

1. It is not useless to recall that the first satisfactory definition of technology that we find is by Max Weber, who sees it precisely as a means: "The technique of an action refers to the means employed as opposed to the meaning or end to which the action is, in the last analysis, oriented. Rational technique is a choice of means which is consciously and systematically oriented to the experience and reflection of the actor, which consists at the highest level of rationality in scientific knowledge. . . . The ultimate meaning of a concrete act may, seen in the total context of action, be of a technical order; that is, it may be significant only as a means in this broader context. Then the "meaning" of the concrete act (viewed from the larger context) lies in its technical function; and conversely, the means which are applied in order to accomplish this are its 'techniques'. . . . The presence of a 'technical question' always means that there is some doubt over the choice of the most rational *means* to an end." *Economy and Society*, vol. 1, p. 65.

2. Regarding that evolution, see Jacques Ellul, *The Technological Society*, chap. 1.

3. Lefebvre clearly saw an aspect of that autonomy in describing the derivation of consciousness and of its social and individual forms from technology, without the mediation of a thinking, a culture to give it meaning. "Through the object, the consciousness reflects technology. . . . The technological object with its both functional and transparent constitution does not receive a determined status": A city becomes a technological object, a package in the modern world of 1968. In reality, however, Lefebvre gives numerous illustrations of the fact that technology has become a mediator.

4. There can no longer be any debate on this topic since the systematic analysis undertaken in West Germany from 1953 to 1969. A single figure for one set of automobiles and the same number of kilometers driven shows thirty-seven percent more fatal accidents and twenty percent more injuries when there is no speed limit. This was confirmed by the traffic "experts" at a round table in Paris during January 1970. France could prevent a thousand fatalities a year by limiting speed. But the round table remained pessimistic about the possibilities of applying such safety measures since they are unpopular.

5. The extreme weakness of H. Marcuse's analysis in *One Dimensional Man* is his failure to see that the appearance of such a man is the most direct result of the technological system, of, among other things, the autonomy of technology. Marcuse's attributing this change to a political or politico-social regime merely proves the inadequacy of his sociology and probably also testifies to his desire to escape by the skin of his teeth and to preserve some hope.

6. And it is as the exclusive mediator that technology ultimately foists its order, as we shall see below. It manages to impose itself even when, at the outset, man desires the opposite. I have shown—and Marcuse then took it up—that National Socialism, starting with a philosophy of the irrational, a mysticism, a conception of the superman, ultimately denied all those things as soon as it became a technological system, a technological rationalization of the apparatus: an irrationalist position is never a force against the system; on the contrary.

7. Hegel realized the beginning of that metamorphosis when he wrote: "The tool as such keeps back man's material annihilation; but in this respect it remains . . . his activity. . . . In the machine, man sublates this formal activity of his and lets it work fully for him. However, the deception he practices on Nature . . . takes its revenge on him; whatever he wins from Nature, the more he subjugates it, the lower he becomes himself. He may process Nature by means of various machines, but he does not sublate the necessity of his labor; he merely puts off his labor, removes it from Nature, and he does not erect himself as living upon Nature as living; instead, this negative livingness flees, and the labor that remains for him becomes more and more machinelike itself." *Realphilosophie* I, 327.

8. Lefebvre has done a remarkable study of this phenomenon in "Le Nouvel Éleatisme," *L'Homme et la Société* (1966), republished in *Position: contre les technocrates* (1967).

9. See John Boli-Bennett, *Technization* (1973).

CHAPTER 3

1. This corresponds fairly to what Habermas calls the "preponderance" in a society (*Technik und Wissenschaft als Ideologie*, 1968).

2. De Lauwe's study, published in 1966, coincides quite remarkably with Raymond Aron's study published in *Progress and Disillusion* (1969). Aron shows that the technological phenomenon is definitely the determining factor for the development of contradictory situations: on the one hand, the formation of new hierarchies, ruling categories; and on the other hand, the

ideology of equality; on the one hand, the socialization of the individual consciousness (with the fear that the individual may vanish in the mass); and on the other hand, the ideology of personal autonomy (with the fear that the individual may lose his identity in solitude). One could truly multiply the examples of these contradictory phenomena resulting from technology, which Aron traces back to the dialectics of equality, of socialization, and of universality.

Furthermore, one of the clearest and most demonstrative works about the primacy of the technological factor over all other factors, including economic ones, is P. Ferraro's, *Progresso tecnico contro sviluppo economico?* (1968).

3. Recent studies go so far as to doubt the growth of the central government's power, which has been dispersed to powers outside the state's jurisdiction. See, for example, Gremion, *Les Pouvoirs périphériques*.

4. See Hamon, *Acteurs et données de l'histoire*, vol. 1 (1970).

5. M. de Montmollin, *Les Psychopitres* (1972).

6. Hartung, *Les Enfants de la promesse* (1972).

7. John Boli-Bennet, *Technization* (1973).

8. Seymour, quoted by Montmollin.

9. See also the collective work, *Civilisation et humanisme* (1969).

CHAPTER 4

1. The point of departure for all conceptions is obviously Ludwig von Bertalanffy, *General System Theory* (rev. ed., 1969).

2. One of the first to present technology as a system without, however, using the term was Ben. B. Seligman: *A Most Notorious Victory*, 1966. See also G. Weippert in his introduction to the collective volume *Technik im technischen Zeitalter*, 1965, which shows technology as a system but without fully grasping the significance of that finding—like Habermas. It is generally the American sociologists who are closest to seeing the reality of the technological world, probably because they live there! Donald A. Schon (*Technology and Change: the New Heraclitus*, 1963) also intuitively senses this reality when he writes—the starting point for any present-day thinking about the technological system—that "technological innovation belongs less to us than we to it." Otherwise, however, though using the word "system," I by no means claim to go along with structuralist thought. I believe that technology is now constituted as a system just as scientists, long ago, spoke of a system of forces or a thermal system. And I am not referring to *the* System, an absolute reality, existing in every social organization, every relationship, etc.

3. Richta regards the deterministic model of society and evolution as tied to the industrial order of things; he felt that everything changes with the scientific and technological revolution. And here he yields to the notion of system: "The situation changes when one or more factors [of industry] are replaced by a general *dynamics* in each of the numerous dimensions of productive forces and in the network of general circumstances, as soon as the *subjectivity peculiar to the planned elements* becomes the fundamental factor that cannot be disregarded, as soon as the simply external rationality of things gives way to a *superior rationality of systems* that are

developing and changing." He concludes, however, that this requires the creative cooperation of men, which strikes me as less certain (*Civilization at the Crossroads*, p. 290).

4. Richta, in line with Simondon and Daumas, remarks that one cannot distinguish the degrees of technological development sharply enough if one prosaically views the machine as a perfected instrument, the automaton as a perfected machine. The machine is not an instrument; it is a mechanism using its own instruments, which implies an inversion of the subject and object. The machine uses man to serve it. And the automatic system is no machine either; it is an aggregate or a process of control utilizing machines. There is thus a new level of subjectivity, and the importance of the automaton for man is quite different from that of the machine.

5. I will not repeat the long discussions I devoted to this topic, concerning the factors that favored its appearance, as well as its characteristics.

6. Habermas's long analysis of the notion of "technocratic consciousness" is nothing but a development of what I studied in *The Technological Society* to explain the transition from the technological operation to the technological phenomenon. Habermas translates this philosophically when he discusses the elimination of the difference between praxis and technology, the blotting out of a desire for communication without domination behind the wish to deal with things technologically.

7. I am obviously in complete disagreement with Habermas (*Technik und Wissenschaft als Ideologie*), who confuses technology (French, *technique*) and technological discourse, and whose idea of what he means by *Technik* strikes me as totally dated! Ladmiral's preface to that book says: "Technologies or technological rules are applications of empirical knowledge formalized by the experimental sciences; they put technological means to work on *any material object* capable of being reutilized systematically within the framework of certain sequences of instrumental activity." A simplistic definition, applicable perhaps to nineteenth-century technology but having nothing to do with the present-day phenomenon! Nevertheless I respect Habermas for his modesty in stressing that his ideas on technology are an "interpretational schema that may be approached within the framework of an essay but not verified seriously as being employable."

8. I do not think that the structure of a given system allows us to interpret other systems. What characterizes each one is precisely its specificity in structure, character, and processing. Hence, I believe that using the structure of the linguistic system to analyze or even explain other systems is an error in scientific method.

9. The aim I am following here is thus very different from the two lines indicated by J. Baudrillard in *Le Système des objets*, 1968. On the one hand, he studies "the processes by which people enter into relationships with technological objects." What are the systematics of the resulting behaviors? On the other hand, he thinks that one can study technology by heeding only the technological objects forming a whole that can be studied, like a linguistic system, by means of structural analysis. Here, I am putting myself on the level of society, and confronting a technology that is made up not only of objects, but also of methods, programs, etc., and whose system

cannot be studied outside of its relation, its integration in the social group. The neglect of those two aspects makes Baudrillard's work useless—subtle and interesting as it may be. He claims to establish the relationship between man and the technological object without precisely situating man in the technological universe. Hence, he ascribes certain attitudes to him, certain behaviors, whose explanation resides in the all-inclusiveness of technology, whereas Baudrillard always makes man a subject. Moreover, the double Marxist and Freudian bias, unadmitted, unelucidated, takes away much of the validity from this system of objects.

10. John Boli-Bennet, *Technization*, pp. 101ff.

11. See, for instance, Le Moigne, *Les Systèmes de décision dans les organisations* (1971).

12. Seligman (*A Most Notorious Victory*) offers a sort of analysis of the main American arguments against the notion that technology has become autonomous. He feels that the authors of these arguments are guilty of "a great distortion of facts, a fundamental ignorance of the new technology, simplistic and archaic conceptions."

13. On this problem, see the remarkable study by Sefez, *L'Administration prospective* (1970).

14. See the report *L'information et les libertés* (1975).

15. Norbert Wiener, *God and Golem* (1964); John von Neumann, *The General Theory of Automata* (1956); De Broglie, *Machine à calculer et pensée humaine* (1953); Toa, *Brain Computer* (1960); L. Couffignal, *La Machine à penser* (1952); Delaveney, *La Machine à traduire* (1963), etc.

16. For a criticism of the so-called results already obtained by the forecasts, one should read: Vacca, *Demain le Moyen Age* (1973); Elgozy, *Le Désordinateur* (1972)—(the latter book is all the more interesting in that the author returns to a certain number of his earlier, far more positive stands expressed in *Automation et Humanisme*, 1978); and J.-M. Font/J.-C. Quinious, *Les Ordinateurs, mythes et réalités* (1968), which offers a remarkable analysis of the myth of the universal computer, a robot ready to do anything, a creator of music and leisure activities, etc.

17. See the excellent study of the problem in Escarpit, *Théorie générale de l'information and de la communication* (1976).

18. This was sharply brought to light in Morris West's novel *Harlequin*. A change in program, subsequently erased, brings out a colossal deficit in a multinational corporation, with a probable embezzlement by one of the directors. Now people are dealing with such astronomical figures and with such complicated business matters that no human being can visualize them, no accounting department fully verify them. Only the computer is capable of all that. Hence, only the computer's result is *real*, and held to be such by consensus, even if the parties involved maintain that they have not done what they are accused of and that the business deal was kosher. But no one can truly check the validity of such undertakings.

19. See the previously cited report on data processing and freedom.

20. B. Charbonneau shows that there is an inevitable contradiction between the technological system and man:

"The pretext of organization is the one thing it cannot give us: freedom. The 'conditions of freedom' are something that organization always achieves by routes opposite to freedom: organization. Hence, any progress left to its own devices will ultimately curtail the autonomy of individuals: freedom presupposes power, hence the power of the apparatus. But the apparatus presupposes the cog: collective power is made up of the powerlessness of individuals. In our increasingly organized societies, we may have more liberty because we are better fed and better taught; but these things are obtained by a proliferation of orders and prohibitions in all areas" (*Le Chaos et le système*).

21. In regard to these facilitation processes, see my *Métamorphose du bourgeois*, "Néo-Romantisme" (in *Contre-point*), and my books on revolution.

22. Ivan Illich (*Tools for Conviviality*) has an excellent view of the technological system when he shows that "the functioning and design of the energetic infrastructure of a modern society impose the ideology of the dominant group with a force and a penetration inconceivable to the priest . . . or the banker." I must endlessly reiterate a warning which I already gave in *The Technological Society*, and which Mumford brilliantly formulates: "Plainly, then, it is not the mechanical or electronic products as such that intelligent minds question, but the system that produces them without constant reference to human needs and without sensitive rectification when these needs are not satisfied." *The Myth of the Machine*, p. 334.

23. L. Mumford, in his rich book *The Myth of the Machine*, p. 184 comes very close to the idea of the technological system, but he actually perceives it as a product of automation, which strikes me as inaccurate. In contrast, he perfectly grasps the constraining and autonomous character of the system: "Once automatic control is installed one cannot refuse to accept its instructions, or insert new ones, for theoretically the machine cannot allow anyone to deviate from its own perfect standards. . . . Here, at the core of automation, lies its principle weakness once it becomes universal. Its exponents, even if they are able to recognize its deficiencies, see no way of overcoming them except by a further extension of automation and cybernation. . . . It is the system itself that, once set up, gives orders."

24. See Wernberg, *Analyse et prévision*, October 1966.

## Part Two

### CHAPTER 5

1. Jürgen Habermas, *Technik und Wissenschaft als Ideologie* (1968), criticizes this autonomy on the basis of Schelsky's work; but he has only a very sketchy and simple view of what technology's autonomy is really all about.

2. It is obvious—and this comment holds for all the rest of this discussion—that when I say technology "does not admit," "wants," etc., I am not personifying in any way. I am simply using an accepted rhetorical shortcut. In reality, it is the technicians on all levels who make these judgments and have this attitude; but they are so imbued, so impregnated with the technological ideology, so integrated into the system, that their vital judgments and attitudes are its direct expression. One can refer them to the system itself.

3. I will not rehash my discussion of this issue. The reader may consult *The Technological Society*. What is presented here is supplementary.

4. "Neuf thèses sur la Science and la Technique" in *Vivre et survivre* (1975). This anonymous text is probably by Groetenduijk. I have summed up the first five theses.

5. Furia, *Techniques et sociétés* (1970), leans toward the same opinion. In contrast, see U. Matz; "Die Freiheit der Wissenschaft in der technischen Welt" in *Politik und Wissenschaft* (1971). But he is actually investigating the freedom necessary *for the scientist* in a technicized state.

6. See Jacques Ellul, *The Political Illusion* (1967), and Finzi, *Il potere tecnocratico* (1977).

7. On the capacity of the state to play the role that is presumed, see Jacques Ellul, *The Technological Society*, chap. 4, and *The Political Illusion*. I will not bother repeating these demonstrations here.

8. Conversely, and without taking up the problem again, we must nevertheless recall that the technological system, in which the state is necessarily integrated, gives the government a power such as no government has ever had. But, as I ought to point out, this power assumes an administrative face (see *The Political Illusion*). It is obvious that computers are integrating all social givens possible with an unimaginable potential of complete control of private life thanks to centralized processing of the totality of stored and utilized data.

9. Naturally, we are confronted with the difficulty caused by the ambiguity of the word *political*. It can refer either to everything concerning man as a social animal, or to the specific activity of the state and of the personnel of the government. Marcuse keeps switching back and forth between the two meanings when he declares that "the technological *a priori* is a political *a priori* to the extent that the transformation of nature involves that of man, to the extent that the creations made by man come from a social ensemble." From there, he allows himself to declare that, consequently, technology is subject to politics. Which is tautological, given that definition. But then he skids over to conclude that the governmental structures have to be modified. . . .

10. Bestoujev Lada, "Les Études sur l'avenir en U.R.S.S.," *Analyse et prévision* (1968).

11. See Vichney, "Le Japon: de la technique à la science," *Le Monde*, June 1972.

12. It appears, quite oddly, in one of the most profound and rigorous thinkers of our time, Bertrand de Jouvenel; he keeps insisting that it is man who decides, and that the overall decisions are made on a political level—technology being merely secondary and subsequent. And yet his admirable book *L'Arcadie* is the best demonstration of the autonomy, the self-sufficience, of technology. This notion runs all through his book, recurring constantly, so that we wonder if the author wrote "on several levels," which are complementary but different and at times seemingly opposed to one another.

13. Of course, everyone agrees that research is the key to (economic) development and that it is therefore worth accumulating economic resources in order to achieve a greater economic advance by means of technological research. But the relation between the two is growing less and less clear. "Research and development" is a source of very great uncertainties. In France, the O. E. C. D. (Organization for Economic Cooperation and Development) has concluded: "The relations of research

and development to economic growth suffer from a paradox. They are both obvious and unmeasurable. . . . Even excluding the money spent on military research, we are unable to bring out the correlation between the expenses of research and development and the growth of the G. N. P." And Closets has a good formula for defining the relationship between economy and technology: One can only speak of an "economy of uncertainty." As for research and development, see the series *Analyse et prévision*, 1967 to 1970—and the writings of Jouvenel.

14. Richta underlines an important turnabout in the Weberian school. At first, with Weber, they asserted that "one can rationalize technologically only in terms of commercial reason. . . . The law of technological reason must always yield to the law of economic reason." But since 1960, the Weber disciples (e.g., Papalakas) have been claiming that this economic rationality is relative and that the relationship between capital and technology is reversing: "It is economic reason that must adapt to the harsh technological reality, it is technological rationality that becomes the primary dimension and that thereby dominates the principal focus of tension in society" (R. Richta, *Civilization at the Crossroads*, p. 80).

15. Also see S. Rose, *L'Idéologie de et dans la Science* (1977), a work of strict Marxist orthodoxy, which tries to prove that science is ideological. Very scholarly and very disappointing.

16. Two very good examples of this autonomy are offered, though on different premises, by G. Vahanian and by H. Orlans. G. Vahanian, *The Death of God*, shows that the "how to do" has become independent of all Christian thought and has, in fact, invaded Christianity, which is subordinated to efficiency. H. Orlans, in *Toward the Year 2000*, Daedalus, 1967, shows that "not all technological development is desirable, of course, but we cannot really see how we can prevent anything technologically possible from being realized."

17. The reader can refer to the excellent analysis of such illusions in Seligman (*A Most Notorious Victory*, 1966), who shows that the tragedy of these illusions comes from technology's having its own strength, capable of destroying the designs of man, of determining his ideologies. And, as he shows at length, this autonomy of technology makes man's autonomy "at best questionable."

18. A. M. Weinberg, "Technologie ou 'engineering' social," *Analyse et prévision* (1966).

19. Nevertheless, since 1968 we have to modify this statement slightly. Certain scientists (but no technicians as yet) are starting to ask moral questions about the legitimacy of their scientific work and its goals, however, with no results.

20. On the autonomy of technology from values, one should read the admirable pages by B. Charbonneau, *Le Chaos et le système*, particularly concerning the atomic bomb. "It is not the most monstrous tyrant that produces the bomb, but the most advanced society. And in 1944, it was not the U.S.S.R. or Nazi Germany, but an evangelical and liberal nation ruled by a president whose goal was to free the earth of fear. Who will have wanted the irreperable if ever it comes? Certainly not the scientists, who are only after knowledge, nor the technicians, who are only after power. As for the politicians, they are only after peace and justice. Unhappily, action commands. It was not Roosevelt who made the bomb: Hitler forced him,

and then Stalin. But the Communists will demonstrate that the bomb is a product of capitalism. The proof is that the U.S.S.R. is exploding even more powerful bombs. Who or what is behind the bomb? Progress (science, technology, the state) left to its own devices. The U.S.S.R. was the second nation to explode the bomb because it was the second power on the globe. Marx has no more to do with this than Jesus."

21. For lengthy treatments on the contents of this ethics, see Jacques Ellul, *Le Vouloir et le faire*, vol. 1, chap. 2 (1963).

22. In regard to man, Mumford shows decisively and at length how and why the series of the most advanced technological inventions has absolutely nothing to do with man's "central historical task, the task of becoming human." If we take the most recent technological exploits—the moon landing, climate control, artificial survival, creation of life—nothing has the least relationship to the project of "becoming human." Everything obeys the internal logic of the system.

23. There are certain studies that contest this autonomy; the most thorough study is by Bela Gold, "L'Entreprise et la genèse de l'innovation," in *Analyse et prévision* (1967). For Gold, technological strides are modeled on preexisting values and by the active convictions of men who decide to devote resources to research. But actually, despite his intention, Gold demonstrates that technological growth has, on the contrary, "brought a modification of principles serving as a guide for managerial decisions." In reality, the "choices" are completely involved in processes ruled by technological imperatives. And, as Gold quite correctly remarks, if progress per se is not made the essential objective of research, if innovation is not consciously desired, then nevertheless "the general opinion is that technological progress is *inevitable* and cannot be neglected."

Gold's study does not strike me as demonstrating his viewpoint, but it does shed very useful light on the framework in which technological progress concretely unfolds. He shows that we obviously must not neglect the pressures acting for and against, the needs to be met, the difficulties of research, the obstacles to communication. In any case, he demonstrates that we are very far from being able to rationally choose and decide upon a policy of "guidance" for innovations and technological growth.

There is not much to be gained from Bookchin's small study, *Vers une technologie libératrice* (1974), for he never seriously investigates the technological system and he keeps confounding the possibilities of technologies with their actual use. He shows that certain technologies would allow decentralizing, reducing small production units, humanizing, economizing on labor, etc. All of which is totally obvious, but accompanied by an implicit "if." If the world and if man were different from what they are, then modern technology would be liberating. But never for an instant does Bookchin perceive that technology as a system has its own law of development, which contradicts the potentials of such and such a technology. Nor does he realize that man's approval of these technologies of power is not accidental, that it is not the capitalist system which makes technology alienating. Never for an instant does he envisage *how* actual technology could turn into liberating technology. The only relevant passage concerns the transformation into an anarchist society. But, alas, he instantly leaps into utopia.

# NOTES 339

## CHAPTER 6

1. A certain number of points that I dealt with in *The Technological Society* (the section on "Monism") will not be taken up again here.

2. The system of interactions among the technologies is called *synergism* by Kahn and Wiener (*The Year 2000*). But since this word is applied to so many other phenomena, I will not use it here. Nevertheless, I will cite this book for numerous examples of interaction among the most diverse technologies and also for analyzing the unpredictability factor in the evolution of technology, which constitutes this synergism.

3. See the amazing study by R. Hublin, "Les Structures gonglables," in "Futuribles," *Analyse et prévision* (1970).

4. Illich sees this connection between technologies perfectly when he shows the correlation between teaching and technological growth, or between the latter and the massive organization of "health." And even in this domain. "Paradoxically, health care per capita gets more expensive as the cost of prevention (hygiene) gets higher: One must be aware of both prevention and treatment to have the right to exceptional care. . . ." And more profoundly: "Americans want to spend the twenty billion dollars of the Vietnam war budget to conquer poverty or promote international cooperation, which will multiply the present resources tenfold. Neither group understands that the *same* institutional *structure* underlies the peaceful war against poverty and the bloody war against dissidence. Everyone is raising by yet another degree the escalation that they would rather eliminate." In the same book, Illich very judiciously observes that "the makers of the green miracle are putting out high-yield seeds that can be used only by a minority disposing of a double fertilization: the chemist's and the educators."

5. For instance, the constructors of artificial satellites had to take into account the extreme temperature differences to which these satellites are exposed at the same time. The surface facing the sun is subjected to extreme heat, the surface in the shade to extreme cold. Technicians had to experiment in chambers recreating the flight conditions. They build a "simulator," whose radiance exactly reproduces the effects of solar light: They "reinvented the sun." This was made possible by applying certain automobile technologies (the creation of reflectors able to resist the ozone generated by the lamps) and cinematographic technologies (the honeycomb condenser for uniform distribution of light intensity). Likewise, Kahn shows the effects of the "synergism" of lasers, holographs, computers, etc.

6. Thus, the study of blood hematin for biological ends led to finding the solution of the fuel cell—producing electric current by cold combustion, with no escape of noxious gas. Hitherto, the prime cost was terribly high. By studying the action of hematin, researchers were able to reproduce its mechanism with an inexpensive product (ferrous phtalocyanine), which allows manufacturing and distributing a new source of energy that will not pollute the atmosphere.

7. A very good example of the unicity of the technological phenomenon in this area is given by Kahn and Wiener, *The Year 2000*, in regard to "social controls." They strikingly point out how in this domain, each

technology reacts upon the others, modifying the body social as a whole by the reciprocity of actions.

8. I agree entirely on this point with J. Habermas (*Technik und Wissenschaft als Ideologie*, 1968) when, in his critique of Marcuse, he shows the unilateral character of technology and emphasizes that there is no alternative for a New Science, a New Technology. His distinction between work (which comes from technology) and interaction (which refers to the practice of experience) is certainly judicious; but he remains fully imprisoned in permanent philosophical concepts without noting the total present-day change. He does admit that technological civilization wipes out the dualism of work and interaction, "as if the practical mastery of our history could be reduced to a technological object disposing of objectivated processes." But this apprehension of reality, this fleeting glimpse are instantly abandoned, and he resumes the politico-philosophical dissertation, as though the philosophical problems completely obliterated the ascertainable reality for him. However, the opposition between work (a rational goal-oriented activity) and interaction (a relation mediated by symbols) is useful and perhaps fruitful for a critique of technology (which is exactly what I did in *The Technological Society*).

9. Bela Gold, *L'Entreprise et la genèse de l'innovation* (1967).

10. Barbichon and A. Ackerman, "La Diffusion de l'information technique dans les organisations," *Analyse et prévision* (1968), with a large bibliography.

CHAPTER 7

1. See *The Technological Society* (1964), the section "Technical Universalism." In this section, I mainly treated the *causes* for the geographic spread of technology, the *effects* of this spread on nontechnological civilizations, the *impossibility* of simply grafting an ensemble of technologies on a traditional society. I will not take up these various items here. Instead, I will sum up my pertinent conclusions.

As Simondon very strongly emphasizes, the various features of the technological system are linked together. Universality is tied to unicity and autonomy. It even results from them, if, obviously, we take rationality into account. "The technological world discovers its independence when it achieves its unity."

2. It is likewise useless here to repeat H. Lefebvre's demonstration of the way technological power invades and subordinates "everyday life." "Nothing escapes and nothing must escape in the regimen of organized everyday life." One must read this book to get a picture of how universal the phenomenon is (*La Vie quotidienne dans le monde moderne*, 1968).

3. "L'Avenir est-il à la machine à tout faire ou prêt à jeter," *Le Monde*, November 1969.

4. This is not the place for an analysis of freedom in the technological society. But Raymond Aron, *Progress of Disillusion*, has stated the problem adroitly by showing both the growing disciplines, the influence of a weighty public opinion, the manipulation, and the philosophy of freedom, the possibility of previously unthinkable choices among a very large number of behaviors for a growing number of individuals. There is a great

deal to say about this "freedom." The pill allows people to do "anything whatsoever" without having to fear consequences or sanctions. Is that freedom? The pill increases one's control over one's own body, personal decision; but is canceling responsibilities a boon? For we should not indulge in sophistry and say that it is very responsible just to be able to choose with no constraint and to make up one's own mind according to one's own taste and desire, etc. Ultimately, this is freedom only in the sense that Hegel described as a negative relation to others. The pill increases the woman's independence and the possibility of her being as irresponsible about her actions as the man used to be, and that does not strike me as having anything to do with freedom.

5. Of course, we know that administration tends to change little by little under the influence of technologies. The best example is offered by Sfez in *Administration prospective*. He shows that it is now impossible to disregard technological management methods and, above all, that the world we live in demands futurology, which transforms the very concept of administration. In particular, his study of "nonfuturological administration in its relations with futurological organs" is remarkably and concretely evocative.

6. A very interesting broadcast by the director of the French Association for Standardization (February 12, 1975) also offers a specific view on the universalization of technology. With a total innocence and an absolutely clear conscience, the director expressed what for him was proof of the excellence of the technologies. Standardization per se is a universal technology. It was applied first to industrial output, which was quite straightforward, in 1918, to ensure the efficiency of wartime production. But standardization has a universal calling: "We have to standardize everything in order to universalize everything." An extremely profound formula, and one that is totally indicative of what technology is all about. Needless to say, language has to be standardized (language being regarded, incidentally, as a first, but primitive and imperfect standardization). The intellectual faculties, intellectual exchanges, and, of course, all the technologies, as well as research and social activities must be standardized. In each case, standardization bears upon two levels of analysis of the object to be standardized: employability and interchangeability. On the basis of this twofold standardizing, the *totality* of the product or service is defined, and they become "standard," "normal," at that moment. A standardized language goes beyond the habitual uses. It aims at all human beings and it makes services noncomparable. Standardization is justified in this discourse by everything that justifies technology itself but that is seldom admitted so plainly. Standardization produces precision, simplicity, efficiency, universality. It prevents disorder. And as this director so finely emphasizes: It is never imposed by a ukase: it imposes itself simply by being taken for granted, as a matter of course. For in order to be applied properly, it demands a *consensus omnium* obtained precisely to the extent that people themselves are standardized!

7. I will not repeat here what I said in *The Technological Society* (1964) about the technological change of the eighteenth century or the traits of geographic universalism. I will simply call attention to an essential book on this subject: *L'Acquisition des techniques par les pays non initiateurs*,

C. N. R. S (1973). Here, in a series of precise cases, a group of historians and sociologists investigate the development conditions of technology and the mechanisms of diffusion. Most of these examples are drawn from Europe (or Japan) and from the nineteenth century. But the parcellary conclusions are so pertinent that they may be generalized in all fairness. The chief conclusions, I feel, were those by: Daumas, "Orientation générale, et acquisition des techniques britanniques en France"; Purs, "La Diffusion asyndromique de la traction à vapeur en Europe"; Ballon and Kimura for Japan; Bairo, "Technique et conditions économiques"; Buchanan, "Innovation technique et conditions sociales."

8. See the fine study by N. Vichney, "Le Japon: de la technique à la science," *Le Monde*, June 1972.

9. This notion that the technological system is ultimately identical in both a communist and a capitalist regime is starting to penetrate the Marxists. Take, for instance, this—highly significant—text:

"Experience has shown that, in its revolutionary energy, socialism was able to speed up industrialization and, to a certain extent, moderate or counteract the phenomena that had traditionally accompanied the industrial revolution: e.g., impoverishment of the masses, expulsion of rural dwellers, formation of an industrial reverse army, etc. Yet even socialism failed to eliminate certain profound and serious consequences of industrialization; it could not prevent: the inherent tendency of industrialization to chop work up into bits and to separate the management activity from the implementation activity; the need to maintain certain social distinctions; the restriction of the progress of consumption by the masses within the limits of the simple reproduction of the labor force, the tendency to devastate the natural environment, etc.

"These trends are inherent in the very nature of industrial civilization; that is why a new life and new human relationships cannot be lastingly founded upon it. In the final analysis, industrialization is not the goal of socialist society, but a preliminary condition, a starting point" ("L'Homme et la société dans la révolution technique," *Analyse et prévision*, 1968).

And Radovan Richta explains this at length in his remarkable book *Civilization at the Crossroads* (1969). He demonstrates that socialism does not escape the consequences of technology, and that, with it, alienation has changed shape but not been removed from the "body of industrial civilization." And he points out that this is found in Marx himself: Marx never limited the revolutionary task to wiping out the relations between capitalist production and capitalist exploitation; his critique bore on *industrial civilization*, of which capitalism was only the creator, the initiator. And as an essential effect upon socialism, says Richta, the intense growth, due to technology, entails a lowering in the coefficient of capital, which, in the capitalist system, permits envisaging the disappearance of the contradiction between the development of production and the growth of consumption.

10. The effects of technicization in the psychological and familial areas have been particularly well studied by a Swiss psychiatrist, Medard Buss, *Un Psychiatre en Inde* (1971). He not only confirms but also deepens what I wrote about this issue in 1950.

11. It is obvious that the transfer of birth-control technologies (sterilization, coils, and even pills) to the third world is producing a fundamental

upheaval, not only in sexual relations but also in beliefs, social structures, etc. This is a true "graft of civilization," as Sauvy puts it. But we are far from having gauged all the consequences. The psycho-sociological "ingredients" of sex, fertility, their equilibrium, are almost totally unknown, and we do not know exactly what tragedies, what disruptions will occur. We are moving rapidly to the stage of application, pressed by urgency, but unable to foretell the consequences or take measures for warding off new misfortunes.

12. One cannot, of course, share the optimism of Ehsan Naraghi (cultural adviser at UNESCO) in *L'Orient et la crise de l'Occident* (1977). This author holds that the nations of Asia and Africa still have a great freedom of choice in regard to technologies, the specific adaptation of technologies, and the maintenance of native cultures. But all this rests on declarations of principles by international assemblies, on philosophical considerations, and it reveals a grand innocence about the reality of technology. The author recurs to the leitmotif that one must affirm the Eastern qualitative against the quantitative. That has been the outlook of numerous Western thinkers since 1920.

13. See, for instance, *The Acts of the Congress of the International Association of Economic Sciences* (1976).

14. In *The Technological Society*, I analyzed the previous causes, which, incidentally, are still operative—namely, commercial universalism, wars (either colonial wars or Western wars in which colonized people have become involved), the rapidity and intensity of the means of communication presupposing an identity of infrastructures and a globalization of relays, the identity of training and education in all countries.

15. B. Charbonneau demonstrates that technology cannot stop short: "It will have to artificially reconstruct the natural totality breached by the intervention of human freedom. When man's power becomes global, science, under pain of death, will have to penetrate the multitude of causes and effects constituting a world. And technology and government will have to sanction its conclusions with the force and scope of the power that assured creation" (*Le Chaos et le système*).

16. The problem of space and its destruction by technology is strikingly exposed by Charbonneau after Mumford. We preened ourselves on our victory over space thanks to technology, for the transoceanic unification of nations! In reality, we are entering the era of "space famine," of "distance and place famine." And we are aware of our victory, Charbonneau demonstrates, only because we are starting to lack space.

17. This "engulfment" of civilization by technology is admirably brought out by H. Lefebvre (*La Vie quotidienne dans le monde moderne*, 1968) when he writes: "The bureaucratic society of planned consumption, certain of its abilities, proud of its victories, is nearing its goal. Its finality . . . is showing through: the cybernation of societies by the roundabout way of everyday life. . . . There is no more tragedy, there are only things, certainties, "values," "roles," satisfactions, jobs, uses, functions. . . . The new is . . . an everyday life programmed in an urban framework which is adapted to that end. . . . The cybernation of society may very well come along this route: a parceling-out of territory, the establishment of vast efficient appliances, the (artificial) reconstitution of urban life according to an adequate model."

18. See Silvère Seurat, *Réalités du transfert de technologie* (1976).

CHAPTER 8

1. And that is why, incidentally, I refuse to present my thinking in the form of a theory or in a systematic fashion. I am making a dialectical ensemble that is open and not closed and I am making sure not to present solutions of the ensemble, responses to problems, theoretical outlets for the future. If I did do these things, I too would be contributing to the technological totalization. But my not doing them leaves the reader dissatisfied and makes it seem that by refusing, I must *therefore* be hostile to technology.

*Part Three*

1. In regard to viewing technology as progress, see Hans Freyer, "Der Ernst des Fortschritts," in *Technik im technischen Zeitalter.*

CHAPTER 9

1. Nonetheless, certain authors feel that there is no longer any such thing as innovation in the precise sense of the term, i.e., the appearance of a new and unexpected element; they hold that all technological progress resides in a combination of economic factors and scientific factors, with the result that innovation as a distinct entity is tending to vanish.
2. On all these questions, see the remarkable study by Daumas, "*L'Histoire des techniques*" in *Documents pour l'histoire des techniques,* VII. In contrast, Tessier du Cros's general and "philosophical" considerations in his *L'Innovation* (1971) do not help us zero in on the problem.
3. See B. Levadoux, *Les Nouvelles Techniques et l'élimination des instruments de travail,* quoted by Beaune.
4. Daumas, *Histoire des techniques,* vol. 1 (1962), p. x; against E. F. Schumacher, *Small is Beautiful* (1973).
5. See B. de Jouvenel's studies on R and D in *Sedeis* and *Arcadie.*
6. See "Human Problems," in Spicer (ed.), *Technological Change* (1952).
7. Good examples of peak technologies in the war in Vietnam can be found in D. Verguese, "Le Banc de'essai des guerres futures," *Le Monde,* October 1972.
8. See the section on "Self-augmentation" in Jacques Ellul, *The Technological Society* (1964). See also Georges Friedmann, *La Puissance et la Sagesse* (1970), chap. 1.
9. George A. W. Boehm, "Des Matériaux qui n'existent pas," *Analyse et prévision* (1968); Dennis Gabor, "Prevision technologique et responsabilité sociale," *Analyse et prévision* (1968).
10. M. Rodes in *Cahiers du Boucau.*
11. See B. Charbonneau's wonderful description of refuse in the urbanized world (*Le Jardin de Babylone*). For technological studies, see M. Neiburger, "La Lutte contre la pollution de l'air," *Analyse et prévision* (1967); and H. Rousseau, "Les Détritus urbains," *Analyse et prévision* (1966).
12. See the excellent demonstration in S. Wickham, *Concentration et dimension* (1966).

## CHAPTER 10

1. To take one single example among a thousand: We know the problem of "medical over-consumption." There is incredible progress in the consumption of not only remedies but above all biological and radiological actions. Now this consumption does not correspond to any true needs or any growth of medical knowledge. Its cause is neither ease nor the National Health Service, but, above all, the improvement in technologies. See Professor Béreaud's "La Surconsommation médicale" in *Le Monde*, January 3–5, 1970. Thus, certain apparatuses can now automatically make a simultaneous quantitative analysis of twelve components for several milliliters of blood. The doctor needs only one analysis, but he will ask for the complete evaluation because it is so easy. In 99% of the cases, the examinations are useless; the technology is there—we employ it.

2. See the excellent study, "La Controverse sur la prévision en U.R.S.S.," *Analyse et prévision* (1971).

3. See M. Crozier, *La Société bloquée* (*The Stalled Society*), 1970, p. 57.

4. Need we recall, in regard to a well-known novel, Dudintsev's *Man Does Not Live by Bread Alone*, that the obviousness of progress, i.e., applying a newer machine to produce pipes, highlights the *wickedness* of the system and of the (Soviet) bureaucracy, both of which oppose it: the nontechnological choice of man appears as a hindrance to obvious progress.

5. In *The Technological Society* (1964), I dealt adequately with judging as positive the economic and social regime that adapts best to technological progress and as negative the one hindering it. It was one of the superiorities claimed for the communist system over capitalism. But during the past ten years, people have noticed that the Soviet regime is also causing blockage in this area and have criticized it accordingly. This, more than any other ideological element, has challenged the regime. Its difficulty in absorbing and applying automation on a large scale has been particularly underlined by Soviet economists like Klimenko and Rakovsky, 1958.

6. See such authors as Diedisheim, *Pour un nouveau mode de penser* (1968), which explains how technological growth demands a profound revision of all the principles and foundations on which the present organizations live; the mode of thinking has to be altered for the sake of a rational adaptation to technology by politics and human groups.

How many works in this connection have to be cited! P. Piganiol's *Maîtriser le progrès* (1968) or Closets *En danger de progrès* (1970) are good examples. Closets writes: "The lag between the dynamics of progress and the resistance of ideologies remains the common denominator in all crises." This reveals what, in his eyes, "progress" is and what resistance is—an illegitimate source of crisis and absurdity.

Likewise Schon (*Technology and Change*) points out the necessity of making the whole economic system, businesses, etc., adapt to technology; except that for him, it does not "go without saying," it is not simple to carry out. He particularly shows that this adjustment is required, probably inevitable, but also negative for individual freedom and identity.

Even a man as concerned about preserving human liberty, the ability to choose, etc., as E. G. Mesthene is obliged to admit: "If no technological change entails a unique and predetermined change, any new technology nevertheless renders certain types, certain ensembles of social consequences more probable. The technological change, in other words, does not lead to just any social change, but rather to a change whose orientation is perceptible" (*Technological Change: Its Impact on Man and Society*, 1970).

7. G. Klein, "L'Influence des techniques de transport sur l'implantation de l'habitat et des équipements commerciaux," *Analyse et prévision* (1968).

8. Jean Parent shows how the concentration results automatically without choice or deliberation, from the growth of technologies: "Certain technologies make it *impossible* for small businesses to exist. Computers, on the other hand, by allowing the processing of great masses of information, make this concentration both *possible* and *necessary* (*La Concentration industrielle*, 1970).

9. C. Freeman, *Recherche et développement en électronique* (1966).

10. Of great significance is a work quoted by B. de Jouvenel, *The Use of Social Research in Federal Domestic Programs*, 4 vols. (1977). Here the most eminent technologists, "consulted on the role of the social sciences, replied on what it means to prepare society to receive the technological innovations."

11. Donald N. Michael, *Cybernation and Social Change* (1964), gives a very concrete, although very incomplete view of these mechanisms of automatic social adjustment, in particular for systems of training and reclassifying not only unqualified but also superior personnel, and not only in industry but also in utilities. In reality, social automatism operates due to the pressure of such phenomena. We obligatorily choose the most efficient, most economic, and least painful solution when facing the challenge of the technological rise. Michael points out that cybernetics is both the *means* permitting these adjustments and the *factor* demanding and entailing them.

12. Closets offers a remarkable scheme for the use of modern technologies in intellectual training and in the total and seamless adaptation of man to technology. He calls it: "Administering human capital." It is quite symbolic as is the dovetailing with Stalin in his celebrated brochure: *Man, the Most Precious Capital*.

13. The French word *organisation*, although equivalent to the *concept* of "organization" or "planning," is often rendered by the *term* "engineering" in English: e.g., *organisation de travail* = "organization of work," "job engineering"; *organisation industrielle* = "industrial engineering"; *organisation de la production* = "production engineering." But: *organisation des données* = "data organization"; *organisation scientifique du travail* = "organization and methods," and so on. In the ensuing discussion, I have used the English cognates for Ellul's *organisation* ( = "organization") and *ingénierie* ( = "engineering"). (Translator's note)

14. Among the many works on engineering, we may point out R. Leclerc, *Les Méthodes d'organisation et d'engineering* (1968).

15. On the technicity of organization and the association between technology and organization, see P. Morin, *Le Développement des organisations* (1976).

16. Once again, we are not speaking about technocrats! We have treated these issues in detail in *Political Illusion*. Barets's research along these lines is highly disappointing and unrealistic. On the other hand, Closets

gives interesting concrete examples of the need to adapt administrations to the computer and modify the processes of political decision-making by the use of multiple technologies. He emphasizes that "a dialogue is becoming more and more difficult between the politicians and the analysts who set up the programs: statesmen must yield to the implacable logic of programming. . . . They will then see the consequences of their decisions largely escaping them. . . ." By contrast, in the sense of a true technocracy, see Finzi: *Il potere technocratico*, 1977. A. and F. Demichel, *Les Dictatures européennes*, 1973, is of great interest for our topic (and for many others as well!). This depicts the trend toward similarity between regimes that are constitutionally and juridically very different, e.g. the Spanish dictatorship and the French Republic, in the form of technicized states. The technization of government effaces traditional distinctions. But these countries are not really technocracies.

17. There are many studies on the necessary adjustment of institutions to new technologies. We can instance Armand, *Plaidoyer pour l'avenir;* Mendès France, *Pour une république nouvelle;* Barets, *Nouvelles Équations politiques;* and so forth. Also, in regard to the ineluctable adjustment of politics, see the series *Politik und Wissenschaft* (1971). Especially H. Kahn's *Politik und Wissenschaft;* Meissner, *Wissenschaft und Politik als kybernetisches System;* Hahn, *Die Bedeutung der Wissenschaft für die Integration der pluralistischen Gesellschaft*, which has good analyses of the inevitable adjustment by both the *structures* and the *tactics* of the political universe.

18. D. Bell sharply analyzes the cultural reaction to efficiency (*Toward the Year 2000*, Daedalus, 1967). The more technological the society becomes, the more the culture will turn hedonistic, self-indulgent, distrustful of authority, organization, technology, and efficiency. He clearly sees that the intellectuals, to avoid entering the mode of technocratic behavior, are launching into the mode of apocalyptic behavior—which is firmly verified by our left-wing French intellectuals. But Bell's description stops persuading me when he maintains that this conflict may lead to serious trouble. I do believe that this situation can cause social problems, but none that are very deep or very challenging to the technological system.

19. R. Blauner, *Alienation and Freedom: The Factory Worker and His Industry* (1964); Dumazedier, *Vers la civilisation des loisirs* (1965); G. Friedmann, *La Puissance and la sagesse* (1970); B. Charbonneau, *Dimanche et lundi* (1966).

20. H. Lefebvre battles against the idea of a technologically "homogenized" society and seeks to demonstrate the opposite, i.e., diversification due to technology (*Position: contre les technocrates*). But he simply makes the mistake of believing that the technological system imposes uniformity, identity; whereas the system can be as total and as rigorous as I have described it, while allowing the survival of, or even causing, cultural differences between groups, which differences, however, will never be significant. The maximum of initiatives within the maximum of organizational rigor: that is the ideal of the technological society!

21. See also Onimus, *L'Asphyxie et le cri*, and our observations on the same problem, above p. 211.

## CHAPTER 11

1. I would also like to point out that in this article, Daumas carries on the work of Maunoury by citing precise examples in order to arrive at a general interpretation of technology, as I do for Simondon: *L'Histoire de la technique, Documents pour l'histoire des techniques* (1969).

2. The most pertinent reflections on this issue were offered by Bertrand de Jouvenel in his admirable and far too unknown study, *Arcadie* (1968). He shows better than anyone else the futility of hoping to assure a better life with technology. And he does an excellent job of pointing out what we can expect when applying technology in this way. But we are remote from that.

3. Hence the success of such justifying books as *And Happiness in the Bargain*, or the boom in titles containing *Happiness* to characterize our society.

4. See Jacques Ellul, *Lucidité de l'an 2000* (1967).

5. Mumford shows perfectly that the triumphant creation of test-tube life will never be anything but an imitation of what has been going on for millions of years. The only new feature is the affirmation of man's control and power. But *who* is he to be invested with such power?

6. Yona Friedmann, an expert in computer programming, has devised a theory of communication and written many works on architecture: *L'Architecture mobile* (1962); *La Théorie des systèmes compréhensibles* (1963); *Les Mécanismes urbains* (1965). These studies, although based on a huge number of historical, sociological, and other errors, are presented as obvious on the technological level. They are utopian in that the author regards certain still problematical technological applications as being immediately realizable.

7. Illich makes the following very significant remark about the Latin American countries: "The building code has standards far below those of rich countries, but by prescribing certain ways in which houses must be built, it creates a rising scarcity of housing. The pretense of a society to provide ever better housing is the same kind of abberation we have met in the pretense of doctors to provide better health and of engineers to provide higher speeds. The setting of abstract impossible goals turns the means by which these are to be achieved into ends."

8. On the contradiction between ends and means, and on the lack of any finality to technological growth, see mainly B. Charbonneau: "When it comes to human ends that might guide a plan, we have to content ourselves with pious generalities about a society 'in which man need only assert himself for the inner satisfaction of his being.' But in regard to the concrete aspects of France in 1985, we learn that she will be 'developed.' Always along the same lines. . . . What is the goal of economic growth? Economic growth."

Likewise, Mumford demonstrates at length that the sole conceivable and real finality of "technics" is the augmentation of power. There is absolutely no other possibility. This brings us back to the problem of the means. Technology is the most powerful means and the greatest ensemble of means. And hence, the only problem of technology is that of the indefinite growth of means, corresponding to man's spirit of power. Nietzsche, exalting this will to power, limited himself to preparing the man predisposed to the technological universe! A tragic contradiction!

# NOTES

9. Shils, *Survivre au Futur*, too, feels that men of science scarcely obey any explicit finalities in their work: "They are motivated by the pleasure of seeking and the joy of discovery; some of them deeply believe in the metaphysical value of attempting to elucidate the nature of existence: nevertheless, those who admit it are rare. They usually say that their work brings material advantages to humanity, whereas they are actually playing a risky and costly game that society should, in their opinion, finance. . . . The relations of science to economic development are obscure," there is no clear and certain economic finality.

10. The present-day historians of sciences and technologies offer analyses that are very different from those current fifty years ago. Thus, for R. Mousnier (*Progrès scientifique et technique au XVIII<sup>e</sup> siècle*), eighteenth-century science was not the necessary inspirer of the technologies, any more than a "response" to social needs. It seems that during the eighteenth century, sciences and technologies progressed separately. The great technological inventions resulted from purely pragmatic research and from the use of means that were available to the practitioners, without the help of scientists (who never saw the technological consequences of what they were doing). And, vice versa, the scientific discoveries had technological results only very gradually and because a "technological spirit" had developed.

Such is also the opinion of M. Daumas, *Histoire générale des Techniques*, vols. I and III. However, he notes that now there *is* an interaction between science and technology. He shows in detail that today technology promotes scientific development; and he calls technology the science assuring the double mutual relationship between science and technology: it is a scientific technology or a science of technology.

I am particularly happy that these two great historians have confirmed the analyses that I did in 1950, coming to exactly these same two results, contrary to the prevailing opinion at that time.

11. The total futility of wanting to subordinate technology to finalities glares out from J. Offredo's superficial and ideological book, *Le Sens du futur* (1971). It contains all the clichés of a plan for a goal-oriented society. The problems are poorly articulated; and the remedies are either perfectly inadequate (dismantling the functions grouped in the notion of property), or simplistic (a new conception of politics), or idealistic (the reconciliation of politicians and scientists). The author certainly has plenty of good will; but such naiveté, such ignorance of the rigorous problems raised by technology, are hard to accept! And to think that he was national secretary of "Objective 1972." It is obvious that these objectives will not, and have no chance of being, achieved in 1992 anymore than in 1972!

12. Closets shows the extent to which an extratechnological objective (military, political, for prestige, etc.) brings trouble and disorder into the harmonious growth of technology. His concrete examples are highly significant. Furthermore, he stresses that the goals of research are becoming more and more uncertain, "people are pursuing a work known as industrial research because 'it can always be of use,' and in any case 'it makes science progress.' " This remark is actually fundamental.

13. It is quite obvious that one can, as Closets does, assert that there are objectives, certain economic, industrial objectives, for which he gives the 1968 budgets: 28% of the overall research and development effort in the

United States; 41% in France; 62% in Germany; 73% in Japan. And military objectives (challenge to other countries, army, space): 65% in the United States; 60% in France and Great Britain; 20% in Germany; 3% in Japan. But there is actually some confusion here. Investing in research and development absolutely does not mean that economic or military objectives are causing technological progress. This finality leads to devoting this money with a view to technological progress—by all means—and hence, it makes it *possible*. But there is only a very indirect and nondetermining relation between the two facts. What is called an "objective" here is a very general view, as also the will to power. But it does not explain technological progress, any more than the discoveries made with a military objective need be useful for the army; they can be useful in so many other sectors; which also goes for the "industrial" objective. The objectives assigned to research determine nothing in the process or the results. They are indispensable merely to justify research to the politicians and to the administration that decides upon subsidies! That is the sole utility of proclaiming the objectives for research and development.

14. Let us be careful not to confuse the wishes of politicians, humanists, philosophers, with the true objectives of technology. To state that "technology must be used to feed the starving nations" is evidence of a good heart. But it will never make technology advance by even half an inch. J. Baudrillard in analyzing the needs, stresses that fulfilling needs is not an end of the technological society either. There are not, there cannot be, autonomous needs in the technological system; there are now only needs for growth. There is no place for individual finalities, only for the sole finality of the system, which is, exactly and precisely, its growth—i.e., the causality.

15. As for having technicians set up objectives, the finest example is furnished by the NASA report of February 1970: "The Post-Apollo Program: Directions for the Future." This is the prototype of the limit between the technological objective and the finality. The program indicates a basic change in orientations. It no longer concentrates on a single mission for manned flights; it focuses on answering the following two questions: How can we lower the costs of missions (which is understandable if they are to become "routine")? How are we to make "man in space" profitable? This marks the second phase of any technological process. The program offers various answers (polyvalent vehicles for varied missions, recycling of used material, simplification of the systems used, etc.). We thus see clearly how the objectives are established. How they really give the meaning of the growth. But, on the other hand, nothing here offers any finality. It is always *because* the means are available that these objectives are mapped out; and everything is integrated in a system that has no finality whatsoever.

Needless to say, government intervention can also be decisive here; but only on condition that the established research program is actually set up by the researchers, with the state as the sleeping partner: a huge government "order" is a first-class incentive. This is becoming more and more obvious in the United States (e.g., C. Freeman, "Recherche et développement en électronique," *Analyse et prévision*, 1966). A technological delay can be very swiftly overcome, so long as there is a technological infrastructure, when the state, by its decision to promote research, concentrates the technological means according to the opinion of the technicians.

16. This thesis, widespread in public opinion, is generally rejected by sociologists and even economists, including those who, like Bela Gold (*L'Entreprise et la génèse de l'invention*, 1967), are convinced that technology is subject to economy.

17. It is acknowledged that the study of only one chemical substance in a hundred leads to a marketable product, and that there is an average delay of five years between studying a medicament and putting it on the market. We can thus understand the reluctance of financiers!

18. B. de Jouvenel raises an essential question when he asks if we should speak, here, about impacts or goals. He notes that an enormous number of Americans writing about research and development discuss only the impacts, the consequences of these innovations, including the technological predictions for which the potential consequences are reckoned. But, he says, in all this, the authors, in sum, consider only that society receives its technological innovations and merely adjusts to them: "It is remarkable," he adds, "that eminent technologists, when consulted on the role of the social sciences, replied that their role was to prepare society for receiving technological innovations" (*Arcadie*, 1968). This submission by these technologists shocks Jouvenel; and of course, as a moralist he is right. He stoutly maintains that we must reverse the terms and pursue the objectives of social well-being in order to adjust research and development. He says that there is a trend of public opinion in that direction. I am willing to go along with this, but no one sees how we can reverse the causalist process that has begun. We would practically have to perform a psychoanalytical operation and go back to the origin in order to reconstruct the history of the last two centuries according to a finalist mode!

19. An excellent article by N. Dangtam, "Les Armes chimiques" in *Science et Paix*, (1973), shows how unaware the researchers and technicians sometimes are of what they are doing. Dangtam delves into the process of discovering a deadly chemical substance, *taboun*, through a series of intercrossing studies done by groups that were unaware of each other. But here, the keystone was the Nazi state.

20. A remarkable analysis of the reasons for the American advance in electronics is supplied by C. Freeman, "Recherche et développement en électronique" in *Analyse et prévision* (1966). Freeman concludes that it is not the importance of funds or aptitudes that makes the difference, but rather the prior technological advance in a large number of technological areas. It was by leaning on the possibilities of these preexistent technologies that Americans could progress very rapidly in electronics although investing relatively little.

Z. Brzezinski points out that people have tried to zero in on the capacity for innovation; scholars have investigated where 139 principle innovations were first used. Nine industrial sectors dependent on innovation were selected (computer, semiconductor, pharmaceuticals, plastics, metallurgy, etc.). The conclusions showed that during the past twenty years, the United States has had the highest rate of innovation: 60% of the 139 inventions were first used in the United States—as against 15% in Great Britain. The United States also gathers 60% of the innovations of the Organization for Economic Cooperation and Development: the industrial *use* of patents is eight times higher for the United States than for the O. E. C. D., whereas the number of O. E. C. D. patents is slightly above that of American patents.

Here we can see how greatly previous growth determines both the possibility of innovation and then the passage from innovation to industrial application.

21. W. Vicheney has done a remarkable survey of Japan, "De la technique à la science" (*Le Monde*, June 1972). In the relation between basic research and technology, the author points out the reverse route of what we are used to. Japan is going back from all-out technicization toward science and basic research. Japan seems a highly interesting model in that technicization has developed here with no scientific underpinning. This is due, no doubt, to the conditions in which technicization took place, the primary aim being to imitate Westerners and adopt their instruments of power; but it may also be due to Japanese psychology and social structure, which are particularly equipped for technological action. Nevertheless, at the moment, Japan is oriented toward basic research in order to gain national industrial and technological independence. But science appears here only as an accessory to technology, the latter being self-sufficient. And this self-augmentation of technology, uncurbed, unadulterated, unlimited, is what *produced* the so-called "Japanese miracle" from an economic standpoint. It was not brought on by what has always been depicted as the key to technological and economic progress in the West: military needs. No indeed. Technology has developed in Japan by itself and in a causal, autonomous, and self-augmenting process.

22. Richta very judiciously analyzes the difference in *nature* between, on the one hand, growth of capital and the resulting economic growth, and, on the other hand, technological growth, which does not rely on accumulation of capital, but on the complexification of experiments and of interconnections between science and technology.

23. Do we not hear today about the use of lunar dust for fertilizer? I will leave aside the marvelous arguments like the one that compares the discovery of the moon to the discovery of America. This author even adds: "Did not America *have* to be discovered?" Come now, that goes without saying! After such arguments, one can doubt the survival of even the slightest critical spirit.

24. This is a phenomenon of causal progression that also usually explains the "mistakes" in forecasting by famous men. We know the peremptory assertions of philosophers or scientists who were in error. Comte, who affirmed that we would never know anything about the nature of the stars, Newcomb, who affirmed that we could never fly any device heavier than air. And in these past twenty years, one scientist has claimed that we could never know anything about the atomic nucleus; another, in 1965, that the era of computer progress was over, etc. Actually, all these errors come from focusing on an objective but not perceiving how to attain it, i.e., maintaining a finalist view—whereas technological progress is due to a combination of means. This conceptual error is what keeps the number of *predicted* and *announced* inventions relatively small.

25. Highly remarkable in this respect, and along these lines, is the study of computer technology development. IBM assured itself an uncontested supremacy, less by exorbitant and brilliant inventions than by a progressive and systematic use of all existing possibilities. Hence, every new type was not "revolutionary," but represented a decisive and rational technological

# NOTES

advance at every step of the way. (See, for instance, Lavallard: "Des circuits intégrés par millions," *Le Monde*, January 1970). It is this causal progression that expresses itself in popular bromides like: "You can't stop progress." If this progress took place in terms of an objective, it could obviously be altered or arrested. You can't stop progress; this means that it has charged forth like a locomotive and that it contains its own cause. Or take Werner von Braun's formula: "The United States is doomed to maintain its technological advance" in *Le Monde*, February 1972: "Maintaining its technological evolution is a matter of life and death for the United States." There is no better way of putting it. What has already been done is what rigorously determines what will be done, and we are no longer masters of the choice. The choice is made in terms of what has been done so far, which is the cause of what we cannot help continuing to do!

26. In concluding, it would help to get rid of a certain confusion. So far, I have spoken about technological progress as a system and in its all-inclusiveness. Of course, I know that ends are proposed in each sector, but even here they are dependent on the means. The most interesting case is the long-term "plan" known as "Horizon," 1985, or the twenty-year plan set up by the Soviet State Committee for Science and Technology, 1961. The Western case uses a futurological method, constructing models in terms of the horizon chosen, expressing the desirable aims, and to which the "intermediary horizons" are then referred. But ultimately, these models express either the personal preferences of the experts or the consequences of the main political and philosophical positions in the society. What we have here is an evaluation of possibilities based on the existing technology, involving, to be sure, a nonrigid possibility of evolution. In the Soviet case, the model is unique, a function of a forecasting attitude. The experts observe, and act upon, the development of present-day trends and hunt solutions for any foreseeable contradictions. But all this is based on the application of Marxist theory, which is regarded as capable of selecting the best model, because it permits having scientific knowledge of the relations between the individual or collective projects and their determination by the social structures. In reality, however, the two systems are not as remote from one another as is claimed, for, among the various models worked out by Western futurology, the decision is based not on the expected ideal, but on the growth of technological means in one sector rather than another!

CHAPTER 12

1. We know that several types exist, from forecasting to futurology, not to mention the futuribles. Simplistic linear forecasting, a mere prolongation of trends statistically ascertained in preceding years by extrapolation. Forecasting with correlation models, with input/output analysis (which is always based on statistical adjustments), analogical models (in which one sets up the great lines of a, perhaps illusory, configuration), and conjunctural models (establishing probable correlations between observations)—all these things are based on the conviction that tomorrow is conditioned by yesterday, and even more that yesterday's progress causes tomorrow's progress.

Futurology proceeds differently. It researches the existing mechanisms, but with the conviction that they will not necessarily produce an acceptable future. It involves estimations, judgments, and introduces a will to change upon the probable, on the level of the possible and the desirable. It also has to evaluate the intervention procedures. Observers have correctly pointed out that all this was already contained in Karl Marx: the forecasting about the evolution of capitalism, futurology about the outcome of the revolution. "Futurologist thinking is a synthesis of several types of approaches: researching the unknown, questioning history to find the vital structural analogies, evaluating political, social, economic, and ecological trends, analyzing the solidity of beliefs and institutions, but also gauging the men whose will and aptitudes express the potentials of an era" (Reszler: *Marx et la pensée prospective*, 1975). See also the remarkable study by R. V. Ayres, *Technological Forecasting and Long Range Planning* (1969).

2. See two good studies on the acceleration of technological progress from an economic viewpoint: Scheurer's "Les Problèmes financiers de l'accélération du progrès technique" and Dupriez's "L'Accélération du progrès technique" in the special issue of *Revue d'Économie politique* (1966) on this question.

3. We must, however, note that this acceleration corresponds to the psychological attitude of modern man and to what B. de Jouvenel calls "the civilization of always more" (*Arcadie*, 1968). As for forecasting, the huge collective American opus *Toward the Year 2000* (Daedalus, 1967) affirms a predictable acceleration of technological progress, albeit without demonstrating it.

4. P. Bertaux, *La Mutation humaine*.

5. Other specialists claim that the interval between scientific invention and technological application in the laboratory, then diffusion, keeps on decreasing. Striking instances are given. It took more than a century to pass from the discovery of the principle of photography to the commercial manufacture of cameras. Half a century for the telephone, and five years for transistor radios.

6. See the interesting special issue of *Le Monde* (July 1972) on energy in Europe.

7. Thus, the extraordinary technological application of plasma at a high temperature to obtain materials armored by overlapping, or even the possibilities of laser use in unbelievably diverse areas, from eye surgery to "micromemories" for storing data by means of an engraving ray with a diameter of five-thousandths of a millimeter, etc. On the countless possibilities of the laser beam, see the books by Closets and Kahn.

8. Everyone has seen the advertising used by one French automobile company to ridicule the huge American cars, caricaturing the disasters unleashed by such a monster in a small village street: "Europe could easily make the same mistake as America." This is a fine example of acknowledging that a technological product, with utmost comfort, speed, silence, and all the perfections possible, can cause so much trouble in its environment as to become a mistake. The adjustment to the environment, which, as we have seen, the system demands, cannot take place at the same speed as progress itself. It is impossible to widen all streets, to build all parking lots necessitated by the growth of the automobile fleet, etc. We will come back to this issue later on.

## NOTES

9. See J. Donnadieu, "La Révolte contre l'efficacité," *Le Monde* (September 1972).

10. E.g., Jay Macculley, "Les Américains se détournent de leur technologie," *Le Monde* (December 1971).

11. See P. Drouin, "Le Travail contesté," *Le Monde* (July 1972).

12. See P. Drouin's very important article, "L'Âge des théories mobiles," *Le Monde*, (December 1970).

13. Illich makes a very important distinction (with, as always, a certain imprecision in the vocabulary—but are his works well-translated into French?) when he analyses the thresholds and limits. The thresholds represent the confines in which the action of man (and technology) must take place if survival is to remain possible. This is a question of necessities. And when we speak of damaging effects, pollution, depleted resources, we are designating thresholds. The amount of drinking water is a threshold for population growth. And decisively, the finite character of our universe is the threshold of technological growth. Thus, it is a question simply of conditions for survival. But this is nothing for the creation of a culture or civilization. Here, man himself must set *limits* which constitute the pattern of a culture. This is where the voluntary and the deliberative come in. The necessity of determining thresholds and not crossing them is spontaneous in the traditional world, but it must be calculated and voluntarily fixed in a technological world. However, this is no control of technology. "Zero growth in no way guarantees the emergence of a new culture, it only marks the possibility. Setting limits is a specific act by which man dominates both his destiny and "Nature." Now, technology must be added. It is not unlimitedness which can be the basis of, or constitute, a culture or person. This is the central issue. It is by establishing voluntary limits that man sets himself up as man. The sole act of authentic, verifiable, and concrete control of technology would be to set limits to its development. But this is the very contradiction of the system. Contrary to what people may think, setting limits creates freedom. Illich's thinking here coincides with mine. And I feel that nothing is as fundamental as this problem of voluntary limits

14. I am quite aware of all the contestations such theses can provoke. Thus, R. Gilpin, *La Science et l'état en France*, (1970), attempts to justify the reverse thesis, namely, that *the state* can, to a certain degree, promote progress. Yet he emphasizes that "despite the efforts" of the French government, France does not succeed in competing with the United States. And it is therefore in the situation of concentrating all its efforts on one or two areas chosen for their commercial value, like Sweden and Holland; or of imitating Japan by creating an industrial basis to exploit American patents; or of falling into step and following the United States (the USSR being a lot less attractive). But Gilpin obviously fails to see that government intervention in France obstructs basic research. The same view is held by Jewkes, Sawers, Stillerman (*The Sources of Invention*) on the importance of the individual researcher and the sterilization by large-scale organizations, huge laboratories, organized plannings, and objects imposed from the outside.

15. But we have also shown that the technological imperative forces itself upon the authorities, who are not free to decide what is "good" when dealing with a program already begun. A good example was offered by

Sweden in September 1976. The Socialists were beaten. One of the important planks in the center's platform was the rejection of the nuclear program, the promise not to build any plants. In Sweden, the safety of life and the protection of the environment are "sacred." "By 1985, there will not be a single nuclear plant in Sweden," declared Falldin. All well and good. Now, Falldin is in power. What is he going to do? His intentions are the same. But he has to suggest that the Swedes greatly reduce their energy consumption. With the very rigorous controls implied. Are the Swedes ready to change their way of life? They are also going to begin research for using other energy sources (but how much time will that take?). Some people will lose their jobs (the nuclear industry employs ten thousand people); and the lowering of energy consumption will curb if not stop the economic recovery (hence, prevent the creation of 400,000 new jobs that were promised). Thus, the resolution is beginning to weaken. It has been decided that the new power plant, which is ready, will not be put to work before spring 1977; and commissions are being appointed to examine the possibilities of carrying out the campaign promises. In reality, when projects have been technologically done by correct technicians, it is almost impossible to cancel them. Wait, there *is* one way: Change the entire direction of the society, alter its mentality, and embark on a period of austerity, deprivation, and nondevelopment!

16. This blockage is perhaps more immediately felt on the business level. As has been correctly pointed out by Schon (*Technology and Change*), business is not made for uncertainty. Its work necessarily consists in transforming uncertainty into risk, offering alternatives to profits and overhead. But it sweeps away the technological factor when this factor creates irreducible uncertainties or when its economic importance is not in keeping with the capital it requires. However, this calculation must also ultimately be made by the planners; hence, the economic factor can constantly operate as a curb, and not only within the capitalist system.

The first man to see the problem as a whole was B. de Jouvenel, and one ought to consult his bibliography in *Arcadie* (1968). Also see B. Cazes and B. Lassudrie-Duchêne and a very good concrete example of the economic viewpoint, Ferhat-Delessert, "Mediterranée an 2000—Eden ou cloaque" in *Analyse et prévision* (1970)—with the ironic note that the increase of public spending for the antipollution struggle appears as a positive aspect in the accounts of the nation!

A typical example in these past few years was the sudden curb on NASA. In 1965, the total NASA budget was 5.25 billion dollars, with more than 400,000 people working for it. The budget and the staff were reduced in 1969, in 1970, and then brought down to 3.3 million dollars and 140,000 people in 1971. The simple explanation is that not even the United States can respond economically to the financial demands of all technological sectors. America has to make a choice. But there is another factor explaining the NASA phenomenon. The United States is now passing into a phase of exploiting technological and scientific achievements, the "routine" phase. One of the constant rules of technological progress is that the peak research sectors cannot always be accelerated. There comes a moment of recuperation, normalization—which is what is happening to NASA. But we may then ask if the same thing might not hold for the entire technological system.

17. We should not, however, overestimate the economic curb. For example, in the United States, the report of the Commission on Electronic Warfare (March 1970) indicated that this warfare had cost three billion twenty-five million dollars in research! It is true that the overall cost of the war was 130 billion dollars, an expenditure that did not shake the American economy.

18. Cf. Mishan's very important book, *The Costs of Economic Growth* (1967). Although often contested, it strikes me as very solid. Mishan states that the solution for controlling unfavorable social consequences of technological progress consists in including the social drawbacks of any product or manufacturing method in their cost price. But there is still the problem of the *real* possibility of such an operation, the scale for calculating economic losses. And incidentally, can anyone truly imagine that this may be done in anything but a totally controlled authoritarian economy? We would have to set the alternative for each industrial producer, etc.: "If you emit this amount of smoke, it will cost you so much to repair the damage—or else you will have to stop your activity." An obviously authoritarian method.

But Schonfield, *Blueprint for Survival*, is right in stating that two kinds of problems are often confused: "How can one measure precisely the growth of costs of the economy?" (One must then pay need to negative effects or simple substitutions.) And also: "It is abnormal to consume for our pleasure goods that are harmful to the collective" (cars, TV, etc.). The first problem is purely technological. In coping with uneconomical factors, it requires paying heed to real savings financed by a new process, which increases the difficulty of calculating. The second problem brings in value judgments and moral judgments. That can involve divergencies of opinion. And Schonfield speaks of the work now being done in London by the Rokill Committee for building the third London airport. This committee is trying to take heed of all damaging effects: the social cost of noise, the potential harm to old apartment buildings and monuments, etc. But a group of local citizens has formed to stop the project for the sake of developing the neighborhood, the activity created by an airport, the enrichment of the people, and so on.

Naturally, all this makes the calculation dreadfully complicated. But in any event, there may be an economic cause here for curbing technological progress. The costs become exorbitant and impossible to support even in a wealthy or socialized economy! (In 1968, air pollution cost the United States four billion dollars just for repairing the damage, not counting the health problems, and of course, without establishing any policy for air purification!)

On all these points, we have to cite Jouvenel's article and the series of works published in *Analyse et prévision* since 1969. Readers should also consult the special issue of *Revue d'économie politique* (1973), on the costs of growth; the report on the *Colloque des Économistes de Langue Française*, 1972, in which there are good things on the indirect expenses, the integration of pullution costs in economic analysis; and above all, case studies (Greece, Iran) on how taking these costs into account influences the economies of developing countries.

19. See P. Massé, *Prospective: l'homme encombré* (1969), an excellent

synthesis of congestion problems, with descriptions of certain elements (e.g., economy, language) and certain effects (on the psychoanalytical level); P. Massé, *Le Plan ou l'antihasard* (1967). But above all, the basic though difficult work of S. C. Kolm, *La Théorie économique générale de l'encombrement* (1969)—a first attempt at evaluating the qualitative return, which is actually the exact opposite of congestion.

20. See a strikingly detailed example in W. L. Libby, "La Fin du trajet quotidien," *Analyse et prévision* (1969).

21. See the 1973 report of France's National Center for Exploiting the Oceans.

22. On these problems, see, in particular, J. M. Treille's excellent study, *Progrès technique et stratégie industrielle* (1972). Treille does a fine job of investigating the problem of the accelerated emergence of new technologies and the ensuing difficulties on all levels, not just on the level of the capitalist structure of market and enterprise.

23. The Diebold Research Program of 1971 correctly notes that "far from simplifying technology of business, the computer has *augmented complexity* and imposed a series of constantly changing constraints on researchers and mangers."

24. Sheldon, "L'Ère de l'espace," *Analyse et prévision* (1966).

CONCLUSION

1. On the transformation of man by the technological environment, see the excellent study by G. Friedman, *Sept études sur l'homme et la technique* (1966).

2. An utterly characteristic book on this topic (and on the confusion between technology and neo-humanism) is Canonge and Ducel, *La Pédagogie devant le progrès technique* (1969). The authors study the intellectual and practical education needed to adapt the child to technological changes and bring him to contributing to technological progress. They show how manual training yields to technological efficiency based on technological thought and made up of logical activity, methodical reflection, and technological research. The child is being schooled to imagine forms, encode all data, while being furnished with the motives necessary for entering the system. This remarkable book demonstrates (involuntarily) that men, thus trained, will never control technology, because they are educated for technology, are perfectly adapted to it, and remain incapable of any critical attitude. Now this is far more decisive than investigations trying to prove that the goal of education is to continue the dominant culture!

3. Richta feels that every man is bound to take part in scientific and technological development as soon as his time is liberated. Against this optimistic outlook, a hard, partisan book by P. Roqueplo (*Le Partage du savoir, science, culture et vulgarisation*, 1974) is far more realistic. There is no truly popular science. What is propagated as knowledge by TV, books, and magazines, has no cultural value. There is no sharing of knowledge. True learning is always above and beyond the parcellary "knowledge" distributed. There is a qualitative difference between this episodic knowledge and scientific learning or critical intellectual training.

All this is fine. But I do not fully agree when the author says that popularization is an "ideological manipulation that serves the ruling class." If we are dealing with a spontaneous function for integrating people into

# NOTES

the technological society, then yes. But if it is a somber Machiavellianism, a deliberate calculation to make the oppressed classes conform, then this is pulp fiction. Nor do I have Roqueplo's slightly simplistic faith that a political change (socialism!) will make a both genuine and generalized sharing of knowledge possible. The problem is, alas, far more complex. Unless—and we keep coming back to this—the new regime is *also* a government of virtue!

4. We should not, of course, neglect the powers of the concrete and voluntary integration of man into technology. For instance, the great fear aroused by a detailed record of each individual's entire background. This problem is correctly stated and analyzed by Messadié, *La Fin de la vie privée*, 1974. The author shows the vast scope of increasing surveillances, the multiplication of files, the "electronic epidemic," all causing both a decline in traditional judicial standards, e.g., professional secrecy, and a growing loss, from a psychological viewpoint, of the sense of privacy. Although this is due not just to technologies, but also to mass society, the "cheek by jowl" society. Young people who "want" to live in communes, who do "everything" in public and lose their sense of privacy, are neither innovators nor revolutionaries. Morally and psychologically, they are simply reflecting the living conditions imposed by technological society. At any rate, the multiplication of computerized files is frightening. But once again, the responses and proposals are feeble. Messadié resorts to judicial measures: setting hard and fast limits, controlling centralization, outlawing advertising (in which case, the government would be doubly privileged!), protecting secrecy and privacy. But who will be able to apply such rules? Who will be able to limit uses? The problem is *not* a good use of technology! We would have to challenge technology from top to bottom, for the system itself is total! Law has lost its grip!

5. And advertising reveals itself as a technology not only in its practical objectives, but also in the very attitude of the advertising men. We need only recall the proadvertising ads: "The man who does not believe in advertising is the same man who, in 1900, did not believe in the automobile (or the movies, or the airplane)." The point of comparison is *always* a technological object. Which implies that the man who does not believe in the advertising technology did not believe in the machine technology in 1900.

6. The enormous change that technology is causing in man has been scientifically studied by P. R. Hofstätter: "Das Stereotyp der Technik" in the collective volume *Technik im technischen Zeitalter* (1965). The author employs the method of connotations revealed by sounding out scales of words, polarizations and oppositions, a method offering a remarkable profile of technological man and his values.

7. Kaufmann and Cathelin, *Le Gaspillage de la liberté* (1964); or Closets, *En danger de progrès*.

8. We must however underscore an essential remark by Jouvenel: Production in earlier centuries had a vital character, hence it was scorned. "Pardoxically, production has acquired an unprecedented moral status in the era in which it increases to fulfill needs that are less and less vital."

9. As for the study of the correlation between need and technology, I must cite an excellent article by E. Leitherer, "Technik und Konsum," in the collective volume *Die Technik im technischen Zeitalter* (1965). The author very judiciously distinguishes between, on the one side, the

emergence of new needs by the mere fact of technology, the modification of the "consumer environment" by technology, and, on the other side, the artificial creation of needs through a voluntary influence by the sellers, the latter circumstance being obviously far less significant than the former. Leitherer is correct in emphasizing that many needs produced by technology (in both cases) are not "antinatural," but seem to announce a different "nature."

10. I will not refer here to Marcuse's theory of one-dimensional man, for it is not new, many others before him have said *exactly* the same thing (the first, perhaps, being Arnaud Dandieu in 1929). Marcuse merely adds a bogus Marxism/Freudianism, which only complicates matters uselessly without contributing anything. He seduces readers with his philosophical parlance—which makes him sound deep, whereas he is really intellectually confused—and by a verbal extremism which makes readers believe in his revolutionary commitment. Luckily, the illusions about him are starting to dissipate.

11. It is obvious that the TV system—E. A. Willener, *Videology and Utopia* (1972)—may look like a means of freedom through technology. But from a different viewpoint, it produces the greatest integration of the participants. It manages to transform spectators into "livers," i.e., while people still have the possibility of distance at a spectacle, they know that the spectacle is not "true." Hence, they remain free. TV makes us enter the thing experienced. It is the process in action that is important, and not the "spectacle product." Hence, by living this work, one coincides precisely with the society suggesting it, and the possibility of reacting and criticizing is accordingly reduced.

12. See A. Toffler, *Future Shock*, chap. 12, and Finzi, *Il potere tecnocratico* (1977).

13. See the fine study by Dennis Gabor, "La Liberté dans une société industrielle advancée," *Analyse et prévision* (1966). With great precision, Gabor shows the possibilities and limitations of choices as well as man's aptitude for judging his *present* contentment, his very restricted right to determine his desires (in regard to the technological society), and his total absence of a "right" to judge the means and long-term orientations. And of course, two essential authors to consult on this theme are: Raymond Aron, *Progress of Disillusion;* and John Kenneth Galbraith *The Affluent Society.*

14. To grasp how greatly modern man is "manipulated" toward technology, how greatly he approves of it, one must read books like A. Touraine, *Les Travailleurs et les changements techniques* (1965); or A. Touraine et al., *Les Ouvriers et le progrès technique, Étude de cas* (1966). Workers react less and less to progress, they mention an increase of their responsibilities, they feel they have a superior qualification; technological innovation is interpreted by them in terms of technological progress. They see this progress positively as opening new possibilities, even though these same workers have a rather pessimistic outlook on their standard of living and their future. This is very revelatory of the way people are made to conform to technology.

Even more remarkably, we note that the East German trade unions in 1975 envisaged the "solution" to the workers' problem only in technological growth and in the computer, and not through a political transformation or a transformation of economic structures.

# BIBLIOGRAPHY

Ayres, R. U. *Technological Forecasting and Long Range Planning.* New York: McGraw, 1969.
Aron, Raymond. *Progress and Disillusion: The Dialectics of Modern Society.* New York: Praeger, 1968.
Baudrillard, J. *La société de consommation.* Paris: Gallimard, 1974. *Le système des objets.* Paris: Gallimard, 1968.
Beaune, Jean-Claude. *La Technologie.* Paris: Presses Universitaires de France, 1972.
Bell, Daniel, ed. *Toward the Year Two Thousand: Work in Progress.* Boston: Houghton Mifflin, 1968.
Brzezinski, Zbigniew. *Between Two Ages: America's Role in the Technetronic Age.* New York: Viking Press, 1970.
Charbonneau, Bernard. *Le jardin de Babylone.* Paris: Gallimard, 1969. *Le paradoxe de la culture.* Paris: Denoël. *Le système et le chaos.* Paris: Anthropos, 1973. *Tristes campagnes.* Paris: Denoel, 1973.
Closets, François de. *En danger de progrès.* Paris: Gallimard, 1972.
Coriat, Benjamin. *Science, technique, et capital.* Paris: Seuil, 1976.
Crozier, Michel. *The Stalled Society.* New York: Viking, 1973.
Daumas, Maurice. *Les origines de la civilisation technique* and *Les premiéres étapes du machinisme.* Histoire générale des Techniques, Vols. I and III. Paris: Presses Universitaire de France, 1962.
Elgozy, Georges. *Automation et humanisme.* Paris: Calmann-Lévy, 1968. *Le désordinateur.* Paris: Calmann-Lévy, 1973.
Font, Jean-Marc, and Quiniou, Jean-Claude. *Les ordinateurs, mythes et réalités.* Paris: Gallimard, 1970, new edition.
Friedmann, Georges. *La puissance et la sagesse.* Paris: Gallimard, 1970. *Sept études sur l'homme et la technique.* Paris: Gonthier, 1966.
Furia, Daniel, and Serre, Pierre Charles. *Techniques et sociétés, liaisons et évaluations.* Vichy: Colin 1970.
Galbraith, John Kenneth. *The Affluent Society.* New York: Houghton Mifflin, 2nd ed., 1969. *The New Industrial State.* New York: Houghton Mifflin, 1967.
Goldsmith, Edward and *Ecologist* editors. *Blueprint for Survival.* Boston: Houghton Mifflin, 1972.

Habermas, Jurgen. *Technik und Wissenschaft als Ideologie.* Frankfurt: Suhrkamp/KNO, 1975.
Illich, Ivan. *Tools for Conviviality.* New York: Harper and Row, 1973.
Jouvenel, Bertrand de. *Arcadie.* Paris: S.E.D.E.I.S., 1969.
Kahn, Herman, and Wiener, A. J. *Year Two Thousand.* Riverside, N.J.: Macmillan, 1967.
Kuhn, Thomas S. *The Structure of Scientific Revolutions.* Chicago: University of Chicago Press, 1962.
Lefebvre, Henri. *La vie quotidienne dans le monde moderne.* Paris: Gallimard, 1970.
Montollin, Maurice de. *Les psychopitres.* Paris: Presses Universitaires de France, 1972.
Mumford, Lewis. *The Myth of the Machine.* New York: Harcourt, Brace, Jovanovich, 1970. *Technics and Civilization.* New York: Harcourt, Brace, Jovanovich, 1963.
Onimus, Jean. *L'asphyxie et le cri.* Paris: Desclee Brouwer.
Reich, Charles A. *The Greening of America.* New York: Random House, 1970.
Richta, Radovan. *Civilization at the Crossroads.* International Arts and Science, 1960.
Rorvik, David M. *As Man Becomes Machine.* New York: Doubleday, 1971. *Brave New Baby.* New York: Doubleday, 1971.
Sauvy, Alfred. *Croissance zéro.* Paris: Calmann-Lévy, 1973. *Les quatres roues de la fortune.* Paris: Flammarion, 1968.
Schon, Donald A. *Technology and Change.* New York: Dell, 1967.
Sfez, Lucien. *L'administration prospective.* Vichy: Colin, 1970. *Critique de la décision.* Paris: Fondation National Science Politique, ed. rev., 1976.
Seligman, Ben B. *A Most Notorious Victory.* Riverside, N.J.: Free Press, 1966.
Simondon, Gilbert. *Du mode d'existence des objets techniques.* Paris: Aubier-Montaigne, 1956.
Toffler, Alvin. *Future Shock.* New York: Random House, 1970.
Touraine, Alain. *Les travailleurs et les changements techniques.* Paris: Organisation de Coopérations et de Développement Economiques, 1965.
Vacca, Roberto. *Demain le moyen age.* Traduit de l'Italien. Paris: Albin Michel, 1973.
Wiener, Norbert. *Cybernetics.* Cambridge: M.I.T. Press, 1961. *God and Golem.* M.I.T. Press, 1964.

Made in United States
Troutdale, OR
06/02/2025